D1383909

EDUCATION
IN THE UNITED STATES

EDUCATION
IN THE UNITED STATES

ITS HISTORY
FROM THE EARLIEST SETTLEMENTS

BY

RICHARD G. BOONE

 BOOKS FOR LIBRARIES PRESS
FREEPORT, NEW YORK

First Published 1889
Reprinted 1971

INTERNATIONAL STANDARD BOOK NUMBER:
0-8369-5924-8

LIBRARY OF CONGRESS CATALOG CARD NUMBER:
70-165617

PRINTED IN THE UNITED STATES OF AMERICA

EDITOR'S PREFACE.

THE editor takes great pleasure in presenting this work to the public, as the first noteworthy attempt at a general history of education in the United States. It forms a tolerably complete inventory of what exists, as well as an account of its origin and development.

Ever since the Oracle uttered the admonition "Know thyself," civilized man has been slowly turning his attention to the importance of studying the deeds and institutions of his race. He finds in them a revelation of human nature altogether above and apart from the self-knowledge that comes to each individual through his own consciousness. For in the history of deeds and institutions there stands out prominently the effigy of human nature in its essential outlines. In contrast to this the individual consciousness offers a picture in which the essential is obscured or obliterated by the complications of the passing moment, which assume undue importance.

Modern science has caught most fully the meaning of the Oracle   It has become fully aware of the importance of knowing every object in the light of its history. How it began and how it developed must lead to a knowledge of what it is. The knowledge of a thing only as a dead result is very superficial. We learn what it is good for

by seeing it in the entire sphere of its action. This reveals
its living force and character.

Practical knowledge, in the eminent sense of the word,
is to be found in this study of history. The statesman or
the teacher knows practically when he knows the trend of
the system which he is to direct or manage.

As a mere inventory, the results of this history will
at first surprise us. We see the broad scope of the educational idea—not merely its school course from the Kindergarten to the university, but its supplementary institutions,
the library, the museum, the reading circle, the scientific
association, the variety of special schools; the wide-spread
impulse toward founding educational institutions, showing
itself in all the colonies at the beginning, and increasing
with the growth of the nation. All this becomes impress-
ive only when seen in the solid mass.

But, more than all, the trend of the movement interests us as it becomes apparent through the contrast of
beginnings with subsequent stages of unfolding:

1. We see everywhere a movement from private, endowed, and parochial schools toward the assumption of
education by the State. The General Government, founded
" to promote the general welfare," as the preamble to the
Constitution recites, has fostered education from the beginning by extensive donations of lands. States first establish
colleges and universities, and next free common elementary
schools; and afterward gradually fill in intermediate links
of the system, and then add supplementary institutions.
By-and-by State systems of education for the unfortunates
and criminal classes arise. Then special schools for the
training of teachers, and the foundation and support of
libraries and museums at public expense begin. Private
endowment and religious zeal initiate new lines of educa-

tional experiment, and as soon as their utility to the general welfare is demonstrated they are adopted into the system of free education supported at public expense.

2. There is a trend away from isolated efforts and toward system and supervision. System has this advantage, that it makes supervision possible. It is the object of general superintendence to discover what is fruitful and promising in the work of individuals or localities, and to strengthen the whole system by making the adoption of these improvements universal. Each shall contribute something worth adopting by all, and, in turn, avail himself of their experience. In this lies the great significance of our national trend toward system.

3. There has been a trend in methods. This appears in several particulars, namely, in the adaptation of the matter of instruction to the mind of the child, so that he assimilates relatively more, and memorizes or stores up in an undigested form relatively less. This adaptation appears most noticeably in the instruction of the primary grades, and, next to this, in the advanced instruction in natural history and physics. The pupil is made to conduct his own researches, and is furnished the material for study. The methods also have improved, in the fact that they widen the investigation into collateral branches. Formerly each subject was isolated from its relations; now it is illuminated by light thrown on it from other provinces. The methods of discipline have generally improved. Corporal punishment has been very much diminished. The entire educational idea of the people has progressed in the direction of divine charity. The institutions for the education of women, together with the mentioned supplementary institutions for unfortunates (the deaf and dumb, the blind, the feeble-minded, etc.), and

for the reform of criminals, the multiplication of means of education for the youngest children—all show this. Again, the opening of free public libraries, museums, and courses of lectures, shows the logical results of the democratic principle in the diffusion of knowledge. Teach the people how to read, and then furnish them what is best to read.

Our national Government bases itself on the ability of the people as people to govern themselves through the ballot-box. The history of education shows how it has seemed fit to make provision for the enlightenment of those citizens. It has grown clear in the process of ages that the only help which may be safely given to individuals or communities is the help that aids and increases self-help. All other help dwarfs the individual and weakens the State. Now, the only infallible aid to self-help that has been found up to this time is education which produces intellectual enlightenment and training in moral habits. This alone is a help that is good alike for sound and perverse. It improves the former and corrects the latter. This view of education has been seen by the fathers of the republic, and preached by the religious founders of our colonies. The conviction has become so generally prevalent that it has produced the joint action—private, national, State, and municipal—looking toward the foundation and encouragement of schools and supplementary institutions, recorded in this book. The patriotic will hope that the results reached are encouraging; at all events, whether gratifying or otherwise, the study of the facts is necessary and salutary to Americans interested in the welfare of their country.

W. T. HARRIS.

CONCORD, MASSACHUSETTS, *May, 1889.*

AUTHOR'S PREFACE.

IT is now generally recognized that any complete study of education must include the historical no less than the critical and practical phases. Neither can be left out of account. Wanting the theory, instruction becomes aimless; without knowledge of means, wasteful. But the teacher who presumes to work without an acquaintance with the record of his profession, is like a ship lacking log-book and compass—progress will be only a happening.

And yet, of general histories of education, there are, in English, less than half a dozen, only two of which are more than primers. In these two, American schools receive the merest mention—*eighteen pages* in one, and *two* in the other. For the only other attempts at a notice of our State and municipal systems, we are indebted to foreign interest. Prominent among these are P. A. Siljeström's "Educational Institutions of the United States" (1855); Rev. James Fraser's report to the Parliamentary Schools Inquiry Commission, on "The Common-School System of the United States" (1865); Francis Adams's "Free Schools of the United States" (1874); and occasional statements drawn from educational exhibits and conferences at international exposi-

tions.   These are all more or less critical estimates of
American schools as seen through foreign eyes; were
all made for special purposes; are chiefly descriptive, and
rarely historical.   Valuable as they are in themselves,
they are imperfect as setting forth American schools to
American teachers.   Profit comes always from a close
and comparative study of current systems, their general
aims, conditions, and accompanying agencies; and the
books named can render an incalculable service to American teachers.   But so vitally is every present related to its
past, that the study of contemporary institutions can be
made intelligent only in the light of their origin.   To
know along what lines in educational experience have
been the great changes, and why, and so what is new and
what old, in current doctrine and practice, serves to
temper undue enthusiasm over real or supposed new de-
partures, and saves from condemning the worthy only
because it chances to be old.

While it can not be claimed that education is more
seriously regarded now than by the thinkers of every
past generation, it certainly is more widely studied.   More
is demanded of the body of teachers—more professionally
and socially.   The inferior teacher has an increasingly
smaller hope of public confidence; the well-informed
one, more of leadership.   This is the meaning of normal
schools, institutes, reading-circles, teachers' classes, and
professional libraries.   It is believed that this history may
help along this impulse—make it possible to study intelligently, and as a whole, the particular but complex institution called the American School.

The book lays no claim to completeness.   It is meant
to be a text-book, suggestive of lines of thought for the
teacher, and sources of information.   One constant aim

has been, avoiding mere description on the one side, and personal criticism on the other, to exhibit faithfully the development of contemporary institutions and educational forces with something of their national setting.

To bring the sketch into a small compass, within reach of the leisure and conditions of the body of teachers, and yet omit no fundamental factor in the educational movement of two centuries and a half, have compelled a frequent readjustment of materials. But it seemed better, all things considered, to cover the whole field of elementary, higher, and special educations, and so give a basis for special studies by individuals. Besides, so interwoven are the interests of the one with those of the others, that no treatment of the common-school system would be complete that ignored the academies and colleges, and *vice versa.*

The author has been placed under repeated obligations to the librarian, assistants, and other officials of Johns Hopkins University, during some months' residence at which most of the present work took shape; and particularly his indebtedness to Dr. G. Stanley Hall, whose long and varied educational experience, and wide reading, through much counsel and suggestion, have contributed to whatever of value the book may have. The Peabody Library, of ninety thousand volumes, including much valuable literature upon special phases of education and educational institutions, and the Maryland Historical Library, both of Baltimore; the Library of Congress, and the Pedagogical Library of the United States Bureau of Education, at Washington—thanks to Librarian A. R. Spofford and Commissioner Dawson—were both freely and frequently used.

The great task, of course, was in the gathering and

sifting of materials. These were found in abundance, but widely scattered; not generally to be had in cyclopædias or compilations, but in journals, both general and educational, often in broken sets; in monographs and addresses; in reports and manuals; in histories; and in the proceedings of educational bodies and learned academies, and in the annual statements of special institutions.

Barnard's "American Journal of Education" (1855–'80), and the "Official Reports of the United States Bureau of Education" (1868–'87), have been the sources of the most, and most valuable, information for the periods they cover. In addition to the frequent mention of them throughout the volume, the author's formal acknowledgment of their services is here gratefully given. Care has been taken to verify facts, where it has been possible, by reference to first and official records. But, as has already been suggested, much has had to be taken at second-hand. Of any errors of statement, either statistical or other, the correction will be gratefully received and cheerfully used.

The bibliography following each chapter is meant to cover, not so much the accepted and standard literature, which may be found in any general catalogue, as in a limited way to call attention to some of the best recent literature, whether of books, pamphlets, or magazine articles. Never was the general press more given to an all-sided discussion of educational interests than now; and the professionally inclined teacher finds it necessary to be acquainted with its contents. As suggesting lines of collateral and special reading, these brief reference-lists are given a place.

R. G. BOONE.

BLOOMINGTON, INDIANA, *April, 1889.*

CONTENTS.

                                                                    PAGE
INTRODUCTION 1

PART I. THE COLONIAL PERIOD.

CHAP.

I. THE EARLIEST AMERICAN SCHOOLS. 9
    1. New York and the Dutch West India Company.
    2. Virginia and the Virginia Company. 3. Early New
    England Schools.

II. COLONIAL COLLEGES 20
    1. Harvard College. 2. The College of William and
    Mary. 3. Yale College.

III. COLONIAL SCHOOL SYSTEMS 43
    1. The Massachusetts Law of 1647. 2. The Connecticut
    Code of 1650. 3. Other New England Schools and
    Teachers. 4. New York prior to the Revolution.
    5. Pennsylvania prior to the Revolution. 6. New Jer-
    sey prior to the Revolution. 7. Colonial Education in
    the South.

PART II. THE REVOLUTIONARY PERIOD.

IV. ELEMENTARY EDUCATION. 61
    1. "Pauper" Schools. 2. Teachers. 3. Common-School
    Text-Books. 4. The Education of Girls.

V. ACADEMIES AND COLLEGES 70
    1. Academies. 2. Colleges.

1

PART III. THE PERIOD OF REORGANIZATION.

CHAP.   PAGE

VI. CENTRALIZING TENDENCIES 79
    1. The Transition. 2. The Creation of School-Funds.
    3. Permanent Funds and Local Taxes.

VII. CENTRALIZING TENDENCIES (*continued*).—School Supervision 94
    1. The District System. 2. State Supervision. 3. City
    Supervision. 4. County Supervision.

VIII. THE PREPARATION OF TEACHERS 117
    1. Educational Associations. 2. Institutes. 3. Nor-
    mal Schools.

IX. THE PREPARATION OF TEACHERS (*continued*) . . . 142
    4. Pedagogical Training in Colleges. 5. Educational
    Literature.

X. RECENT COLLEGES 158
    A. The Curriculum.
        1. The Physical Sciences. 2. Modern Language
        Studies. 3. Institutional History. 4. Economic
        Studies.

XI. RECENT COLLEGES (*continued*) 186
    A. The Curriculum (*continued*) . . . .
        5. Elective Courses and Studies. 6. Graduate
        Courses.
    B. University Organization.
        1. State-established Colleges. 2. Privately Endowed
        Institutions.

XII. THE PROFESSIONS 209
    1. Theological Education. 2. Legal Education. 3. Med-
    ical Education.

XIII. TECHNOLOGICAL EDUCATION 221
    1. The Beginnings of Industrial Training. 2. The Cur-
    riculum. 3. Agricultural Education. 4. Military
    and Naval Education.

CHAP.   PAGE

XIV. EDUCATION OF UNFORTUNATES AND CRIMINAL CLASSES . 243
    1. Deaf-Mute Education. 2. Education of the Blind.
    3. Education of the Feeble-Minded. 4. Reforma-
    tories. 5. Indian Education. 6. Education in
    Alaska.

XV. SUPPLEMENTARY INSTITUTIONS 264
    1. Private Schools. 2. Denominational Schools. 3. Even-
    ing Schools. 4. Museums of Art and Science. 5.
    Clubs and Circles.

XVI. LEARNED SOCIETIES AND LIBRARIES 285
    1. General Societies. 2. Libraries.

XVII. THE GENERAL GOVERNMENT AND EDUCATION . . . 307
    1. The Bureau of Education. 2. The Smithsonian Insti-
    tution. 3. Special Scientific Work. 4. Special Pub-
    lications.

PART IV. CURRENT EDUCATIONAL INTERESTS.

XVIII. COMPULSORY SCHOOL ATTENDANCE 326

XIX. THE GRADATION OF SCHOOLS 331
    1. Primary Schools. 2. The Kindergarten. 3. The
    High School.

XX. EDUCATION IN THE SOUTH 347
    1. The Ante-war Period. 2. The Period of Reorganization.
      A. The Freedmen's Aid Society. B. Government
      Agency. C. Denominational Agencies. D. The
      Peabody Fund. E. The Slater Fund. F. Public-
      School Systems. G. Normal Schools. H. Col-
      leges. I. Professional Schools.
    3. General Conditions.

XXI. THE HIGHER EDUCATION OF WOMEN 362
    1. Ladies' Seminaries. 2. Colleges for Women. 3. Co-
    education of the Sexes in College. 4. Examinations
    and Annexes. 5. Association of Collegiate Alumnæ.
    6. The Professional Education of Women.

CONCLUSION 382

EDUCATION
IN THE UNITED STATES.

INTRODUCTION.

OF the underlying notion of the colonists who instituted the American school system, Dr. D. C. Gilman has asked:* "How far was it a natural evolution from the social usages and laws of England? How far from those of Holland?"

For an answer to this query, one of which Lieber says "it must be of interest to every American," the future gives continually less of promise. Every day loses something of record. The question remains. It recurs perennially. It must be asked by every thoughtful mind. Every day's experience enforces the belief that no life is dissociated from its past—of government or man. Whence, then, the American idea of control, of society, and the family? of education and industry? of place and character? For these are the flower of culture for which institutions exist. Of whom and where were learned the lessons of self-mastery and direction, of distributed sovereignty and co-operation? For these make a general education, not so much possible, as safe. They can not be supposed wholly unknown to Puritan and Huguenot Europe; and yet the want of them has made her the battle-ground of the centuries.

---

* "Education in America," D. C. Gilman, "North American Review," January, 1876.

"Puritan" and "Huguenot," "Saracen" and "Protestant"—the very names recall the birth in Europe, of the
impulse whose developments in the newer West have out-
stripped the best in the Old World. They mean what modern dissent and the independence of a growing individual-
ism have led us to understand by them. They mean mod-
ernism wherever found—in institutions or the personal life,
in education or industry.

Mr. Eugene Lawrence says: "The true parent of the current system of teaching was the Reformation." It was the
world's recoil from authority; the renunciation of servitude;
the assumption of personality. Protestantism meant, not so
much independence, as a growing fitness for independence.
We have learned to think of the race, in every period, as
growing toward its manhood; and America is a step in that
growth, a phase of race-development; a long stride may be—
Americans believe it is. Horace Mann insisted, and his life
enforced the thought, that "the transference of the fortunes
of our race from the Old to the New World was a gain to hu-
manity of a thousand years." It was the opinion of Froebel,
to which he gave frequent expression, that "the Kindergarten
could only have its full development in America, where the
national principle is self-government ; in perfect freedom,
but according to law."

Here were to be found the more favorable conditions, freedom from established customs and precedents, and an absence of fixed public institutions, giving room to invention,
a field for new and, in the light of a larger independence,
more rational adventure.

The period itself (seventeenth century) was one of vigorous social and intellectual activity. The invention of printing, and the consequent and rapid multiplication of books—
equally multiplying the resources and occasions of mental
culture—were more than paralleled by the coincident increase in the facilities of commerce, the extension of geographical discoveries, the increase not less than the diffusion
of physical knowledge, and the expansion of industries. It

was a period in whose activity every people and every sort of human interest more or less participated. Society became eclectic. The past was studied and drawn upon for its wisdom. Nations began to take note of their neighbors. Governments were remodeled. New inventories were taken, and men came to read history with a new purpose. In the awakening education shared richly.

"The idea that education must be coextensive with sovereignty," says Dr. E. E. White, "was not original with our fathers. This has been," he continues, "the favorite doctrine of aristocracy the world over" ; and "despotism clamors for a restricted education, because she would have a restricted sovereignty." That control should be intelligent is older than Plato, and is denied by no people.

In the Zealand school law of 1583, education is insisted upon because "it is the foundation of the commonwealth." And Charlemagne, eight centuries before, had required that the children of all persons participating in the government should be educated, "in order that intelligence might rule the empire."

Nor is the idea of universal freedom less ancient or more Western in its origin. It has been the inspiration of poet and statesman ; the dream of Roman gladiator and Greek slave ; of Israelitish brick-maker and Russian serf. The idea of local self-government was already historical at the time of the colonization of North America. Among the Germanic ancestors of the colonists, the custom was so general for the inhabitants of a district to control their local affairs, that it has been said : "One leading principle pervaded the primeval polity of the Goths ; where the law was administered, the law was made." *

In ancient England, local self-government was found along with the common political and territorial division of tithings, hundreds, burghs, counties, and shires, in which the body of the inhabitants had a voice in managing their own

---

* Frothingham's, " The Republic of the United States," p. 14.

affairs.   Local self-government was the germinal idea of Anglo-Saxon polity.

So is the notion of universal education common to all philosophy.   That it is yet to be realized, only emphasizes the aspiration.

John of Nassau, in the sixteenth century, urged upon the States-General that they should " establish free schools where children of quality as well as of poor families, for a very small sum, could be well and Christianly educated and brought up."   He saw the fruitfulness of a wise and state-administered system of universal education.   This he said to his subjects " would be the greatest and most useful work you could ever accomplish, for God and Christianity, and for the Netherlands as well." *

In the middle of the tenth century, the Arabian Caliph Alhakim, at Cordova, besides schools in every village, established twenty-seven others at his own expense, where the children of indigent parents were instructed free of charge. Prior to this even, Abderrahman I. had established, in addition to the usual agencies, high-schools for girls, taught by female teachers.   The expulsion of the Jews, the effects of the Inquisition, and the limited opportunities and means of education, prevented the influence of this early Arabian learning from being immediately felt in the colonies of the early Spanish explorers.†

The very barbarism of the uninstructed but self-dependent Saxons and Germans attracted Alfred and Charlemagne, and schools and universities attest the faithfulness of their service.

Charles X and Gustavus Adolphus did for Sweden and their generations what America, with all her achievement, has failed to do since—made education so common that in

---

* Motley's, " Rise of the Dutch Republic."

† See, in the " Report of the United States Commissioner of Education," a collection of facts relative to the Old World early ideas of education, 1875, p. 13.   Also " Circular of Information," No. 1—1873.

the year 1637 (the year of the founding of Harvard) "not a single peasant's child was unable to read and write." *

In the previous century, under William, Holland, having founded the universities of Leyden and Frankfort, supplemented them by Latin or "great schools," and lower, or public, or "small schools," for the elementary training. Fixed salaries were paid to such as, by an examination before the magistrates, had shown their competency. Following the Union of Utrecht (1579), it was ordered that "the inhabitants of towns and villages should, within six weeks, find good and competent schoolmasters." Two years later, it was further provided that "such as neglected to do this should be bound to receive the schoolmasters sent to them," and provide the usual compensation.† In the year 1618 the Synod of the Protestant Episcopal Dutch Church of Dort urged that schools be instituted, "not only in cities, but in towns and country places." So common was the impulse, it is said, that "neither the perils of war, nor the busy pursuit of gain, nor the excitement of political strife, ever caused them to neglect the duty of educating their offspring. Schools were everywhere provided at the public expense, with good schoolmasters to instruct the children of all classes in the usual branches of education." ‡

Motley, the historian, is authority for the statement # that in 1635 the Latin school at Dordrecht had been in existence for some centuries, ‖ and was one of the most famous institutions of Northwestern Europe. It frequently instructed six hundred students brought from all parts of the continent. It was a training-school for a nation of merchants, and, though classical, was eminently practical as fitted to the social conditions. "The one linguistic need of the boys,"

---

* Schmidt's "Geschichte der Erziehung."

† Compare this provision with that of the Massachusetts law of 1642, p. 16.

‡ Broadhead's "History of New York," vol. i, p. 462.

See his "John De Witt," p. 35.

‖ Founded about 1290.

said Motley, "was instruction in Latin and French. No progress in public life was possible without a knowledge of these tongues."*

Mr. Motley concludes that the New England colonists gained their educational impulse more from the Netherlands than from their own country. And a recent writer,† after asserting that the influence of the Dutch in shaping our educational life has not been enough regarded, says: "Our free public-school system of which we are justly so proud seems to have its beginnings distinctly traceable to the earliest life of the Dutch colonies here in America, and to have had its prototype in the free schools in which Holland had led the van of the world."

It was a favorite doctrine of the protesting Luther that every child was worthy to have the best education—languages, history, music, mathematics — everything that can contribute to his highest development. And in a "Letter to Magistrates" (1524), after recounting the advantages to the Church and to the religious life of the individual, he insists that, "if there were no soul, no heaven, no future after this life, and temporal affairs were to be administered solely with a view to the present, it would yet be a sufficient reason for establishing in every place the best schools, both for boys and girls ; that the world, merely to maintain its outward prosperity, has need of shrewd and accomplished men and women." Taking the sentiment as typical of a national idea, Hon. Henry Barnard speaks of the "common school" as "only an improvement on the parochial schools of Germany."‡

Once more : John Calvin, at Geneva, in the sixteenth century, made education, so far as he might, obligatory upon all ; and, to-day, the thrifty cantons of Switzerland enjoy

---

* It would seem as if the founders of the Boston Latin School adopted the form of this, without the social demand (see p. 338).

† H. B. Adams, in "Johns Hopkins Studies in History," series iii, p. 15.

‡ "American Journal of Education," vol. x, p. 32.

the beneficent influences of a law of whose significance the author little dreamed. Tracing the growth of this impulse, George Bancroft says : "The common-school system was derived from Geneva, the work of John Calvin ; introduced by Luther into Germany ; by John Knox into Scotland ; and so became the property of the English-speaking nation."*

So instances of old ideas clustering about this common sovereignty and universal education might be cited indefinitely. No stronger word, however, has been said in the interests of the latter, and the enforcement of school provisions and attendance, than by Plato, in his "Laws." Indeed, throughout both this and the "Republic," one frequently falls upon ideas peculiarly modern, and especially so of education.

In the "Laws," as a part of a discussion on schools and their importance to the state, the Athenian stranger is made to say : "In these several schools let there be dwellings for teachers who shall be brought from foreign parts by pay ; and let the frequenters [learners] be taught the art of war, and the art of music ; and they shall come, not only if their parents please, but if they do not please ; and, if then education be neglected, there shall be compulsory education, of all and sundry, as the saying is, so far as this is possible ; and the pupils shall be regarded as belonging to the state rather than to their parents."†

That these sentiments can not be more definitely derived, only marks their universality. They form a kind of ideal of civilization ; and the problem that the states were set to solve had been a long-established theory of thinkers and statesmen. The English, as the later born of European nations, was the heir of all the East ; and among the early colonists to this country were specimens of both individuals and families from the highest level of English thought. There

---

* "History of the United States," vol. iii., p. 100.

† "Laws" (Jowett's translation), book vii, p. 732. A presentation of Plato's "Theory of Education" appeared in the "Presbyterian Review" for July, 1887, by Prof. J. Watson.

were English Churchmen in Virginia, English Puritans in Massachusetts, English Catholics in Maryland, and English Quakers in Pennsylvania. And, not ignoring the early educational attitude of Dutch and Swede, Spanish Saracen and modern German, the united colonies were founded and school systems organized by somewhat homogeneous forces —a people of common stock, having common political instincts, and with the tradition of common institutions. In England they sprang from a superior class : a rank that produced Milton and Sir Walter Raleigh and Locke; Hampden and Cromwell ; Carver, Eaton, and Winthrop ; Robinson, Cotton, and Davenport. Of the first six hundred who landed in Massachusetts, one in thirty, it is said, was a graduate of the English Cambridge. These and their companions were rare men. They had the schooling for a service the like of whose execution, in completeness and good sense, the world has never equaled.*

"With matchless wisdom they joined liberty and learning in a perpetual and holy alliance, binding the latter to bless every child with instruction, which the former invests with the rights and duties of citizenship. They made education and sovereignty coextensive, by making both universal."†

---

* Two interesting papers were published some years ago : the one in 1859, " The American System of Education," by Dr. E. O. Haven ; and the other the " Common School Historically "—a most valuable summary made in 1873, by Prof. David Putnam, and read before the Ohio Teachers' Association. Both are well worth reading on this point.

† E. E. White, " Proceedings of National Education Association," 1882.

PART FIRST.

THE COLONIAL PERIOD.

CHAPTER I.

THE EARLIEST AMERICAN SCHOOLS.

IN a prefatory note to a recent oration, the Rev. Phillips Brooks records that "the Public Latin School of Boston enjoys the distinction of being the oldest existing school within the bounds of the United States." *

As frequently happens of sweeping statements concerning "first events" and "oldest institutions," this one of Dr. Brooks seems questionable. A similar claim has been made for Dorchester, Hartford, Brooklyn, and Virginia. Indeed, it is known that various schools had been established prior to that in Boston, one of which, the school of the Reformed Dutch Church in New York, founded as early as 1633, continues to the present.

Those in Virginia, though established earlier, had generally a short existence. Schools in the three sections † were very unlike, and were typical of very dissimilar institutions.

1. The New York Settlements.

The Dutch West India Company, organized in 1621, received, nine years after, instructions from the States-General

---

* Founded 1635. † New England, New York, and Virginia.

of Holland, among which occurred the following order, "to all founders of colonies": Patroons should particularly exert themselves "to find speedy means to maintain a clergyman and a schoolmaster, in order that divine service and zeal for religion may be planted in that country."* And it was required that to this end "each householder and inhabitant should bear such tax and public charge as should be considered proper for their maintenance."

Four years later, in an official estimate of the company's expenses, the schoolmaster is entered at three hundred and sixty florins per annum (just one fourth that of the clergyman).† Under these provisions, the educational policy of New Amsterdam was unbroken, and for many years more or less uniform. The second Director-General of the new province was Wouter Van Twiller, who arrived at Manhattan in the year 1633, and with him Adam Roelandsen, the first schoolmaster. The latter remained nine years. With the advent of the new administration, the first school-tax was levied, four pounds being collected. This would seem to give color to Brooklyn's claim to have had the first *free public* school in the United States.‡

Corel de Beauvois, a recent arrival from Holland, was called to take charge of the school ; adding to his duties as instructor those of grave-digger, court bell-ringer, and precentor. During this period, and for many years thereafter, indeed until 1808, when a special board of trustees was appointed, this school, both for support and management, was in the hands of the local congregation of the Protestant Reformed Dutch Church. It was perhaps only an elementary parochial school, receiving now and then aid from the public treasury, and, while controlled by the Church, was maintained

---

* "Colonial History of New York," vol. i, p. 99. These volumes are valuable not alone for New York, but for all the early colonies.

† Ibid., p. 155.

‡ See article "Brooklyn" in Kiddle and Schem's "Cyclopædia of Education."

for the use of the general public. From its founding it has a continuous history,* through a long line of teachers, legislative and ecclesiastical provisions, and educational progress.

Though Stuyvesant wrote in 1642, "Nothing is of greater importance than the right, early instruction of youth," no care seems to have been shown for more than the rudiments, including, besides reading, writing, and arithmetic, the doctrines of the Church,† and the fundamental "Freedoms, Privileges, and Exemptions," granted to the colonists, through the West India Company. ‡

But in the year 1658, while yet Stuyvesant was Director, the burgomasters petitioned "for a fit person as Latin Schoolmaster, not doubting that the number of persons who will send their children to such teacher will, from year to year, increase, until an Academy will be formed, whereby this place to great splendor will have attained." The petition was granted, and the first classical school was instituted—nearly a quarter of a century after the founding of the Boston Latin School. The first principal was one Dr. Alexander Carolus—a professional teacher—who was paid out of the public treasury five hundred guilders ($187.50) annually, was given the use of a house and garden, received six guilders from each scholar, and was privileged, in addition, to practice medicine !

During this early period, from the first, teachers, whether of private, parish, or public schools, were subjected to an established and formal examination ; and, while licensed by the council of "nine men," must be sanctioned by the deacons of the Church.

---

* This has been well and fully written by H. W. Dunshee, in " A History of the School of the Reformed Protestant Church in New York."   .

† It was ordered (see " New York Colonial MSS.," edited by George Bancroft) that " no other religion should be publicly admitted in New Netherland, except the Reformed, as it was then preached and practiced by public authority in the United Netherlands."

‡ Dunshee, p. 51.

Besides Roelandsen and Cornelison, of elementary teachers, there were others. Mr. Dunshee, the historian of the school, speaks of certain private schools, of Jan Stevenson and Aryaen Jansen, and "other teachers in hired houses," prior to 1649. By the middle of the century, New Amsterdam had a population of eight hundred. This was doubled in the next decade, and, by the close of Stuyvesant's administration, fifteen teachers are recorded as having served in the settlement, some of them with long terms. As early as 1650 they were paid regularly out of the public treasury; the excise money being set apart for this purpose. The pay there as elsewhere, then and since, was probably poor enough; for a few years later one William Vestens headed the long line of petitioners for "an increase of salary."*

2. Virginia and the Virginia Company.

Even prior to New Amsterdam and Boston, the needs of education were being considered by the older colony of Virginia. These also were an earnest body of men. In 1619 Sir Edwin Sandys, treasurer to the London Company, moved in the English Parliament, the grant of fifteen thou-

---

* It has frequently happened that the services performed and the wages received by the common-school teacher have been sadly disproportioned. Concerning the former it is interesting to note the functions of the teacher in the early colonial period. He was usually, both in New England and the middle colonies, clerk of the town, chorister of the church, and official visitor of the sick. Indeed, far into the last century, the teacher was scarcely differentiated from the preacher. The Rev. Gideon Sheets, when engaged as minister at Rensselaerwick, New York, was required among other duties " to bring up both the heathens and their children in the Christian religion; to teach the catechism; and to pay attention also to the office of schoolmaster for old and young." The following extract from the " Town Book," indicates the manifold duties of a New England schoolmaster of 1661 : 1. To act as court-messenger ; 2. To serve summonses ; 3. To conduct certain ceremonial services of the church ; 4. To lead the Sunday choir ; 5. To ring the bell for public worship ; 6. To dig the graves ; 7. To take charge of the school ; 8. To perform other occasional duties.

Adam Roelandsen not only taught the youth, but took in washing also i

sand acres of land for a university. It was to be a great Episcopal college—a preparatory school to English learning and English religion. The grant was made. The king appealed to the churches for contributions. Interest was aroused. Schools as well as a college were projected. Fifteen hundred pounds were contributed "toward the erecting of some churches and some schools for the education of the children of those barbarians." Two years later, upon the arrival of the Royal James, a subscription was opened by the chaplain, Rev. Mr. Copeland, for the erection of a free school. The company gave "one thousand acres of land, five servants, and an overseer, for the maintenance of a master and an usher." * Toward the erection of the house, also, the company subscribed one hundred pounds, to which were afterward added other small amounts of money, and a few books. About the same time (1621) two English crews gave nearly sixty-seven pounds;† and the year following a bequest of three hundred pounds was left to the proposed college. Matters were promising. Affairs, educational and commercial, were shaping themselves to the profit of both the company and the settlers. School and college were in sight; buildings and land had been provided. But the terrible Indian war of 1622 came on. Settlements were laid waste, houses and property destroyed, and lives lost. Education was out of the question; rather, the education most needed was that of arms and self-defense. Neither school nor college, however, was forgotten. Immediately steps were taken to increase the funds and replace the buildings. Collections were made throughout the kingdom, in English factories, and on board ships. But the summer following, it was ordered that "all the moneys collected be deposited, *until the plantation be so settled as there may be use of a school there.*" ‡

---

* E. D. Neill, " Virginia Company of London," p. 211.

† Warren and Clark. " Public Libraries of the United States," p. 22.

‡ " Virginia Vetusta," Neill, p. 180.

2

In the Bermuda (Somers) Islands there was already a considerable population—some five thousand inhabitants— and a school regularly established. The bequest (three hundred pounds) noted above, failing of its purpose because of the Indian massacre, was turned (1622) to the Somers Island Company, on condition that they "educate three Virginia Indian children, and, when they were of proper age, put them into business or send them back to convert their relations." The Bermuda school, both then and later, had a reputation on two continents, and claimed the thought of the philosopher Berkeley, who sought to found a college there. Richard Norwood, writing from the island (1645), stated that he had been teaching in that place for thirty years, and at that time had twenty pupils.*

That on the continent also the efforts stand as something more than vain attempts, appears from an extract made from a thoroughly entertaining description of Virginia, 1649. The writer says: "I may not forget to tell you we have a free school, with two hundred acres of land, a fine house upon it, forty milch kine, and other accommodations to it; the benefactor deserves perpetual memory; his name is Mr. Benjamin Symmes, worthy to be cherished. Other petty schools we have too." †

3. Early New England Schools.

On the 13th of April, 1635, the people of Boston, in town-meeting assembled, impressed not less with their need of schools than with their appreciation of education in general, requested "Brother Philemon Purmont to become schoolmaster, for the teaching and nourteuring of children" in the town. In part pay for his services, thirty acres of land were

---

* It was here thăt Bishop Berkeley proposed founding his college, and in anticipation of which he spent some years at Newport, R. I. For further notice of the schools of the island, see Neill's "Virginia Company of London," p. 214.

† "Massachusctts Historical Collections," vol. xix, p. 119.

voted him by the young colony. Almost immediately "a garden plot was voted to Mr. Danyell Maude, schoolmaster," also. Both of these occurred within less than a year from the founding of the town. John Winthrop, writing, 1645, said: "Divers free schools were erected at Roxbury (for the maintenance whereof every inhabitant bound some house or land for a yearly allowance forever), and at Boston, where they made an order to allow forever fifty pounds to the master, and an house, and thirty pounds to an usher who should also teach to read, write, and cipher. Indian children were to be taught freely. The charge to be by yearly contribution, either by voluntary allowance, or by rate of such as refused; the order being confirmed by the General Court."

Sixteen years before, wild and warlike natives alone stood between Virginia and the proposed Charles City school and Henrico College; three years before, the infant school of the Reformed Church was beginning its long career. Looking back upon these events, it is easy to see that they were big with promise of the marvelous achievements of the first half of that great seventeenth century, destined to do so much for liberty and intelligence. These three settlements were civilization centers for a continent.

Little can now be definitely known of the first few years of the Boston school or schoolmaster. They were brave, and not the less scholarly men, who were laying the foundations of a new commonwealth. Posterity is left to infer the greatness of the deeds of those years from the outcome.

Other Massachusetts towns also showed a vigorous and liberal spirit of culture. Rehoboth was set off from Weymouth as a colony about 1643, and the fifth man upon the list was a professional schoolmaster, who taught the village urchins twelve months in the year. Plymouth Colony had ordered schools, 1650; while, ten years before, Dorchester had petitioned for some islands "for and toward the maintenance of a free school."* Ipswich and Salem each, had

---

* "Records of Massachusetts Colony," vol. iii, p. 139.

schools as early as 1641, Cambridge the year following, and
Roxbury in 1645.*

In the year 1642, in an attempt to make the privileges of
the few towns general, the Colonial Court enjoined upon all
towns the duty of seeing to it in their localities. The order
is comprised in the following extract from the Massachusetts
law of 1642: †

"This court," so the record runs, "taking into serious
consideration the great neglect of many parents and masters,
in training up their children in learning and labor, and
other employments, which may be profitable to the commonwealth, do hereby order and decree, that in every town, the
chosen men appointed to manage the prudential affairs of
the same, shall henceforth stand charged with the care of
the redress of this evil; so as they shall be sufficiently pun-
ished by fines, for the neglect thereof, upon presentment of
grand jury, or other information of complaint in any court
in this jurisdiction: and for this end, they or the greater
number of them shall have power to take account, from time
to time, of all parents and masters, and of their children,
especially of their ability to read and understand the principles of religion and the capital laws of this country, and to
impose fines upon such as shall refuse to render such account to them when they shall be required; and they shall
have power, with the consent of any court, or the magistrate,
to put forth apprentices, the children of such as they shall
find not able and fit to employ and bring them up. They
are also to provide that a sufficient quantity of materials, as
hemp, flax, etc., may be raised in their several towns, and
tools and implements provided for working out the same." ‡

---

* For a history of this school, with much additional contemporary matter of interest, see C. K. Dillaway's "History of the School in Roxbury."

† Taken from the "Records of the Massachusetts Colony," vol. ii, p. 6.

‡ From almost the beginning of New England settlements it seems to
have been common to transact the current public business in a meeting of
the people assembled. By such body Mr. Purmont was called to be Boston's
first teacher; Mr. Cheever, in New Haven; and Mr. Lenthrall, in Provi-

What grave educational and social questions were then sprung by the Boston fathers, that subsequent generations have had to answer! Parental responsibility, the general viciousness of indolence, the educative office of labor, the state's relation to individual need, compulsory employment and schooling, the function of courts, and the state ownership of child-life, were all suggested by the act quoted. The town—society in its organized capacity—was commissioned to secure to the child its rights, and to the community protection.

The selectmen of every town were further required "to have a vigilant eye over their brethren and neighbors, to see that none of them shall suffer so much barbarism in any of their families, as not to endeavor to teach, by themselves or others, their children and apprentices, so much learning as may enable them perfectly to read the English tongue and [obtain] a knowledge of the capital laws ; upon penalty of twenty shillings for each neglect therein." *

"If, after admonition, parents were still neglectful of their duty in these particulars," children might be taken from their parents, and servants from the custody of their masters, and bound to such masters as the selectmen might deem worthy to supply the place of "the unnatural parent" —boys until the age of twenty-one, and girls until that of eighteen.

---

dence. In these meetings all were freemen, and all equal in privileges. The voice of each was individual and stood for one only. As early as 1632, however, twelve men of Dorchester were selected to meet statedly, and hold in consideration public interests. Two years later, Boston chose a like number, and Charlestown the year following ; Watertown, Newton, and others soon did the like. And Mr. Palfrey says ("History of New England," vol. i, p. 372) that, "at the fifth General Court of Massachusetts, twenty-four persons appeared delegated by eight towns." It was such a representative body of freemen, fit type of the later administrative republicanism, that passed the school act of 1642, from which the extracts are taken.

* See Horace Mann's comments upon this in "Tenth Report of the Massachusetts Board of Education," 1849.

Commenting upon this act and the primitive Boston idea of barbarism, Horace Mann was led to say that, "tried by this standard, many a man who now glories in the name and prerogatives of a republican citizen would, according to the better ideas of the Pilgrim Fathers, be known only as the barbarian father of barbarian children." *

It would seem that the first school in Connecticut was at New Haven, during the year 1638.† Prof. G. B. Emerson says Ezekiel Cheever left Boston with those who founded the settlement, and "began his services as schoolmaster in that year ; the pastor, Mr. Davenport, together with the magistrates," according to the records, being invited to consider what yearly allowance was "meet to be given him out of the common stock of the town." Two years later a second and higher grade school was established, and Mr. Cheever, then a young man of twenty-seven, was made its principal. This also was supported, in part, out of the "common stock."

Besides Mr. Cheever's, there were other schools in New Haven. Care was even then taken that every child should have its just deserts. In a year from the date of settlement, one Thomas Fugill appears on the public records, charged by the court to keep Charles Higinson, an indentured servant or apprentice, "at school one year ; or else to advantage him as much in his education as a year's learning would come to."

With the exception of Mr. Cheever's school, instruction was chiefly elementary, comprising only reading and ciphering. The former was called a grammar-school, in which were taught, besides the common higher branches, Latin, rhetoric, grammar, etc., corresponding nearly to the modern high-school, but with relatively more of the classics.

The first school appearing on the town records of Hart-

---

* "Lowell Institute Lectures," 1869, p. 351.   Also "American Journal of Education," vol. i, p. 297.

† Report for 1846.

ford was a somewhat famous one in that day, in operation as early as 1641, and kept by a not less widely known teacher, Mr. William Andrews. He was employed to teach the school for one year (twelve months) for fifteen pounds; each patron to pay at the rate of twenty shillings per year, the poor being paid for at the town's charge.

In Rhode Island, Newport had a public school in 1640, and Providence one, twenty years later.

Throughout the colonies, schools were endowed ; first with lands, very early with bequests, rents, and donations, and supplemented by taxation. They were not free. Tuition was paid for all. The abuse of the principle is an interesting historical study.

Bibliography.

Consult "The School of the Reformed Dutch Church" of New York, by H. W. Dunshee, which contains also pertinent information of other schools and colonies ; "Documents of the Colonial History of New York," in eleven volumes ; and manuscripts of the New York Historical Society ; the "Virginia Company of London," "Virginia Carolorum," and "Virginia Vetusta," three volumes, by E. D. Neill, comprising original documents and records ; the "History of Education in Rhode Island," edited by T. B. Stockwell ; the "Roxbury Grammar-School," by C. K. Dillaway ; the "Massachusetts Historical Collections," and the official "Colonial Records" of Plymouth, New Hampshire, Massachusetts, Connecticut, and Providence Colonies. A series of articles also by G. G. Bush in the "Yale Review" for 1885, affords a general view of "Early Education in New England." In the "Atlantic Monthly" for January, 1885, is a description of the "Dame School," such as the early English colonies had a few curious examples of.

CHAPTER II.

COLONIAL COLLEGES.

1. Harvard.

In the autumn of the sixth year of the settlement of Boston, the General Court* of the colony, with a far-seeing liberality, and a wisdom of sacrifice such as shall be for years to come a monument to it and its people, voted† the sum of four hundred pounds " toward a school or college ; whereof two hundred pounds shall be paid the next year, and two hundred pounds when the work is finished, and the next Court to appoint where and what building."

The following year twelve of the most trusted men of the whole colony, previously appointed, magistrates and ministers, of political foresight and abundant learning, were set to execute the official mandate, " to take order for a College at New Towne." Among these early educational leaders were such men as the Rev. Thomas Shepard, John Cotton, and John Wilson, Jr. ; all clergymen and all college-bred ; ‡ Stoughton; Dudley, the Deputy-Governor, and above all " Winthrop, the Governor, the guide and the good genius of the colony." #
Such were the men and the sources of greatness of the infant colony, and pledge of the college. Here were learning and character ; world-wisdom and refinements of the heart ; breadth and wholeness of culture, such as could alone justify the boldness of their attempt. " It is questionable," says

---

* This Massachusetts Assembly, over which Henry Vane presided, has been said to be " the first body in which the people, by their representatives, ever gave their own money to found a place of education." (Quoted by Palfrey, vol. i, p. 247.)

† September 8, 1636.

‡ Mr. Savage estimates that in 1638 there were in Massachusetts and Connecticut not fewer than forty men who had been more or less educated at Cambridge, England.

" History of Harvard University," Josiah Quincy, vol. i, p. 9.

Mr. Dwight, " whether a more honorable specimen of public spirit can be found in the history of mankind."

Institutions of learning are expected among men of intellect and refinement, but not in poverty ; in leisure, but not surrounded by public dangers. " These early settlers," wrote Quincy, " waited not for affluence, for days of peace, or even domestic concord." Neither narrowness of territorial limits, nor fear of savage enemies, nor scanty subsistence, nor meager population ; neither religious dispute, nor uncertain abode, nor lack of leisure restrained their unbounded zeal for an education that to them seemed not so much desirable as necessary, that " the light of learning might not go out, nor the study of God's Word perish."

Notwithstanding their own learning, however, and solicitude for their children, they must have failed in their undertaking had it not been for the generous gift of John Harvard.

A citizen of Boston, writing back to friends in 1643, says : " After we had builded our houses, provided necessaries for our livelihood, reared convenient places for worship, and settled the civill government, one of the next things wee longed for and looked after was to advance learning and to perpetuate it to posterity ; dreading to leave an illiterate ministry to the churches, when our present ministers shall lie in the dust. And as wee were thinking and consulting how to effect this great work, it pleased God to stir up the heart of one Mr. Harvard (a godly gentleman and a lover of learning, then living among us) to give the one half of his estate (it being in all about £1,700) towards the erecting of a colledge, and all his library. After him another gave £300; others after them cast in more, and the publique hand of the State added the rest." * The official record is similar.

Of John Harvard little is known. The institution founded is his best monument. This much may perhaps be said: He was a son of Robert and Katharine (Rogers) Harvard, and was

---

* " Massachusetts Historical Collections," vol. i, p. 242.

born in the parish of Southwark, London, November 29, 1607.
His father was a butcher by trade, dying while John was yet
a youth. He entered Emmanuel College, Cambridge, at the
age of twenty-one, his name appearing on the registrar's book
as a pensioner. He received the bachelor's degree in 1631, and
was made a master four years later. Beyond these meager
facts, concerning his life in England, it is only known that
he was a dissenting clergyman, and set sail for this country
some time in the early part of 1637. Almost immediately
upon his arrival in Massachusetts he was admitted a freeman of the village—Charlestown—along with his co-laborer,
Mr. John Fisk, and others. He continued his ministry, as
appears from the records, and was wealthy beyond his surroundings. His small bequest was almost double what the
whole colony besides was able to give. Thirty years old, and
a finished scholar, after the severe standards even of that ul-
tra-classical period, his counsel was sought outside the field
of theology also; for, almost immediately upon his arrival,
he was appointed one of a committee "to consider of some
things toward a body of laws for the town." After a year
in the colony he died of consumption, September 24, 1638.
He has been called "reverend" and "godly." Henry Barnard says of him, "He was the greatest benefactor of education in America."

"It was given," said Edward Everett, "to the venerated
man whom we commemorate this day"* (1828), "first to
strike the key-note in the character of this people ; first to
perceive with a prophet's foresight, and to promote with a
princely liberality, considering his means, that connection
between private munificence and public education which,
well understood and pursued by others, has given to New
England no small portion of her name and praise in the
land."

His books, which formed the nucleus of the present Harvard Library, were solid and standard. The catalogue is still

---

* Upon the erection of a monument at Charlestown to his memory.

preserved, showing two hundred and sixty volumes, and is one window into the intellectual habit of the man. As might be expected, they were chiefly theological and polemical. They were also classical, and mark the thoughtful bias along with general culture. There were Aquinas and Chrysostom and Calvin; Duns Scotus, Luther, and Pelagius ; but there were, besides, Bacon and Homer, Isocrates and Plutarch, Pliny, Juvenal, and Horace. John Harvard * was a fit benefactor of the first American university.

The colony caught his spirit. Among the magistrates themselves two hundred pounds was subscribed, a part in books. All did something, even the indigent. One subscribed a number of sheep ; another, nine shillings' worth of cloth ; one, a ten-shilling pewter flagon ; others, a fruit-dish, a sugar-spoon, a silver-tipped jug, one great salt, one small trencher salt, etc. From such small beginnings did the institution take its start. No rank, no class of men, is unrepresented. The school was of the people.

The institution was as yet only a modest school ; not till later did it aspire to be a college, much less a university. The first principal, during whose administration the Harvard bequest was received, was Nathaniel Eaton. " Of this man," says Josiah Quincy, " nothing has been transmitted worthy of being repeated " ; a thought emphasized in the statement of Hubbard, that " he was fitter to have been an officer in the Inquisition than the instructor of Christian youth." †

Eaton was succeeded (1640) by Mr. Henry Dunster, with the title of " President." A scholarly, painstaking, pious, earnest man, he, of all the early friends of the college, after its founder, deserves most thoughtful notice. Under his direction was formed the first code of laws, regulations were

---

* The remains of John Harvard lie buried on Harvard Hill, in Charlestown, where (1828), almost two centuries after his death, a monument was erected to his memory ; it was upon this occasion that Hon. Edward Everett pronounced his famous oration on the founder of Harvard College. (See " Orations," vol. i, p. 176.)

† " History of New England," p. 91.

adopted, and degrees established. Like John Harvard, Mr. Dunster was educated in Emmanuel College, and, like him also, had been a nonconformist clergyman.

From his own early training, he patterned the Harvard course largely after that of the English universities, though variously modified to suit the new conditions. After nineteen years of only informal management the policy began to be more fixed, and the requirements for admission were announced as follows : "When any scholar is able to read Tully or any like classical Latin author, *ex tempore*, and make and speak true Latin in verse and prose (*suo ut aiunt Marte*), and decline perfectly the paradigms of nouns and verbs in the Greek tongue, then may he be admitted to the college ; nor shall any claim admission before such qualification."

The course covered three years, and, in the nomenclature of the day, was both "liberal" and comprehensive. It must be remembered that for sixty years the institution was little more than a training-school for ministers, managed as a theological seminary, having religion, of a more or less well-defined type, as its basis and chief object. Yet, as Prof. Emerson has put it,* "It is one of the most remarkable things in the history of Harvard, that, in all the constitutions of the college, there is nothing illiberal or sectarian ; nothing to check the freest pursuit of truth in theological opinions, and in everything else; and this, too, while the founders of the college were severely and strictly orthodox; often exclusive in their own opinions, and while their object was unquestionably to provide for the thorough education of ministers of the gospel of like views with themselves."

The course † included two years of logic, and something of physics; two of ethics and politics; two of mathematics (including, however, only arithmetic and geometry), the equivalent of four years of Greek, and one year each of He-

---

* " Lowell Lectures," 1869, p. 293.
† Richardson's " The College Book," p. 8.

brew, Chaldee, and Syriac. Latin was excluded as something that must have been mastered before entrance, its conversational use being obligatory upon all within the limits of the college, in place of the mother-tongue, which was "to be used under no pretext whatever, unless required in public exercises." The Bible was systematically studied for the entire three years, Ezra, Daniel, and the New Testament being specified. A year was given to catechetical divinity. Daily prayers must be attended "at six o'clock in the morning and five o'clock at night all the yeare long"; at which time students were required to "read some portion of the Old Testament out of Hebrew into Greek, and the New Testament out of English into Greek, after which "one of the Bachelors or Sophisters should logically analyze that which was read."

History was taught by lectures a few weeks in the winter, and botany in like manner in the summer. Allowing even for this last, science was practically unknown ; all profane literature was excluded ; and even "philosophy, such as is worthy of the name," says Richardson, "was untouched."

Not less exacting were the requirements of studentship. President Dunster seems to have been head and body of the whole institution. No possible conduct escaped his eye. Class deportment, plan of studies, personal habits, daily life, private devotions, social intercourse, and civil privileges, were all directed.

Concerning degrees it was ordered that "every scholar that on proof is found able to read the originals of the Old and New Testament into the Latin tongue, and to resolve them logically; withal being of Godly life and conversation; and at any publick act hath the approbation of the overseers and master of the Colledge, is fit to be dignified with his first degree." *

For a second degree, it was required, in addition to the

---

* See " New England's First Fruits," a quaintly entertaining sketch of Harvard, written 1643, and to be found in " Massachusetts Historical Collections," vol. i, p. 245.

above, that the applicant should "give up a system, or synopsis or summe" of logic, natural and moral philosophy, arithmetic, geometry, and astronomy ; and defend his thesis.

The first commencement was held in 1642, when nine young men took their degrees. The first doctorate conferred was upon the famous Increase Mather (1692), a distinction "as well deserved," says Quincy, "as it was acceptable to both father and son."

Under President Dunster the college grew and prospered. Few men have done so much for American education as he. In a chaotic period he gave it form. Amid distracting religious and political claims, he secured to the college a union of interests and a co-operation of forces that, aside from formal education, did much to shape and fix a common New England sentiment. During his office, Harvard acquired such repute that " in several instances youths of opulent families in the parent country were sent to the American Cambridge for a finishing education." *

In the year 1647 the population of the Massachusetts Bay Colony was about four thousand, and that of all New England something more than five times as much. There were in all, fifty towns and villages, as many ministers, and half as many churches. Of the twenty graduates in the first decade, twelve found their life-work in Europe ; but of the five hundred alumni during the seventeenth century, fully one half, it is estimated, entered the ministry, and chiefly in New England. After Chauncy, successor to Dunster and second president of the college, "both presidents and tutors were chosen from its own graduates." †

The four colonies had, in the first decade, given Harvard thirteen hundred dollars—Boston, one third of it. Connecticut, about this time, projected a college ; but, failing in the undertaking, the money raised was generously turned

---

* Palfrey's " History of New England," vol. i, p. 290.
† George C. Bush's " Harvard College," p. 63.

over to Massachusetts. Indeed, it is on record that, up to the founding of Yale, the one settlement of New Haven had furnished one thirtieth of the Harvard graduates.

The institution was intrusted to a managing board in 1642, and eight years later received its first and only charter, sealed by Governor Dudley, and ratified by the Constitution of 1780. Fellowships were introduced by President Dunster, and, about 1725, two professorships founded by a London merchant. Aside from the latter, the salaries were, for a hundred years, paid out of the colonial treasury.

In an official paper signed by Governor Endicott, bearing date 1655, and addressed to the General Court, information was given that "all the estate the college hath (as appears by the inventory thereof), is only its present building, library, and a few utensils with the press,* and some parcels of land (none of which can with any reason, or to any benefit, be sold to help in the premises), and in real revenue, about twelve pounds per annum (which is a small pittance to be shared among four fellows), besides fifteen pounds per annum, which by donor's appointment is for scholarships."

During the next fifty years the embarrassments of the college were numerous, both financial and official. Salaries—small as they were—were repudiated ; the buildings were decayed, and the political influences of the English Restoration were noticeable in the diminished support accorded the college. Added to all this, the president proved inefficient, and the attendance greatly decreased. But for timely help from New Hampshire, and occasional private aid from England, the institution must have been seriously impaired.

Under the provincial reorganization of William and Mary, a strong effort was made to revive the college interest. A royal charter was repeatedly sought. It was a period of extreme religious controversy and political unrest, witchcraft

---

* The printing-press brought from England, and set up at Harvard by Stephen Daye in 1639. (See Thomas's "History of Printing," vol. i, pp. 203, 231).

was at its highest, Calvinism and the newer New England Congregationalism were in conflict.* The college was without a recognized charter, and for twenty years without a resident head.† The once unquestioned power of the clergy was waning. There was faction without, and sometimes incompetence within. A child of the people, and expecting little from royalty, it received less. Having only a provincial charter, with no English authority, the institution lacked permanence. The management was various and unequal. A fixed constitution was indispensable. This came, as has been noted, not from the queen, but from a royal Governor, Joseph Dudley, of whom and whose service to the college, Mr. Quincy has said, "Of all statesmen who have been instrumental in promoting the interests of Harvard College, Governor Joseph Dudley was most influential in giving its constitution permanent character."

President Leverett (1707–1724) was a man of rare intellectual attainments and dignity of character. Rich in scholarship, he was at the same time, what was far more common then than now, both theologian and statesman. He was one of the earliest, if not the first, among American recipients of election to membership in the Royal Society of London. Under his somewhat uneventful service were initiated certain improvements in the curriculum, which, while not completed for many years, ultimately made the Revolutionary Harvard very different from that of the seventeenth century.

First, Latin ceased to be required in conversation, and through Virgil and Cicero became a part of the instruction. Chaldee and Syriac were omitted, though Hebrew long remained. After a time there was added to the course, something of geography, and in a limited way of physics. Not

---

* This is well treated in Quincy's "History of Harvard University," vol. i, p. 366.

† Both Increase Mather (except for a few months of the sixteen years he held the office) and Samuel Willard, residing in Boston and having ministerial charges.

until near the Revolution was any attempt made to organize the instruction into a system, by establishing departments or courses. This change marks an epoch in the development of the Harvard curriculum. All instruction was thrown into the four groups : 1. Latin. 2. Greek. 3. Logic and metaphysics. 4. Mathematics and natural philosophy ; each of which was put into the exclusive charge of one man.

By benefactions during the century prior to the Revolution, the college received in money nearly fifteen thousand pounds, of which Thomas Hollis, an English Dissenting friend, and his son, gave one half. It received also one thousand acres of land, and a few books. Nevertheless, the management all these years had to do with poverty and faction and antagonisms. Dunster was compelled to resign his presidency through the jealousies of Pædobaptist fanaticism. Chauncy lived in grinding poverty ; Mather and Willard both depended upon pastoral relations to eke out a pinched maintenance ; and Leverett died bankrupt.* But most of all and most serious, the institution was for years disturbed by being brought into the religious controversies of the time. In a controversial age this was inevitable. The conscience of dissent begot a habit.

The very foundation idea of the college was the theologic want. The presidents and members of the corporation were generally the prominent scholars, the theologians, and political leaders, of the community and time. The college easily came to be the arena upon which, or the interest about which, were fought those terrible logomachies of dogma and doctrine. These required, as they had, the best learning, the shrewdest insight, the most politic minds of the day.

---

* The president's salary during this period never exceeded two hundred pounds a year, and usually was but one hundred and fifty. The total grants made to the college during the first century, by the colony, amounted to about eight thousand dollars. At the close of the century (1732), the total annual income from all sources was but seven hundred and fifty pounds.

3

In the controversies sustained by the Mathers; in the New England scheme for establishing a chair of divinity by Hollis; in the conflict of Puritans and Episcopalians; Whitefield and Wigglesworth; Chauncy and Edwards, the college was repeatedly shaken to its foundations. Yet, through it all, it accomplished a much-needed work, with manifold wholesome reactions upon society and government, so that it has been affirmed, with show of truth, that "the founding of Harvard College hastened the Revolution half a century."*

2. The College of William and Mary.

Ten years after the settlement at Jamestown (1617), the English king, James I, addressed the following letter to the bishops of the English churches:

"Most Reverend Father in God, right trustie and well-beloved counsellor, wee greet you well:—

"You have heard, ere this time of the attempt of diverse worthie men, our subjects, to plant in Virginia (under warrant of our letters patent), People of this Kingdom, as well for the enlarging of our Dominion, as for the propagation of the Gospel among Infidells: wherein there is good progress made, and hope of further increase; so as the undertakers of that Plantation are now in hand with the erecting of some churches and some schools for the education of the children of those barbarians; . . . in which we doubt not but that you and all others who wish well to the increase of the Christian religion will be willing to give all assistance and furtherance you may, and therein to make experience of the zeal and devotion of our well-minded subjects, especially those of the clergy.

"Whereby we do require you, and hereby authorize you to write your letters to the severall Bishops of the Dioceses of your Province, that they do give order to ministers and

---

* Concerning this controversial period and its relations to the college, read chapters vii, x, and xxii of Quincy's "History of Harvard University."

other zealous men of their Dioceses both by their own example in contribution, and by exhortation to others to move our people within their severall charges to contribute to so good a work in as liberal a manner as they may; for the better advancing whereof our pleasure is that those collections be made in the particular parishes four severall times within these two years next coming; and that the severall accounts of each parish together with the monies collected, be returned from time to time to the Bishops of the Dioceses, and by them transmitted half-yearly to you; and so to be delivered to the treasurer of that Plantation, to be employed for the Godly purpose intended and no other." *

Two years afterward (1619) Sir Edwin Sandys, treasurer, reported fifteen hundred pounds, one half of which had been loaned to the company as an investment, whose interest should be applied to the support of the school.

He recommended, however, that the building of the college be temporarily postponed; that a piece of land be laid out at Henrico, which should be called the " college land," one half the returns from which should go to the company, and be set apart as a "college fund." † It was so ordered. A hundred laborers were sent over, a superintendent of buildings was appointed, and Rev. Patrick Copeland made first president of the college. The enterprise was promising. Everything was planned on a large scale. These were loyal English subjects and had the patronage of the throne. In the year 1621 the preparatory school at Charles City was ordered open, with its lands and servants and revenue. The college was to follow.

The massacre, the next year, put a stop to every enterprise, except that of self-defense. Superintendent Thorp, nine of the college laborers, and more than three hundred

---

* Neill's " Virginia Vetusta," p. 167.

† The story of the efforts in Virginia during these years to found a college is told with much interest and a fund of original material, in Mr. Neill's " Virginia Company of London."

colonists, perished in a day. It seemed as if years must elapse before anything further could be even attempted. Dangers were all about. The Virginia savages were at their cruelest, crops were uncertain, disease had numerous victims, and for many months the company's reports abounded in disappointment and defeat. Of ten thousand colonists, old and young, said to have arrived in the first sixteen years of the Virginia settlement, but two thousand remained.

Yet the colonists were not disheartened. The only people on the continent asking immediate means of schooling, their sacrifices become heroic. New England existed in four towns. Davenport, Winthrop, Eaton, and John Harvard were still in England. As yet Virginia was America. Ambitious beyond their means, there was no Berkeley to oppose. Almost immediately after the massacre the idea of the college was revived.

One Edward Palmer, an educated Englishman, and holder of a Virginia patent, provided by will for the founding of a university and school of art, on an island near the mouth of the Susquehanna River. He is said to have spent many thousand pounds improving the island, and the immediate site, that it should be at once a quiet retreat for the studious, and afford security from the attacks of the savage. It was to be called "Academia Virginiensis et Oxoniensis." * Of all this, however, nothing remains but the memory of a misplaced æstheticism, the vagary of an educational enthusiast. The Indian was a poor subject for a school of art ; and the Indian seemed to rule.

In 1660 the founding of the college was again revived, this time by the settlers themselves. The Virginia Company had dissolved, nearly forty years before. It had sought to colonize the country, make a profitable investment, convert the heathen (the infidels), and magnify the king. On every point they came out bankrupt : money had been sunk in the experiment, lives lost, and the gains to religion, to learning,

---

* "Virginia Vetusta," p. 183.

and to human comforts, were painfully small. The settlers were now few, and in poverty. Harvard was flourishing, paying her president one hundred and fifty pounds a year, and fighting heresy through anti-pædobaptism. In the year named, the Virginia Assembly, moved by the want of able and faithful ministers, enacted that "for the advance of learning, education of youth, supply of the ministry, and the promotion of piety, there be land taken for a colledge and free schoole." Subscriptions were taken, and others invited by magisterial order and sanction.* They came from every class and of varying amounts.

In this first appears the spirit of the people as distinct from the administration and the Church. It marks a feeling of confidence and self-helpfulness wholly new to the Virginian. Although nothing came of it immediately, it constituted the beginning of an interest that culminated in the founding of William and Mary College thirty years later. The institution was as yet without name—only known as the "college"—but referred to in frequent communications, public documents, bequests, and legislation; and universally so recognized throughout Virginia, the Bermudas, New England, and in Parliament, for fifty years prior to the reign of William and Mary.

Finally (1688), certain wealthy planters subscribed for the college twenty-five hundred pounds, and the preamble to the charter then sought, and obtained five years later, was largely in the words of the act of 1660. The Winthrop of Virginia was Rev. James Blair, for many years a minister of the Established Church, first in England, then in the colony; and later an educator, a scholar, and an author, he was familiar with the people, their institutions, and their ignorance, as few others could be. He presented the cause to the queen in person, receiving her enthusiastic support. King William co-operated. Both generously gave aid in money, promising a charter.

---

* Henning's "Statutes at Large" (Virginia), vol. ii, p. 25.

When Seymour, the attorney-general, was presented with the royal order for a charter, he refused. The home country was involved in a war with France; and Virginia and the barbarians could wait for their college. Mr. Blair urged, by way of manly appeal, that, as "Virginians had souls to be saved as well as their English countrymen," the institution was needed to prepare young men for the ministry. "Souls !" cried Seymour, "damn your souls ! make tobacco." Notwithstanding official profanity, however, the charter was granted—the first royal educational charter in America. Aid was abundantly given. A provisional board was constituted, Mr. Blair was made first president, and the college of William and Mary became the second colonial school. By charter the college was established in the Middle Plantation, now Williamsburg, where it remains ; was given twenty thousand acres of land, a penny a pound tax on all tobacco exported from Virginia and Maryland, and the fees and privileges of the Surveyor-General's office.* It further provided for a chancellor, who should hold his office seven years; a president (in terms of the charter, a commissary); the education of Indians ; immunity of the college belongings from taxation, and a representative of the college in the colonial Legislature. In respect of the last point, at least, the history of William and Mary is peculiar among American institutions of learning. This representative might be one of the faculty, or a member of the board of visitors, or "one of the better sort of inhabitants of the colony," but, in any case, the selection was by the college faculty. The bishops of London were the chancellors down to the Revolution. George Washington, chosen to the office in 1789, was not only the first American, but the first layman, to receive the honor.

The institution came into existence rich. In three months it was given more than Harvard received for the first fifty

---

* Washington and Jefferson both received their surveyor's commission from the College of William and Mary.

years. In twenty years, while Harvard was in poverty and Yale had yet no fixed existence, the property of William and Mary included, besides buildings and grounds, 22,450 acres of the richest of Virginia river-bottom land, a large tobacco revenue, the fees and profits of the Surveyor-General's office, together with a considerable cash income. In its royal foundation, its generous endowment and liberal patronage, it stands in sharp contrast to the early years of Harvard. This was established by Puritans and stood for the severest of ultra-orthodox though dissenting Protestantism ; that was founded to be and was an exponent of the most formal ceremonialism of the Church of England. The one was nursed by democracy; the other befriended by Cavaalier and courtier. Endowment for the one came from the thin purses of an infant and needy settlement; the other was drawn from the royal treasury. The one was environed and shaken for a hundred years by the schisms of a controversial people; the roots of the other were deep in the great English ecclesiastical system.

In the organization, besides the grammar-school for teaching the Latin and Greek, and a school of philosophy, including mathematics, there was designed to be a third, and one to which these were to be in the main supplementary and subordinate, in which should be taught divinity and the Oriental languages ;* for it was part of the original plan, running back through the years to 1619, that the college when established should be " a seminary for the breeding of good ministers."† Governors and visitors were required to be members of the Church of England, professors to subscribe to the Thirty-nine Articles, and students to know the catechism.

Of the curriculum up to the Revolution, less even is known than of that of Yale of the same period, and far less than of Harvard. All were of English pattern, though

---

* To these was afterward added the " Indian school."

† See " Massachusetts Historical Collections," vol. v, p. 164.

modified in time by local conditions. History seems to have had an earlier prominence in Virginia than in the colonies North.* The general course covered three years, and included the five departments—Greek, Latin, mathematics, moral philosophy, and divinity. It was classical and prescribed. For a hundred years the speaking of Latin in original composition was required twice a month. Meager as it all seems in the light of inadequate records, it was nevertheless a "school of the prophets," outside divinity. It was a place where independence grew, but where tolerance also thrived. Its teaching has been described as after the Oxford order of humanities: the abstract as the foundation of the concrete; everything for discipline; the ancient languages before the modern; the laws of right rather than those of matter.

Whatever it was, the historic product is worthy of consideration. Jefferson and four other signers of the Declaration of Independence were graduates; three Randolphs, Monroe, Judge Blair, and Chief-Justice Marshall. This, too, from a school whose annual average enrollment for the entire period was less than seventy-five students.

With an annual revenue of £4,000 it was by far the best equipped institution in America; but its buildings were twice burned, its libraries lost, and it came out of the war (1783) with entire loss of its landed interest, and, in the depreciation of currency, of all its endowment, revenues, etc.

The regulations of William and Mary College were no less severe than those of Harvard already noted. Laws were passed (1754) prohibiting students "keeping or having to do with race-horses," against "playing or betting at the billiard or other gaming table," or being concerned in "keeping or fighting cocks," under pain of severest animadversion or punishment. Everything was prescriptive and mandatory. Even the faculty had no escape. Just prior to the

---

* See Adams's " College of William and Mary," and " Study of History in American Colleges."

Revolution, the Professor of Divinity and the master of the grammar-school having married and taken up their residence outside the college grounds, it was resolved by the Board of Visitors that it was " the opinion of this visitation that the professors and masters, their engaging in marriage and the concerns of a private family, and shifting their residence to any place without the college, is contrary to the principles on which the college was founded and their duty as professors." It was further ordered that *thereafter*, upon the marriage of a professor or master, his professorship be immediately vacated.*

3. Yale College.

With John Davenport,† one of the founders of the New Haven Colony, it was a design from the first to provide them a college. He had assisted in the establishment of Harvard and lost no opportunity to give like direction to the newer colony. In 1647 a lot was set apart for a college. Within ten years the need was so urgently felt that New Haven had subscribed three hundred pounds and adjoining settlements nearly as much more. The project however, halted. The "college" was not begun. The people were few, and the embarrassments attending all new settlements pressing at New Haven. Besides, the support of all the colonies was needed at Cambridge. The cost was counted, the returns from two small colleges put beside the influence from one vigorous and well-supported one; and it seemed to them more wise to be content with something less than a college at home, and wait for a more favorable season.

Of course, it could not long remain that the colony of Davenport and Eaton should be dependent upon another for the best education. The inconveniences of a journey to Boston, the extra expense, and the importance of a sufficient

---

* See " Sketch of William and Mary College," anonymous, p. 50.

† He was a member of the committee, 1637, to carry into effect the order of the General Court locating Harvard College.

and thoroughly and wisely educated ministry, all served to
keep alive the original design. In 1698 a plan was proposed, and embraced with great unanimity. It contemplated
a college founded and directed by a general synod of the
churches. It should be called the "School of the Church,"
and receive from them toward its support, and an oversight
"as far as should be necessary to preserve orthodoxy in the
government." * The synod seems not to have been formally
constituted; but the ministers, among whom, all the while,
the design was concerted and cherished, held it in remem-
brance and discussed it in their councils. In the year 1699
ten of the principal clergymen of the colony were agreed
upon to be "trustees to found, erect, and govern a college."
They met the year following with invited counsel, and
formed a society, to consist of eleven ministers, to take initial
steps.

At a second meeting, but in the same year, each trustee
brought a number of books, and, laying them on a table, presented them to the body, saying in substance, "I give these
books for the founding of a college in this colony." These
forty volumes, and the acts of the trustees at this meeting
(1700), constitute the beginning of Yale College. Like that
at Cambridge, sixty-three years before, it was without dis-
play; and, except for the magnanimous character of the
founders, without promise.

The colony had a population of fifteen thousand (about
one fourth that of Massachusetts), a tax-list of two hundred
thousand pounds, and fifty or more college men, including
the clergy.

The whole of New England had a population of less
than one hundred thousand, whose patronage must now
be divided not only between Harvard and Yale (with the
advantages three to one in favor of the former financially),
but more or less also with the recently founded William

---

* On this point see a "Sketch of the History of Yale College," by Prof.
Kingsley, 1835.

and Mary College. With limited means and a scattered population; little royal support, and the taxing industry of a pioneer life ; exhausted by Indian wars, and no established commerce, the prospect was anything but encouraging.

The beginning was made, however; a charter was obtained the year following (1701), and Rev. Abraham Pierson chosen first rector. The school (it was not called a college—sometimes a collegiate school) was opened in March, 1701, and, until the following September, one Jacob Hemingway was the sole student. The first fruits were largely gleanings from Cambridge. The school increasing in numbers, a tutor was elected in 1703, and the school took on something of organization. The regulations, for the most part, were those at Harvard, as also the course of study.

There was nothing in the charter concerning any religious test for trustees, rectors, or tutors. It was early required by the trustees, however, that no instruction should be given in any other system or synopsis of divinity than such as the trustees should order ; and that students should recite daily, and be examined in, the "Assembly's Catechism" and Ames's "Cases of Conscience," and "Theological Theses."

To add to the first year's embarrassments, the school had no fixed existence. It had been decided (1701) to open it at Saybrook, "if it could be done without too much inconvenience." Inasmuch as the rector lived at Killingworth, however, where he had his clerical charge, the school was first located there. At Mr. Pierson's death (1707), Rev. Samuel Andrews was made acting rector, with whom, for nine years, the seniors resided and were taught, at Milford. For most of this time the under classes were with two tutors at Saybrook, the nominal seat of the school, and where for fifteen years the commencements were held.

Factions had been at work for a permanent location. In 1716 the trustees being unable, financially, to decide the question at once, allowed to students (except seniors) the privilege of finding their own instructors until the next

commencement. Seniors were required to reside with the
rector. The school, small as it was (about twenty-five students), was scattered in half a dozen towns of the colony.
The provision was extremely unsatisfactory. The institution was really no institution. Its work was inconsiderable
in amount, and lacked every element of system, or unity,
or pervading purpose ; and yet, even then, next to the
churches, it was the one object of concern for clergy and
educated laity ; the one interest, universal and ever present ; whose discussion was destined to unite the Connecticut colonies as nothing else could. The factions were bitter enough in seeming, but they were superficial. It was
finally decided to locate the school permanently at New
Haven. This was effected in 1718.

As yet little has been said of the financial condition and
growth of Yale College, and nothing of the event which
finally gave it a name.

Elihu Yale * was born in Boston, April 5, 1648. At ten
years of age he was taken to England to be educated.
Twenty years he spent in the schools and in special study.
He afterward went to the East Indies, acquired a large
fortune, was made Governor of Madras, and, later, Governor of the East India Company. In 1718 he was elected
a Fellow of the Royal Society of London. His donations
to the college at New Haven, largely in books, amounted to
about five hundred pounds.

Next to John Davenport, also, the college owed much
to Rev. Cotton Mather, of Boston. Somewhat disaffected
toward Harvard, on theological grounds, † both he and his

---

* A good biography of Elihu Yale, including so much as is known of
his life, may be found in the " Yale Literary Magazine," April, 1858.

† The Saybrook school was opened the year after the unsuccessful attempt at Harvard to impose a religious test; and it has been frequently
affirmed, with some show of truth, that the first movers in the Connecticut
school alleged this as a reason : *that the college at Cambridge was under the
tutelage of latitudinarians.* (Quincy's " Harvard University," vol. ii, p.
462.)

father had, from the beginning, encouraged the Connecticut venture. A private letter from the younger Mather to Governor Yale probably suggested the Yale donation, and led, at the commencement, 1718, to affix to the now established institution its present name. Besides Mr. Yale, others, both in this country and in England, contributed to the college, prominent among whom was the Rev. George Berkeley, who gave ninety-six acres of land in Rhode Island, and one thousand volumes for the library. The conditions and circumstances of this gift are interesting. Dean of Derry, and afterward Bishop of Cloyne, he was a man of outward as well as intellectual rank. Though a High Churchman, he was a liberal-minded, scholarly, generous-hearted lover of learning. He came across to America early in the century, hoping, with the promise of a parliamentary grant, to found a college in the Bermudas. His property accumulated ; but, his scheme failing, he returned to England, leaving in America many nonconformist friends to whom and for whom it was easy to make generous gifts.

The entire contribution of every sort made by the Commonwealth of Connecticut prior to the Revolution was less than twenty-five thousand dollars, and in a century and a half had not reached one hundred thousand dollars. Indeed, the institution has been chiefly supported, as it was originally founded, by private means.

Of the course of study not much can be given from these earlier years—even less than of Harvard of the same period. As might be supposed, it was chiefly theological, though an occasional tutor seems to have injected somewhat of science into the common routine. Dr. Samuel Johnson (1718) broke away from the established cosmic doctrine, and introduced the Copernican theory. Mr. Ezra Styles, a little later, made simple experiments with an electrical machine which had been presented to the college by Benjamin Franklin. Rector Clap (1740), "to keep the college abreast with what were thought to be the demands of the age," made certain additions to the curriculum. The work in physics and mathematics was increased; the latter comprising instruction in conic sections and fluxions, surveying, navigation, and the calculation of eclipses. While there was not, for many years, such a thing thought of as modern history, Dr. Clap announced, and regularly delivered for a number of years, "lectures upon all those subjects which are necessary to be understood to qualify young men for the various stations and employments of life." Here was an attempt at least, whatever its success, to fit culture to living. The "Great Awakening," also, of 1740, through the preaching of Whitefield and Jonathan Edwards, led to the founding (1755), after years of bitter excitement, and tract and pamphlet war, of a professorship of divinity. Earlier in the century, Rector Cutler and part of the tutors had gone over to Episcopacy,* and had been "excused from further service." This was sufficient cause for alarm throughout the New England congregations, and led in 1722 to the introduction of a religious test in Yale, for rector and tutor, that lasted for a hundred years. All officers of the college were required to assent to the "Saybrook Platform" of 1708, giving satisfaction of "the soundness of their faith in opposition to Arminian and prelatical corruption." This was reaffirmed in 1753, and was followed by the divinity chair noted above.

Bibliography.

Of the colonial colleges, Harvard is best known, and has best preserved its history. The earliest, Part I, of "The First Fruits of New England," published in 1642, and to be found in the "Massachusetts Historical Collections," is a brief but detailed sketch of the first American college. One published in 1833, by Prof. Benjamin Peirce, covers the colonial period only. The best of all is the "History of Harvard University," by Josiah Quincy, 1840. Information of William and Mary College is very meager. An anonymous sketch, published in 1874, gives a brief history, a list of the alumni, and what is known of the faculty

---

* This defection of Mr. Cutler and his friends, and the former's relations to Harvard College, as well as to the theological controversies of the day, are well depicted by Mr. Quincy in his first volume (see pp. 364–376.)

and curriculum from its founding. Consult also "De Bow's Review," August, 1859, "Scribner's Monthly," vol. xi, p. 1, and a recent sketch by H. B. Adams, published by the Bureau of Education. Somewhat more is known of Yale College, though far less than of Harvard, and the "Annals of Yale College," by President Thomas Clap (1766), a "Sketch of the History of Yale College," by J. S. Kingsley (1835), and "Yale University," by T. B. Dexter (1885), contain most that is authoritative. Next to these, perhaps first in importance, because dwelling upon certain details, are the numerous articles that have appeared in the "Yale Literary Magazine," begun 1836.

CHAPTER III.

COLONIAL SCHOOL SYSTEMS.

ACCORDING to Horace Mann, there are three fundamental propositions upon which the common-school system of Massachusetts rests. These he gives as—

"1. The successive generations of men, taken collectively, constitute one great commonwealth.

"2. The property of this commonwealth is pledged for the education of all its youth up to such point as will save them from poverty and vice, and prepare them for the adequate performance of their social and civil duties.

"3. The successive holders of this property are trustees, bound to the faithful execution of their trust by the most sacred obligations; and embezzlement and pillage from children have not less of criminality, and more of meanness, than the same offenses perpetrated against contemporaries."*

This was written but forty years ago, and so belongs to the present; but the sentiment was scarcely less true of Massachusetts two hundred years before.

New England early adopted, and has, with a single ex-

---

* See his "Lectures," vol. ii, p. 549. (Report for 1846.)

ception, constantly maintained the principle that the public should provide for the instruction of all the youth. That which elsewhere, as will be found, was left to local provision, as in New York; or to charity, as in Pennsylvania ; or to parental interest, as in Virginia, was in most parts of New England early secured by law. "For the purpose of public instruction," said Daniel Webster, "we have held, and do hold, every man subject to taxation in proportion to his property; and we look not to the question whether he himself have or have not children, to be benefited by the education for which he pays." That it was not always so only serves to define the growth of the educational idea. The act of 1642 in Massachusetts, whose provisions were adopted in most of the adjacent colonies, was admirable as a first legislative school law. It was watchful of the neglect of parents, and looked well after the ignorant and the indigent. But it neither made schooling free, nor imposed a penalty for its neglect. It provided employment for the idle, and so early recognized the dependence of social institutions upon individual thrift; it admitted the force of intelligent citizenship, and sought to make the school also serve the uses of the State, enjoining upon all towns provision for universal education. The spirit of the law was progressive. But schools were largely maintained by rates, were free only to the necessitous, and in not a few of the less populous districts closed altogether or never opened. This led, five years later, to more stringent legislation.

1. The Massachusetts Law of 1647.

As the Colonial Assembly, in the founding of Harvard, was moved by a consideration of the interests of the Church, so the preamble to the first compulsory common-school-enactment of Massachusetts urged the necessities of the religious life as its occasion. As suggesting the general scope and tenor of the law, the following extract is made:

" It being one chief project of that old deluder, Satan, to keep men from the knowledge of the Scriptures, as, in former times, keeping them in an unknown tongue, so in these later times, by persuading from the use of tongues; so that at last the true sense and meaning of the original might be clouded and corrupted with false glosses of deceivers; and to the end that learning may not be buried in the graves of our fore-fathers, in church and commonwealth, the Lord assisting our endeavors: It is therefore ordered by this Court and authority thereof that every township within this jurisdiction, after the Lord hath increased them to the number of fifty householders, shall then forthwith appoint one within their town to teach all such children as shall resort to him, to write and read; whose wages shall be paid, either by the parents or masters of such children, or by the inhabitants in general, by way of supply, as the major part of those who order the prudentials of the town shall appoint; provided that those who send their children be not oppressed by paying much more than they can have them taught for in the adjoining towns.

"And it is further ordered that where any town shall increase to the number of one hundred families or householders, they shall set up a grammar-school, the master thereof being able to instruct youths so far as they may be fitted for the university; and if any town neglect the performance hereof, above one year, then every such town shall pay five pounds per annum to the next such school, till they shall perform this order." *

In this law, it is evident, the school system of Massachusetts had its birth. Schools did not spring up all at once, and throughout the State; nor were all of equal efficiency; the school course was not yet fixed; resources were limited; teachers were poorly prepared; there were no elementary texts and no school organization. With every possible support of the law, there were many hindrances. As a matter of fact, if perhaps Sweden be excepted, there was no precedent in the world's history for such universal

---

* " Massachusetts Colonial Records," vol ii, p. 203.

4

education, through the agency of free schools as a civil institution.   The attempt must have seemed, to the nations
looking on, as the irrational presumption of a youthful
colony.

The law was a public measure and sought the schooling
of all: not the poor alone, or of preference; nor select
schools for the sons of ministers and magistrates ; nor
family schools; but common schools, upon the principle,
then efficient, but formulated later, that " they must be cheap
enough for all, and good enough for the best." It should be
noted that the law makes provision for grammar-schools;
that is for schools which should give instruction in Latin and
Greek; and, indeed, in whatever should be necessary to fit
young men to enter Harvard.   They belonged to a type of preparatory school, characteristic of New England, the original
of the best modern secondary institution.   Still further, the
law was mandatory; a penalty was attached for a town's
neglect.   The original forfeit, five pounds, was increased in
1671, 1683, and 1718, successively, to correspond with the increasing wealth of the towns, to a penalty of sixty pounds
for a town of three hundred families.*

---

* Mr. Joseph B. Felt, in his " Historical Account of Massachusetts
Currency," has been at some pains to estimate the relative cost to the community of these forfeitures, measured by the community's resources.   It is
known that, in early American times, grains were used as tender in payment
of debts.   New Haven for many years paid her annual quota to Harvard by
sending " one peck of wheat to each man." For the payment of obligations, the law fixed the value of the product in terms of its standard unit.
The average rate for Indian corn for the last half of the seventeenth century (the period under consideration), Mr. Felt estimates at less than three
shillings per bushel.   To pay a fine, therefore, of sixty pounds, to which a
town of three hundred families was liable, would require four hundred and
twenty-three bushels.   At sixpence a day (the wages provided by law,
1630, and in force many years), it would take a man forty days to pay a
fine of one pound.   The penalty imposed upon towns by the law of 1647,
was five pounds ; equivalent, at the above rate, to the work of a common
laborer for two hundred days.

2. *The Connecticut Code of 1650.*

Three years after the law just cited Connecticut passed a very similar one. A difference will be seen in the reasons assigned for the enactments in the two colonies; and it is a significant fact that the "indifference and indulgence of many parents and masters" is made a sufficient reason for the colony's interference in the interest of the child.

This enactment continued in force, substantially unchanged. until the close of the last century, and, excepting that of Massachusetts, marks out the only system of schools during the colonial history. It is given almost entire, first as a means of comparative study, and as a specimen also of the severe ethical standards of the day:

"Forasmuch as the good education of children is of singular behoof and benefit to any commonwealth, and whereas many parents and masters are too indulgent and negligent of their duty in that kind: It is therefore ordered by this Court and the authority thereof, that the selectmen of every town, in the several precincts and quarters where they dwell, shall have a vigilant eye over their brethren and neighbors, to see first: that none of them shall suffer so much barbarism in any of their families, as not to endeavor to teach, by themselves or others, their children and apprentices, so much learning, as may enable them perfectly to read the English tongue, and knowledge of the capital laws, upon penalty of twenty shillings for each neglect therein: also that all masters of families do once a week at least, catechise their children and servants in the grounds and principles of religion, and if any be not able to do so much, that then, at the least, they procure such children or apprentices, to learn some short, orthodox catechism, without book, that they may be able to answer to the questions that shall be propounded to them out of such catechism by their parents or masters, or any of the selectmen when they shall call them to a trial of what they have learned in this kind. And further that all parents and masters do breed and bring up their children and apprentices in some honest, lawful calling, labor, or employment, either in husbandry or some other trade profitable for themselves and the commonwealth, if they will not, nor can not, train them up in learning to fit them for higher employments : and if any of the selectmen, after admonition by them given to such masters of families shall find them still negligent of their duty, in the particular aforementioned, whereby children and servants become rude, stubborn and unruly, the said selectmen with the help of two magistrates, shall take such children or apprentices from them, and place them with some masters—boys till they come to twenty-one, and girls to eighteen years of age complete—which will more strictly look unto, and force them to submit unto government, according to the rules of this order, if by fair means and former instruction they will not be drawn into it." *

In addition to the provisions quoted, the code required of every town of fifty families an elementary school, and every town of one hundred families a grammar-school, as provided in the Massachusetts law.

The enactment in the colony of New Haven (1655) was very similar to this, differing perhaps only in being, if equally considerate, more exacting. The same watchful eye over their brethren was enjoined upon the deputies of the Court or other officers. Negligent parents and masters were to be warned, and, if still remiss, pay a double fine. For a third offense the Court might " proceed to a greater fine," or, " taking security for due conformity to the scope and intent of the law," might take such children or apprentices and bind them out " both for the public conveniency, and for the particular good of the children and apprentices."

Ten years afterward the two colonies were united, the Connecticut " code of 1650 " becoming operative for the whole province. The law was revised when the civil or-

---

* Extract from Code of Laws, 1650, paragraph 19, " Colonial Records of Connecticut," p. 520.

ganization was perfected (1672), each of the four county towns, irrespective of population, being required to maintain a grammar-school.

Elementary schools were later required of towns having thirty families, and in those of seventy householders must continue eleven months in the year.

It was a vigorous system among a thrifty and self-denying people. It betrays no loose sentiment of tender-hearted indulgence. Children should be brought up, not left to grow up. It was the sternest kindness, participation in whose benefits was incident to citizenship.*

These laws of Massachusetts and Connecticut † remained in force for many years—of the former practically till the State Constitution of 1780, of the latter eighteen years longer, until school societies and petty districts were formed.

3. Other New England Schools and Teachers.

In Rhode Island there was no attempt at a school system prior to the efforts of John Howland about 1790. There

---

* As illustrating further the severity of the ethical idea current at the period, two extracts are presented from the capital laws of the colony of the same date :

" SEC. 14. If any child or children above sixteen years old and of sufficient understanding, shall curse or smite their natural father or mother, he or they shall be put to death ; unless it can be sufficiently testified that the parents have been very unchristianly negligent in the education of such children, or so provoked them by extreme and cruel correction, that they have been forced thereunto, to preserve themselves from death or maiming.

" SEC. 15. If any man has a stubborn or rebellious son of sufficient understanding and years, viz., sixteen years of age, which will not obey the voice of his father or the voice of his mother, and when they have chastised him, he will not hearken unto them ; then may his father or his mother, being his natural parents, lay hold on him and bring him to the magistrates assembled in the court, and testify to them that their son is stubborn and rebellious and will not obey their voice and chastisement, but lives in sundry notorious crimes ; such a son shall be put to death."

† " Blue Laws, True and False," by J. H. Trumbull (1876), is an excellent exposition of the spirit of discipline and its consequences, in early Connecticut.

were schools in both Providence and Newport; but the colony was small (with a population of less than ten thousand
in 1700), broken into feeble settlements, and offering little
opportunity for organization.   Up to 1820, as a matter of
course, the school history of Maine was the same as that of
Massachusetts, from which it was then set off as a separate
State.   A like remark may be made of New Hampshire.
United with Massachusetts in 1641, it was subject to the law
of that colony until 1693, when, having become an independent province, and copying the spirit of the Massachusetts system, the selectmen of the towns were required to
raise money "by equal rate and assessment on all the inhabitants for the support of schools," the penalty being put
at twenty pounds.   In Vermont, as the first white settlement
dates from 1724, no schools were maintained during the
period other than occasional and chance ones.

Education to the New England of this period was a public responsibility— part of an exacting religious duty.
Viewed from the individual side, it was to many a privilege.
It claimed the public's second attention; and, next to the
pulpit, commanded the best talent in every settlement.

Among the New England teachers there were men of
both learning and ability.   Not a more cultured body of
men ever formed a colony than settled about Boston, Salem,
New Haven, and Hartford.   They coveted the best advantages for their children, frequently making the best men
their teachers.   It is on record that of the twenty-two masters of Plymouth from 1671 to the Revolution, twenty were
graduates of Harvard.   The like was true of Roxbury.*
Such men, next to the functionaries of church and state,
commanded the highest respect.   In the churches, they had

---

* It was this school whose memory has been perpetuated in the " Free
School of 1645 in Roxbury," by C. K. Dillaway ; and of which Cotton
Mather said, " It had afforded more scholars, first for the college, and then
for the public, than any town of its bigness, or, if I mistake not, of twice its
bigness, in all New England."

special pews provided for their use beside those of magistrates and the deacon's family. In every community was usually one who was the teacher professionally, so considered as much as was the minister or physician. But, among them all, Ezekiel Cheever stood, and stands pre-eminent.

Born * in 1614, he came to this country at the age of twenty-three, joining Eaton and Davenport at New Haven the year following. Here he taught twelve years, first in the free schools, and later in the grammar-school, with a " scholarship and force of personal character which left a permanent mark on the educational policy of New Haven." For eleven years he taught at Ipswich, nine years at Charlestown, and thirty-eight years as master of the Boston Latin School. Cotton Mather links his name with that of Master Corlett's, in the couplet :

> " 'Tis Corlett's pains and Cheever's, we must own,
> That thou, New England, art not Scythia grown."

Mr. Cheever was the author of an " Introduction to the Latin Tongue," popularly known as the " Latin Accidence," which was the hand-book of Latin instruction in New England for more than a century. President Quincy said of it: " For simplicity, comprehensiveness, and exactness, I do not believe it is exceeded by any other work." Under his guidance, the Boston Latin School became the principal classical institution, not only of Massachusetts Bay, and New England, but, according to Dr. Prince, " of the British colonies, if not of all America."

He died in 1708, aged ninety-four, after having taught seventy years.

Women were not formally recognized as teachers until after the Revolution, not generally so till late in the present century, though dame's schools were not infrequent through all the earlier period.

---

* For an extended and appreciative biography of Mr. Cheever, see " American Journal of Education," vol. i, p. 297.

Salaries varied, much as they do now. Exceptional ability always commanded extra remuneration. In considering this question it must be remembered that schools then continued, nominally, twelve months in the year ; the salaries, ranging from two pounds, paid to Thomas Fox, in Newport, some time before 1700, to sixty pounds paid Ezekiel Cheever (1670) as Master of the Boston Latin School. Mr. Barnard is authority for the statement that previous to 1800 the wages of a master varied from four to ten dollars per month, besides board, which was generally " given." Mistresses received from fifty cents to a dollar and a half per week, and board.

The kind and amount of instruction have already been broadly marked out for the whole of New England by the legislation quoted. The classics required in the grammar-schools were, no doubt, well taught. But the elementary instruction, limited to reading, spelling, writing, and the simplest calculations, was very meager. Its content can best be shown perhaps by enumerating the school-books used. Prior to 1665, Richard Mather's Catechism * was, aside from the Bible, almost the only one known. Then, and later, the New Testament was in common use ; and the Psalter, containing—1, the Psalms; 2, Proverbs; 3, the Sermon on the Mount ; and 4, the Nicene Creed. The Horn-Book was very early employed in this country, as it was in England, while the historical " New England Primer " was not introduced until near the close of the seventeenth century, then taking the place of the Catechism.

By these books was determined the organization of the schools, as follows :

---

* " A Catechism, on the Grounds and Principles of the Christian Religion, set forth by question and answer, wherein the summe of the Doctrine of Religion is comprised, familiarly opened, and clearly confirmed from the Holy Scriptures. By Richard Mather, Teacher to the Church in Dorchester in New England, 1650."

1. Psalter class—beginners.
2. Testament class.
3. Bible class.

Of the education of girls almost no mention is made, though they were now and then admitted to the dame's schools.

4. New York prior to the Revolution.

Outside the localities already described, there was little that could be dignified by the name of school system, though here and there, as in the early days of New England, regard was had for education both elementary and advanced, with like courses of study and in the same texts.

It is claimed that, at the surrender of the Dutch in New York (1664), so general was the educational spirit, almost every town in the colony had its regular school and more or less permanent teachers. After the occupation of the province by the English, little attention was given to education ; the settlers were robbed of their revenues; and the new government was not forward to aid Dutch schools in the control of a nonconforming church. While many of the parochial schools were broken up, that in New York city insisted on its chartered rights, maintained its privileges, and is still in existence. Thirteen years after the surrender, a Latin school was opened in the city ; but the first serious attempt to provide regular schooling was in the work of the "Society for the Propagation of the Gospel" (1704) in the founding of Trinity School. The society kept up an efficient organization, for many years, and at the opening of the Revolution had established and chiefly supported more than twenty schools in the colony. About 1732, also, there was established in New York city a school after the plan of the Boston Latin School, free as that was free, and which became, according to eminent authority,* the germ of the later King's (now Columbia) College.

---

* " New York Colonial Manuscripts," vol. viii, p. 486.

From all which it would appear that while the Dutch settlers in New York were earnest in the support of their principal schools, the English officials, either in London or in the
province, showed little interest in the matter. The whole
attitude was in sharp contrast to what was found in New England. Rev. Dr. Samuel Johnson, President of King's College,
writing (1762) to the English archbishop, complained that,
when royal patents were granted for large tracts of colonial
land, "no provision was made for religion and schools."
These, he insisted, should be encouraged, whatever else be
neglected. It is safe to say that, prior to the Revolution,
hundreds of acres had been appropriated in New England
for schools, and in Virginia many thousands.

In one other respect, also, the educational influences in
the two sections were different. Lieutenant-Governor Col-
den, petitioning for aid for King's College, seeing "that dissenters from the Church of England had the sole education,
not only in seminaries of learning in New England, but like-
wise in New Jersey and elsewhere," argued that it was
"highly requisite that a seminary founded on the principles of the Church of England be distinguished in America
by particular privileges ; not only on account of religion,
but of good policy, to prevent the growth of republican
principles which already too much prevail in the colonies."

5. Pennsylvania prior to the Revolution.

Here, as in the last-mentioned colony, no system of
schools existed until the present century. In this province,
however, some attempts at education are worthy to be noted,
both because of occasional individual success, and the fact
that, in the social and civil conditions of that period, recent
educational sentiments have received their impulses.*

The original draught of the Penn Colony charter required

---

* In Sypher's "School History of Pennsylvania," chap. xxxvi, on
"Education," is a very satisfactory summary of the schools and school
legislation of the colonial period.

that the Governor and Provincial Council should erect and order all public schools, and "reward the authors of the useful sciences and laudable inventions in said province." In the fifteen years following the settlement, a few schools were opened in other parts, and in 1698 the Society of Friends established one in Philadelphia. This was the now famous Penn Charter School, to which all children were admitted, male and female, even servants ; and provision made that while the children of the rich might attend at reasonable rates, "the poor should be taught gratis." Though a Friends' school, it was open indiscriminately to children of all denominations, and for fifty years was the only public school in the province.

Near the middle of the last century (1754), urged by the interests of the large German population of the colony, Dr. Franklin and others, aided by contributions from Europe, were instrumental in organizing the "German Society," in Philadelphia, whose purpose was "to found and maintain schools for the numerous children of German settlers." It had a long service, instructed at times nearly one thousand pupils, and proved a powerful civil as well as educational factor in the development of the colony.

It is a matter of history that the Swedes early took possession of fertile valleys along the Delaware, and even in proximity to the mountains, in what is now Pennsylvania. A thrifty, industrious people, they acquired property, and exerted a far-reaching influence on the State's institutions. Others came—Hollanders and English, Catholic and Protestant, Churchmen and Quakers. A book,* descriptive of the Swedish churches of this section, includes a characterization of the people and social conditions of the time, which is suggestive. "The people," the author says, "are a mixture of all sorts of religious belief ; the schoolmasters have a different faith from their pupils, and the children, in like manner, differ from each other. Hence, Pennsylvania is known

---

* "History of New Sweden," by Israel Acrelius, p. 357.

all over the world for its lamentable destitution and deficiency in the instruction of its children in the knowledge of Christianity." Forty years before, about 1725, his people, he claimed, scarcely knew what a school was. While this will be admitted, or it should be, as an exaggeration, it is still only an exaggeration of an actual state, having a foundation in fact, that persisted through the colonial period. A heterogeneous population, and the idea that public education was a form of charity, obstructed schools generally.*

Among all the early teachers of the province, the reputation of none is more worthy to be perpetuated than that of Christopher Dock. A simple but scholarly man, a Mennonite and teacher, exceedingly conscientious, little acquainted with the ways of the world, but devoted to his school, he acquired a reputation as an instructor and companion of the young that, if the record of his life be true, makes him a veritable Pestalozzi in his way. He taught for many years in Germantown; then, dividing his time with a neighboring village, gave three days to the one and two to the other each week, and so continued for twelve years.

His life is historical, though little known. He used a blackboard as early as 1725, instructed in music, and had a well-developed method of primary numbers. He was an author a century and a half ago, and one of the fathers of American pedagogy. His "Schul-ordnung," † published about the middle of the century, must have seemed to most of his contemporaries very strange and unreal, so modern and orthodox it seems now. Mr. Dock is an excellent representative of the best colonial Pennsylvania teaching everywhere. Service and success were individual, intermittent, and local. There was no system, no uniformity.

---

* Of successful private and church schools there were some excellent examples. Prominent among these were those of the Moravians and Quakers. Most German settlements had schools; of public schools there were none.

† See page 149.

6. New Jersey prior to the Revolution.

Although the settlers of New Jersey, Delaware, and Pennsylvania, were of similar tastes and antecedents, and one would expect a kindred educational history, they are found to differ greatly. Schools were established in Newark, and (1683) an island in the Delaware River was appropriated to education in the Burlington settlement, the revenue from which by rent or sale was to be enjoyed "by all the families equally." The fund is certainly one of the oldest permanent school-funds in America, the income of which is yet enjoyed by the town.

Ten years later (1693) a general law was passed, legalizing schools in any town of the colony, "the consent of the major part of the inhabitants to be binding upon all," to pay their shares for the maintenance of a school, "*even to the distress of their goods and chattels.*" This seems equal to the best New England interest, and was withal thoroughly republican. Within ten years schools had been established in all the counties, and, for a sparse and pioneer population, were generously supported. But the law, at best, was only permissive, and subject to annual defeat in each community. There was no permanence, and for more than a century no further attempt to perfect a system of schools.

In New Jersey also, as in Pennsylvania, what is most significant of the general condition is the individual service rendered by the occasional teacher. Typical of the wholesome but unorganized educational spirit, and the influences that were working, were the labors of Rev. William Tennent. An Irishman by birth, a clergyman by profession, a teacher of choice, and liberally educated, he probably did more to shape the first sentiments of culture and morality about him than all others combined. After preaching for a Presbyterian congregation in New York, and later in Bucks County, Pennsylvania, he was called (1726) to the charge at Neshaminy, twenty miles north of Philadelphia, where he soon established what has come to be known, through the writ-

ings of George Whitefield and others, as the "Log College."
In a rude school-house, uncomely and secluded, the reputation of his great work is justified, as that of any school, by
its service to society. Mr. Tennent was a classical scholar,
conversing in Latin with the ease of his vernacular, and
proficient in other languages as well. He is described as a
man of integrity and industry, with great piety, and drawing
students from adjoining provinces. He taught for twenty
years, most of the time in the "Log College," * the germ of
the now famous Princeton, the College of New Jersey.

7. *Colonial Education in the South.*

The colonies of the South were settled, on the whole, quite
as early as those farther north—Virginia and New York
about the same time; South Carolina a dozen years before
Pennsylvania. Maryland made a permanent settlement a
year before the Boston Latin School. Except Georgia, then,
lateness of colonization can not be urged as a reason for delay in establishing schools. As a matter of fact, however,
there was no school system in any colony south of Connecticut before the Revolution, and no enterprise of the kind to
speak of before the present century. As elsewhere, there
were isolated and transient schools, throughout the provinces,
which had a commendable influence in forming public sentiment. In both Virginia and South Carolina, however, the
sons of those who could afford it were sent abroad to be educated, or put under tutors at home; and parents, assisted by
settled clergymen, and an occasional transient teacher, furnished all the elementary instruction of the period.

Indeed, it was a part of the policy of the colonies, characteristic of the class who settled them, though not unknown
also in Rhode Island, Delaware, and Pennsylvania, to leave
elementary instruction to the family. Of Rhode Island,
Mr. Barnard says, "Her people tolerated no legislative inter-

---

* See a sketch of the "Log College and its Founder," by Archibald
Alexander, 1851.

ference with religious belief or practice, or with the education of children, which, like religion, was considered strictly a parental and individual duty." When the English Commissioners of Foreign Plantations asked what course was taken in Virginia for instructing the people in the Christian religion, Governor Berkeley replied, "The same that is taken in England out of towns, every man according to his ability instructing his children." But he also added, what has become historic, though little understood in its connections : " I thank God there are no free schools nor printing-presses, and I hope we shall not have them these hundred years; for learning has brought disobedience, and heresy, and sects into the world, and printing has divulged them and libels against the best of governments: God keep us from both!" And the hope of Berkeley was fulfilled, for he spoke in 1671, and there was no system of schools in Virginia attempted before Thomas Jefferson.

There was one school in South Carolina whose founding and career are deserving of mention. It was the Dorchester Seminary, established by a body of Massachusetts Congregationalists who colonized in the South about 1734. This seemed more like the New England academy than any other school in that section; and, with the four other grammar-schools claimed for the colony, probably justified Mr. Ramsay's assertion that, " from this time, all who wanted might find in South Carolina the best of classical instruction."

The Battle Creek School of Maryland, also, was older even than this last, and of nearly equal rank, and was the type, both in function and organization. of the later county academies.

It can not be said that any of the colonies were indifferent to education of any grade, any more than they were to the claims of religion and individual honesty. But to some of them these were not matters of public control. It was not *schools*, but free schools, which Governor Berkeley denounced. During his short administration he was more

than once a generous subscriber to funds for private academies—a policy of conduct entirely consistent with his own
and the South's views concerning the means of education;
consistent too, with the practice of all the colonies, or parts
of them at some period, even in New England. Only seventy
years ago in Boston, primary instruction was first made public, and elsewhere even later. As a fact, the taking on of
general education as a function of government was yet an
experiment, well into the present century. The question of
how much, has carried with it a multitude of others, whose
answers are the way-marks in the growth of American educational ideas.

Bibliography.

The only comprehensive reference on the colonial schools and school
systems is Barnard's "American Journal of Education," begun 1855.
Its republication of original papers, legal enactments, and early educational documents, gives it a peculiar and unquestioned authority.   Consult also "Ezekiel Cheever and his Descendants," in "New England
Historical Register," vol. xxxiii, p. 164, and "Colonial Education in the
South," "De Bow's Review," vol. xx, p. 622; also "Local Government
and Free Schools in South Carolina," by B. J. Ramage, 1883.

PART SECOND.

THE REVOLUTIONARY PERIOD.

CHAPTER IV.

ELEMENTARY EDUCATION IN THE REVOLUTIONARY PERIOD.

FROM the first vigorous colonial resistance to English aggression it took America fifty years to establish an independence among nations. The Revolutionary War and the War of 1812 were two culminating incidents in the conflict. How much more than this was necessary before national equality was granted, how much of diplomacy and invention, advancement in learning, and domestic control, can scarcely be estimated. The period was not altogether one of revolution; but the ideas and the type of men dominant in 1783 ruled still in civil and administrative and social affairs for a quarter of a century. They enacted laws, erected schools, shaped education, and gave direction to sentiments of industry and refinement and the means of progress. In a history of culture, the period of the Revolution in America may be said to include the War of 1812. Indeed, the next period, that of reorganization, can not be said to have had a recognized beginning until twenty-five years later (1837).

The two chapters following seek to sketch the conditions of elementary, secondary, and collegiate education during the period named.

5

1. "*Pauper Schools.*"

Francis Adams, speaking for his own country, recently (1875) said: * "Our public elementary schools of England have always been regarded as charitable schools."

The same idea prevailed for many years in this country, in Pennsylvania, almost wholly throughout the South, rarely in the West, but more or less in New England, though not extensively in Massachusetts and Connecticut. Rhode Island held that elementary instruction might not safely be interfered with by the State except in the interest of those who were unable to provide for their own; and, contradictory as it seems, when John Howland and his mechanic friends undertook (1785) to establish the free school in Rhode Island, it was objected to chiefly "by the poorer sort of people."

A generation later, Governor Hammond, of South Carolina, in his annual message, animadverting upon the common schools, but evidently speaking in the atmosphere of a local unfriendly sentiment, took occasion to say: "The free-school system has failed. Its failure is owing to the fact that it does not suit our people, our government, our institutions. The paupers for whose children it is intended need them at home to work." † The sentiment was not peculiar to this State: Governor Hammond was only more emphatic. In half the original colonies the idea was a ruling factor in more or less of the educational legislation through the early constitutional period. By the Maryland act of 1723, and following, visitors for the counties were empowered to select certain children to be taught gratis. The literary fund of Virginia (1810) was set apart for the exclusive benefit of the poor, as was a special Georgia appropriation of two hundred and fifty thousand dollars seven years later. In the same year also New Jersey began the foundation of a

---

* " Free Schools of the United States," p. 52.

† Rev. James Fraser's report, p. 10 ; quoted there from an address by Dr. B. G. Northrop, delivered 1864.

school-fund, but almost immediately provided for an optional taxation of townships " for the education of paupers." Even Ohio, as late as 1821, attached a charity clause, and so defeated the purpose of an otherwise liberal enactment. In Pennsylvania, also, throughout both the colonial and the early constitutional periods, the public-school idea was compassed by the care which it was thought the State should take of the dependent and unfortunate classes. Public schools in the early history of Pennsylvania were "pauper schools." This appeared in the Penn School, Philadelphia, and was reaffirmed in the Constitution of 1790.

Such schools raised and maintained a well-meant, charitably intended, but unfortunate distinction between rich and poor, so as in time to frustrate the design of the schools and the generous charity of their founders. The poor despised the provision as a public badge of their debasement; the wealthy shunned them as degrading. That this was not merely the bias of legislation imposed upon the public appears in the constant misinterpretation of the spirit and function of the common schools by the people themselves. Not till far into the present century was even Philadelphia freed from the invidious distinction, while the emancipation of the rural districts came later.

Elsewhere a similar antipathy resulted from very different conditions. The "school fees" in England and the "rate-bills" in the United States were designed to throw a part of the burden of maintaining the schools upon patrons. While doing this they had the effect in every State where tried either to exclude those from the privileges of the school who could not afford them, or to subject them to the odium of "pauper patrons" when school fees were remitted. In either case the "odious rate-bill" has been the occasion of setting off society into classes, excluding some, and so limiting the efficiency of the schools.*

---

* See this question of rate-bills discussed, in the light of both English and American experience, in Mr. Adams's " Theory of Free Schools," " Free-School System," pp. 45-57.

These fees took on various forms. They were not always assessed in money, though in cities they were usually so. In country districts in most States, both East and West, the rate frequently included board for the teacher. In Rhode Island, pupils were assessed for fuel as late as 1833, fee-bills being entirely abolished fifteen years later. In Vermont they remained until 1864, in New York three years and in Connecticut four years longer, and in New Jersey until 1871.

2. Teaçhers.

In general, the teachers of the last century were poorly qualified for their work. But of the majority of the teachers, of what generation, since Adam Roelandsen, Dutch schoolmaster under Wouter Van Twiller, at Fort Amsterdam, and Brother Philemon Purmont, in Boston, might the same *not* be said ? The cause is not difficult to find. What with the material urgencies of a new country, the dangers without and want within, a professional spirit was not to be expected. Contemporary conditions show less excuse. In a pamphlet, published in 1791, the teacher of the period is characterized as generally "a foreigner, shamefully deficient in every qualification for instructing youth, and not seldom addicted to gross vices."* Dr. William Darlington, also, of Pennsylvania, describes the country school-teachers (1788) as "often low-bred, intemperate adventurers of the Old World," but generally on a par with the prevalent estimate of the profession. For some years before, and again soon after the War for Independence, the Atlantic States were at times overrun with English adventurers or Irish immigrants, many of whom occupied the interval till they should find employment, in teaching. Some came, as did other laborers, indentured for their passage-money. One Boucher, a royalist, in an address (1763),† is reported as saying that

---

* See "American Journal of Education," vol. xiii, p. 752.

† See Neill's "Maryland Colony," p. 212. Thomas Scharf, in his "History of Maryland," vol. ii, p. 22, says, of the same period, "Probably much

"at least two thirds of the contemporary Maryland education was derived from instructors that were either indentured servants or transported felons. Not a ship arrives," he said, " either with redemptioners or convicts, in which schoolmasters are not as regularly advertised for sale, as are weavers, tailors, or any other tradesmen."

With such standards of intellectual and literary excellence among the people, no prominence could be expected among their servants—the teachers, and yet the case was not wholly bad. In each of a dozen colleges were a few men of ability and noble influence—men to know whom, and to live in whose atmosphere, was an education. Of this character, without exhausting the list, or excluding others, were Dwight and Stiles, of Yale, and a little later Prof. Silliman ; Dr. David Tappan and Prof. Sewall, of Harvard; Maclean, of Princeton; President Wheelock, of Dartmouth; and, somewhat earlier, Prof. Hugh Jones, of the College of William and Mary. In the academies there were Masters Moody and Doddridge; Ebenezer Adams, of Leicester; and Dr. Thomas Rowe, the teacher of Isaac Watts. Benjamin Abbot began in this period, also, his long career at Exeter.

Concerning the common or elementary school-teachers, however, the story is different. Exceptions were few. The learning of the day was not of the school-room. The period was one of activity, not thought. Life was conduct: culture was valued, not less; but doing, more. The years were full of a wisdom suited to the times. The needful teachers were new institutions, an unbroken continent, impoverished treasuries, menacing neighbors, and the care that belongs to venture without precedent. All these the period had; and from their influence, in season, came both men and scholars.*

more than half the population, not including slaves, were totally illiterate and grossly ignorant," and still further that there was " no general education, no free circulation of books, no emoluments and distinction of literature."

* For a vivid and entertaining sketch of life and culture in the Revolutionary period, see McMaster's " History of the People of the United States."

3. Common-School Text-Books.

The subjects of the school course remained much the same as in the first century, with this difference: whereas then there were almost no books but the Bible and Catechism, scarcely had the war closed, when texts were published in such numbers and quality as revolutionized the methods of teaching. The change was fundamental.*

Spelling at first was not distinct from reading; or, rather, reading had not differentiated from spelling. The "New England Primer," first published some time during the seventeenth century, had already gone through fifteen editions in 1720, been many times revised and enlarged, and, in the reissue of 1777, dedicated to the "Hon. John Hancock, President of the American Congress." It was used until the close of the century, but was probably valued more for the abridgment of the Catechism it contained than as a speller. The "New England Psalm-Book," after fifty editions, was still in use during the Revolution. The Dilworth "Spelling-Book," published about the middle of the eighteenth century, with a little elementary grammar, furnished all the instruction given upon this subject for three generations. Besides these were half a dozen other spellers of various grades, including John Woolman's "First Book for Children," Daniel Fleming's "Universal Spelling-Book," and one by Mr. Pierce, a Pennsylvania teacher, which contained a tolerable English grammar. Of course, the eminently popular, successful and influential speller of the period was Webster's "Spelling-Book," published in 1783. The author planned "A Grammatical Institute of the English Language, comprising an Easy, Concise, and Systematic Method of Education, designed for the Use of English schools in America." It was to be in three parts—a Speller, a Grammar, and a Reader. The first contained, besides appropriate word-lists, much geographical knowledge of countries and towns, to be taken occasionally

---

* McMaster, vol. ii, chap. vii. Also, Thomas's " History of Printing."

as spelling-lessons. The wide use of this book almost justifies the author's assertion that "the Spelling-Book does more to form the language of a nation than all others combined."

The readers of the period were a great improvement on those previously used. Webster's "Third Part" came first (1785), and, like the speller, was very comprehensive. Its modest title—"An American Selection of Lessons in Reading and Speaking; calculated to improve the Mind, and refine the Taste of Youth; and also to instruct them in the Geography, History and Politics of the United States. To which are prefixed Rules in Elocution and Directions for giving Expression to the Principal Passions of the Mind"—marks its scope. Its only rivals for many years were Bingham's "American Preceptor" and the "Columbian Orator," about the close of the century. Of others, having less sale, were Murray's "English Reader," reaching its fifth edition; Chipman's "American Moralist"; Stanford's "The Art of Reading" and Goldsmith's "Roman History," all published about the opening of the century. Another book of merit, and used as a reader, was an "Account of the Historical Transactions of the United States after the Revolution" (1788), by Webster.

Hodder's "Arithmetic, or that Necessary Art made most easy; being explained in a Way familiar to the Capacity of any that desire to learn it in a Little Time," the first of a long line of similar texts, had passed through twenty-five editions in 1719, and was practically the only book in use until the publication of Pike's "Arithmetic" (1785). This claimed a "new system," was somewhat more pretentious, and contained an appendix of forty pages, or an "Introduction to Algebra," for the use of academies. Daboll's "Arithmetic" was published about the same time, and, a few years later (1790) the "Schoolmaster's Assistant," by Thomas Dilworth, an English teacher at Wapping.

Of works on language there were many, from Bailey's "English and Latin Grammar," in its fifth edition, 1720; new ones being published at the rate of two to a generation for the century. Mr. Cheever's "Latin Accidence," first issued in 1645, was republished about the middle of the next century, and again in 1838, with the commendation of distinguished scholars throughout New England.   The "Young Lady's Accidence," by Mr. Caleb Bingham (1790), is notable as one of the first books on English grammar, "the first ever used in the Boston schools," where it was continued many years. Besides these were South's "Short Introduction to English," and the much-used "Grammar" of Lindley Murray.   Mr. Murray was never a teacher, but, watchful of the progress of education, gave, about 1790, a series of informal lessons, on the teaching of English, to the assistants in a girls' school in York.   These were afterward put into form and published, and, later still, reissued in the United States.

Of all the other texts of the period, the only one claiming attention is the geography.   Except the incidental information gathered into readers and grammars, no instruction was afforded in this subject before the "Universal Geography" of Jedediah Morse (1784).* This was an 18mo book, contained four maps, and, excepting in a limited way Nathaniel Dwight's "Catechetical System of Geography," it was the only available text for nearly half a century.

4. The Education of Girls.

By a kind of "traditionary blindness," few among the colonial fathers saw the contradiction of the most fundamental of their religious and political principles in disregarding or thwarting the intellectual life of their daughters. The independence which they claimed, carried implicitly the emancipation of all mind—if in holy things, certainly in secular; but, with a bias born of generations, while democratic in government and Protestant in religion, in a few things they exemplified the most conservative aristocracy.

---

* An abridgment of this book was made seven years afterward, in which were added historical accounts of the European settlements in America, the thirteen States, and of Europe, Asia, and Africa.

Before the close of the last century, most New England towns had made some provision for the education of girls, either in short summer terms, or at the noon hours, or other interval, of the town (boys') school. But no such opportunity was afforded girls to make the most of themselves, as had been forced upon most boys for a half-dozen generations. There were certain schools that were not only eminently successful as schools, but were agencies of wide influence in educating public sentiment, and at the same time of service in publishing the possibilities of the female mind.

For a hundred years the Penn Charter School, Philadelphia, had admitted both sexes on equal terms. The Moravians had established a school for girls at Bethlehem, Pa., as early as 1745, while the Philadelphia Female Academy dates from the Revolution. Among the earliest in New England were Dr. Dwight's Young Ladies' Academy, at Greenfield, Conn. (1785), and the Medford School, near Boston (1789) ; the latter is said to have been for many years the resort of young lady students from all the Eastern States.

The most vigorous and systematic experiment, however, and the most vigorously and systematically antagonized was in Boston. As early as 1700 there had been "writing-schools," to which girls were admitted. They were irregularly maintained for nearly a hundred years, but to no definite purpose. Instruction was usually given by the teachers of the common schools, but between the regular sessions.

About 1787 Mr. Caleb Bingham,* with an illustrious reputation as a teacher, proposed to open a real school for girls, where, besides writing, they should be taught reading, spelling, arithmetic, and English grammar. Immediately upon opening, his room was filled. The supply created a demand. More sought admission than could be accommodated. With the selectmen's daughters in school, female educa-

---

* For a biography of Mr. Bingham, and much interesting matter concerning the early education of girls, see "American Journal of Education," vol. v, p. 325.

tion was becoming popular. It was proposed to establish three new schools for girls, called "reading-schools." Now was introduced a curious organization. Pupils attending a writing-school in the morning in one building, were, in the afternoon in another building, by another set of teachers, instructed in the "reading-school." While the girls were in one school, the boys were in another ; and, to avoid too great hazard, the girls were only allowed to attend school six months in the year.

This came to be called, very appropriately, the "double-headed" system, and continued until near the middle of the present century. A like separation of sexes in the same building, without the alternation of rooms and teachers, is yet practiced in Baltimore and in many Eastern and some Southern cities.

Bibliography.

On "Social Life in the Colonies," just prior to and during the Revolution, see "Building the Nation," by C. C. Coffin, chapters vi, vii ; and on the text-books of the period, the "History of Printing in America," by Thomas; the "Christian Examiner," vol. vi, p. 130 ; and "De Bow's Review," vol. xxviii, p. 434.

CHAPTER V.

ACADEMIES AND COLLEGES.

1. Academies.

ALONGSIDE each of the first colleges, frequently antedating them, sometimes forming part of the organization, was a grammar-school. This was true of Harvard, William and Mary, Yale, Princeton, the University of Pennsylvania, and Dartmouth. Such schools served the double purpose of fitting for the college and supplementing with a classical training the meager elementary instruction of the common schools and the home. They were the only preparatory schools of the time and of uniform type, their courses being fitted to the time-sanctioned curriculum of the college. They taught much Latin and Greek, an extended course in mathematics, and were strong generally on the side of the humanities as these were understood. Theirs was an eminent service, making the severe training of the college possible.

But within a century there had been established schools of a high order which did not, and were not designed to, in any special manner, prepare for the universities. These were independent institutions of extended courses, some of them endowed in a limited way, presided over by the best scholarship and teaching in the State, and altogether deserving the name of the people's college. During the period these rapidly multiplied, and with changed social conditions came new academic functions.

The academy, both name and institution, was evidently borrowed from Great Britain. Scotland had such schools in her principal towns as early as the twelfth century, while the so-called middle schools of the Continent, the classical drill-schools of Germany, and the great public schools of England—Rugby, Eton, and the like, "the most English institutions of England," venerable with age—are their European antecedents.

The Edinburgh High School dates from 1519. In 1644 John Milton, after describing, in his "Tractate," a complete and generous education as "that which fits a man to perform justly, skilfully, and magnanimously, all the offices, both private and public, of peace and war," recommended that "less time be bestowed on grammar and sophistry," and that an academy be established which should be both school and university. Immediately upon the "Act of Toleration," academies were set up by Dissenters, who subsequently introduced them into the colonies. Indeed, Harvard, Yale, and William and Mary were for many years not superior to the best classical schools of English Dissenters. The Dummer School, Massachusetts (1763), Flatbush Academy, "Erasmus Hall," on Long Island (1787), and a few years earlier, Ger-

mantown Academy, Maryland, Phillips Exeter (N. H.),
Phillips Andover, and Leicester academies, Massachusetts,
all belong to this period, and, while the most famous, constitute but a small proportion of all.   Of the Moravian
academies at Bethlehem and Nazareth, Pa., the historian
Winterbotham asserts (1795) that they were "among the
best establishments of any schools in America."

At the close of the century New York had nineteen of
these schools and Massachusetts about an equal number.
They were to be found in almost every State, both North and
South, and were the one characteristic educational agency
of the time.   In these and their like, sometimes followed
by a college training, oftener not, were educated the "boys
of '76" and the generation following.   Franklin, for a
time, both the Adamses, and John Hancock, were trained
in the Boston Latin School.   Prof. Tappan, of Harvard,
Chief-Justice Parsons and Sewall, prepared for college under Master Moody at Dummer Academy; while Benjamin Abbot and John Adams, masters at Exeter and Andover, made for themselves and their schools a lasting reputation.*

The English academies were usually well endowed.   (Eton
has an annual revenue of one hundred and fifty thousand
dollars, and pays the head-master twenty-five thousand dollars.)   The Americans of the last century were in no condition to endow so well their schools, though possibly they did
better.   The academies were kept near the people, breathing
the spirit of the time.   Most of them were incorporated ultimately.   Some were founded by returns from lotteries, more
by appropriations from the public treasury, and yet more by
private munificence.

An interesting characteristic of these academies and peculiar to the oldest colonial grammar-schools is the signifi-

---

* The New England academies, typical of such agencies throughout the
States, have been well characterized by Mr. C. W. Hammond in the "American Journal of Education," vol. xvi, p. 423.

cance of the term "free" as applied to them. They were not at all "free" in the modern meaning of the word; the privileges of attendance involved the payment of a fee. The larger the endowment, however, the smaller the fee usually; and to most of them, in whatever State, admission might be had by the needy without charge. The Dummer School was for those specified in the bequest, chiefly the inhabitants of Byfield, Mass. So the Hopkins grammar-schools in the seventeenth century were free to the towns of Hartford, New Haven, Hadley, and Cambridge, in which they were situated. Later, the Phillips Academies were opened to all from whatever State in the sense that no race, nor rank, nor limitations of residence, nor religious distinctions, were made conditions of admission. Equal privileges were given on the same terms. They were free, then, in contrast with the like schools and seminaries of England, admission to which required membership in some particular church or other organization, and so were exclusive.*

2. Colleges.

After the three colonial colleges already noted, sixteen others were founded before the close of the century, six of which preceded, by a few years, the Revolution.

Of these, the earliest was Princeton, already referred to incidentally as the local outgrowth of the "Log College" of Rev. William Tennent. Though founded by Presbyterians, and still supported by them, it stands as the representative of the State's higher education in New Jersey.

Following Princeton was King's College (now Columbia), New York. It was founded by royal charter (1754), and was meant to be an Episcopal seminary. Initiated by a legalized lottery—the usual step in such moral and educational enterprises then—it received local excise money, private benefactions, and the "King's Farm," a valuable grant

---

* See a second view also offered by Mr. Hammond in his "New England Academies and Classical Schools."

held by "Trinity Church" for religious and educational
purposes. Started upon an Episcopal basis, it met the antagonism, not only of Dissenters, of whom President Johnson bitterly complained, but of the Dutch, also, who naturally opposed anything English. Nevertheless, it prospered. Prior to the Revolution it received liberal grants
from King George III, and generous contributions from the
nobility and gentry of England, besides substantial aid
from the "Society for the Propagation of the Gospel in
Foreign Parts." Its curriculum had been expanded in the
few years, even beyond that of Harvard and the older
institutions. In addition to the usual subjects it included
"divinity" and medicine, something of natural science, the
modern languages, and "whatever else of literature may
tend to accomplish the pupils as scholars and gentlemen."*
Predisposed to royalty, the college was closed early in the
war, and not reopened until 1784, when it became Columbia
College, with its general control in the "Regents of the
University of the State of New York."

Even before the agitation in New York city about King's
College, Pennsylvania, led by Franklin, began to talk of an
institution in Philadelphia. In the year 1749 was opened
the Philadelphia Academy, with a kind of charity-school
attachment. In the former were taught Latin, English,
and mathematics. It immediately took on the functions
of a high-grade seminary, at the same time fitting young
men for college. Within a decade, it had four hundred students, was chartered with the privileges of a college, had an extended course of study, a department of
law, and drew patronage from half the colonies. At the
close of the war it was merged in the University of Pennsylvania.

Brown University, though founded (1764) as a Baptist
institution, was, nevertheless, one of the first schools of the
period to emphasize the growing sentiment for a thoroughly

---

* "Historical Sketch of Columbia College," 1884, p. 3.

undenominational collegiate training. Dartmouth College*
developed from the Indian school of the honored principal,
and first president, of the college, Rev. Dr. Wheelock. It
was chartered 1769, and had a few years later a large landed
interest (twelve thousand acres in one body, and valuable),
yielding even during the last century a considerable revenue. A second college was founded in New Jersey (1770)—
Queen's, now Rutgers ; and sixteen others, in various States,
before the close of the century. Of these, three were in
Maryland, two each in Virginia, Tennessee, and Vermont ;
and one in each of the six States—Maine, Massachusetts,
North Carolina, New York, Pennsylvania, and South Carolina, with one in the District of Columbia.

A marked feature of the period is the rapid multiplication of colleges that followed the first flush of independence.
Four were established during the war ; twelve immediately
following. By the close of the century the country had
more colleges in proportion to the population than it has
now. Massachusetts was the first to protest. When it was
proposed to found Williams College, Harvard filed a long
and formal remonstrance. It was urged that "Harvard was
properly a college of the whole government ; and that the
Commonwealth would do its people an injury by taking the
support from one old and established institution, and encouraging a new and feeble school." † The protest failed,
and the college (Williams) was established (1793). It still
remains true that the Harvard principle was sound. Will-

---

* Dartmouth has a very excellent history in a work published 1878,
written by B. P. Smith. Chapter xii, p. 100, contains a succinct statement
of the celebrated " Dartmouth College Case " touching the charter of the
college. Consult also the " Dartmouth Causes and the Supreme Court,"
by J. Shirley, St. Louis, 1879. Works of Daniel Webster, vol. v, p. 462.

† Tennessee at this time, Pennsylvania, Maryland, and New Jersey,
had each two, and Virginia three, colleges. On the " Multiplication of Colleges and Education in Smaller Colleges," see the " Ninety-fifth Report of
the University of the State of New York " (1882), p. 333; also, " Education and the State," by F. A. P. Barnard, p. 30.

iams has a record of which to be proud ; but, of the sixteen institutions founded between 1776 and 1796, the present conditions of five only, hint at even passable thrift. The current average attendance of the others falls below eighty, with a present aggregate endowment of less than three million dollars.

This was a time of general expansion. More or less unsettled, society was necessarily less given to formal and prescribed culture, but devoted to organization and attempts at practical readjustments.

Harvard now first assumed the name of university ; for, though there had been collateral professorships, these were maintained by assessments upon students, were not co-ordinated into departments, and left the institution only an academic school of art. Signs of catholicity also appear, in that students were no longer required to attend the divinity lectures, except they were preparing for the ministry. The democratic tendencies of the time were shown in many ways. Students from about the beginning of the Revolution (1770 in Yale) were catalogued alphabetically, and not as previously by the social rank of their families. Literary societies, voluntary associations for social and general culture, were multiplied ; and at William and Mary College was formed (1776) the first Greek fraternity in this country —the Phi Beta Kappa—the parent of both secret and open college fraternity organizations in America.*

New interests were arising. The New England colonial conflict had been a theological one. The opposition and divergence of sects—freedom from which, in Virginia, had constituted, in the estimation of President Blair, one of that colony's commending social features—were rapidly being obscured, in the greater immediate civil and political interests which all the colonies shared in common. Less importance was attached to the formal subscription to creeds ; re-

* For a sketch of this organization, its origin, and occasion, see Quincy's "Harvard University," vol. ii, p. 397.

ligious tests were less frequent and insistent. William and Mary elected a lay chancellor ; Yale, also, though nominally on a Congregational foundation, received aid (1792) from the State, and gave place in her corporation to State representatives.

The college, once an appendage to the Church, was seen, in view of imminent State dangers, to have an equal value to the Commonwealth. First encouraged because it provided an educated ministry, there was coming to be recognized an opinion, despite the deficiencies in culture, that education is something more—that it has a value in itself ; that schools might well be maintained apart from the Church as an organization, and in no way lessen their usefulness. Of the four colleges established during the war, two were nonsectarian, as were three fourths of the sixteen colleges founded in the twenty years after 1776.

Colleges founded prior to 1800.

INSTITUTIONS.	State.	Date.	Character.
1. Harvard	Massachusetts....	1637	Congregational.
2. William and Mary.........	Virginia..........	1693	Episcopal.
3. Yale.....................	Connecticut......	1701	Congregational.
4. Princeton................	New Jersey......	1746	Presbyterian.
5. University of Pennsylvania*	Pennsylvania	1749	Non-sectarian.
6. Columbia	New York	1754	Episcopal.
7. Brown............	Rhode Island.....	1764	Baptist.
8. Dartmouth...............	New Hampshire..	1769	Congregational.
9. Queen's (Rutgers).........	New Jersey......	1770	Reformed.
10. Hampden-Sidney..........	Virginia.........	1776	Presbyterian.
11. Washington and Lee.......	Virginia	1782	Non-sectarian.
12. Washington University....	Maryland........	1782	Non-sectarian.
13. Dickinson................	Pennsylvania	1783	M. Episcopal.
14. St. John's	Maryland........	1784	Non-sectarian.
15. Nashville*...............	Tennessee	1785	Non-sectarian.
16. Georgetown..............	District of Col....	1789	R. Catholic.
17. University of N. Carolina.*	North Carolina...	1789	Non-sectarian.
18. University of Vermont*...	Vermont........	1791	Non-sectarian.
19. University of E. Tennessee.	Tennessee	1792	Non-sectarian.
20. Williams.................	Massachusetts....	1793	Congregational.
21. Bowdoin.................	Maine...........	1794	Non-sectarian.
22. Union	New York	1795	Non-sectarian.
23. Middlebury	Vermont........	1795	Congregational.
24. Frederick College.........	Maryland........	1796	Non-sectarian.

* State.

6

Bibliography.

The "New England Academies," by Rev. Charles Hammond; the "Old Academies," "New-Englander," January, 1885; "Academies in New England" (1830), "American Quarterly Register," vol. ii, p 131, and vol. iii, p. 288; the "Relation of Academies to Colleges," "Congregational Review," vol. ii, p. 50, and "Putnam's Magazine," vol. ii, p. 169. The colleges of the period are well represented in "A History of Harvard University, 1636–1776," by Benjamin Peirce; a "History of the College of New Jersey," by J. Maclean; an "Historical Sketch of Columbia College," 1754–1876, by J. Van Amringe; "History of the University of Pennsylvania," by T. H. Montgomery; the "Early History of Brown University," by R. A. Guild (1864); the "First Half-Century of Dartmouth College," by N. Crosby (1769–1820); and "Descriptive Analysis of the Society System in Colleges of the United States," by W. J. Baird.

PART THIRD.

THE PERIOD OF REORGANIZATION.

CHAPTER VI.

CENTRALIZING TENDENCIES.

1. The Transition.

THE transition from a colonial dependence to national independence was a costly one. The States came out of the contest bankrupt financially ; disorganized in industries ; a Government without precedent ; the real War of Independence yet to fight, and the civilized world looking on to see the failure. Not three decades had passed from the inauguration of Washington when the final conflict was over. The War of 1812 was fought, a substantial independence achieved ; and the States, no longer engrossed with conflicting and unsettled foreign interests, turned their attention to economic and industrial questions at home. Trade began to revive ; commerce had found a way ; social and governmental forces were active and planning. The period was one of great change and much growth.

In four decades population had trebled. The six cities of 1790 had grown to twenty-six in 1830 ; then, one thirtieth of the entire population, they were now one sixteenth. The acquisition of territory had been enormous. The scarcely more than eight hundred thousand square miles of 1783 had expanded to upward of two million square miles in 1819, or

five times the total area of the original thirteen States. The
increase alone was equal to one hundred and fifty-eight States
such as Massachusetts. The Mississippi was open to American
commerce its full length, leading to a rapid extension of settlements in the Southwest. It was the era of new States.
Eleven had been added to the first thirteen. Trade was
opened with the West Indies. In the census of 1820, statistics began to be taken concerning manufacturing interests.
Appropriations were made by Congress, as well as by several
of the States, for internal improvements, in the year 1816
three hundred and fifty thousand dollars being set aside by
congressional act for this purpose. Virginia, Delaware, and
Maryland established "improvement funds." Manufacturing associations and trade leagues were organized in Pennsylvania and North Carolina. Congress voted one hundred
thousand dollars annual appropriation to the navy. A system of coast defense was projected, and the pre-emption land
act passed. The year 1830 opened upon twenty-five canals,
including the great Erie, with an aggregate length of sixteen
hundred miles ; while, five years later, one thousand miles
of railroad had grown from the Quincy (Mass.) four-mile
granite line of 1826.

Already the slavery question was forcing itself upon the
public mind, leading directly to the founding of the American Colonization, and other manumission societies, and end-
less political readjustments. Academies of science, philosophy, and history, the "North American Review," in Boston,
and thirty colleges, took their start in this period. It was
in these years when most of our educational systems originated or began their reorganization. Professorships of
science, law, medicine, and the modern languages were
added to the existing faculties. In place of the thirty-five
newspapers of 1775, there were three hundred and twenty-
three in 1810, and one thousand two decades later. It was a
period of great awakening and great activity. In the atmosphere of the Revolution were born and reared statesmen
and soldiers; not less did the years following give scholars

and authors and teachers, tradesmen and benefactors, professional and scientific men.*

It was the period of the Adamses and Jefferson; of Franklin and Webster; of Governor De Witt Clinton; of young Denison Olmsted; of Horace Mann and Joseph Henry; of Everett and Story; Gallaudet, of Connecticut; Guilford, of Ohio; Grimke, of South Carolina; and Frelinghuysen, of New Jersey. Wayland, in Rhode Island; Peers, in Kentucky; and Shaw, in Virginia, were planning school systems in their several States. Chancellor Kent was in his prime, and Randolph and Marshall and Jackson and Clay were contemporaries whose like the modern world has rarely seen.

In the presence of such men, one ceases to wonder that the young nation was growing confident and aspiring. To the vigorous young the future is always promising. To them the maintaining of a free government seemed, if not easy, at least possible. How possible? The wise men—these and others—set themselves to answer the question.

They differed in their views about the Constitution, and wrangled over the dangers of centralization; the best men were fearful of the inroads of slavery and the dangers to commerce; but all agreed that intelligence was necessary to citizenship. Look through the writings of Washington and Jefferson, and it will be found that the best thought was given to the importance of a right training of mind. "In proportion as the structure of a government gives force to public opinion," said Washington, "it is necessary that public opinion should be enlightened." So Mr. Jefferson repeatedly urged, and made it the guide of his later years, that "the diffusion of light and education are the resources most to be relied on for ameliorating the condition, promoting the virtue, and advancing the happiness of man."

---

* On the general culture, the refinement, the progress of institutions, etc., Holmes's "American Annals," first published at the opening of the century and reissued a generation later, contains much material not to be found in later books covering the same period.

The sentiment was no forced one nor exotic. It was familiar to the best men in every State and station; to John Adams, and Madison, and Rush; to lawyer and statesman and clergyman. It was so general, that the memorable saying of Chancellor Kent, that "the parent who sends his son into the world uneducated, defrauds the community of a youthful citizen and bequeaths to it a nuisance," * was not more a personal opinion than the expression of a wide-spread public faith. Out of such patriotic and exalted sentiments, that of universal and liberal education had an easy birth. Not that intelligence sprang suddenly out of ignorance, or that sufficient schools were at once provided. History can hardly be so set off into periods. Most "turning-points" are curves; improvement is growth. But, in the fifty years after 1800, there was a time when progress noticeably accelerated. Organization was upon a higher plane. Institutions took on new significance. New arts and industries, thronged cities and an active press, the exaltation of personal and cooperative life, and the increased recognition of humanitarian interests, were, both logically and chronologically, accompanied by a large and wholesome enthusiasm for education. The time was pregnant with half-seen possibilities.

In this awakening was the American renaissance—a return to vigorous life, such as had not been enjoyed for a hundred years. Something of the early enthusiasm for learning and the means of learning came in with Jefferson and Mann, Mark Hopkins, Denison Olmsted, Mary Lyon, and their contemporaries.

Early in the century (1805) the Public School Society of New York city was formed; the claims of public primary education were urged—Boston, 1818; and New York provided for the county supervision of schools. Within the

---

* " In the United States, he who does not send his child to school (which he should do, for the same reason as he pays his taxes, or fights in time of war) must be regarded in a peculiarly insidious sense as an enemy of the State."—DR. G. S. HALL.

period were introduced or discussed the first high-schools, manual training-schools, and mechanics' institutes, seminaries for teachers, associations, institutes, and the publication of educational journals. Independent professional schools and departments, technological institutions, and learned societies, school and general public and free libraries, were multiplied. Evening and special schools for laboring classes, and the whole list of institutions for the defective and dependent classes—institutions for the blind, the deaf, the imbecile, orphans, and the wayward—took their rise during these years.

There were without doubt great agencies at work looking to general education. "A broad philanthropy," says Mr. Bicknell, "rather than a deep philosophy, ruled the hour; when men consulted their instincts more than formulas of logic in their educational policy." But they were impulses well rooted and guided, out of whose working have come the current systems.

This enlargement of educational interest was accompanied further by certain tendencies toward centralization peculiarly modern, and which claim a fuller treatment. These appear in the creation of school-funds by the States, and the accompanying boards of control, superintendents, commissioners, etc. Begun with a purpose, they show a far-reaching wisdom, and an understanding of the educational problem, rare enough in any age; surprising, *then*.

2. The Creation of School-Funds.

The sources of income for the support of schools have been various. Local, State, and national taxes ; municipal and legislative appropriations ; city, State, and congressional land-grants; land-rents, students' fees, rate-bills, and private benefactions; swamp and saline lands; bank-tax and surplus revenue funds; fines, forfeitures, and escheats; excise tax and vender's license, have all contributed to the support of education.

Speaking generally, most early funds were local and

annual. This is especially true of New England and Pennsylvania, where the idea of local self-government was strong.
For a different reason also the same statement applies to parts
of the South, where, as in Rhode Island, education was put
alongside of religion as a matter of personal and domestic
concern. The district system, as will appear elsewhere, is a
phase of this same early tendency to divide authority, dis-
tributing the school control among many small and independent corporations. First appearing in New England, it
has, at some time, been upon the statute-books of more than
half the States of the Union. It was part of the general impulse toward the sharing of administrative power, educational, political, and religious, which was a vigorous and long-
lived reaction against the unreasoning monarchism which
had prevailed into modern times, and been imposed upon
our forefathers.

The later years—the last half-century—in education show
a bias toward a larger and more central control. The co-op-
erations of an industrial life in a populous country not only
require a general likeness of interest, but a homogeneity of
culture and participation in a common experience. This
disposition of the public, in the direction of organization and
concerted action, is manifest in most civil affairs. It is
shown in the consolidation of industry into corporations;
in the inauguration of fraternities and lodges, and guilds
and granges; in the organization of charity and the union
of church agencies in the service of missions, Christian associations, benevolent exchanges, etc. It appears also in the
endowment of research, and the multiplication of learned
societies, as set over against individual investigation; while
the constant aggressions of legislation upon territory once
recognized as individual grounds has led Herbert Spencer to
say: "The old superstition was the Divine Right of kings;
the modern one is the Divine Right of Parliaments."
Among all representative governments the mark of centralization is upon contemporary interests. Education is no exception. Questions of compulsory school attendance, re-

formatory training, and the treatment of bodies of illiteracy,
reveal, in their discussion, a like sentiment. Care for the
defective classes, once regarded as a private charity, is now
made a State interest almost without exception.

Speaking historically, the first step in all this centering
of educational control was the creating of permanent school-
funds.

A. THE BEGINNINGS OF PERMANENT FUNDS.

As has already been seen, Massachusetts and other colonies both North and South, made appropriations of land, some
of which, held by leases, ultimately went into the general reserve.* Connecticut as early as 1733 had set apart her public
lands lying in the northwestern part of the colony "to the
perpetual use of the schools." A portion of the proceeds was
distributed to the town and parish school societies, and now
constitutes a part of their permanent funds. To these have
been added at different times "excise moneys," local bequests,
and forfeitures, forming in some towns considerable sums.
In the year 1786, upon the cession of Connecticut's Western
domain to the United States, a State reservation was made
of what is now northeastern Ohio, and called the "Western
Reserve." This (except a small tract) was sold 1795, for one
million dollars, which was turned into the school-fund.

By a law of 1786, New York † State set apart two lots in
each township of the unoccupied lands, for "gospel and
school purposes," and fifteen years later ordered that the net
proceeds of half a million acres of vacant and unappropri-
ated lands should be devoted to a permanent fund for the
support of common schools.

New Hampshire, 1821, began a similar fund, by exacting

---

* A very exhaustive study of the "Origin and History of the Massachusetts School-Fund" is presented by Hon. George S. Boutwell, in the Report of the Board of Education, 1859.

† For a statement of the New York School-Fund (for the Common
schools) and the Literary Fund (for the benefit of academies), see "Historical and Statistical Records" of New York, 1888.

one half of one per cent upon the capital of all banks within
the State. And Maine, about the same time, devoted the proceeds of the sale of twenty townships of public lands for a
like use; a part of which was distributed to the towns, as in
Connecticut, but held as invested capital whose income only
might be used for schools. Certain bank-stock held, and the
funded debt of the State, were made in New Jersey a permanent fund whose revenue, since about 1820, has been applied
to the public schools.

Rhode Island, Vermont, and Pennsylvania have no invested school-funds. The first supplements the local revenues by an annual appropriation of one hundred thousand
dollars, and the last by not less than one million dollars.

As might be supposed, and as has been frequently asserted by historians, little was accomplished in the South
during this period; little even attempted. Yet the principle
of State responsibility, and somewhat of State control, was
admitted, and became a factor of legislation in half the
Southern States.

A beginning was made by Delaware as early as 1796, it
seems, though no definite results came of it; the present
fund dates from 1837, and rests upon bank-stock, and a bond
of the State, together amounting to about one hundred and
fifty thousand dollars. Virginia (1810) began the constitution of her "Literary Fund" by legislative appropriation,
which was augmented from various sources, until, at the
close of the War of 1812, it amounted to two million dollars.
South Carolina followed (1811), but feebly, and North Carolina (1825). Any substantial benefit from the funds was
negatived in all three of the States by conferring them
chiefly upon the poor. Alabama, Florida, and Georgia
made large appropriations of land, and maintained, especially the last, flourishing academies, but upon special endowments or local support. At the prompting of Congress
(1806), grants of reservation lands were made in Tennessee,
one hundred thousand acres each to colleges and academies,
and one thirty-sixth of the remaining unoccupied territory

for the use of the common schools. All this, which later would have yielded such abundant revenues, was almost wholly wasted, and the present fund began with an investment in Bank of Tennessee stock (1846). This was increased both by legislative enactments and bank-stock dividends, amounting in 1858 to one million five hundred thousand dollars. Large grants of land were made by Kentucky and Louisiana also. In the former (1821), one half the net profits of the Bank of the Commonwealth were made a "Literary Fund," to be distributed annually for the maintenance of common schools under State control. The land-grants in Louisiana were, in the year 1847, consolidated, aggregating nearly eight hundred thousand acres, and forming a large and for some years a productive investment.

B. LOTTERIES.

An interesting feature of school administration, fifty to seventy-five years ago, was the lottery. It came in for all sorts of uses, and some which to-day would be counted very questionable. Those referred to here, however. were legalized, had the sanction of public opinion, and were considered altogether an honorable means of raising funds. Their proceeds were in some instances considerable; and contributed to increase the common-school fund, and the endowment of colleges; to aid in the erection of buildings, furnishing apparatus, and paying salaries.

The first steps taken (1747) toward the founding of what is now Columbia College were in the grant of a system of lotteries. Williamstown Academy, Massachusetts, was partly so founded (1790), and two years later, four lotteries were granted to the Regents of the University of the State of New York, one eighth of whose proceeds should go to the academies, and the remainder to the common-school fund. Upon Union and Hamilton Colleges, and the College of Physicians and Surgeons, Vincennes University, Indiana, and academies throughout the West, was bestowed such aid. The Catholepistemiad, first University of Michigan, and the

General Board of Education, were granted four lotteries, fifteen per cent of whose proceeds should be applied to the
general fund.   William and Mary College and Brown and
Harvard* Universities were recipients of like favors.   Indeed, for the half-century following the Revolution there
was almost no public enterprise requiring pecuniary aid
that did not receive more or less State recognition and
assistance through lotteries, at some time and in some
section.   From municipal improvements to founding and
equipping colleges, establishing libraries, initiating and augmenting school-funds, and building churches, the lottery
has been a common source of relief.   One writer, speaking
for Rhode Island alone, says lotteries were made " to contribute to churches in Providence, Newport, Bristol, and
half a dozen other towns ; by Baptist, Methodist, Presbyterian, and Congregational faith."   They were the church
fairs of our grandfathers—a device whose function, as a
source of general revenue, possesses a decided historic interest.

C. CONGRESSIONAL LAND-GRANTS.

A more important source of school revenue, in the form
of permanent investment grows out of the provisions of the
famous " Ordinance of 1787 " and subsequent acts.

The several colonies, upon establishing independent governments, and even before the " Articles of Confederation,"
laid claim to the undeveloped territory lying west of them
and extending nominally, to the Pacific.   Virginia owned
Kentucky and the territory north of the Ohio River, except
some reserves in Ohio.   Tennessee was held by North Carolina ; Alabama and Mississippi by Georgia ; Maine by Massachusetts ; and Vermont claimed by both New York and
New Hampshire.   The claims of Pennsylvania and Con-

---

* Harvard, 1775, took two thousand tickets in a public lottery, and
realized eighteen thousand dollars toward the erection of Stoughton Hall.
Again, in 1811, Massachusetts Hall was almost wholly built from the proceeds of a lottery that brought twenty-nine thousand dollars.

necticut also were conflicting, and the dispute was finally submitted to Congress (1775).

The offer of Virginia, in the year 1781, to cede her territory, was accepted by the General Government (1784). Two years later (1786) Connecticut withdrew her claims, reserving to herself a section in the northeastern corner of Ohio, from the western boundary of Pennsylvania, one hundred and twenty miles westward and from the forty-first parallel of latitude north to the lake, called in the early days " New Connecticut." The school-fund to which reference has been made elsewhere began in the sales of this " Western Reserve."

For the organization and control of this Northwest Territory Congress provided in 1787. In the year 1784, Mr. Jefferson, as chairman of a committee, had presented to Congress the draught of a bill respecting the disposition of the public lands, in which one is surprised to find no reference to schools or education. Eleven months later another bill was reported, containing the provision that " there shall be reserved the central section of every township for the maintenance of public schools, and the section immediately adjoining the same to the northward for the support of religion." After several amendments and prolonged discussion, the clause referring to the support of religion was stricken out. The remaining provisions were confirmed two years later in the " Ordinance for the Government of the Territory Northwest of the River Ohio," * along with which was given the fundamental declaration which has since been incorporated into almost every State Constitution that " religion, morality, and knowledge, being necessary to good government and the happiness of mankind, schools and the means of education shall be forever encouraged."

Ohio, the first State admitted to the Union from this Territory, received three townships; one as a Territory, and two upon admission as a State (1802), for the support of a univer-

---

* Of this ordinance it is said Nathan Dane was the author.

sity, and subsequently the sixteenth section in each township toward the maintenance of common schools. Prior to 1821, Indiana, Illinois, and Michigan had received like grants. In the South, under the general provision for the disposition of public lands, Louisiana, Mississippi, Alabama, and Tennessee received three townships each. Maine, Missouri, Arkansas, Florida, Texas, Wisconsin, and Iowa, respectively, received the sixteenth section only (one square mile out of each township of thirty-six square miles).

In the year 1841, by act of Congress, sixteen States—Alabama, Arkansas, California, Florida, Illinois, Iowa, Kansas, Louisiana, Michigan, Minnesota, Mississippi, Missouri, Nebraska, Nevada, Oregon, and Wisconsin—each received five hundred thousand acres, of which three million in the aggregate went to augment the common-school fund. Upon the organization of Oregon Territory, 1848, the reservation for schools was doubled, whereby California, Minnesota, Oregon, Kansas, Nebraska, Colorado, and Nevada have each received both the sixteenth and thirty-sixth sections. The provision applies, indeed, to every new State since 1848, except West Virginia.

By act of Congress (1849), supplemented by legislation the year following, and again in the year 1860, thirteen States — Alabama, Arkansas, California, Florida, Illinois, Iowa, Indiana, Louisiana, Michigan, Minnesota, Mississippi, Missouri, and Wisconsin—received an aggregate of 62,428,413 acres of swamp-lands, 14,000,000 acres of which were appropriated to the use of schools.

The total land-grants made by the United States for educational purposes up to 1876—one century of its existence—amount to nearly eighty million acres, or one hundred and twenty-five thousand square miles; a territory greater than the landed area of Great Britain and Ireland, and more than half that of all France. Of this it is estimated that more than eighty per cent has contributed to permanent funds for the elementary schools.

In addition to the appropriations of land, it has been the

policy of the Government to turn into the State treasuries, also, a percentage of the net proceeds of the sale of public lands within their borders. At first this was three per cent (later made five per cent), and was known as the "Three-per-cent Fund." In the year 1818 Congress ordered that one sixth of it should be given to the founding or maintenance of a college or university in each. The disposition of the remainder being left to the option of its holders, in a dozen States it was diverted to education ; Missouri realizing one million dollars' increase of the permanent fund.

Arkansas, Indiana, Missouri, and a few other States, received saline lands, the proceeds from the working or sale of which were added to the school-fund. In New Jersey (1871) the income from the sales and rents of riparian lands between high and low water were made a part of the school-fund, a sum the future possible revenue of which has been estimated at millions.

In some of the newer States school lands have been sold in part only. Nebraska has two million five hundred thousand acres, none of which can be sold for less than seven dollars per acre. Texas has about twenty-four million acres.

D. THE SURPLUS REVENUE FUND.

In 1836, by act of Congress, a large surplus in the United States treasury, amounting to over $42,000,000, was ordered to be deposited with the several States, in proportion to their representation in Congress. On account of subsequent financial embarrassments, the amount actually distributed was something less than $30,000,000. Sixteen of the twenty-six States then organized (1837) set aside their quota of the deposit, in whole or part, as a fund whose revenue should go to the maintenance of the common schools in their respective States. Eight of these * so appropriated the whole

---

* Alabama, Delaware, Kentucky, Missouri, New York, Ohio, Rhode Island, and Vermont.

of their shares, amounting in the aggregate to $9,855,134.
Eight States,* of the $9,462,798 they received, added a part to
their school-funds, the other going for internal improvements
and general purposes. In ten States receiving the deposits
none was given to education. These were Arkansas, Louisiana, Maine, Massachusetts, Mississippi, New Hampshire,
New Jersey, Tennessee, and Virginia, receiving in the aggregate $8,793,713, which went, as named above, to general pur-
poses or internal improvements. New York received most
and Delaware least, in both of which it was set apart for
education.

3. Permanent Funds and Local Taxes.

Notwithstanding the large common-school endowments †
considered in the last paragraph, they furnish but a limited
part of the total school revenues.

By the United States Commissioner's report for the year
1886–'87, it appears that the expenditures for education in
the United States, by States and Territories, was $115,103,886;
of which less than six millions was received from permanent funds. More than sixty millions of dollars were collected in local taxes, a revenue representing a capital of a
billion and a half of dollars. With all the large funds,
it is, after all, the willing citizens' tax that supports the
schools. Pennsylvania appropriates $1,000,000 annually
from the State treasury, but raises $9,000,000 from local
sources. Illinois, with a permanent fund of over $12,000,000,
makes an annual expenditure nearly as large, all but half
a million being from local taxes.

In the table have been grouped the ten States having the
largest school-funds, in which the annual income, at four
and a half per cent, from this source, is compared with their
respective school expenditures for the academic year 1885–'86 :

---

* Connecticut, Georgia, Illinois, Indiana, Maryland, North Carolina,
Pennsylvania, and South Carolina.

† The aggregate of the invested school-funds of the thirty-five States
approximates one hundred and twenty million dollars.

Resources and Expenditures of Public Education in ten States, 1885–'86.

	STATES.	Invested fund.	Revenue.	Expenditure.
1	Illinois...............	$12,049,000	$542,205	$10,136,000
2	Missouri...............	10,475,000	471,375	4.328,000
3	Indiana...............	9,458,000	425,610	5,314,000
4	Minnesota.............	6,731,000	302,895	2,372,000
5	Nebraska..............	4,904,000	220,680	2,351,000
6	Ohio..................	4,375,000	196,875	9,328,000
7	Iowa..................	4,100,000	184,500	4,660,000
8	New York.............	4,083,000	183,735	13,285,000
9	Michigan..............	3,838,000	172,710	4,333,000
10	Wisconsin.............	3,015,000	135,675	3,645,000
	Total..........	$63,059,000	$2,836,260	$59,752,000

Bibliography.

For a picture of society at the opening of the century, see Schouler's " History of the United States," vols. ii and iii; also, " Building the Nation," by Coffin, chapters xvi, xvii, xviii, xxxi, and xxxiii, and "Historical View of Education, its Dignity and Degradation," by Horace Mann, lecture v. Consult " Public Lands for Schools," J. Sparks, " North American Review," vol. xiii, p. 310; "History of Land Grants in the Northwest Territory," G. W. Knight, 1885; the "Ordinance of 1787," Hon. John Eaton, " Education," February, 1887, " Educational Influence of the Ordinance of 1787," " Proceedings of the National Educational Association," 1887, p. 118; "Dr. Cutler and the Ordinance of 1787," W. F. Poole, " North American Review," 1876; " American State Universities," by A. Ten Brook, including interesting matter on " Congressional University Land Grants"; "Land Grants in the United States for Educational Purposes," by Prof. H. B. Adams, "Proceedings of National Educational Association, Department of Superintendence," 1889; "History of the Surplus Revenue Fund " of 1837, by E. G. Bourne (1885), and the " Division of School Funds for Religious Purposes," by Dr. W. T. Harris, " Atlantic Monthly," August, 1876.

A curious bit of history is to be found in a sketch of the " Pious Fund of California," in the publications of the California Historical Society, vol. i, Part I, 1887. See also the " Origin and History of the Massachusetts School Fund," by Secretary George S. Boutwell.

7

CHAPTER VII.

CENTRALIZING TENDENCIES.—(Continued.)

SCHOOL SUPERVISION.

THE development in this country of systems of school supervision was inevitable. It is the normal result of public interest in the child. Division of labor in education, as in other human industry, works out its own economy. And the authoritative management of schools is justified, not alone because the training of mind is of overmastering importance, but on the plain business principle that the economical use of resources is the first step to success.

It has been said there are three stages in the development of school systems as known in the United States: 1. The conviction made general, that every child should receive a fair share of education. 2. The later but equally fundamental idea, that the property of the State should be responsible for that education. 3. That of school unity and system as secured by supervision. How slow has been the progress along these lines is evident at a glance. The enforced patronage of the schools is a phase of the first not yet generally accepted. Under the second is the—to many—doubtful question of free, secondary, and professional education; while with an abundance of supervision, the public is not wholly convinced of the importance of wise direction.

Bishop Fraser, visiting this country (1865), was constrained to say, " The great desideratum of the common-school system, both in Massachusetts and the States generally, was adequate, thorough, impartial, independent inspection of schools "; and more than twenty years afterward, an editorial in the " New England Journal of Education " declared, " The most important question of the hour in matters of education is that of supervision. "

In the earlier years, when there were few schools, and

scattered, control was chiefly local, and exercised, in New England especially, by the selectmen of the towns; later, and until late in this century, by committees and local school-boards. Each individual school was a law unto itself; uniformity was out of the question. Schools were efficient or neglected according to the local management. To a greater or less extent this must always be true, even in cities. It is the personal and localized effort that brings success. But the extension of the powers of the committee (or board) to administer a system of schools, or the fixing of a general control in a specialist, while minor and executive interests are left to the community, has great advantages. A close organic connection of the stronger schools with the weaker may advantage the one while offering no hindrance to the other. This is the function of a well-ordered supervision. The co-operation of all gives efficiency to each.

Again, the early supervision, if it may be so called, was chiefly prudential and economical. It regarded the expenditure of moneys and the erection of houses; the levying of taxes, making repairs, fixing the school terms and salaries; and, in general, had to do with the administration, the business, as opposed to the professional side of education. It was the infancy of control, necessary but incidental to the real work of the school. It was a care for the scaffolding rather than the structure. The oversight of methods and courses of study; of teachers and their selection; of individuals, and grades and classes; of discipline and sanitation, is a matter of half a century's growth. While, in a more comprehensive view of the office, there must be added to these its function in respect to the school's broader economic relations as a social institution, a factor in civilization, its ethical bearings. This is the philosophical side of education, and belongs appropriately to the office of general inspection. It has been said by Dr. Hall, " If teaching is to become a profession, it is superintendents, supervisors, etc., who must first make it so, by becoming, as their high position demands, strictly professional themselves in their work."

In tracing the rise and development of this systematic supervision, it will be convenient, after a notice of the "district system," the extreme of decentralization, to consider it in its three forms * as: 1. State supervision which was the occasion of, and has developed into, *State systems.* 2. County supervision, occasionally appearing as township control. 3. City supervision.

1. *The District System.*

The district system of school management took its rise in the colonial period of New England, and implies the setting off of towns and townships into smaller bodies, and the erection of these into independent corporations. They were possessed of legal powers of holding property, levying taxes, etc., and filled a large place in the life of the time. The town, in New England, was the unit in all civil affairs. The recognition of its functions gave character to the only two school systems formed before the Revolution. The substitution of the district, in educational matters, and the rise of " school societies," † form an interesting piece of history.

First introduced into Connecticut (1701) and half a century later into Rhode Island, the principle was incorporated into the revised Code of Massachusetts in the year 1789. It was the provision of this act, concerning "school districts," which Mr. Mann pronounced the most disastrous feature in the whole history of educational legislation in Massachusetts. Vermont seven years before, and New Hampshire in 1805, made like changes.

In Rhode Island these minor districts were called "squadrons," and were given the entire "management of their school-houses and lands, leasing out the latter, and employing schoolmasters as was most agreeable to them." Massa-

---

* The supervision of the General Government will be found considered elsewhere. See, in index, Bureau of Education, Indians, Alaska, etc.

† For a history of these school societies, see "Educational Documents of Connecticut, for 1853," p. 141.

chusetts soon (1800) authorized district taxation—a measure
from whose mischievous implications the State did not free
itself for seventy years. New York, with Ohio, Illinois, and
other Western States, passed similar enactments. Throughout New England at the opening of the century the district
had become the educational unit, while outside of New England (excluding the South), in a single generation, it pre-
dominated in half the States. The system represents the
extreme of self-government. A study of its development in
Connecticut will perhaps best reveal its character and influence.

An act of the General Assembly of Connecticut (1701)
provided that " the inhabitants of each town in the colony
shall pay annually forty shillings in every thousand
pounds in their respective lists toward the maintenance of a
schoolmaster." Some of the towns were large and contained parishes or ecclesiastical bodies—churches ; and elev-
en years later it was ordered that, " for the bringing up of
their children and the maintenance of a school," they (the
churches) should receive the money collected among them.
The ecclesiastical body thus became a civil organization
holding an official relation to the management of schools
sustained by public funds.

Originally, in New England, the parish was coextensive
with the town; the two were coincident indeed. The citizens in the one were members in the other. The same in
constituency, the same in territorial limits, and co-ordinate in
functions, there was no more occasion for friction, or difference of opinion, than among the members of either. The
interests of one were the interests of both. But, with the
growth of towns, religious care led to their division into distinct parishes; with diversity of religious belief came the
affiliation of those of like sentiments, without regard to geographical limits. The parish had lost its fixed existence,
while maintaining its functions and organization. It was
under these conditions that the Connecticut law was enacted.
The step was a new one, and away from the common-school

idea of New England—amounting practically to the establishment of school districts within towns. Authority was divided, and the direction of education put into the hands of a
class. It pointed to a delegation of authority that is ruinous. The parish was as yet, however, only a district, deriv-
ing all its power, as did other districts, from the civil body.
It could initiate nothing; it levied no taxes; it changed no
law. Forty years after, it was enacted that, when a town
consisted of but one ecclesiastical society, the selectmen of
the town should manage the schools; but that, when it included more than one, a committee from each society should
be empowered to manage lands and funds. By 1767 these
parishes were allowed each a separate treasurer; and, before
the close of the century, towns had been authorized, by the
new State Legislature, to incorporate themselves into " school
societies." In the revision and codification of laws, 1799, it
was ordered that they should have full power " to grant rates
for building and repairing ; to appoint their own committees; to provide teachers ; and to manage the prudentials of
their schools." This seems the extreme of deterioration.
So wide-spread was the influence, that few States in the
Union escaped it.

Growing out of these applications of the principle of
decentralization were two evils that were vicious in every
way, and call for special mention.

The first, though an incident of the system in Connecticut, and not found in most States, was the farming out of
school revenues to religious bodies.* It was subversive of
civil and social unity. It was yet one more encroachment
of the ecclesiastical upon the civil and personal life,
because of which Puritan and Huguenot had left their
European homes. So disastrous have been felt to be its
implications, by the newer States and in recent years, that

---

* The claims, on behalf of the Roman Catholic Church, for participation
in the control of school revenues, suggest that the question has a present
significance also.

seventeen of the thirty-eight States have seen fit to incorporate into the body of their Constitutions the provision that
"no religious sect or sects shall ever control any part of the
common-school or university funds."

But, aside from its ecclesiastical aspects, the district system seems generally to have worked mischief except in an
occasional thriving and homogeneous community. Along
with the unequal distribution of wealth, the system leads to
great inequality in the means and provisions of education; to
an unwise distribution of school-houses, many and poor ; to
short terms or poor teachers, or both; and, in imposing upon
indigence and improvidence the education of its own, tends
directly to class distinctions. In Massachusetts, for example,
it is said that one third of the State's taxable property is found
within a radius of ten miles about Boston. Without appor-
tionment equalizing the revenues, schools in the more distant parts must be very insufficiently supported.

The system, moreover, in its ultimate development makes
each school an independant organization, assigns mixed
classes to the same teacher, obstructs gradation, and, besides
being a wasteful practice financially, ignores the plainest
pedagogical principles of instruction. During the administration of Horace Mann, certain townships "abolished their
districts, assuming control of their schools in a corporate
capacity," but twenty years later it was said: "So fully are
most citizens attached to this system, so fully persuaded that
centralized power is dangerous, that the township ought not
to be intrusted with the entire care of schools (although its
officers preside in every other department), and that the
reserved right of having an agent to have the care of their
school-houses, and to employ the teachers of their children,
is a privilege of vital importance and not lightly to be re-
linquished—that there was little hope for better things." *

In New York, but two decades ago, there was an almost
entire disappearance of the township. Whatever local

---

* " Twenty-eighth Report of the Massachusetts Board of Education."

taxes were raised came through the districts ; of one of
which it was said (1865) " it had not taxed itself nor raised
one cent by rate " during three years of the previous four.
These small and weak but more or less independent districts
in parts of New England, Delaware, some of the States West,
and one or two others South, have constituted the greatest
hindrances to the maturing of school systems.   Strength
comes from co-operation; differences are equalized, and public administration is made to contribute to a homogeneity
that is civil no less than political safety.

But the influence of this division of authority is sometimes felt in States where the right to levy school-taxes has
not been reserved to the district.   With more or less of
central organization, it frequently occurs that the right to
select, examine, and hire teachers, rests in the neighborhood,
while the township authorities are held to answer for the
school's success.   Inferior teachers, and favoritism in their
selection, indifference in some neighborhoods, and the frequent shifting of instructors, are very serious evils, and all
cluster about district management.

The great diversity in State administration, and in local
administration among the States, makes any attempt to clas-
sify them as to local organization impracticable.   In some,
both township and district control are combined in respect
to different though more or less conflicting functions.
Nevertheless, there are certain general distinctions apparent.
In twelve States the district system predominates, though in
most of them the union of districts is legalized.   In general
this form characterizes the older colonies, or those whose
institutions are of the New England cast.   The organization by counties prevails in the South, as it did in the
days of Jefferson.   In eighteen States, chiefly Western,
the township is the unit in most civil affairs, education
included.

Not until 1856 were " school societies " and parish educational corporations abolished in Connecticut, and many years
later the union of districts authorized.   In Massachusetts the

change occurred less than twenty years ago, and in Rhode Island soon after. In the reorganization of schools during the middle of the century, while this change came after State management and supervision, and partly as a result of these, it was also in part an outgrowth of causes which led to these, and so exhibits one form of the wide-spread tendency of the period toward centralization.

2. State Supervision.

The Massachusetts law of 1647, and the Connecticut Code of 1650, were the only successful attempts at systems of education prior to 1800. Other States had tried: Rhode Island, under John Howland; New York, under Clinton; Pennsylvania, and, about the same time, Virginia, under Jefferson. But in every instance the laws failed of any efficient results.

Of the States named, New York approached soonest to a working plan. In 1795, Governor George Clinton had recommended the establishment of schools, and an act was passed, one of whose provisions was a supervision by local commissioners and trustees, reporting to the Secretary of State. The act applied, though, to cities and towns only. Seventeen years later (1812) was passed the first act contemplating a permanent system, and creating the office of "Superintendent of Common Schools." Gideon Hawley received the appointment, holding the office for nine years— until it was abolished, the Secretary of State becoming Superintendent of Schools *ex officio.*

Although the first State to move in the matter of State oversight of schools, the legislation of 1821 left New York far behind. Few Secretaries of State gave them any considerable attention; the duties of the two offices having no organic, much less any logical connection. Hon. John A. Dix was perhaps an exception. Made Secretary of State in 1838, and so charged with a kind of school auditorship, he gave the system a large place in his thoughts. It was during his term that the District Library act of the State was

passed. In 1841 the office of deputy-superintendent was created, and the duties largely turned over to him. With this
exception, nothing was done in New York toward State
supervision for thirty-three years; and by the time the office
was revived (1854), and the State had set earnestly about
the task of developing a system of schools, eighteen other States had already done the like ; among the earliest
being Maryland (1823, the office was abolished after two
years) ; Vermont, 1827 ; Pennsylvania, 1834 ; Michigan,
1836 ; Massachusetts, Kentucky, and Ohio, 1837 (the duties in the last being, after three years, in 1840, imposed
upon the Secretary of State);* and Missouri and Connecticut, 1839.

For a time most States combined the general educational
duties with those of officers already provided for. The former
were often regarded as nominal only. In the newer States
there were few schools, sessions were short, the finances
could easily be managed by existing agencies, and, East
and West, with few exceptions, the office was subordinated
to the current administration. Missouri, Ohio, Pennsylvania, Vermont, and Louisiana merged it, as had New York,
into that of Secretary of State. In Colorado, the duties were
performed by the State Treasurer; in Oregon, for thirteen
years, by the Governor.

The service was not easily set off from that of other
administrative agencies, as, in certain States, the office of
city and town trustee is not yet; as, for many years also,
and now for the smaller places, the city superintendent was
only a successful teacher or disciplinarian. And while the
chief State school officer is now, *usually*, one chosen for the
place, he is far too often a general student only, a specialist,
an ambitious young man or a politician, in place of the
practical, educational philosopher and wise organizer, which

---

* A very interesting sketch of the " Origin of the Ohio School System "
appeared in the " Magazine of Western History " for January, 1888, from
the pen of General M. D. Leggett.

the schools need. In a few instances the Constitutions or school acts require that he be a professional teacher or educator, though the same result is perhaps best attained, if at all, by an educated public sentiment.

The best State systems are principally what they are through the careful and unbiased administration of more or less imperfect laws by sensible and professionally spirited superintendents and Boards of Education. Not only States but the nation delights to honor the names of Horace Mann and Henry Barnard; Peirce in Michigan, Lewis in Ohio, Mills and Hopkins in Indiana, Burrows in Pennsylvania, and Beers and Northrop in Connecticut, besides more recent officers in these and other States. Such wise directors are the hope of the schools. Order and harmony and efficiency come from settled rational law, friction and waste and confusion from aimless unassociated efforts.

A. MASSACHUSETTS AND HORACE MANN.

When Massachusetts, in 1837, created a Board of Education, then were first united into a somewhat related whole the more or less excellent but varied and independent organizations, and a beginning made for a State system. It was this massing of forces, and the hearty co-operation he initiated, in which the work of Horace Mann showed its matchless greatness. " Rarely," it has been said, " have great ability, unselfish devotion, and brilliant success, been so united in the course of a single life." A successful lawyer, a member of the State Legislature, and with but limited experience as a teacher, he has left his impress upon the educational sentiments of, not only New England, but the United States.

At the time named (1837), Mr. Mann was President of the State Senate, a position which he resigned to accept the secretaryship of the new board; withdrawing from financially paying professional and business engagements, abstracting himself from political parties, that he might in singleness of aim do the best things in the line of duty, with timely need.

He entered upon his duties in June * of that year, and, for the rest of his life, was known as an educator. The office was no sinecure. The gnarls of a century's growth were to be smoothed; not all of the large number of private schools were in accord with the new movement, and the churches were naturally watchful of the encroachments of unsectarian education. Incompetent teachers were fearful, politicians carped, and general conservatism hindered. Much was to be accomplished, also, within the school. Teachers had to be improved, interest awakened, methods rationalized, and the whole adjusted to the available resources. Moreover, school architecture had to be studied ; school-funds must be found, regularly provided and husbanded, and legislators instructed. All this and more Mr. Mann did. It was at the beginning of his administration, and by his wise counsels and persistent pleadings, that the system of normal schools was originated. The annual appropriation for schools was doubled; two million dollars expended on houses and furniture; the number of women teachers increased; institutes introduced and systematized; school libraries multiplied; education provided for the dependent, and young offending classes, and the first compulsory law of the State enacted. His volume of lectures and twelve annual reports are already teachers' classics.†

B. CONNECTICUT AND HENRY BARNARD.

The securing of general control in two other New England States also, is so important, because of the comprehensive benefits resulting to education, and the wisdom and magnanimity which brought them about, as to call for special notice.

---

* Rev. John D. Peirce, eleven months before, had become Superintendent of the Public Schools of Michigan.

† For an exhibit of the present Massachusetts school system, see special report by the Bureau of Education on the Educational Conference at the New Orleans Exposition, Part II, p. 130.

At the time when Mr. Mann resigned his seat in the Massachusetts Senate (1837), Mr. Henry Barnard, a young man of twenty-six, a lawyer, and recently returned from two years of European travel, was elected to the Connecticut Legislature. He originated, and in less than a year had carried through the Assembly, an act for the control of the common schools, under which the "State Board of Commissioners" was organized. Mr. Barnard was made its first secretary. His duties were to gather and disseminate information, and to discover, devise, and recommend plans of improvement.

His first report, in 1839, was a graphic and painstaking exposition and summary of the local and general condition of the Connecticut schools. No point of failure seemed to escape his criticism, no success his commendation. Horace Mann said of him: "No better man for carrying out the Connecticut measures of reform could be found." He devoted to them both time and means. This first report made some startling revelations, and emphasized the need of an efficient general inspection of local schools. The twelve thousand pupils in private schools cost more than was expended for the forty thousand in public schools with equally good instruction. Primary children were neglected in both; there was almost no gradation of schools; public money had been misappropriated; and, while in the cities and populous districts Connecticut was doing as well as other parts of New England, progress over the State was represented as very unequal. The influence of Mr. Barnard and his coadjutors was soon felt. Much and most valuable information was diffused through lectures, periodicals, and tracts. Teachers were awakened, associations for mutual improvement were formed. In the fall of 1839, was called at Hartford one of the first teachers' classes in this country. He established an educational periodical as a vehicle of official and current educational information, which together with the institute of teachers, was made a private enterprise wholly at the expense of Mr. Barnard.

Suddenly, in an evil hour, and seemingly without occasion, the board was abolished, and the wholesome laws repealed (1842). The only vestige of the office remaining was
that of the commissioner of the school-fund, who was, *ex
officio*, a nominal superintendent for seven years.* In the
year 1849, Mr. Barnard being made principal of the newly
founded State Normal School at New Britain, was also by
legal provision Superintendent of Common Schools, both
of which positions he held for six years. In the year 1865,
the State Board was reconstituted, and Mr. D. C. Gilman †
was made its first secretary.

C. RHODE ISLAND.

One year after the repeal of the Connecticut law and his
retirement, Mr. Barnard was invited to Rhode Island, to
assist in devising plans for the organization of schools in
that State. For sixteen years there had been in force a
permissive law, but indifferently accepted and inefficient.
There were many private schools and expensive. The public terms were short, and the work was without system. A
bill was drawn up largely at his dictation, submitted to the
Legislature, passed unanimously by both Houses, and Mr.
Barnard, before he could leave the State, was invited to become " Commissioner of Public Schools" in Rhode Island.
He accepted, and in December of that year (1843) began a
work of six years, in magnitude and detail, in permanency
of result and general co-operation, scarcely second to that
of Horace Mann in Massachusetts.

It is not extravagant to say that the services of Mr. Mann
in Massachusetts, and Mr. Barnard in Rhode Island and
Connecticut, have been the models, in comprehensiveness

---

* Mr. Seth Beers became, in 1825, commissioner, and to him belongs
much of the credit of preserving and augmenting the school-fund, during
a quarter of a century, when the State organization was the most imperfect.

† Since President of Johns Hopkins University.

and system, and general spirit, of most of the inspection and oversight of State schools in the United States for nearly fifty years.

D. GENERAL VIEW OF STATE CONTROL.

Delaware, of all the States, has no superintendent. The last to create the office (1875), after eleven years, the legislature repealed the law, and at present the three county superintendents report (nominally) to the Secretary of State. Among the Territories New Mexico has an officer appointed annually to receive the educational reports, but without supervisory powers. With these exceptions the form of State supervision is universal. Its functions are variously exercised.

The average official term is a fraction over three years. In fourteen States it is four years. Of these last, eight have established the office in the last two decades ; while but five State enactments in that period have made it two years— hinting at a tendency to lengthen the official service. In Massachusetts, Connecticut, and Rhode Island the appointment is annual, being in the first two a secretaryship in the State Board. As a matter of fact, however, the terms of service in these States have been longer than the average. Uniformity of administration through a fairly established tenure of office is fruitful of good in all departments of education ; in supervision it is fundamental.

In most of the States the services of the superintendent are supplemented by a general Board of Education, of which he is, *ex officio*, a member, and whose two chief functions are the examination of teachers, directly or indirectly, and the management of the State school-funds. Of the thirty-eight States, twenty-three have such boards. Three others —Arkansas, New Hampshire, and West Virginia—provide bodies corporate for the control of the funds ; and Illinois, Iowa, and Ohio each a Board of Examiners only. In Minnesota the Board of Commissioners on Preparatory Schools is constituted of the Governor of the State, the Superintend-ent of Public Schools, and the President of the University of Minnesota, for the encouragement of higher education in the State.

The first board organized, so far as known, was that in North Carolina, in the year 1825, under the name of the "Presi-dent and Directors * of the Literary Fund." From this act and the services of this board, dates all that was attempted toward a system of schools in North Carolina prior to 1861. Ten years after the North Carolina law, Missouri instituted a similar organization, to be known as the State Board of Education, † and to consist of the Governor, the Auditor, and the Treasurer of State.   Besides these, and the Massachusetts and Connecticut Boards already noticed, the only other State with similar provisions before 1850 was Maine, whose board was abolished six years later, and has not since been re-vived.

Of the twenty-three State organizations, ten are com-posed chiefly of State officials, and can only be regarded as administrative in a business way.   The constitution of the other thirteen is mainly professional, and points to better things.   It is certainly a matter of grave importance that, whatever the educational office, persons shall be chosen for their fitness . to discharge its functions.   If super-visory powers—general or local—are to justify themselves, they must be administered in the light of the maturest, all-sided educational thought.   State control, both corpo-rate and individual, may otherwise be only so much ma-chinery.

The following table shows not only the date of the first ap-pointment of a superintendent in each State, but in some cases also the successive modifications of the idea of supervision.

---

* Consisting of the Chief-Justice of the Supreme Court, the Speak-ers of the Senate and the House of Commons, and the Treasurer of the State.

† This was eighteen years before the appointment of a State Superin-tendent.

State School Control.

No.	STATE.	Supt.	No.	STATE.	Supt.
1	New York.............	1813	14	Maine.................	1846
	Secretary of State....	1821	15	New Hampshire........	1846
	Superintendent.......	1854		Sec. of the County Bd.	1850
2	Maryland.............	1825		Superintendent.......	1857
	Abolished	1827	16	Louisiana.............	1847
	Revived	1864		Revived	1868
3	Vermont.............	1827	17	Wisconsin	1849
	Abolished	1833	18	California.............	1851
	Revived	1845	19	Indiana....	1852
	Abolished	1851	20	North Carolina........	1852
	Revived	1856	21	Alabama...............	1854
4	Pennsylvania	1833	22	Illinois	1854
5	Michigan	1836	23	Minnesota	1858
6	Massachusetts.........	1837	24	Kansas	1859
7	Ohio	1837	25	Colorado..............	1861
	Secretary of State.....	1840	26	Nevada...............	1866
	Superintendent.......	1853	27	Tennessee	1867
8	Kentucky.............	1837	28	Georgia...............	1868
9	Missouri.............	1839	29	Florida...............	1868
	Secretary of State....	1841	30	Mississippi............	1868
	Superintendent.......	1853	31	South Carolina........	1868
10	Connecticut...........	1839	32	Nebraska..............	1869
11	Iowa	1841	33	West Virginia..........	1869
	Abolished	1842	34	Virginia	1870
	Revived	1846	35	Texas	1871
	Abolished	1858	36	Oregon	1872
	Revived	1864	37	Arkansas	1874
12	Rhode Island	1843	38	Delaware	1875
13	New Jersey....	1845		Abolished	1886
	Made general.........	1846			

3. City Supervision.

Next to some form of State control, as most general and best defined, is that of cities. Now so common that the attempt to maintain a system of schools in any city of large size, without some responsible directive agent, is looked upon as an anomaly, it is easy to forget—many seem not to know—that the experiment itself is but a generation old.

In the year 1837, Buffalo (New York), made a city but five years before, with a population of about a thousand, and six school districts, was authorized to appoint a superin-

8

tendent.* The step appears to have been without precedent
in this country. Within two years there were fifteen districts, a school in each, a central school for the higher English branches, and a superintendent.

About the same time in Rhode Island one Thomas W.
Dorr, known in history as the leader of the Dorr Rebellion
of 1842, was a member of the Providence School Committee
and, as chairman, drafted a plan for the more vigorous
management and inspection of the town schools. It is
claimed that he got his idea from the State and local factory
system, whose directors, as in all large industrial enterprises, select some skillful, trusted, intelligent workman as
foreman or superintendent. The plan was adopted in Providence as a similar one had been in Buffalo, and others were
later in most enterprising communities. Indeed, from the
material standpoint, any objection that may be made to
school supervision may be made to foremen and overseers
and master-workmen anywhere. Hon. Nathan Bishop was
elected to the new position (1839), a place which he honor-
ably filled until his promotion twelve years later to a similar
one in Boston, where also he had the honor to inaugurate
a work so admirably established at Providence.

In the mean time, however, in other cities and sections,
the suggestion was being adopted. The city of New Orleans
was incorporated in the year 1804. Thirty years later, having about one hundred thousand population, it was set off
into three independent municipalities. By State law (1840)
they were authorized to establish schools. The second district organized (1841) with twelve citizens as a board of
directors with power to act. Mr. John A. Shaw was chosen
superintendent. Within three years the enthusiasm was
transmitted to the other wards, and the system became (1844)
uniform throughout the city. For the same year also Cleveland, Ohio, specified the secretary of the board as "acting
manager of the schools," who served twelve years, when the

---

* Steiger's "Cyclopædia of Education," article "Buffalo."

name was changed to "Superintendent of Schools," and Andrew Friese elected to the office. Springfield, Massachusetts, the year following made the experiment, but almost immediately adandoned it. Mr. J. N. McJilton was elected superintendent of Baltimore, 1849; and Nathan Guilford, of Cincinnati, 1850. This last was by popular vote, though since 1853 the office has been filled by appointment of the board. The decade from 1850 to 1860 shows a general reorganization, one of whose elements was the choice of a superintendent. Boston made the change, as has been seen, in 1851, leading to a State law in that year authorizing supervision in towns throughout the State. Under this law Gloucester immediately made an appointment. New York city reorganized the same year, San Francisco and Jersey City in the year 1852, Newark and Brooklyn in 1853, and Chicago and St. Louis in 1854. In Jersey City the office was for several years an unsalaried one, and was held by merchants and other business men, the duties being performed, if at all, in a perfunctory manner, and with no public expectation that thought or time would be put into the service.

But the most unique city system in this country for many years was that of Philadelphia. Until 1883, it, among all the cities of the United States, was without a superintendent. In the midst of the enthusiasm aroused by the centennial exhibit, leading citizens of the city organized somewhat informally, but with capital and enterprise, the " Public Education Society." Meetings were held, lectures were provided, educational systems and questions were studied, teachers were consulted, the papers used, and the city officers and general public educated. Finally, with a school census of one hundred and sixty thousand and a school enrollment of ninety thousand, with twenty-five hundred teachers and more than five hundred schools, the city was asked to provide some effective supervision. The ward committees, the Central Board, and municipal officers, readily consented; and (1883) Superintendent James McAlister, with six associates, was given the schools in charge to work out a system.

No one, who would understand the functions and relations of school supervision in the United States, can afford to miss a comparative study of Philadelphia schools in the years before and since 1883.

From recent reports it appears that of four hundred and seventeen cities, containing five thousand inhabitants or over, but thirty-eight are without superintendents. Among these the duties are nominally performed by some officer of the board, as was the case in the early experiment in Cleveland, Ohio.

It would seem as if this phase of centralization, for bringing which into New England Horace Mann was severely censured, had become a fixed principle in educational economy. Wisely managed the investments here yield the richest of all returns. It is skilled labor that pays best ; next to this must be esteemed skilled oversight of average labor. Three fourths of the teachers of the country at large have had no professional training ; of the others, many have had but little. For years to come, then, it must remain true that, on an administrative basis alone, the success of schools can be predicted only upon the maturest, far-seeing direction.

But this is only the infant stage of school control ; it is primitive and prudential. It has to do with the accessories of school management, whose officers are stewards and keepers. There is a higher stage, in which organization and system, the regulation of the machine, and the general subordination of parts, are themselves seen as means ; and the effect of all this upon the learner, the real object of inquiry. This phase is interrogative and inductive. Facts must be gathered as data—facts of mind, and child-mind ; knowledge of the race and its environments ; observations of men, and institutions and customs, as culture-yielding agencies ; systems of education ; the bearings of science. Out of such study by fearless inquirers, free from the bias of adopted theories, must come, ʼif at all, a science of education. This is the particular function of a city superintendent. Philbrick in Boston, Harris in St. Louis, Pickard in

Chicago, and Rickoff in Cincinnati and Cleveland, have each in turn given the schools of their cities distinctive features ; and, what is far more to the purpose of an advisory supervision, have contributed measurably to the body of the educational doctrine of the present.

When the superintendent was only a successful teacher or principal promoted, there was unavoidably little philosophical study of the problem and conditions of education ; but with the professional aspect of teaching is recognized a demand for educators fitted for supervision and criticism ; for men whose comprehensive training, habits of scientific thinking, a careful and continued study of the historical aspects of education and its kindred philosophies, entitle them to speak with authority on current questions and in the organization of systems. No one can better render this service to education than the city superintendents, because under no other circumstances are the opportunities of manifold observation and repeated comparison and verification of pedagogical facts so numerous or available,

4. County Supervision.

The need of careful school inspection in rural districts is implied in conceding any supervision. The best school, other things equal, is the most wisely supervised school, of uniform administration and professional direction. No interests need this more than those of the outlying districts, subjected to hindrances peculiar to sparsely settled and widely separated neighborhoods.*

The earliest attempts at this local supervision were almost wholly confined to the management and investment of funds, the control of school-lands, and the services which concerned the institution as a material organization. As early as 1824 in Missouri, the civil commissioners of the

---

* A general discussion of the conditions and possibilities of rural schools may be found in " A Graded School System for Country Schools," by L. S. Wade, 1881. See also " Courses and Methods," by John T. Prince.

county were required to appoint "visitors to the schools,"
nine in each district, who were to visit their respective
schools once in three months, to examine teachers, grant
licenses, and to exercise "general supervisory power." Ten
years later, three trustees were made to take the place of the
nine visitors, but with like duties. The control was of the
district. In Vermont, about 1837, and in Massachusetts the
same year, superintending committees of towns (townships)
were appointed, with functions similar to those of the selectmen in Massachusetts and Connecticut towns a century before. The very literal way in which the duties of these
early committees have been adopted by the more recent
county supervisors well illustrates the evolution of the
office ; it has been in most instances a process of fixing an
existing function in fewer hands. In North Carolina also,
for many years deficient in execution, but forward among
States to recognize and adopt the best current thought on
education, the principle of more or less general control of
local school affairs was early incorporated into the school
law. In the year 1839, counties were directed to divide
themselves for educational purposes into six districts, each
six miles square, over all of which should be appointed not
less than five superintendents; and for each of whose school
corporations should be chosen by the county court not less
than three "school committee-men." This provided a more
general control than that in Missouri fifteen years before,
but it was still of limited districts. The belief was growing
that a more centralized administration of schools would
conduce to their efficiency. County control (occasionally
as noted above, including or implying township or district
control) was the next step in the development of school systems.

In New York, county superintendents were authorized by
the law of 1841; their chief function being, however, confined to hearing appeals from local officers. There was no
attempt at even advisory control. The law was repealed six
years later, and before its revival in the act of 1856, creating

the district commissioner's office, four other States had tried, and proved the efficiency of the plan. California's first law incorporated it, and Pennsylvania, always fearful of centralized authority, seemed (1884) wholly to forget her past, or to read it more wisely, and abolishing sub-district committees, introduced county control, uniformity of text-books, and a minimum school term. Michigan (1867) adopted the county system, but after eight years' trial abolished it, and now maintains township school inspectors, who report to the secretary of the County Board of Examiners, the county clerk acting as the local agent of the State in financial affairs.

Taking county supervision as a general term, including all forms of local direction, narrower than the State, and outside of cities, there appears much diversity. In seven States, comprising Michigan, and all of New England, it becomes township supervision. In Arkansas, North Carolina, and Texas, it is almost entirely of the district; with the two combined in Louisiana, Mississippi, and West Virginia. Altogether, thirty States and five Territories have a fairly well-defined county organization.

The diversity in the modes of selecting the supervising officer, especially county superintendents is striking. In one State only, Alabama, they are appointed by the State Superintendent, for a term of two years; in Delaware and Florida, by the Governor; in Mississippi, New Jersey, and Virginia, by the State Board. The County Board elects in Georgia, Maryland, North Carolina, and Indiana; the school directors in Pennsylvania; and the town (township) superintendents in Vermont. In thirteen States the office is subject to general election; these are California, Colorado, Illinois, Iowa, Minnesota, Missouri, Nebraska, Nevada, New York, Oregon, South Carolina, West Virginia, and Wisconsin. In accounting for this diversity, something must be ascribed to differing social and political conditions, something to official inheritances, but far more to an imperfect understanding of the means and resources of real education.

In most States one of the duties of the office is to visit schools, though this is not universal by any means. Why it should not be is difficult to say. Less than this makes a business office only. If supervising schools means anything, it implies familiarity with the management within the room, methods, discipline, and the means and character of instruction. It means counsel and criticism. Less than this may be needful as precautionary and economic measures; but these are in no sense professional, and contribute only indirectly to the school as an agency of culture.

Another duty usually assigned to the local supervisor is that of examining and licensing teachers. This, indeed, has been one of the functions of school inspectors for two hundred years. In twenty of the States, of very unlike organization, the offices of supervisor and examiner rest in the same person. Whether this is well, has been questioned; but the practice widely prevails.

Bibliography.

"School Supervision," by W. H. Payne; "School Inspection," by D. R. Fearon, 1876 ; the "Supervision of Schools," in "Proceedings of National Educational Association," 1887, p. 512; "Supervision of Schools in Massachesetts," by A. D. Mayo, "Unitarian Review," vol. vii, p. 400; "City School Systems of the United States," by J. D. Philbrick, published by the United States Bureau of Education as Circular 1—1885; "City Supervision," by R. W. Stevenson, in "Proceedings of National Educational Association," 1884, p. 283, also "Proceedings of the National Council of Education," 1884, p. 26 ; and the Annual reports of Dr. W. T. Harris, St. Louis, 1867–'79. The "Inspection of Country Schools," by J. D. Philbrick, in "American Social Science Journal," vol. ii, p. 11 ; and, in general, "The School, its Rights and Duties," by J. H. Hoose, in "Proceedings of National Educational Association," 1876, p. 167. See "Life of Horace Mann," by Mrs. Mary Mann (1881), and his collected "Lectures and Reports," 1872.

CHAPTER VIII.

THE PREPARATION OF TEACHERS.

THE changes already noted as accompanying the educational awakening were administrative. The transformation on the professional side, in the school course, the teacher, the objects and character of discipline, etc., was not less complete. The administrative function preceded, not because it must—logically, the changed function of the school should work out its own adapted organization—but because the former want, being professional and technical, was not generally recognized. A few men fifty years ago, fewer yet ten years earlier, saw both the need and the remedy; crudely it may be, and vaguely, but well in advance of the common mind. From their lectures and addresses and sermons, their books, the classes they taught, and their persistent influence on public and legislative sentiment, have developed, not only normal schools, but the earlier occasional classes, institutes, associations, journals, etc.

It is a large interest and, from the pedagogical standpoint, of the first importance.*

1. Educational Associations.

The principle of co-operation is fundamental in a republic; it is the soul of both its individual and institutional life. Social friction and the free interchange of experience presuppose a degree of equality; and equality, in turn, incites to combination. The individual is strong in proportion as he takes to himself the experience of all; each is increased as he gives to all.

Societies, then—combinations of individuals founded upon a like interest, looking to the accomplishment of the same

---

* " Good teachers," said Dr. Philbrick, " and what next? There is no next."

object, and that a general good—are in consonance with the organic law of our government. In a sketch of the people's culture, to leave out of view their organization, and the joint services of individuals, would be to miss a powerful agent in the upbuilding of our national life. Associations may be classified, according to their objects, as—

1. Those looking to the general good, through the establishment and efficient administration of institutions and organizations.

2. Those whose purpose is the promotion of professional or class interests.

3. Those organized to investigate, discover, invent; to add to the sum of human knowledge.

To the first belong missionary organizations, school and manumission societies, and political parties. It includes most organized effort, indeed, as lecture associations, village improvement societies, temperance and other reforms, etc. It is a potent agency, and, well used, one of the most fruitful means of progress. With the second may be classed professional associations, conventions made permanent, industrial guilds, fraternities, and sects. Philosophical and scientific societies are representative of the last, and form a large class. A consideration of such of these, in so far as they are educational from the school or professional side, is the aim of this section. The consideration of the third class will be left mainly to a subsequent paragraph.

A. SOCIETIES FOR THE PROMOTION OF SCHOOLS.

To one who is familiar with the current governmental administration of schools only, the recital of how large a part in education voluntary association played fifty years ago in this country, must seem an exaggeration. It built up schools, and supplied houses, and found and prepared teachers ; it manipulated parties and draughted laws; it formed public opinion, and initiated reforms. Whatever was best done in New York and Pennsylvania, in Rhode Island and the South, and especially in the newer States of the North and West, in Ohio and Indiana and Kentucky, was the work of organized societies. The earlier habit of Massachusetts and Connecticut is in this respect in strong contrast with that of other colonies and States, and even with their own later history.

Rhode Island had no attempt at a school system until the Mechanics' Institute of Providence took it in hand. In New York city, the "Free School Society" established the first permanent schools (1805), and through the law of 1812 secured the present system. The Philadelphia Society for the Support of Charity Schools (1790) was the prime mover in all the important school legislation, not only of Philadelphia but of Pennsylvania, for forty years.

Of a like general nature, but of broader field, was the College Society formed at Yale, 1829, to assist collegiate and theological students in the West. Illinois College, at Jacksonville, was founded and for many years supported by it. The Western Baptist Educational Association organized a little later "for the promotion of schools and education generally in the valley of the Mississippi," sent teachers to both Indiana and Illinois ; and ten years after (1844) a society, formed and controlled under the counsel of Miss Catherine E. Beecher, the Board of National Popular Education, sent West not less than five hundred teachers, several of whom became eminently successful and widely known.

About the same time was another organization * whose services deserve mention, for it operated in half a dozen States, and aided twice as many colleges that must otherwise have succumbed to misfortune. Nowhere were the financial reverses of 1837–'42 more seriously felt than in the then new West ; and by no institutions more than by the colleges and schools. Twenty institutions for superior instruction had been founded in Iowa, Illinois, Michigan, Indiana, Ohio, and Kentucky, in the fifteen years after 1825. Not

---

* The Western College Society.

one of them was endowed, few had even a moderate support at best, and, as the little property they held was chiefly in unimproved land, it was unproductive. It seemed as if numbers of these colleges must surrender their charters. Most of them, of course, were denominational, and in 1843, delegates of churches representing Wabash, Illinois, Marietta, and Western Reserve Colleges, and Lane Theological Seminary, met representatives of Eastern churches to confer on the state of Western education. The heavy losses of these institutions (approximating two hundred thousand dollars), already greatly aided by the East, were strong appeals for renewed help. An organization was effected, under the name of the Western College Society, "to afford assistance in such manner and so long only as, in the judgment of the directors, the exigencies of the institutions may demand." Besides the five colleges first aided, nine others received help at various times in thirty years. More than half a million dollars were contributed at the East, and twice as much in the West, to promote the objects of this management. Half the institutions became independent before 1860, and the others soon after. The Western College Society did an eminent service.

B. SOCIETIES FOR THE IMPROVEMENT OF TEACHERS.

Supplementing these general endeavors, sometimes following them, were special organizations of teachers for mutual improvement and professional advancement. Members of the first class (A) were frequently not teachers, but business men, lawyers, public officers, and especially the clergy. The second class was composed of teachers. Indeed, membership in the profession was, at first, a condition of membership in the association. These were local and, largely, expedients. They were at once a product and a sign of the awakening interest in education and educational institutions in the third and fourth decades of the century. Reference has been found to but one earlier.

The Middlesex County School Association of Massachusetts was in existence in 1799. A generation later, Essex County formed a like society, and, among States, Florida, followed by the Utica Convention of "teachers and friends of education" in New York. About the same time (1829), in Cincinnati, was organized, under the lead of Albert Picket, the "Western Academic Institute and Board of Education," merged three years later in the "Western Literary Institute and College of Professional Teachers," which for ten years was almost the one regenerative agency in Ohio education.* It sought to promote, by every laudable means, the diffusion of knowledge in regard to education, and especially by the elevation of the character and qualifications of the teachers. Among the members were Lyman Beecher, Prof. C. E. Stowe, B. O. Peers, and Samuel Lewis. Money was contributed, and a school agent appointed to visit the schools of the State. This was an attempt at a general supervision ten years before the first State Superintendent. Ladies were not admitted as members; though Mrs. L. H. Sigourney (1836), and again Mrs. Emma Willard, were allowed to submit papers on female education, which were read by men.

The work of these societies, and of such men and women in behalf of education at the West, was having its effect. Associations of teachers were held in Kentucky, Georgia, Tennessee, Illinois, and Michigan prior to 1840. The State Associations of Massachusetts, Connecticut, and Rhode Island were all organized in 1845, and still exist. Established later (1863), but of the same class of State organizations, is the "University Convocation of the State of New York," than which perhaps no State Association has performed a more eminent and lasting service for good. It concerns secondary and collegiate interests chiefly, and admits: 1. Members of the Board of Regents. 2. Instructors in colleges,

---

* At the second meeting occurred Thomas S. Grimke's arraignment of the classics and mathematics, as subjects of study, and his enthusiastic commendation of science.

normal schools, academies, and other institutions under
the care of the regents and their trustees.   3. The president, vice-presidents, and secretaries of the New York State
Teachers' Association.   In 1867 representatives of colleges
in other States were invited to membership.*

The "Northwestern Educational Association" originated
in a teachers' institute held in Chicago 1846.   Nine States
were represented.   It marked an era in Western school experience, consolidating the interests of these States.   They
were compacted into a section.   What was best anywhere,
the sooner became common property.   Free schools, gradation, teachers' seminaries, institutes, State appropriations,
and supervision, were all made easier by the common recom-
mendation and support.

The earliest settled, New England preceded most other
sections in professional agencies.   Almost a score of years
before the association last named, the "American Institute
of Instruction" was organized in Boston.   It was incorporated (1831) "for the diffusion of useful knowledge in regard
to education."   In its earlier meetings, and regularly for
many years, were Goold Brown, Warren Colburn, Judge
Story, Horace Mann, D. P. Page, Denison Olmsted, and
Bishop Huntington.   Charles Northend talked on "Common Schools," and Hermann Krüsi told the story of Pestalozzi.   It was a veritable teachers' school, when such were
few.   While its meetings have been chiefly confined to New
England, its influences were long general, and for thirty
years it was the only recognized national organization.

Out of this, perhaps urged by the apparent insufficiency
of it, grew the "National Educational Association."   Its general purposes were set forth in the first inaugural address of
President Richards, 1858, as: 1. The union of all sections in
friendly associated action. 2. The creation of a teaching

---

* A history and *résumé* of the work of the Convocation since its organization may be found in the "Historical and Statistical Record of the
University of the State of New York, 1885," pp. 789–834.

profession, by professional methods. 3. The accrediting of
teachers by proper examining boards. 4. The establishment
of departments of pedagogics in connection with all schools
which send out persons to teach. In thirty years the work
of the association has been much specialized, and doubtless
to advantage. Besides the general body, there are now nine
departments : 1. School Superintendence. 2. Higher Instruction. 3. Normal Schools. 4. Industrial Education.
5. Art Education. 6. Music Education. 7. Kindergarten
Instruction. 8. Elementary Schools. 9. Secondary Instruction. Besides these also is the "Council of Education," a
deliberative body whose members are chosen from the general association. This was organized in 1881, having for its
object " to reach and disseminate correct thinking on educational questions." It has standing committees as follows :

1. On State School Systems.	7. On Technical Education.
2. On City School Systems.	8. On Pedagogics.
3. On Higher Education.	9. On Education of Girls.
4. On Secondary Education.	10. On Hygiene in Education.
5. On Elementary Education.	11. On Educational Literature.
6. On Normal Education.	12. On Educational Statistics.

The modern Industrial and Scientific Exposition also has
come to be utilized as the occasion for conference on educational questions.

2. Institutes.

Somewhat more specific in aim than the associations and
conferences, but more general than normal schools, is the
"Institute." This has been characterized * as a peculiarly
American institution. Yet to an American it is not easy to
formulate the sufficient distinction between it and other
agencies for the training of teachers. Its function varies in
different States. It is all things to all sections. An eclectic
agency, it supplements the normal school with something

---

* Francis Adams, " Free School System of the United States," p. 65.

of the function of the annual conference, but, more frequent and local, is also more personal.* Under present conditions with few institutions for formal training, and three hundred thousand teachers, uncertain employment and temporary, and an unsettled professional code, it must long remain that these, and every contributing means, will be needed for the better fitting of teachers.

As early as 1834 an institute was reported to the "College of Teachers," as held in one of the counties in Ohio ; and, in the same year, perhaps, one assembled in Boston for the instruction of teachers of music. Five years later, and just prior to the first State normal schools, Mr. Barnard, then School Commissioner of Connecticut, called his teachers together at Hartford, and again in the spring of the following year. These gatherings were at his own expense, and enrolled twenty to thirty teachers, with a faculty of seven instructors.†

The first institute, *so named*, was held in Tompkins County, New York, by Superintendent J. S. Denman, 1843. It continued two weeks, under the instruction of Hon. Salem Town, and was, says the school report for that year, "a revelation of the large sphere of this new agent in school improvement." Two years afterward, the State reported institutes in seventeen counties. They were introduced into Rhode Island in 1844, and into Ohio, Michigan, and Massachusetts the next year. In certain States they began to receive financial aid, and so became a part of the general system. Before 1850 they were common in a dozen States, and reached hundreds of teachers who must otherwise have had no reliable professional training.

There are now ‡ State and district organizations main-

---

* Prof. Payne has described it as a " normal school with a very short course of study."

† Among them, besides Mr. Barnard, were Prof. Charles Davies and Rev. T. H. Gallaudet.

‡ For a very complete exhibit of " Teachers' Institutes," see " Bureau Circular of Information," No. 2, 1885, prepared by Hon. J. H. Smart, of Indiana.

tained in Alabama (for colored teachers), Arkansas, Florida, Massachusetts, Minnesota, Nevada, New York, North Carolina, Rhode Island, South Carolina, Texas, and West Virginia ; and county institutes in half of the States. Twelve States—Colorado, Connecticut, Delaware, Georgia, Kentucky, Louisiana, Maine, Mississippi, Missouri, New Hampshire, Oregon, and Tennessee—report neither, regularly held. Sixteen make State appropriations in their aid, and six, county appropriations.

In seven States—California, Maryland, Nebraska, New Jersey, North Carolina, Virginia, and West Virginia—attendance is compulsory. It is estimated that not less than one hundred and fifty thousand teachers receive annually, an average of six days' instruction by means of these State and local institutes.

In addition to these also, are those in cities, more or less regularly held, generally under the direction of the superintendent, and, in the larger cities, set off into sections, each doing the particular work of its department. Of ninety-six cities reporting teachers' meetings, forty-four make attendance upon them compulsory. Some of them have informal courses, which, pursued for successive years, would do credit to many a so-called normal school. Almost no agency, excepting a formal and established course of training, can do so much for the right guidance of the teacher, the sharpening of her understanding, and the full rounding of her professional character, as the frequent meeting, under wise direction, of a body of teachers in daily co-operation and intercourse.

3. Normal Schools.

From the earliest times, the fitness of the teacher has been held as one condition of the learner's advancement. Adaptation to the work of instruction is one measure of the best service. Not knowledge alone, nor maturity, nor a faithful conscience, can excuse inaptitude and want of skill in address and presentation. " The art of well delivering the knowledge we possess," said Lord Bacon, " is among the

9

secrets left to be discovered by future generations." This "delivering the knowledge we possess" has since been developed into a system, whose like even the fertile mind of Bacon, but dimly perceived. There has come to be among every civilized people a more or less specialized class, whose business it is to instruct, and whose preparation is the work of a particular institution.

That it was not always so—that it is, indeed, of comparatively recent times—needs only to be mentioned. Harvard had been founded fifty years before the first known teachers' seminary; the school systems of New England were in operation; and Mr. Cheever, now an old man, had been himself the most famous master of his time, and had educated many others. The teacher then, and long since, was himself only the best instructed ; now he was the parent, and then the pastor; here, the young man fitted or fitting for the professions, and so possessed of a real or supposed superiority among his fellows; there, again, he was any one whose leisure or inclinations led him to choose this as a business.

But, along with other social and economic interests, teaching, in its vital importance, worked a specialization of institution—an organization adapted to the new function.

A. ITS EUROPEAN ORIGIN.

As with many another institution, so with this, it had its genesis in the older civilization and more closely discriminated social interests of Europe.

The earliest school of the kind of which record is had was that founded at Rheims (1681) by the Abbé de la Salle.* This developed, three years later, into the now famous Christian Brothers' School, and became widely influential. By Hermann August Francke, the distinguished German

---

* A man of progressive, modern thought, he introduced, besides normal schools, gradation, and object-lessons, and established industrial schools, polytechnic institutes and reformatories.

educator, and Johann Julius Hecker, his follower, it was introduced into Germany—by the latter into Berlin (1748). Before the century closed, Prussia had six normal schools, and became the center from which radiated the professional spirit to other European systems and to the United States.

B. BEGINNINGS OF THE IDEA IN THE UNITED STATES.

As early as 1789 Elisha Ticknor had urged, in the "Massachusetts Magazine," that steps be taken for the improvement of education and the common intelligence, and to this end recommended the establishment of a system of " county schools to fit young gentlemen for college and school-keeping." It was claimed by Noah Webster also, about the same time, that "the principal defect in the plan of education, in America, was the want of good teachers in the academies and common schools." Without doubt these were the expressions of a common feeling, whose development and realization belong to the present century.

(1.) Lancasterianism.

The monitorial system of instruction, originated in 1797, by Dr. Andrew Bell, and elaborated and promoted by Joseph Lancaster, was early introduced into the schools of the United States.* Ten years before Lancaster visited this country, the method had gained a foothold in half a dozen States—a ground which it held for half a century in New York and Philadelphia, and in Maryland and elsewhere even longer.

As early as 1810 the Public School Society of New York city, employing the system, opened a school for female monitors, and six years later a similar one for males. By invitation of this society, Mr. Lancaster, on his tour through the States (1818), lectured in New York, and so impressed his hearers with the efficiency of his system that leading edu-

---

* See Gill's " Systems of Education," p. 162, and " History of the Elementary School Contest in England," by F. Adams, p. 48.

cators regarded it as marking a new era in education. Though falling short of the early claims for it, its history in this country exhibits one phase of the development of teachers' training that can not be ignored.

(2.) Early Promoters of the Normal Schools.*

There were as yet no very definite ideas as to the systematic and thorough training of teachers. Lancasterianism was only a device, at best, for the crudest of information-giving. Schools were at a low ebb and instruction mediocre. Nevertheless, forces were shaping themselves for the greatest educational event of the century.

Upon taking his master's degree at Yale, 1816, Denison Olmsted read a thesis on "The State of Education in Connecticut," in which he elaborated a plan of an "Academy for Schoolmasters." In New York, since 1787, the incorporated academies, along with the colleges, had been under the supervision of the Regents of the University. About 1821 the State making an annual appropriation to such of the academies as were judged worthy, they came to be looked to for a supply of teachers for the common schools, this being made the basis, two years later, of a claim for a generous distribution of funds. Almost simultaneously, William Russell, of Massachusetts, and W. R. Johnson, of Pennsylvania, Rev. Thomas Gallaudet, of Connecticut, and Dr. Philip Lindsley, of New Jersey, all submitted, each unknown to the others, petitions and plans for teachers' preparatory schools.

Previously, however, Prof. S. R. Hall, of New Hampshire, minister, teacher, and writer, called to a church at Concord, in that State, accepted the invitation, on condition that he be allowed to open a "teachers' school." Here, in the year 1823, he opened a private seminary, chiefly for those who would teach, but admitting a class of children,

---

* The "American Journal of Education" is full of information touching the rise of teachers' seminaries, especially vols. ii, iii, and v.

which he used, in instruction and discipline, as a model and practice school. In this village, away from libraries and great teachers and the universities, were first delivered the talks and lessons which, published in 1829, as " Lectures on School-keeping," were spread broadcast through New England and the central States. He continued in this school seven years. From 1830 to 1837 he was at Andover, and the next three years at Plymouth, New Hampshire, at both of which places he was principal of the only established teachers' seminaries outside of New York, until the Massachusetts Normal School was founded in 1839. At Andover the "Normal Department" had a three years' course, including fifty lectures on the "Art of Teaching." At Plymouth, during the year when Massachusetts got her first normal school, it had two hundred and fifty students, and was furnishing teachers for all the adjoining towns. Mr. Hall is the American Hecker—the pioneer in the work which most distinguishes recent from early schooling in the United States.*

(3.) Acquaintance with European Systems.

Another efficient influence of the period was the spreading of a knowledge of German and other foreign schools. Rev. Charles Brooks, visiting Europe, in 1834, became acquainted, through friends, with the Prussian system, and especially with their training of teachers. Returning in 1835, he urged the establishment of normal schools in this country, enforcing the need and the advantage by a vigorous exposition of Prussian teaching ; lectured in every New England State, in New York and Pennsylvania, and addressed the Legislatures of most of them. Prof. A. D. Bache, President of Girard College, also went abroad (1836) on a

---

* Mr. Hall was the author of a number of school-books, some of which were much used in their day—a " Child's Geography," a " School Arithmetic," the " Grammatical Assistant," and a " School History of the United States," besides a volume of " Lectures to Female Teachers."

professional tour, visiting and inspecting the schools of
England, Scotland, Germany, Holland, Switzerland, France,
and Italy ; and upon his return published a volume of
six hundred pages on "European Educational Institutions," Chapter IX of which, "Seminaries for the Education of Teachers for Primary Schools," is especially valuable, and was then most timely, as characterizing the training system of the principal European countries. Prof.
Calvin E. Stowe had recently returned from a similar
visit to those countries, and his report to the Ohio Legislature, on the "Elementary Schools of Europe," set new
standards for the West.

Later, the studies of Mann and Barnard and Gallaudet
in the same schools, added to the contributions, and made
the improvement of American teaching an easier task.
Events were shaping themselves with more definiteness.
Grimke, of South Carolina, Pickett and Lewis, of Ohio,
Emerson, of Massachusetts, Gallaudet, of Connecticut, Johnson, of Pennsylvania, and Clinton, of New York, were fixing
public sentiment in their respective States.*

C. STATE NORMAL SCHOOLS.

But the one man to whom, more than to any other, must
be credited the permanent public normal school, and the
systematic training of teachers, is the Rev. James G. Carter.
All other service was good ; beside his it was occasional, or
an expedient, and, at best, suggestive. Prof. Emerson calls
him the "Father of Normal Schools." Born in the last
century, he graduated at Harvard, 1820, and at once began
writing upon education. In 1824 he published "Essays on

---

* In March, 1834, there was opened the Indiana Teachers' Seminary,
one express design of whose founding was, in the words of the trustees, "a
provision for the qualification of school-teachers' ; and three years later
there was formed in Maine the "Teachers' Association of Bowdoin College," composed of students, and which was, in all but name, a teachers'
class, or club.

Popular Education "; and two years later a second volume, including an elaborated plan * for the education of teachers. The same year he memorialized the Massachusetts Legislature on the subject of teachers' seminaries, and addressed the American Institute of Instruction at its first meeting (1829), on "Raising the Qualifications of Teachers." Mr. Carter's greatest work, however, was done as a member of the State Legislature after 1835. He was usually on the Educational Committee, and for a time its chairman. In 1837 he sought to divert the State's share of the surplus revenue to the uses of education, but failed. He draughted the bill providing for the State Board of Education, and was the one man within the Legislature to whose exertions and speeches was due the passage of the Normal School Act of 1838.

(1.) Massachusetts.

Next to Mr. Carter, the establishment of the Massachusetts Normal School was due to Mr. Edmund Dwight, who offered ten thousand dollars toward it, provided the State would give a like sum. As so frequently happens, the general advancement was due to the benevolence and enterprise of individual interest. The school was opened (1839) at Lexington (afterward removed to Framingham), with Cyrus Peirce as principal. Women only were to be admitted, and *three pupils entered.* The number increased, however, and the same year, later, another school was opened at Barre, (now at Westfield), to both sexes. The year following another was established at Bridgewater.

That there was not perfect confidence in normal training, though, is apparent from the action of the Boston School Committee. It was recommended that a suitable person be employed to visit the schools of the city, confer with the teachers, and "to instruct and qualify a class preparing to

---

* This was reviewed in the "North American Review," May, 1827.

teach." * The committee made two objections: 1. Such instruction would "lead to repeated experiments of new
methods, and so tend to disorganization." 2. "It would lessen the respect of pupils for their teachers, when it should
be found that, like themselves, they were the subjects of instruction." †

(2.) New York.

Notwithstanding the work done in teachers' classes by
the New York academies, the feeling was growing that the
system lacked uniformity and thoroughness and completeness. "They contributed," says Dr. Potter, "to supply instructors for select rather than for common schools." The
work was academic, and but incidentally didactic. Teachers were needed who, in addition to their scholarship, were
familiar with the theories and best-known methods of
teaching.

It was recommended to the Legislature (1843) that there
be established an institution devoted exclusively to the preparation for teaching. Massachusetts schools were inspected,
European systems studied (by a legislative committee), and
a school was ordered as an experiment for five years. David
P. Page became, in 1844, its first principal. At the expira-
tion of four years the school was made permanent.

The New Britain (Connecticut) school was established
in 1849, with Hon. Henry Barnard as principal; the Michigan Normal School 1850, opening two years later, and one
in Philadelphia 1853.‡ Altogether, the almost half-century
of discussion, and the personal and public influence of the
highest scholarship and best statesmanship, resulted in nine

---

* Boston had not a superintendent of schools for fourteen years after.

† Wightman's "Annals of the Primary Schools of Boston," p. 180.
This is very suggestive on the growth of primary education in New England.

‡ This was the reorganization of another, established 1818, to fit teachers
for the schools of Philadelphia, and of which Joseph Lancaster, the English
educational reformer, was first principal.

schools outside of academies, whose leading purpose was the training of teachers. Six of these were public—four in New England, and one each in New York and Michigan. The Oak Grove Seminary, Missouri, and Mount Vernon College, Ohio, had normal departments; and the Evangelical Lutheran Church had opened a normal school at Addison, Illinois.

D. THE MODERN NORMAL SCHOOL.

In organization, contemporary policy makes the normal school a part of the common-school system. In some sections this has long been true. Elsewhere the public is only coming to recognize the common dependence of the two. This does not so much imply that the ratio of public to private schools is increasing, as that the first are increasing. It appears that there are in the United States (1887) one hundred and sixty-eight institutions admitted as normal schools, of which one hundred and nineteen are public, either of the State, county, or city.

These are found in thirty-two States, Arizona, Dakota, and the District of Columbia. Colorado, Delaware, Florida, Georgia, Kentucky, and Nevada, report none; Ohio, none under State control. Ten States, including the six in New England, Pennsylvania, New York, North Carolina, and West Virginia, support half (fifty-six) of them; while eleven States have but one each. Of the whole number, but thirteen were founded in the first twenty years. Each one came more as a concession than a recognized necessity. Not with those who knew, but with the great body of the people—teachers even—the normal school was an experiment. The public is convinced slowly. Before 1860, however, almost one thousand teachers had graduated and themselves became exponents of the idea; more had taken partial courses, and in the single decade from 1859–1868, twenty-nine schools were established, nineteen of them in States which had previously had none. In the nearly twenty years since, the multiplication has been rapid, chiefly

in the South and West. Of the twenty-six schools founded
in the last eight years, half have been in the South, eight in
North Carolina alone.

Besides the public normal schools, there have been many
private ones, though information regarding them is incomplete and unsatisfactory. That their academic work has
been of incalculable service in the absence of true professional schools, is the uniform testimony of educators. They
have extended the meager advantages of local common
schools, have furnished many excellent teachers, and men
and women of studious habits; but they have rarely been
professional.

Not too great praise can be spoken of the few really good
schools of the class that have pioneered the work in the
newer and in the Southern States, and made a thorough,
critical teachers' training so much in demand as to enlist
the public interest. The need for such schools will probably
not grow less. They will at least long be required to supplement those of the State and of cities. But some of them
which have not even the semblance of the considerate, accurate habit, either of student or teacher, can not be too
vigorously condemned. Quality is far more important than
the number of institutions. It is not enough that there be
normal schools, either public or private. It rests with the
profession itself to adjust them to the highest professional
needs.

Although it appears that much has been already accomplished, a comparison of the number of teachers required,
with the total normal school supply, makes equally apparent the inadequacy of the present provision. The table sub-
joined is an attempt to exhibit the normal school as to numbers, both of institutions and pupils (those in professional
classes only), making a distinction between public and private foundations; and, of the former, between State schools
and local (city or county). It is admitted that there are
numbers of private, well-established schools from which no
reports are available:

Normal Schools, State, Private, and City, in the United States, 1885–'86.

STATES.	State.	Pupils.	Private.	Pupils.	City.	Pupils.	Total enrollment.
Alabama	5	525	4	198			723
Arkansas	1	46					46
California	2	750			1	76	826
Colorado							
Connecticut	1	266			2		266
Delaware							
Florida			1	8			8
Georgia							
Illinois	2	658	3	833	1*	425	1,916
Indiana	1	909	6	2,910	2	22	3,841
Iowa	1	432	2	630	2	20	1,082
Kansas	1	431	1	580			1,011
Kentucky							
Louisiana	1	75	2	200	1	100	375
Maine	4	581	2	191	1	223	995
Maryland	1	272	1	170	1	32	474
Massachusetts	5	1,128			5	233	1,361
Michigan	1	628			1		628
Minnesota	3	891					891
Mississippi	2		4	453			453
Missouri	4	1,091	1	46	1	138	1,275
Nebraska	1	248	2	80			328
Nevada							
New Hampshire	1	50			1	12	62
New Jersey	2	128	1	270	1	60	458
New York	9	2,693			5	1,684	4,377
North Carolina	4	559	1	3			562
Ohio			3	385	3	289	674
Oregon	2	100			1		100
Pennsylvania	11	3,537	2	373	1	1,218	5,128
Rhode Island	1	153					153
South Carolina			3	276	1	105	381
Tennessee	1	154	4	250			404
Texas	2	215	2	41			256
Vermont	3	191					191
Virginia	3	493			1	350	843
West Virginia	6	702					702
Wisconsin	5	1,185	2	118			1,303
Arizona	1	50					50
Dakota	2	241					241
District of Columbia			2	50			50
Total	87	19,382	49	8,065	32	4,987	32,384

* Cook County Normal School.

1. Professional *vs.* Academic Studies.

But, far more than organization, the curriculum of a training-school is important. Current tendencies seem to show that it is becoming more professional, if not less academic, emphasizing the model and practice schools, and directing original studies in mind and philosophy.

The earliest institutions seem not to have differed materially in function from the academies, and more special academic courses, of which they were the outgrowth.

The time devoted to the study of school economy, methods of instruction, and the history of educational theories in the Canandaigua Academy (1832) was scarcely exceeded by that in any established normal school for twenty years.

The Millersville (Pennsylvania) Normal School (1859) offered three courses—elementary, scientific, and classical; the first only of which was meant to be professional. In this the academic work was supplemented by two courses of "Lectures on Teaching," and practice in an elementary school attached, for six months.

As late as 1865 the curriculum of the Massachusetts schools comprised essentially * a shorter course of one year, covering only such studies as were taught in the common schools; and a course of two years, adding to the elementary branches general history, mental philosophy, music, the Constitution and history of the United States and of Massachusetts, natural philosophy and astronomy, natural history, the principles of piety and morality common to all sects of Christians, and *the science and art of teaching with reference to all of the above-named studies.* In the Westfield (Massachusetts) institution (1862), of twenty subjects required in a two years' course, the school laws of the State, and the theory and the art of teaching, with one term on mental philosophy given to seniors, constituted the professional matter.

---

* For the full course see, " American Journal of Education," vol. xviii, p. 657.

This academic work was necessary, perhaps, in all the first schools. Right methods were given in the process of correct teaching, subject-matter being held central. An advance was made when these studies came to be taught as a means to illustrate modes of instruction, or the process of learning. The course of study of the Winona (Minnesota) Normal School, adopted soon after its opening (1860), is typical of this enlargement of the special exercises. The scholastic work included English, mathematics, physical and natural science, graphics, and political economy; the professional outline specified intellectual and moral philosophy, the principles of education, the history of education,* didactic exercises, observation in the model school, preparation of sketches, criticism, lessons in teaching, teaching in the practice-school, and the school laws of Minnesota.

In the Kansas State Normal School, opened some years later, but in the same decade, six terms (twenty weeks each) were given to the science, method and history of education.

A forward and helpful impulse was given by the Oswego Training-School (1861) also, that is yet apparent throughout most of the States, not only in the cities, but in rural districts as well. From 1853 the city schools had maintained Saturday classes for their own teachers. The need of something more permanent and systematic being felt, Miss M. E. M. Jones, of London, England, was employed to arrange and give direction to a course of training for primary teachers. Miss Jones remained a year and a half, and shares with Superintendent Sheldon the credit of having first systematically established the principle of object-teaching in this country. The original course of one year has been extended to four, with shorter courses for special classes, and the school has been adopted by the State.

In Michigan great latitude is offered in the selection from five regular and five special courses, each covering four

---

* One of the earliest appearances of a subject of fundamental importance to the teacher.

years (except the English course, which is three years), and
each including, during the last two years, a large introduction of special exercises, both theoretical and practical.

Indiana offers six courses, as follows :

1. Regular English course .... 3 years.
2. English and Latin course........................... 3½ years.
3. Course for graduates of high-schools................ 2 years.
4. Course for graduates of high-schools................ 1 year.
5. Course for college graduates....................... 1 year.
6. Post-graduate course .... 1 year.

The following table of the regular English course is
given as showing fairly the proportion of professional and
academic work in the better public normal schools :

Terms.	Subjects of Instruction.			
I...	Theory.	Penmanship and Reading.	Arithmetic.	Grammar.
II...	Methods in Reading and Numbers.	Reading.	Arithmetic.	Grammar.
III...	Mental Science.	Geography.	Physiology.	United States History.
IV...	Mental Science.	Geography.	Composition.	United States History.
V...	Methods in Grammar, Geography, and Composition.	Music.	Chemistry.	General History.
VI...	Practice.	Drawing.	Physics.	General History and Rhetoric.
VII...	Practice.	Physics.	Algebra.	Literature.
VIII...	History of Education.	Astronomy or Geology.	Algebra.	Composition.
IX...	Science of Teaching.	Botany.	Geometry.	Theses.

(2.) Model and Practice Schools.

A further mark of the professional character of the
schools is found in the general recognition of model and
practice schools as factors in their organizations. These
are not peculiarly modern, although the use made of them is.

The first Massachusetts schools early provided practice classes ; the Albany and Millersville institutions, at their organization ; while the Oswego school was itself the outgrowth of a model or training class.

The number of these departments, and the amount of practice-work, seem to have constantly increased. Of one hundred and three schools, 1872, fifty-seven reported model departments ; in fifteen years the latter had increased to eighty-three, out of a total of one hundred and seventeen schools, or at twice the rate. In the first experiments, the courses being short and chiefly academical, the practice-work was taken along with the other. In contemporary schools there is an obvious tendency to condition the observation and practice upon a thorough grounding in the study of mind, and the general principles of instruction and learning.

In a few institutions, notably the State Normal School at Worcester, Massachusetts, a system of apprenticeship is practiced which serves a like purpose. For half a year the student is allowed to teach in some selected public school as an assistant.

The system is designed to give the student practical acquaintance with the work of teaching, and at the same time furnish the faculty a standard by which to judge of her teaching ability.

(3.) Child-Study.

One characteristic of very grave importance, though less conspicuous than others, is the prominence given in a few schools to psychological principles, and in fewer yet to the systematic observation and patient, scientific study of child-mind. It has been recently well said : * " The study of psychology lies at the foundation of any substantial building for high excellence in the profession of teaching. It is this body of principles more than all else, which makes teaching a profession and not a mere trade. All the reasons that

---

* G. S. Albee, " Proceedings of the National Educational Association," 1887, p. 500.

force upon physicians the study of physiology may enforce the study of psychology upon professional teachers."

For many years, however, in normal schools, lessons on mind were given in no other way than might have been found in any college and in many secondary schools, and to little better purpose for the teacher. But, as the study of plants at first hand is better than conning names, and the inspiration from work in a laboratory of matter is fresher than of books, so does the teacher's efficient study of mind differ from the reflection upon theories and controversial psychology. And the ocasional recent texts upon educational psychology, and the culture of mind, point to better things. A dozen normal schools throughout the country are doing somewhat original work in this respect, as their courses show ; and the Worcester (Massachusetts) school has been, for some years, quietly pursuing an investigation into child experience, both unique and suggestive. It was begun in 1884, by a single section of the school ; at present all the classes take part in it. About seven thousand records have been preserved, each representing a particular observation, the whole classified under twenty heads.

(4.) Specialization in Training.

The impulse toward specialization belongs to the training of teachers not less than to other industries and professions. First, the conditions in cities considerably modify the preparation given in their training-schools. The course is generally shorter, is more purely professional, involves relatively more practice-work, and frequently fits for particular grades.

The inauguration of city training did much to systematize and adjust the instruction, to rationalize the courses. Their influence upon State and other institutions has been a wholesome one. The Normal School in Boston, established in 1852, and that of St. Louis (1857), are among the oldest in cities, and examples of an efficient direction.

Davenport, Iowa, early followed (1863), San Francisco (1865), New Haven (1866), and Fort Wayne and Indianapolis the same year, the last two directed by graduates of the Oswego Training-School. There are now twenty-five such institutions in the United States, established in most of the large cities, and in a few of the second class. Besides these there are forty-one Kindergarten training-schools, normal, art, and music schools, and, in New York city, a system of special training of teachers for instruction in science, in charge of the director of the Central Park Museum, and an Industrial Training-School recently opened.

Bibliography.

" History of Normal Schools in New England," Rev. Charles Brooks; "Normal Schools, their Necessity and Growth," Thomas Hunter, " Education," vol. v, p. 235; " Normal School Work and the State," S. N. Fellows, "Education," vol. i, p. 180; the " Nature and Limits of the Normal School," F. Louis Soldan, "St. Louis School Report," 1875; " The True Function of the Normal School," General T. J. Morgan, 1886; "Teaching as a Profession, Inadequacy of the Present Normal School," Dr. E. H. Magill, " The American," March 5, 1887; " Methods in the Normal Schools of the United States," Thomas J. Gray, " Proceedings of the National Educational Association," Chicago, 1887, p. 472.

Concerning the nature and method of child-study, consult the " Contents of Children's Minds," by Dr. G. Stanley Hall, " Princeton Review," May, 1882; " Biographical Sketch of an Infant," by Charles Darwin, " Mind," vol. ii (1877), p. 285; " About the Minds of Little Children," M. A. Powers, "Education," vol. vi, p. 26; " Observations on Infants," by E. S. Holden, " Transactions of the American Philosophical Society," 1875; the " Growth of Children," by H. P. Bowditch; and " The Mind of the Child," by W. Preyer, 2 vols., D. Appleton & Co.

10

CHAPTER IX.

THE PREPARATION OF TEACHERS.—(Continued.)

A SYSTEM of education comprising elementary secondary, and collegiate schools, viewed pedagogically, is incomplete, if it fail to provide competent instructors and supervisors for any of them.   If this be true, how imperfect is the best State system we yet have!   In the large cities the management usually provides teachers for the graded schools.   For the rest, normal schools supply, perhaps, from one fourth to one third of the places.   But with the most generous allowance, many thousands of positions, in the elementary schools even, in cities of the second class and smaller, and in rural districts, must be filled from chance selection, or from non-professional sources.

1. Pedagogical Training in Colleges.

The danger from the blunders of inexperience, or want of knowledge, or both sometimes, might be provided against by the employment of disciplined principals and masters, wise supervision, and a leadership schooled in the problems of education and the machinery of its institutions.   But, while some little provision has been made to fit teachers for the elementary schools, almost nothing had been done, until recently, to prepare for instruction in secondary and collegiate institutions.   The high-school could not do it, nor with fairness could most normal schools attempt it.   This appears in the fact that the average curriculum of one hundred and fifteen public normal schools is a fraction over two years in length, and the conditions for entrance such as would admit to the better high-schools.   This need for a broader scholarship for secondary teachers has been met generally by the colleges.   But discipline of mind and wealth of information are but two of the three factors concerned in the right training of the teacher. The only one which makes the teacher to be a teacher, and not a lawyer or a journalist, has been omitted.

How to combine this needful academic study with the professional training is a question of grave importance. That in the present social conditions it belongs, in part, to the college, is already widely recognized. In sixty-eight colleges (degree-giving institutions), in thirty States and Territories, more or less instruction is given in the theory of education. These have about two thousand students pursuing such courses, varying from one to four years in length.

A. REVIEW COURSES.

Among the earliest provisions of these schools was the introduction of "review courses," whose only aim was to combine, with more or less college study, a systematic and somewhat critical survey of the elementary branches. In the absence of other means, this has advantages, and is not to be wholly condemned.

B. COURSES IN DIDACTICS.

The presentation, by lectures, or an occasional text, of the principles of school management, questions of school-room economy, and the few best known theories of education, was a considerable step forward in the college training of teachers. The young man of average graduate training and maturity, who has learned to look at social questions from his business point of view, and make them an object of patient study, has made no small beginning. It is little enough; but it is the recognition of a teaching class, with a special function, and is significant.

C. THE UNIVERSITY NORMAL SCHOOL.

Of a different sort, more systematic and comprehensive, is the normal school, equipped and complete within itself, but co-ordinated with other "schools" in the university. These differ in no essential from the independent normal school. They usually teach the same subjects, have the same length of course, and employ (occasionally) both model and practice schools. Further than this, their connection with the college secures them students better instructed, makes available the advantages of libraries, and lectures, and the specialist's discussion of related questions. These are so much clear gain to the normal school, and must favorably react, not only upon the instruction, but upon the general public estimate of education.

As types of the university normal school may be named (not excluding others) those connected with the Central Tennessee College at Nashville; the University of Missouri, and Drury College, Missouri; Hillsdale College, Michigan; De Pauw University, Indiana; and the university of Colorado. Connected with the "University of the Pacific" at San José, California, is a "School of Psychology and the Science and Art of Education," with a faculty of three, and nine courses, entirely professional, including one on "Human Development and the Psychology of Childhood," and another on the "Science and Art of the Froebel Kindergarten."

D. PROFESSORSHIP OF PEDAGOGICS.

Somewhat different, in respect to both organization and aim, is the university professorship of Pedagogics.

"The distinctive function of the university," says Rev. R. H. Quick, "is not action, but thought. And the best thing the university can do for schoolmasters is to employ some of their keenest intellects in considering education on the side of theory, and in teaching such principles respecting it as have been or can be established."

Both the normal school and the professorship have like educational bearings. The former, however, is special; the latter general. The one seeks to influence elementary training directly through its teachers; the other mediately, through the more advanced. Each is needed, as appears from the history of both. The European experience is longer than the American, and altogether reassuring. Not only in Germany, but in other Continental and the insular states, especially England and Scotland, university training in education has commanded the ripest learning.*

In the United States its introduction is comparatively recent; its development slow, but on the whole forward and continuous. It could not but be that the universities, supplying the principals and assistants in secondary schools, supervisors and directors, local and State commissioners should ultimately find a demand for a preparation for such positions.

As early as 1850, Prof. S. S. Green, then superintendent of the Providence schools, was made Professor of Didactics in Brown University, Rhode Island. He held the position five years.

Ten years later (1860) Dr. Gregory (State Superintendent of Michigan) gave a course of lectures to the seniors in the university on the " Philosophy of Education, School Economy, and the Teaching Art." It was afterward given in Kalamazoo College, Michigan, and in the Illinois Industrial University (1867).

The first permanent chair of the kind in this county, so far as known, though shared with the professorship of General Philosophy, was that established in Iowa University (1873).† A department was organized in the University of Wisconsin (1881), followed three years later by somewhat similar ones in the University of North Carolina, and Johns Hopkins University, Baltimore. Since then, four others have opened: in Ottawa University, Kansas (1885); Indiana University, and Cornell, New York (1886); and the University of the City of New York (1887).

---

* The New York Regents' Report for 1883 page 342, contains a very fair statement of the " English and Scottish University Work in Pedagogy," and some liberal suggestions as to its introduction into the colleges of the United States.

† In the March issue of " Education," 1881, Dr. Fellows has an excellent statement of the work offered for many years, in his course in didactics. See p. 393.

In line with the purpose of these departments, though having no immediate dependence upon any institution, were "Pedagogical Lecture Courses" given for three years in Boston. At the suggestion of a Boston master, and official of Harvard, Dr. Hall (1881), then a member of the university faculty, was invited to deliver to a body of Boston teachers a course of lectures on professional subjects. These were the so-called "Harvard Lectures an Pedagogy," and were maintained thoughout the winter, and also for the winter of 1883-'84. A course was given by Dr. Harris in Boston University in 1881, and a second in 1882-'83 in Wesleyan Hall, in the same city. The lectures were well attended, and the experiment as a whole serves admirably to illustrate the readiness with which the best thought everywhere finds listeners.

Perhaps Michigan University first demonstrated what could be done in a strictly professional way, on a high plane, to fit young men and women for the best positions in the school system, where scholarship and discipline and a comprehensive knowledge of the means and ends of education are needed. The department * (1879) is that of the "Science and Art of Teaching," and from two series of lectures has been enlarged to include seven courses, covering the practical, theoretical, and historical phases of the subject. The work is entirely elective, falls largely into the later terms of the course, and has been taken, in the last half-dozen years, in whole or in part, by forty per cent of the graduates, besides partial courses by undergraduates.

Lectures on pedagogics were first given in Johns Hopkins University during the collegate year 1884-'85. Dr. G. Stanley Hall had been recently elected to the chair of General Philosophy, and with this the instruction in pedagogics was incorporated. The course covers three years: the first being historical ; the second devoted to problems

---

* The work and growth of this department are set forth in detail, in Prof. Payne's " Contributions to the Science of Education," p. 335. See also chap. xv, p. 257, " Education as a University Study."

of elementary and secondary education ; and the third to higher and special education. The pedagogical work of Dr. Hall has, throughout the course, been given with reference to its philosophical bearings, and has been discussed in a comprehensive way, and in the light of universal principles. His resignation * leaves vacant a position not easily filled.

The course projected for the department in the University of the City of New York is somewhat more extended. Begun in the year 1887, with three lectures a week on the history of education, it now includes: 1. Psychology; 2. The psychological basis of education ; 3. Methodology ; 4. Economy as applied to education; 5. Bibliography with criticisms ; and, 6. Sociology in so far as it has reference to education.

It need scarcely be said that the work as a whole, and in this country, is yet only tentative. A few of the courses are painfully narrow and barren ; others are subordinated—made to share both time and attention with unrelated subjects. Nevertheless, the movement is assuring and is, almost without exception, favorably regarded by educators.

"The great need of the hour," it has been said,† "is to ascertain what has been done in the line of educational effort, what plans have succeeded, and what have failed, and the conditions under which success or failure has come." This is one of the most stimulating services of the contemporary college—the large contributions it has made to the intelligent and systematic and comparative study of history; and now, especially, the history of education and its institutions. This involves not only the education of the states, ancient and modern, but the accompanying social and political forms, custom and creed, antecedents and evironment, and the physical and other conditions which deter-

---

* Dr. Hall has just recently accepted the presidency of the new Clarke University at Worcester, Massachusetts.

† Prof. Payne, "Contributions to the Science of Education," p. 265.

mine the institutional life. It is a work, viewed from the pedagogical side, peculiarly within the province of the university.

Again, as the principles of instruction are to be sought in the nature and functions of mind, and the general spiritual life, the conditions of education, in its deeper content, presuppose the broader co-ordinations of knowledge included under anthropology, ethics, and the indefinitely complex sociology, in the study of institutional life. Philosophy of education is, then, a phase of general philosophy, rests upon its constituent knowledges, borrows its deductions and is conditioned by them. Theories of mind, and the individual responsibility; prevalent estimates of the social life and the functions of the State; the changed interpretations of natural phenomena and forces, all contribute to the shaping of educational doctrine and its ultimate creed. The enlargement of university pedagogy on the side indicated is one of the hopeful signs of the day. Never was it more needed than now. And if the present movement shall result in calling to the universities throughout the country its best men to study these questions in their universal relations, study education as philosophy, and mark its bearings, it will have done the generation an eminent service.

2. Educational Literature.

One of the conditions of professional efficiency, at the present day, is familiarity with the contributing literature. It marks economy in service, and is the starting-point for any sound original study of current conditions. This is neither less nor more true of teaching than of law, medicine, or theology. Paraphrasing the famous dictum of Matthew Arnold, it may be said the right acquaintance with the best that has been thought and said touching one's profession is a liberal professional education.

Incomplete and unsatisfactory as this literature is in the United States, most departments of modern inquiry have made some contributions.

A. WORKS ON PEDAGOGY.

Historically, educational literature in the United States belongs almost wholly to the period of reorganization. Christopher Dock,* in Pennsylvania, had published his "Schul-ordnung," Joseph Neef † his "Plan of Education," and "Methods of Teaching," and Rafinesque, ‡ the eccentric naturalist, a pamphlet on the "Improvement of Universities, Colleges, and other Seats of Learning in North America."

Besides these, and the movements which they represented, it has been said of this period (the first fifty years of our national history), that there were only two men whose efforts to promote general, and especially higher education, are worthy of note—Jefferson and Washington.# Within two decades from the accomplishment of Jefferson's plan in the founding of the University of Virginia, came the "educational revival" that touched all the States, and in which began, along with school systems, supervision, normal schools, etc., a school literature, descriptive and critical, if not constructive, and of very general influence. Some of it, though used with a local purpose, has yet a permanent value. Such were the writings of Mann and Stowe; Abbott, Page, and Hall. President Wayland's study of the "Collegiate System of the United States," is well worth a careful reading by contemporary teachers, and, among expositions of foreign school systems, Prof. Bache's "Report on Education in Europe," which has been pronounced "one of the most influential educational works ever published in this country."

---

* For a biography of Mr. Dock, and a summary of his book, see Penny-packer's "Historical Sketches," p. 95. A copy of the first edition of the "Schul-ordnung" may be found in the Library of the Historical Society of Pennsylvania.

† Mr. Neef was connected with the "Community School," at New Harmony, Indiana, then and now one of the most cultured, progressive neighborhoods in the West.

‡ See "Science Sketches," by Dr. Jordan, p. 143.

"Washington and Higher Education, a Monograph," by C. K. Adams.

To these and other more recent works reference will be found in the bibliographies upon the several topics. Espccial attention, however, should be called to the few works on infant and child education, on graded and rural schools, on city school systems, and occasional books on methods that are especially valuable. There are a half-dozen State histories of education that are of value outside their localities; as those of Rhode Island, New York, California, Pennsylvania, and Michigan. Histories, longer or shorter, of colleges, are quite numerous; but of city schools very few. Some valuable special studies have appeared in the last years on normal schools, something of the science of education, industrial and reformatory training, and the general relations of education.

One of the most fruitful sources of educational literature has been the translation and republication of foreign works. By this means have been made available to the English (American) reader, Froebel and Pestalozzi, Rousseau, Rosenkranz, Compayré, Radestock, Preyer, Perez, and others; as well as Quick, Browning, Payne, Sully, Fitch, Tait, Laurie, and Spencer; to master whose pedagogical writings would be a liberal training for any teacher.

Ten years ago was published the "Cyclopædia of Education." One or two supplementary volumes have been added since; and, while it is exceedingly defective and incomplete in parts, it is nevertheless, to the reading and thinking teacher, an invaluable source of much-needed information. But the one comprehensive reference on educational matters—a library in itself—thoroughly American, though all-sided in its fullness, is Barnard's "American Journal of Education."

Among reference works for teachers, also, should be named two bibliographical texts recently published. The one, "Bibliography of Education," * by Dr. Hall, and the

---

* Including twenty-one hundred and sixty-five entries. These are put under sixty headings. The Mac Alister "Catalogue of the Philadelphia

other a "Catalogue of the Pedagogical Library of the Philadelphia Public Schools," by Superintendent Mac Alister, are timely and suggestive. Both include bibliographical and critical notes which, for busy, ambitious teachers are not the least valuable part.

B. PERIODICALS.

When the complete history of general education in the United States comes to be written, it will be found that the rise, growth, and influence of educational periodical literature fill a long chapter. School journals * early began in this country the campaign against ignorance and unreasoning conservatism. The inferiority of some in no wise detracts from the incalculable services of the few timely and well-managed ones, adaptable, working with a purpose —and that the enlargement of public views on education.

The first published journal in the United States (and Mr. Barnard is authority for the statement that it was the " first in the English language " devoted to the advancement of education) was that of Wait, Green & Co., Boston, 1826. Its editors were William C. Woodbridge, William A. Alcott, and William Russell, with such men for correspondents as Prof. Emerson, Horace Mann, Joseph Story, Caleb Cushing, Francis Wayland, and Bronson Alcott.

The " Massachusetts Common-School Journal " (1837) and a similar paper in Connecticut (1838) were started, the one by Horace Mann, the other by Henry Barnard, when State School Commissioners of their respective States. They were used as organs of the administration, disseminating school and legislative and official news, and embodied in both cases their editors' maturest thoughts and most unselfish service. Very early such periodicals were made the organs of local

---

Pedagogical Library," noticed in the text, comprises thirteen hundred and forty-eight entries.

* In the Government report on the educational exhibit at New Orleans, 1885, is published a sketch of " Educational Journalism in New England," by T. W. Bicknell.

or State associations of teachers. The "Massachusetts Teacher" was so begun (1847), the "Ohio School Journal" (1852), the "Pennsylvania School Journal" (1853), and the "Indiana School Journal" (1856). A file of the periodicals al ready named would afford a fairly complete exhibit and summary of American education for more than sixty years. Of something more than one hundred and forty such papers started prior to 1870, twenty were organs of State Teachers' Associations.

The Barnard "American Journal of Education," established 1855, has already been referred to. At first published monthly, it now appears quarterly, each number containing about two hundred pages, and in educational biography, national and foreign school systems, it is very full. Upon the whole, no American journal devoted to education has had a more general or salutary influence upon the higher education, or has done more to dignify the cause of liberal culture.

Of more recent journals (of which there are about three hundred) it is well known that their undue multiplication has left some of them of indifferent quality. Editorial inexperience and ignorance and carping bias have crept in at times and bemeaned the true service of journalism. Mere devices and formulæ, which have filled so large a place in these papers, are rarely constructive. They are expedients at best, and of themselves add neither power nor insight. Such literature has given the profession neither credit among thinking men nor confidence with the people. Much of it seems both trifling and puerile. In the opposite of this appears the great power of school journalism forty years ago; it was uncompromisingly in earnest. It was one with the spirit of co-operation that carried reform through communities and States and Legislatures; that established systems and rationalized methods.

But much current periodical literature is creditable also. There is a manifest tendency to combine journals of limited patronage, to the great improvement of the matter. Each

State can well support one paper, rarely more, as a medium
of frequent local communication, on legal and administrative matters, with which every State teacher should be familiar. But to every teacher's desk there should be brought
(and it is not impossible among contemporary journals)
abundant and intelligent comparative studies of home
schools, with the best thought of neighboring and foreign
states gathered and focused upon them. It is believed the
tendency is strong in this direction.

But there is apparent, also, and on the contrary, a parallel
drift toward specialization in educational and academic
papers. This is shown in the multiplication of Kindergarten records, health journals, and exponents of manual
labor, primary and normal schools, etc. More especially it
appears in a class of journals published as the representatives of departmental work in the universities. Of this
class are published, in Columbia College, "The School of
Mines Quarterly," now in its ninth volume, and the "Political Science Quarterly," begun in 1886, and devoted to scientific investigation in the field of economics and public law.
Of a similar nature are the Johns Hopkins "Studies in History and Political Science" (1882), and the "Quarterly Journal of Economics," published at Harvard since 1883. From
Johns Hopkins are issued also journals of mathematics,
chemistry, biology, and philology, and the recently established "Journal of Psychology"; each in a way representing the work and being under the control of the
department whose name it takes. How large a field is
opened here for the increase and dissemination of knowledge can only be roughly estimated. Such journals must
make easier the work of every student and instructor in
these lines.

Altogether, then, periodical literature of whatever kind,
bringing together and publishing the freshest information
and established generalizations in special and general fields,
remains, as it has ever been, one of the teacher's readiest
means of improvement.

C. EDUCATIONAL REPORTS.

Of the reports of school officers and educators it may be said briefly that they include by far the largest part of America's contribution to the literature of education. They are valuable as furnishing statistical and other data,* for comparative studies of school systems; and as a medium of information between institutions and the public. But as supervision in city and State has developed toward a profession, employing a trained and special class, the annual statement frequently takes the form of a monographic treatise on some one or more phases of education or schooling.

Among State reports those of Horace Mann easily stand first. They grew out of the system and, in an interesting way, reflect his own labors. After a general view of the administration, they were usually didactic, discussing vital questions in educational philosophy, with a vigorous mind. Of the twelve reports some have become historical. The fourth and ninth gave a comparative exhibit of the Massachusetts system. The seventh discussed European schools, and especially the Prussian seminaries for teachers. (It was this report which called out the celebrated "Common-School Controversy" between Mr. Mann and the "Thirty-one Boston Schoolmasters.") In the tenth is traced the origin and growth of the free-school system, in which he formulates the now familiar sentiment that "the property of a commonwealth is pledged to the education of all its youth."

"To be appreciated," says Mr. Barnard "these reports must be read." No abstract can exibit the fullness of thought, or the familiarity with which the questions are handled. "We know of no series of educational reports,"

---

* It is of the first importance that something of uniformity be secured in the taking and manipulation of census items; the records of attendance, including continuance, the school period and age; and the relation of the two classes; those entitled to school privileges, and those attending.

he continues, " by one mind, in any language, so readable or so instructive." The Massachusetts Board (1887) made its fiftieth report, and with it published both a sketch of the legislation of the State on leading matters, and an index—very complete—to the entire set. It compasses the educational history of a large part of New England. The Connecticut reports are almost equally valuable, and those of Rhode Island, especially under Stockwell. The New York, Illinois, and Michigan reports are authorities outside their respective States. The interchange of such literature among the States promises to unify the systems, and to equalize the opportunities as no legislation can do.

Of city reports, those of Boston being among the oldest, are also among the most valuable, particularly those under Dr. Philbrick. Excellent features are to be found in those of Chicago, San Francisco, Cincinnati, Providence, etc., as doubtless in others. But the most complete and systematic presentation of educational philosophy is to found in the annual reports of Dr. W. T. Harris, as Superintendent of the St. Louis Schools (1867-'79). The following analysis * of the discussion is appended, both as illustrating their scope, and as a somewhat connected outline of educational philosophy:

1867-'68. Discussion of Pestolozzianism and object-lessons.

1868-'69. Discussion of Leigh's phonetic system of teaching reading. English orthography and how to teach it with the least loss of time. Defects of the graded school system. What a pupil gains by a mastery of the three R's.

1869-'70. Discussion of the co-education of the sexes. Industrial education. German-English instruction. Library classification, a scheme for it. How the branches of the course of study givé the pupil a mastery of the world. How to conduct recitations. A plan for local supervision of principals.

1870-'71. Moral education as involved in the school discipline. Education and crime. Eulogy on Ira Divoll, Superintendent of Schools,

---

* Taken from Hall's " Bibliography of Education," p. 242.

St. Louis. Syllabus of oral lessons in natural science, and directions for teaching it. Music instruction.

1871–'72. A classification of occupations in the United States proposed, and a discussion of the occupations represented in the St. Louis schools. The injury to the district schools caused by a too strict examination for admission to the high school. Corporal punishment. German-English instruction. Arithmetic *versus* Grammar as a culture study. The psychological significance of the several studies.

1872–'73. Method of promotion and classification adopted in the St. Louis schools. Discussion of the psychological effect of Latin and Greek in education, their containing the embryology of our civilization. Elaborate discussion of the branches necessary in a course of study in district schools, high schools, and colleges ; what each branch adds to the mental structure in the way of discipline and knowledge. Identical co-education of the sexes discussed in the light of the history of the three epochs of industrial civilization. The library and its significance in modern civilization. Outline of educational psychology.

1873–'74. Discussion of school hygiene and the lessons furnished by statistics taken in the St. Louis schools. Grading, classification, class intervals, and promotions. Suspension of pupils *versus* corporal punishment.

1874–'75. History of the public school system of St. Louis.

1875–'76. The school architecture best adapted for good hygiene. The philosophy of the kindergarten. The Centennial Exposition educationally considered.

1876–'77. German-English instruction, its uses for towns and cities where there is a mixed population of English and Germans. What the common schools teach to fit pupils for their future vocations. Half-time schools for primary pupils, its economy and hygienic effect. The proper school age. The results of the kindergarten in St. Louis.

1877–'78. Teaching United States history.

1878–'79. The age of withdrawal from school. Industrial education. The educational influence of works of fiction drawn from the library. History of the St. Louis kindergarten system, the philosophy of its methods, and the practical devices necessary to make it a part of the public school system. Oral lessons in history, syllabus of lessons for all the grades of the common school. Bird's-eye view of the entire organization of a system of city schools, with remarks and commentary on the practical working of different devices in vogue.

In this day of growing interest in higher education, its distribution and means, it is encouraging to note the adjustment of college reports also to the public demand for a better acquaintance with these agencies of culture. The Harvard publications, especially the official annual statements of President Eliot, have left in large measure the formal exposition of the early days, and have shown a disposition to study the practical questions which concern the university and not less the community. The report of 1883–'84 gives in a terse, plain statement the history of elections and the evolution of the curriculum in that ancient institution. The annual statements of Cornell also, as a representative of the "open system" of studies, of Columbia and Johns Hopkins and Michigan, and the Universities of Pennsylvania and California, have contributed much in ten years to a better public understanding of the relations of higher education.

Bibliography.

"Normal Training in Colleges," "Proceedings of New York University Convocation" (1883), p. 342; "Collegiate Instruction in Pedagogics," "Report of Superintendent of Public Instruction of New York" (1862); "Chairs of Pedagogics in Colleges," Harris, "Proceedings of the National Council of Education" (1882); "Psychology as a Branch of Education," "American Journal of Education," vol. iii, p. 125; "Education as a University Study," chapter xv of "Contributions to the Science of Education," by W. H. Payne (1886); "Philosophy in Education," "Mind," vol. iii, p. 225. "Educational Psychology," by Dr. W. T. Harris, in "Journal of Speculative Philosophy," vol. xiv, p. 225 (1880). See also "Educational Reports," by J. D. Philbrick, in the "United States Commissioner's Report" (1884–'85), pp. xiv–xxiv; and on "Educational Literature," "Popular Science Monthly," vol. ii, p. 713, and especially Poole's "Index to Periodical Literature." No other knowledge can excuse ignorance of the uses and suggestions of this last source of information.

CHAPTER X.

RECENT COLLEGES.

A. The Curriculum.

In no respect has the modern college changed more than in its academic constitution. Between the average curriculum of 1800, and that of the most conservative institution of to-day, there is a great disparity. Practically speaking, it is the difference between the sums of knowledge then and now. The Harvard of 1700 was rich in contemporary learning. The statement would apply to the same and other institutions at the beginning of this century. But how has the world of fact enlarged! Then the "organization of knowledge" was comparatively simple. That it is less so now is one mark of progress.

Biology belongs to the present century. Chemistry in the same time has been much developed along the old, and worked out in new lines. Geography in its comparative study is very recent—from Ritter, indeed—and in its descriptive aspect has been enriched by vast territories within half a century. Ethnological investigation, the natural systems of botany, together with its numerous economic bearings, and the indefinite multiplication of our knowledge of physical forces and their phenomena, come within the ages of men yet living. Whole fields of science have been discovered and inclosed, and others reclaimed from the dominance and uses of mediæval dogmatism. Both geology and astronomy have been reconstructed and enlarged. College programmes have been made over by the claims of such new and comprehensive interests.

Further, the current and recent magnifying of the humanities, the growing recognition of an altruistic and co-operative spirit in civil and social and political life, the increasing complexity of social forces, new aspects of government, the fundamental oneness of all life, and the sequent idea of the solidarity of human society, have created for the student new lines of investigation. The history of customs and institutions, the growth of opinions and sentiments as crystallized in social forms, the study of governments and religions, of art and industry, are clamoring for place in the curriculum. Comparative philology, with the enlarged interest in modern languages, belongs to the present period.

The rise of new sciences, dependence upon other interests, and this multiplication of facts and relations, have changed the nomenclature of learning. The other day only, a liberal education meant fitness for the professions. But in no service has modern thought been more busy or more iconoclastic than in the silent but ceaseless readjustment of the professions. In a period of limited knowledge and the universal rule of authority, a course of study was easily made and as easily interpreted. The wants of a homogeneous life were met by a conventional training. But new views of nature and mind, the aging of institutions, and the interminable complexity of custom and impulse, give direction to indefinite individual divergence from the common plan. The history of higher education for half a century is largely a record of the readjustings of the curriculum to the life—or the one to the other—an attempt to adapt the means of culture to the highest ends.

1. The Physical Sciences.

Speaking generally, and not confined to mere chronological sequence, the earliest, and certainly one of the most comprehensive and conditioning modifications of the traditional curriculum is found in *the large infusion of the physical sciences.**

---

* A valuable contribution to this question was made by the publication of Circular 6-1880, by the Bureau of Education, Washington, on " Physics and Chemistry," in the United States. Not greatly historical, it is still suggestive.

Though having twenty-four colleges, the century opened with the merest excuses for nature-study. Whatever was known of the physical universe, little was taught. No subject better illustrates the marvelous development and accompanying specializations, which have gone on in the field of knowledge, than what has come to be known as physical science. Science, among the early colleges, was either natural philosophy or natural history. The latter was little regarded, and the former generally a branch of or companion study to mathematics. The term was generic, and made to include not only physics (to which it is yet sometimes applied), but chemistry, geology, and astronomy, and had frequently associated with it, in the first professorships, both botany and zoölogy.

A. PHYSICS.

The department in Harvard, known as the Hollis Professorship of Mathematics and Natural Philosophy, and established in 1727, had, in forty years, accumulated several pieces of apparatus. How well this was used can only be conjectured. Mr. Quincy furnishes a list of those lost in the fire of 1764, which included apparatus illustrative of the mechanics of gravity, hydrostatics, pneumatics, and optics ; an orrery, a number of microscopes (magnifying-glasses), dials, a twenty-four-foot telescope, and instruments for surveying. Some of these were subsequently replaced by Mr. Hollis and friends, but it was many years before the physical laboratory was more than an appendage to mathematics.

After Harvard, Dartmouth (1782) and Union College (1797) were the only institutions prior to 1800 that could be said to have given any respectable attention to physics, much less to the other sciences. But within fifteen years after this half a dozen colleges had gone beyond them. The University of Georgia, during the year 1800 ; Yale and Williams Colleges, 1803; Dickinson College, 1808; William and Mary, and Hobart Colleges, 1812 ; followed by Colby University, Maine, and the University of North Carolina,

1818—had established courses in mechanical physics, and possessed more or less of illustrative apparatus.

In the year 1827, James F. Dana, a professor in Dartmouth College, gave a course of lectures on electro-magnetism, then a new and little understood topic. The lectures were popular only in the sense that they were properly illustrated by experiments—a method of instruction quite as new as the subject, and the audiences were general as well as academic. Mr. S. F. B. Morse, an artist in New York, heard Prof. Dana, took practical suggestions, and says that from that course he had his "scientific birth." Seven years later, Prof. Albert Hopkins was sent to Europe with a commission to procure both philosophical and chemical apparatus for Williams College. Returning, he was thought to have furnished a rival for Harvard even, which in 1840 was described as possessing a " complete outfit," including, besides the usual apparatus in hydrostatics, pneumatics, and the mechanical powers, electrical and electro-magnetic pieces, an air-pump, and somewhat in illustration of the polarization of light. Besides these, the general contributions of the Rensselaer School at Troy, New York, are well known. Industrial and material interests were being everywhere augmented. Surrounded by an infinite diversity and potency of physical phenomena, and material products, it was easy for the American mind to be inquisitive and objective. Private interest, the national character, and physical environment, were all helping the impulse along. But the greatest advance of science along the line of physics for recent times, began with Prof. Joseph Henry in Princeton, and later in the Smithsonian Institution, and Prof. Pickering's laboratory in the Massachusetts Institute of Technology (1867). Deserving of special mention are the more recent services of Yale in mathematical physics, of Harvard and Cleveland (Case School); and especially of Prof. Langley, of the Smithsonian Institution, in the study of heat and light ; the principal original work of the period being done in light and electricity. The making and using of machinery, in-

vestigation into little understood forces, their application to
industrial uses, and, finally, the study of them from a love of
science, mark not always successive but closely interrelated
steps in the growth of physical knowledge.

B. CHEMISTRY.

Though chemistry was originally a branch of physics, it
was early put into the colonial medical schools, and the first
chemists were medical students or practitioners. In this
way, as belonging to materia medica, it became a part of
the course in the University of Pennsylvania, 1768; of Harvard, 1782 ; and of Dartmouth, 1798.

But in the year 1795, Princeton College instituted an independent chair of Chemistry—the first in this country—
under Dr. John Maclean, a young Scotch medical graduate.
William and Mary, and Dickinson Colleges had combined
chemistry with natural philosophy twenty years before.
But that in Princeton was regularly co-ordinated with the
other departments, and so marks an era in the development
of chemical studies in American colleges. Columbia College, five years later, established a like professorship; and in
1801 Prof. Silliman was elected to a chair of Chemistry,
Geology, and Mineralogy, at Yale. While a mixed department, it immediately became known under the young instructor for the thoroughness and originality of the work in
chemistry. Directly upon his election, he visited Dr. Maclean,
at Princeton, went through his laboratory, and afterward
said that there were then performed the first experiments
in chemistry he ever saw.* Bowdoin College provided for
chemical instruction in 1805, and the University of Georgia
some years earlier. But candor requires the statement that
most institutions offered but lectures, and *the best of them*
experiments performed by the instructors only. Laboratory

---

* " I regard Prof. Maclean," said Prof. Silliman, " as my earliest master
in chemistry, and Princeton as my starting-point in its pursuit." Fisher's
" Life of Silliman," vol. i, p. 109.

practice of students was almost wholly unknown. Among the better courses were those of Dr. Cooper, first in Dickinson College, and later in South Carolina College ; and those of Dr. William H. Ellett, also of South Carolina, who did initiate his students into some little handling of materials and manipulating of simple experiments. "Silliman's Journal" also was a university in itself, and from its founding, in 1818, has exercised a directive and conserving influence upon chemistry and chemical instruction, sadly wanting in most other sciences.

Chester Dewey studied under Silliman some time at Yale, and through him fitted up his laboratory at Williams College in 1812. The next year Prof. J. F. Dana was employed to go to England and select and purchase for Harvard the furnishings of a chemical laboratory. The next quarter of a century was a period of general activity, no less than of individual inquiry and the increase of knowledge. The scientific schools of Harvard and Yale, and other Eastern colleges, were making experimental chemistry better known, the Smithsonian Institution was founded, and the American Association for the Advancement of Science; and, in the year 1862, the greatest recent impulse of all, to both physics and chemistry, was given in the congressional act providing for agricultural and mechanical instruction, in that it opened the way for laboratories on a more comprehensive scale, and created a demand for experimental physicists and chemists.

C. GEOLOGY.

Next to physics and chemistry, one of the earliest developed of the sciences was geology—not always distinct from geography on the one hand, or from mineralogy, which was a branch of chemistry, on the other. It was included in Prof. Silliman's department at Yale in 1802, and so continued until after the middle of the century, when it became a distinct chair under James D. Dana. Among the older geologists, and one of the first to study nature in the field, was

Prof. Amos Eaton, of Williams College. He has been called the "Father of American Geology," was the instructor of Hall, Dana, and Williams, and initiated the interest in a half-dozen States. Under the patronage of Hon. Stephen Van Rensselaer, he made a systematic examination of the section of the Erie Canal (1823), and explored other parts of New York. During the same period, Prof. Olmsted was doing a like service for North Carolina and the general advancement of the science in the South.

Another phase of the development of geological study and instruction is shown in the beginnings of museums—botanical, geological, mineralogical—in this period. Specimens had been gathered, in a way, by various institutions for many years; but in 1827 Williams College set about doing it systematically. During the summer of that year an exploring party was sent out—professors and students—to Nova Scotia, and a quantity of mineralogical and geological specimens collected, making an excellent start for a museum. These expeditions were kept up for many years, and all parts of the country visited, South and West, and a place established for Williams College among the originators of scientific museums.

D. ASTRONOMY.

Theoretical astronomy was taught, in connection with mathematics, in the better institutions, even in the last century. Some of the minor instruments, indeed, were used. More than a hundred years ago Harvard boasted a telescope; but it all effected little of culture, less of discovery, and scarcely more of illustration. Princeton provided a room for instruments as early as 1803. Yale had an improvised observatory in 1830, and, but seven years later, Williams College, a separate building, and specially equipped under Prof. Albert Hopkins. The Hudson Observatory, at Western Reserve College, was founded in 1839, and one for the Philadelphia (boys') High School the same year. A few years later the National Observatory was established at Washington, and shortly after, one at the Military Academy. Up to this time astronomical instruction, and the science, so far as Americans had contributed to it, had only a nominal existence. The instruments were but ordinary, and the methods those of authority and prescription; inquiry was dependent and subservient. Its emancipation was coming, but slowly. In 1844 was completed the Cincinnati Observatory, and Prof. Mitchell made director. Here began a truly scientific and efficient study of astronomy. Not more for what it did, than for the spirit it exampled to science, is its service honored. The Cambridge (Massachusetts) Observatory was erected in 1846, and that of Michigan University, at Ann Arbor, in 1854. This last was generously equipped, and furnished with the most modern conveniences; and, when measured by the first Williams College foundation, exhibits the rapid growth of seventeen years. Miss Maria Mitchell was for some years connected with an observatory at Nantucket, Massachusetts; and later, for nearly twenty years, director of one at Vassar College, where she made for herself a name of more than national reputation.

A few years earlier than the last events recorded, just prior to the civil war, the Clarks, manufacturers of optical instruments, had established themselves at Cambridgeport, Massachusetts, and have, in a quarter of a century, done much to dignify and promote astronomical study.* In 1862 they furnished a glass for the University of Mississippi, but which, because of the misfortunes of war, was ultimately set up at Chicago. It was eighteen and a half inches in diameter, and was thought to be a large glass. Ten years later, they erected a twenty-six-inch telescope in Washington at the Naval Observatory, and took orders for another of the same size, which was finished and set up four years since (1885) at the McCormick Observatory, the University of Virginia.

---

* The American method of recording astronomical observations by means of electro-magnetism, it is acknowledged, has greatly increased the efficiency of the practical observer.

Princeton and Yale both erected large telescopes in 1882—in the latter institution Denison Olmsted had taught astronomy fifty years before. The famous Lick Observatory, California, has a thirty-six-inch glass, and the largest in use in this country.* The Warner Observatory, at Rochester, is a private institution, but one of the most efficient in important discoveries and verifications. Princeton, the University of Minnesota, and a few other institutions, have separate, endowed and especially equipped foundations for the use of students.

E. BIOLOGY.

Natural history, which was for many years the all-inclusive science, comprising even chemistry, physics, and astronomy, later became restricted to minerals, plants, and animals, in their normal condition, as objects of observation, but not of experiment. Biology is narrower, resting fundamentally upon the observations and comparative studies of the organs and phenomena of life. It has been said that biological study (in the universities) began with Huxley in England, and later in this country.

But it does the English scientist no discredit to say that American learning, both in colleges and outside, presented instances of the true scientific spirit, in the study of life-forms, many years prior to 1875.† These instances are individual, it is true, and were not always connected with institutions of learning. As the first laboratories were private or medical, so the first museums and studies of nature in the field were of personal preference and interest. Through individuals they got into the colleges—how slowly, is emphasized by a study of a few names.

---

* A contract has just been completed for a forty-inch glass, for the observatory to be built for the Leland Stanford, Jr., University, in California.

† It is well known how revolutionary and regenerative was the influence of Agassiz in all biological studies, substituting the comparative for the merely descriptive method. The Penikese school and the Harvard Museum are works of his wonderful genius.

Thomas Herriott, an English scientist, a man of wide culture, the teacher of Sir Walter Raleigh, and an author, made a voyage to America in 1585. He is described as astronomer and mathematician, but also as botanist and zoölogist. His natural history writings were numerous, and included careful descriptions from personal observation of twenty-eight mammals, and more than thirty birds. John Smith, it has been said, would have been a scientist if he had not had a continent to rule; Dr. James Logan early lectured on physiological botany; and John Bartram, the Quaker naturalist, built a botanic garden, the first in this country, on the banks of the Schuylkill. Linnæus called him the greatest natural botanist in the world. In Harvard's first course botany was included—to be pursued for one term each year by lectures only, but during the summer term. About the middle of the last century lectures were also given on the subject, in connection with materia medica, in the College of Philadelphia. Of the same general character were Dr. Hunter's lectures on comparative anatomy at Newport, Rhode Island, 1754; those on natural history to the medical classes in Harvard, 1788, and by Dr. Mitchell in Columbia College four years later.* About the same date Dr. David Hosack was made Professor of Botany in the same institution.

But, with all this, colonial instruction in science was scarcely scientific. It was meager, almost wholly by lecture, chiefly theoretical and classificatory, as it remained even down to the present generation. There were but few books, and upon the part of students no field study. Nothing satisfactory is known of any better instruction prior to 1800. Prof. Eaton lectured on botany in Williams College 1810, and was succeeded by Prof. Chester Dewey. Among later men have been Gray and Dana and Baird and Agassiz; Martin and Brooks in Johns Hopkins, and Jordan and Coulter in Indiana, not to name others widely known, and large origi-

---

* Six years after this (1798) he established a scientific journal, perhaps the pioneer in this country.

nal contributors to biological science. The subject has been greatly enlarged. Besides the first descriptive and structural botany, there have been developed the whole field of microscopic botany, paleontological and geographical botany, and its various economic phases, as in agriculture, medicine, and the commercial arts. Zoölogical science also, along with the doctrine of evolution, has specialized into new fields and answered many of the old questions. The greatest present activity among institutions and individual scientists, of this class, seems to be in the study of marine forms—absolutely and relatively a large field.

F. THE GENERAL RESULTS.

Chemistry has been greatly developed, and, so far from being a branch of physics merely, has its own large divisions, the prosecution of whose single interests occupy men a lifetime. Moreover, besides medical chemistry, and organic and inorganic chemistries, forms thoroughly distinguished, it has developed along both quantitative and qualitative lines, from general chemistry into agricultural, domestic, commercial, and other applications.

In physics * also, have been constructed almost bodily the accepted doctrines of force, and of particular forces, electricity, magnetism, etc.

So in geology, beyond the older divisions into dynamic and static has been carried on the study of particular periods, particular structures or processes ; and historical geology in its broader developments, economic geology, microscopic geology, etc., have been added. Biology is wholly a product of this century's thought. Resting upon a large previous knowledge of animal and vegetable life, there has followed an enormous increase in particular zo-

---

* Inasmuch as the university study of physics is more or less dependent upon the preparatory work, teachers of high and normal schools and academics should see the little book, "Harvard Preparatory Physics," recently published.

ological and botanical and comparative studies, to the enlargement of the curriculum many fold.

Of the several courses in Harvard, thirty per cent are in science, and in most other contemporary institutions a similar large ratio obtains. All this has had its influence upon the accepted curriculum. It could not be otherwise. It is so much net addition to the sum of instruction offered in the older courses—even those of a century ago. It has come to be universally recognized in the colleges, says Dr. Noah Porter, that "the facts, the laws, the theories, the experiments, with the changed conceptions of matter and spirit which they warrant, the new view of the nearer and distant universe ; the discoveries and the arts which the microscope, the telescope, and the spectroscope have made possible; the altered conceptions of matter living and dead, and of spirit in its relation to both—all these should be familiar to the man who aspires to the culture of the scholar." *

Not less pronounced have been the modifications of the curriculum along the line of philosophy, psychology, and ethics.† The enlargement of their meanings, comparative studies, scientific methods of inquiry and exposition, and the humanizing of interests, have, in the best sense, increased the serviceableness of the course on this side. How much has been accomplished by a few institutions is only equaled by the much that remains to be done by most colleges, before the study is rationalized.

2. Modern Language Studies.

A second characteristic of contemporary courses is the emphasis put upon *the modern languages*. The impulse has had a twofold confirmation, first in the general service-

---

* "The Ideal Scholar," in "The New-Englander," June, 1886.

† For a presentation of the current work in philosophy, see "Science" for May, 1886, or the "Library Magazine," May 29, 1886, "Philosophy in American Colleges," by John Dewey.

ableness of those languages, but equally and directly in their disciplinary value, as culture-giving studies.

Necessarily the record of current science must be made, and must therefore be studied, in the half-dozen more or less of living languages representing the field of original investigation. These become a medium of preserving and transmitting the products of investigation into not only the physical but institutional world as well. It is reported of the classical scholar, Prof. Seeley, that while "recognizing most strongly the value of the classics," he thought "the needs of modern life were peremptorily demanding very much more devotion to the modern languages than has ever yet been accorded them." * Indeed it is this supreme utility, it has been claimed, which is the prime agency in raising their study "from the status of an accomplishment, or of a commercial art," and making them to take rank as "an integral portion of a liberal education."

This highest recognition of them—the scientific study of a language for its own sake, and for the accompanying mental discipline—was the outgrowth of, as later it supplemented, the study of vigorous living tongues from a persuasion of their economic functions.

How great is this divergence from the traditional defense of the classical curriculum, can perhaps best be appreciated by first taking a view of the older course.

Naturally, the introduction of the European languages into our Western schools would find neither encouragement nor occasion during the colonial period.   But, with independence once achieved, the new relations fixed new obligations. Such, for example, were the reciprocal influences between France and the United States in the period immediately following the American Revolution; the frequent social and general intercourse; the growing and mutually profitable commercial interests; and the necessary and ruling diplomatic relations resulting, that the study of the French lan-

---

* "Modern Language Notes," February, 1888, p. 74.

guage naturally followed. Their incipient republican impulse, and a waxing protestant spirit, made an alliance with the new European thought and literature both easy and important.

Columbia College, under Charles Bellini, established a chair of French in 1779, and one of German five years later. Two years before the latter, William and Mary College had included modern languages in a single chair. Not for almost half a century, however, was any study made of their literatures. Harvard had provided incidental instruction in French, even during the heat of the Revolution, but with no professorship until 1815. Union College, New York, had a professor of French in 1806, another of German a generation later, both of which had been merged into a chair of Modern Languages by the middle of the century. The one inexplicable official act of the time is that of Williams College, whose formal acknowledgment of its importance, in the establishment of a chair of French (1793), antedates the professorship of Greek and Latin by a quarter of a century.

The affiliations of the South being generally more foreign and less provincial than those of the North, except in the institutions named, earlier introduced the study of the European tongues, especially the French. With the opening of the century South Carolina College had a well-defined and established two-years' course; as did William and Mary, already noted, at least two of the colleges of Maryland, and an occasional academy and high-grade seminary.

After all, little had been accomplished beyond a few instructorships in French, and an occasional tutor in German; both taught after the method of the classics, and omitting all literature. In this, as in elementary education, the greatest activity has been since 1825. This period includes the work of the Grimm brothers, the rise of historical grammar, and the comparative and critical studies in language. The rapid increase of German immigration gave a peculiarly practical aspect to the demand for the language, and led to its introduction, not only into the college curriculum, but into many secondary and elementary schools even. This two-fold impulse to modern language study lent it a new importance.

Lafayette College, Pennsylvania, known for sixty years for its modern language, Old English, and something of philological interest, led out in the newer curriculum. To the French and German of Columbia College were added Spanish and Italian, Princeton provided modern languages, and Longfellow went to Bowdoin, all within five years. The University of the City of New York opened in 1831, with four separate chairs. Michigan also organized, ten years later, with a modern language department, which in 1867 was erected into separate professorships of French and German. Yale, noticeable among the older colleges, long contented herself with only elementary and tutorial instruction, estab-lishing her first chair of Modern Languages but twenty years ago. As early as 1825, when Harvard, to the Smith profess-orship of French and Spanish had appended Italian and German, Yale was led to consider the propriety of modern language instruction, but, with characteristic conservatism, hesitated to endanger the dominance of the classics, and, while having a chair of Arabic and Sanskrit (1873), voted to strengthen the course in Greek instead.

In most of the older institutions now, and in all of the recently established ones, two or more of the modern lan-guages, either in a single department or separately, are recog-nized as both a desirable and necessary part of any finished course of study. In the University of California, Cornell, Wellesley, and Bryn Mawr, Tulane University, and Johns Hopkins, the new State institutions West and North, and slowly throughout the South (the University of Virginia since 1825), these languages are accorded a place beside the older classics, mathematics, and philosophy ; taking the place of the first in the curricula of industrial and mechani-cal institutes, schools of science, commercial and political departments, etc.

It would be gratifying if as much could be now said for the increased attention given to the university study of English as belongs to other modern languages. Whatever argu ment of utility applies to other tongues applies equally to our own. As latest developed it is richest in the possibilities of comparative studies ; historically it has a very practical aspect. And yet no college in this country gives anything like so comprehensive instruction in the philological or critical or even the practical study of English, as in that of most other languages, or as it concedes to science or mathemat ics. Perhaps students are not properly fitted for this work in the lower schools. If not, let it be remembered that the raising of the standard must originate with the higher faculties. Progress in education (it is emphatically true of the United States) is downward from the universities. The initiative must be taken by the colleges ; and no phase of American learning shows more present neglect than the university study of English.

Supplementary to this prominence of the languages, and as its logical sequence, is the increasing attention given to advanced philological studies. Initiated by the great learning of Leibnitz, the recognition of a universal kinship of languages found a deserved and formal justification at the close of the last century in the Zimmermann "Comparative Grammar," under the patronage of Catharine II of Russia, and its first authoritative development forty years later in Bopp's studies among the Indo-Germanic languages, and Grimm's "Historical Dictionary." The easy freedom of our institutional life, and the uniform encouragement given to new and promising interests, paved the way slowly for phil ological studies in American institutions also ; * the study of language, not as a means to the prosecution of other studies, nor yet as a mere mental discipline, but as a legitimate field for original investigation, an open door to the ethnological and institutional kinships of mankind.

* " Harvard Report," 1883-'84, p. 8.

12

Bowdoin early established a chair of Oriental Languages, Yale, of Arabic and Sanskrit; and Lafayette, of English and Philology.* But, compared with the more recent instruction, much of the earlier was both superficial and diffuse; descriptive rather than comprehensive and critical. In Columbia courses are offered in Greek, Latin, French, Italian, Spanish, Portuguese, German, and English, with at least one in each chiefly for senior or graduate study in the higher critical literature and philology. Cornell offers a course on ethnographical philology, and general linguistic science ; Hamilton College, on comparative philology, with special reference to Greek, Latin, and English ; Johns Hopkins, a course in comparative philology and classical antiquities, and in connection with the classics, but having a special professor ; and Harvard one each in Greek and Latin, comparative philology, and Romance philology.

3. Institutional History.

One of the most pronounced changes in the scope and quality of the average course, and which has become, if it was not originally, characteristically American, is that which has enlarged it on the side of *history, the study of social agencies, and the growth of institutions.*†

Very early in the Harvard course history, such as it was, shared with botany, such as *it* was, the honor of one hour on Saturday afternoons for half the year. No considerable advance upon this, either as to amount or kind of work done, is shown by the records before the present century. Both Harvard and Yale had, from about the time of the

---

* An Essay by Thomas Jefferson, " Toward facilitating Instruction in the Anglo-Saxon and Modern Dialects of the English Language," is a quaint production (1790), and well worth an examination. It was republished half a century afterward, for use in the University of Virginia.

† " The institutional history of political states is at the present moment, perhaps, the subject which attracts the most lively attention of scholars."
—J. C. Morrison.

Revolution, included ecclesiastical history in an incidental way, but with no particular reference to other social institutions. Williams College, forward also in this as in the study of modern languages, provided in the original organization (1793) for instruction in "natural law and civil polity." Columbia College, the only other institution which seems to have made any serious attempt to encourage the study of history in the last century, was fortunate both in subject-matter and method. The course is described by Dr. Adams as "history with an ancient and geographical basis, but with a modern political outlook." For the most part history had not been set off from the anciently allied studies of language on the one hand, and philosophy on the other. The historical expositions of Prof. Anthon, of the chair of Greek and Latin, and Prof. McVickar, of Philosophy, Rhetoric, and Belles-Lettres, both at Columbia ; Prof. Hadley, of Yale ; and Prof. Gross, of the department of German and Geography, and later of Moral Philosophy, illustrate the subordinate place of history during this period, as late as 1835.

In the year named, Francis Lieber, a political refugee from Germany, and but a few years in the United States, was elected to the chair of History and Political Economy in the University of South Carolina. In the twenty years following, besides onerous class-room duties, he wrote his manual of "Political Ethics," enthusiastically commended by Kent and Story, and made the text of all best instruction elsewhere; "Great Events described by Great Historians," the "Study of History and Political Economy as Branches of a Superior Education," and his chief work, "Civil Liberty and Self-Government." Chiefly known in the field of economics and the studies of government, his influence in directing the educated mind, and in bringing about a rational view and presentation of the living fruitful facts of history has been of inestimable service.

Four years later (1839) the first professorship at Harvard was established, and Jared Sparks, pioneer representative in the study of modern and current, and especially American history, was elected to the new chair.

Two centuries had worked a revolution in the attitude of culture toward historical instruction. In Michigan Dr. Whedon taught "Philosophy of History," succeeded a few years later by Prof. (afterward President) Haven in the new chair of "History and English Literature." But the long step forward for Michigan, in respect to this subject, was taken when, in 1857, Andrew D. White, of New York, graduate of Yale, 1853, student of President Woolsey in this country and of Laboulaye in France, was called at the age of twenty-five to a separate chair of History. In half a dozen ways President Tappan had shown a comprehensive appreciation of the university function, and a far-seeing management of local affairs, but greater wisdom in nothing than in the strengthening along these lines. Prof. White remained in Michigan five years, and set national standards for study in political administration. Agencies of progress were singled out and made the objects of both particular and comparative study. Foundations were taken in a liberal estimate of the social, physical, and culture conditions, antecedent and contemporary, of political and other institutions; and it is safe to say that with the Michigan service and twenty years as President of Cornell, few men have exerted a wider and more wholesome influence upon higher education, and particularly upon national and social studies than Dr. Andrew D. White.

The year 1857 has been recognized as a way-mark in American political culture. While Prof. White was entering upon his new duties in Michigan, Francis Lieber had gone from South Carolina to Columbia College in a similar department. He remained in New York eight years, giving lectures not only upon history and economics as such, but upon international, civil, and common law, as well. In 1865 Yale instituted her first chair in this subject, which came to include, besides courses in general and ancient history, lectures and class-room work on modern and constitutional history and in 1868, optional exercises in Bancroft's United States.

Great changes have occurred in the twenty years since, in the multiplications of courses and the accompanying specializations of study. These years include Dr. C. K. Adams's work in Michigan, Dr. White's at Cornell, the enlargement of the course in Harvard, Prof. Dexter's lectures on American history at Yale, the revival of the course at Columbia (that had been abolished in 1865), and all of the Johns Hopkins instruction.

Of the forty-seven higher institutions, whose reports are given by Dr. Adams,* including Harvard, Columbia, and Brown, and ten leading State universities, forty-six report an aggregate of one hundred and eighty-nine courses in history and closely related studies. The development of the subject in half a century, and the really prominent place (small enough) which it holds in the progressive college of to-day, are rendered apparent by this multiplicity of courses, their thoroughly practical character, and the comparatively new but vital lines of inquiry in economic questions. A look through a dozen college manuals reveals the fact that to the limited traditional course in ancient and mediæval history, once so common, have been added new lines of lecture and research, in modern and local and institutional forces and phenomena, many times enlarging its scope and fruitfulness : forms of government and political constitutions ; history of political theories ; history of diplomacy in general, and of particular periods and peoples ; comparative history of religions, of constitutional law and governmental administrations ; constitutional and political history of contemporary governments, and especially of the United States ; American history, etc. How large a field ! To these have been added also those newer subjects growing out of the commerical character of contemporary society ; mercantile and administrative law, and the financial his-

---

* " The Study of History in American Colleges," p. 268.

tory of contemporary nations ; State and municipal finance, and international history.

Of a piece with this new interest in modern history in general is the increased recognition of the importance to our schools of studies in American history. After repeated recommendations by President White, Cornell established (1881) a full professorship in this subject ; according to Dr. White,* the first department of the kind in this country. During the same year, however, similar provisions were made at Harvard and the University of Pennsylvania. Besides these three schools, courses varying in definiteness and scope are offered at Yale, Columbia, and Michigan. From the department in the University of Pennsylvania, the literature of American history has been enriched by McMaster's "History of the People of the United States," and from Harvard a "Short History of the English Colonies in America," by Henry Cabot Lodge. Not immediately growing out of the department, but intimately associated with, and re-enforcing it as it re-enforces such interests everywhere, is the "Narrative and Critical History of America," by Justin Windsor, Harvard librarian. The work is to be complete in eight volumes, each division of the subject being treated descriptively for general use, and, for the scholar, critically. Supplementing both, are admirably arranged and very full bibliographical references, and classification of original documents and rare sources of information.

Following are the divisions of the work, vols. ii to vii, inclusive, being already published:

    I. America before Columbus.

    II. Spanish Discoveries and Conquests in America.

    III. English Discoveries and Settlements in America.

    IV. French Discoveries and Settlements in America.

    V. The French and English in North America (1689–1763).

---

* " Official Report for Cornell," 1882–'83, p. 20.

VI. The American Revolution.
VII. The United States (1783–1850).
VIII. Canada and the American Outgrowth of Continental Europe.

4. Economic Studies.

Not less striking in the development of the historical idea, and its presentation, is the kindred growth of *political, social, and economic studies.*

The need for political education began to be felt with our national birth. The peculiar national life early became a subject for study in college, academic, and other assemblies where citizens were schooled. For forty years some form of economic instruction has been more or less common in the leading colleges. A few of the representatives of the early day are historical. McVickar taught political economy at Columbia College as long ago as 1817 ; and the well-known author and economist, Dr. Cooper, was elected the same year to a like position in William and Mary College. Francis Lieber, to whom reference has already been made, began his political lectures and writings in South Carolina College just half a century since. Torrey and Bowen initiated the work at Harvard, and President Woolsey at Yale.

In general, however, it may be said the instruction showed its metaphysical presuppositions in an *a priori* dogmatic treatment that left it barren of any insight into institutional life. Not until within a recent period has it come to be studied as is geography or ethics for their higher economic connections. The current decade (1880–'90), indeed, includes nearly all the organized effort in this direction, and is worth studying, both for its own results, and as an illustration of the change that has come over the college course.

The principal activity is shown in Columbia College and the Universities of Pennsylvania, Michigan, Cornell, and Johns Hopkins, having special schools ; and in Harvard and Yale offering extensive courses in political and economic studies.

A. COLUMBIA SCHOOL OF POLITICAL SCIENCE.

The Columbia school was organized October, 1880, by the combination of forces already at work, and which had been directed to this end. A special faculty was selected, and a course of study covering three years, and embracing a history of philosophy and political literature as the basis for a rational study of the specific questions of the new department. These were made to include, besides much historical matter, a study of Roman law and derived codes, constitutional and comparative administrative law, public and private international law, statistics, and communistic and social theories.

The purpose of the school was and is to give a complete general view of all the subjects, both of internal and external public polity, from the threefold standpoint of history, law, and philosophy.

B. THE WHARTON SCHOOL OF FINANCE AND ECONOMY.

The Wharton School in the University of Pennsylvania is rather a school of trade and the principles of finance than for political science and economics in the usual sense.   Its functions are peculiar. It is more professional than political, and looks to the manipulation of industries rather than the administration of government.   Nevertheless, it has economic bearings. The school was founded by Joseph Wharton in 1881, aiming to give, in addition to a purely business training, an extended study of economic principles, as a foundation for a correct political economy which shall " command the respect of thoughtful business men who are skeptical concerning the worth of that usually taught." The course covers two years, and is re-enforced by a library particularly full in industrial, commercial, and economic literature.

C. THE MICHIGAN SCHOOL OF POLITICAL SCIENCE.

As one effect of the experiment in Columbia College (1880), and the general drift toward the university idea, was the establishment of a School of Political Science at Ann Arbor (1881). Similar in fundamentals to the Columbia school, it developed certain new lines, which give it an individuality. Lectures were given in general historical study, and the method of original investigations, political economy, international law, civil and political rights, sanitary and social science, and forestry. Subsequently were introduced some very practical and fruitful lectures and discussions on public surveys, the economic development of mineral resources, the historical development of educational systems, municipal government, modern diplomacy, and local government in Europe and America.

D. THE WHITE SCHOOL OF HISTORY AND POLITICAL SCIENCE.

Instruction at Cornell was organized into schools at its founding. It could not well have been otherwise. It was part of a wide-spread tendency. Culture should no longer be bolstered and petted. All learning should stand upon its merits. Alongside a full presentation of the dead languages and traditional systems were offered the modern languages and their discipline. The emancipation of the sciences from metaphysics, and history from the Church, and politics from monarchism, was a task worthy of, as it has commanded, the best thought and most liberal means everywhere. As the plan developed at Cornell, history rapidly appreciated. Social and institutional life were dignified with the profoundest study. Goldwin Smith and James Anthony Froude and Edward A. Freeman were invited to lecture on English history and related topics, Theodore W. Dwight on "Constitutional Law," and others on their specialties; but the leading spirit of the new school, as for twenty years he was the administrative head of the university, was President White, dean of the school, and lecturer upon French history and institutions, and general economics. His course was suggestive. It paved the way and laid the foundation for the recent and contemporary political and economic studies recommended by the president in his first reports.

The school was formally instituted in 1882, with a course extending over four years, two of which were to be chiefly devoted to a thorough preparation in modern languages, mathematics, and history. At present the department offers fifteen courses, with five alternates, as follows:

1. The history and civilizations of Greece and Rome.
2. The private life of the Romans.
3. Private, political, and legal antiquities of the Greeks.
4. Political and social history of Europe to the French Revolution.
5. Political and social history of England through the Napoleonic wars.
6. General history of Europe to the Franco-German War.
7. History of America to 1783.
8. Constitutional and political history of America, 1783–1861.
9. Problems in American constitutional and political history.
10. History of political and municipal institutions.
11. Growth of the English Constitution.
12. International law and diplomacy.
13. Literature of political science.
14. Historic achievements in statesmanship.
15. Political and historical questions.
16. Elements of political economy.
17. Problems in political economy and finance.
18. History and management of industrial, penal, and charitable institutions.
19. Economic questions.
20. History and significance of the Roman law.

E. THE JOHNS HOPKINS HISTORICAL-POLITICAL SCHOOL.

This course is No. 6 of the seven groups of studies constituting the academic work of Johns Hopkins University. The department employs six professors, and, in addition to a study of the general history of institutions, provides lectures and seminary discussion on European politics, historical jurisprudence, political economy, modern historical criticism, historiography, and modern methods of historical research, administrative and comparative politics, and concrete problems of social science.

The work throughout is carried on in a comprehensive, familiar, and practical way; libraries and original research, both in Europe and the United States, being made to contribute to its efficiency.

F. OTHER INSTITUTIONS.

Yale maintains a strong department also, with characteristic courses upon the industrial organization of society, sociology with an elementary study of human paleontology, archæology, and ethnology, railroad administration, industrial legislation, etc. The courses in Harvard are similar. Mention should not be omitted, also, of the like instruction and a commendable interest manifested among Western institutions, particularly at the Universities of Wisconsin and California.

G. HISTORICAL LIBRARIES AND SEMINARIES.

Besides the lectures and conventional class-room work, most of these schools sustain, in fact if not in name, seminaries, or organized, more or less formal societies, of students and instructors, for the carrying on of original studies, chiefly among advanced students.

Dr. H. B. Adams is authority for the statement that the seminary was first introduced in a simple form into this country, through Michigan University, about 1869. The idea was further applied in Harvard the next year; but received its principal impulse in the department of the Johns Hopkins University in 1876. Cornell has three such seminary bodies, one for American history, one for political studies, and one for economics.

A necessary accompaniment of this seminary work, whether in history and economics, or, what is not less common, in psychology, in physical science, or philology, is a working collection of selected books. The Cornell library for such use is one of the richest in this country in original and standard materials for economic and historical studies. It contains the Goldwin Smith library of English, and the Sparks library of American history, a large collection of documents on American slavery, and the generous gift of President White's own historical library of thirty thousand volumes. Prominent also among the numerous originally valuable features of the Johns Hopkins Seminary of History and Politics are the admirably managed and well-used special library of twelve thousand volumes, containing valuable manuscripts and rare treatises, the newspaper, Geographical and Statistical Bureaus, and the Historical Museum. Few similar schools have collections, either so valuable in themselves or so directly and without restriction available upon occasion, and certainly none more industriously used. In 1882 was begun the publication of the "Johns Hopkins University Studies in Historical and Political Science." Six volumes have been published, including papers on social institutions; economics; Maryland, Virginia, and Washington ; municipal government and land tenure ; and like questions, and represent the best results of individual and organized original inquiry by the department.

At Harvard also as an organ of the department is maintained the "Quarterly Journal of Economics," supported by the income from a fund of fifteen thousand dollars.

Bibliography.

"Science in American Colleges," the "Century Magazine," April, 1882; "The Beginnings of Natural History in America," by G. Brown

Good, "Proceedings of the Biological Society," Washington, D. C., February, 1886; the "Teaching of Chemistry and Physics in the United States," F. W. Clarke, "Bureau of Education," Circular No. 6, 188▶; "Biological Teaching in Colleges," W. G. Farlow, "Popular Science Monthly," March, 1886; "The Growth and Development in the Teaching of Science in the Schools and Colleges of New York," in ninety-eighth "Report of the Regents of the University of the State of New York" (1884); "A Century of Abstract Science in America," Simon Newcomb, "North American Review" (1876). A valuable contribution to the discussion of this question was made in the "Culture demanded by Modern Life," E. L. Youmans (1867), and its companion volume, as a sort of reply, "Classical Study, its Value illustrated by Extracts from the Writings of Eminent Scholars," by S. H. Taylor (1870).

Consult also "Modern Language as a College Discipline," by A. M. Elliott, "Education," vol. v (1884); the "Position of Modern Languages in Higher Education," "Proceedings of the National Educational Association" (1876), p. 111; "History of Classical Education," by C. S. Parker, in Farrar's "Essays on a Liberal Education"; "A College Fetich," by C. F. Adams, Jr., "Independent," August 9 (1883); the "Study of Language in a Liberal Education," by J. Bascom, "Proceedings of National Educational Association" (1884), p. 273; "On the Function of the Study of Latin and Greek in Education," by William T. Harris, "American Journal of Social Science," vol. xx, p. 1; "The Classical Question in Germany," by E. J. James, "Popular Science Monthly," January, 1884; the "Place of English in the College Curriculum," "Yale Review," February, 1886; and "English in our Colleges," by A. S. Hill, "Scribner's Magazine," April, 1887.

See "Manual of Historical Literature," by C. K. Adams (1882); "Methods of Historical Study," by E. A. Freeman (1886); "Methods of Teaching History," by G. S. Hall (1885); and the "Study of American History in Schools and Colleges," by F. M. Thorpe; also, a "Plea for the Study of American Institutions in American Schools," by F. M. Thorpe, "Education," November, 1886; "A Narrative and Critical History of the United States," by Justin Windsor; "Outline of a Proposed School of Political and Social Science," E. J. James (1885); "Economic Science in America," C. F. Dunbar, "North American Review" (1876); "Of the Study of Politics," Woodrow Wilson, "Princeton Review," March, 1887; and "European Schools of History and Politics," by Andrew D. White (1887).

CHAPTER XI.

RECENT COLLEGES.—(Continued.)

5. Elective Courses.

SUPPLEMENTING these modifications, and in some degree made necessary by them and marking their culmination, is the *large privilege of option* accorded students in following a course of study.

The conditions leading to this changed attitude of the educated and general public toward, and the newer ideas of a liberal education, are manifold. Something may doubtless be ascribed to a very general withdrawal of authority in all matters, domestic, civil, and political, as well as educational. That this influence is one whose working and effect are not calculable, and is indefinitely and variously estimated, but universally recognized, only serves to dignify the fact. Besides, the fundamental American trait, protestant and confident, initiates a zeal for change, an impatience of tasks and restraints ; and, along with a very natural intolerance of the wisdom of experience, suffers a confidence in untried methods, a wealth of risk, and speculation, and hopefulness, which, to a people of ancestral foundations, forebode only ill.

The growth of a people also, surrounded by and within reach of abundant material resources ; stirred by constant exhibitions of material progress ; influenced by present considerations ; early forced into competitions for place, and personal aggrandizement, and local advantages ; in a country where the virtues of party and sect are exalted ; and, intoxicated by an almost unbroken record of achievements— easily divorces the public regard from the traditional regenerations of a pronounced humanistic culture, and breeds a warranted but sometimes unwise demand for the merely expedient and useful. Further, the early training in self-control which lies at the basis of our individual sovereignty and the rapid maturing of American youth, suggest a limited prescription and freer appointments throughout society. A citizenship at twenty-one must rest upon a previous training in self-direction, making the assumption of that citizenship rational. That the sentiment may be unwise though soundly inspired, and yet find a general indorsement, is not improbable. The imminence of citizenship to every student sets limits to authority, and fosters the tendency to early independence.

It has been aptly said by a recent writer: * " The American college curriculum, at the time when most of us became acquainted with it, was a very definite thing, time-honored, and commanding a certain respect from its correspondence with the theory on which it is based. Its fundamental idea was discipline of the mind. Its mode of effecting this was, in large part, by shutting the student's eyes to the distracting and inconsequential present, and fixing his gaze on that which was great and good, and hard to understand, in the past. The main work of the course consisted of drill in grammar and mathematics ; and the results of this training were bound together, at the hands of the president, by a final exposition of such of the speculations of philosophers as seemed to him safe and substantial. This work lasted—for reasons so old as to be long since forgotten—just four years, and was preceded by a certain very definite amount of drill of much the same kind, which was regarded as a necessary preliminary to the other work."

This is no caricature, but a statement of recorded fact ; not all the merit belongs to the new education ; the old-time learning, too, was worth treasuring ; but that such education would no longer be called " liberal " has the most scholarly testimony. With the changed human relations have come new estimates, and the growing impression that " the languages of Greece and Rome can never again be

---

* Dr. David S. Jordan, " Science Sketches," p. 230.

considered—as they were once—almost the sole requisites of a liberal education." *

The enlargement of the curriculum, due to the great increase of the field of knowledge—both spiritual and physical science—has already been suggested as historically conditioning the lapse of the prescribed course. Science, history, and their comparative studies; philosophy that is not metaphysics and is more than speculation; anthropology —the comparative study of races, language, and customs; the evolution of laws, and ideals of culture—all represent legitimate lines of development and perfection. Neither can all be included nor these omitted.

A. BEGINNINGS OF THE OPEN SYSTEM.

It can not perhaps be said where or when the freedom to select studies was first formally allowed to students in our American schools. Indeed, it is a matter of no great importance; it grew. The privilege has been granted; is now used in every State, perhaps in a majority of all our colleges —in some institutions, too, where it should not be found. But the change is made, or making, and is part of an impulse as old as the century. This change in the curriculum, which in the older institutions has been brought about through years of experiment, and at the expense of much halting and indecision, the newer colleges possess as an inheritance. Sixty years span most that is historic in the question.

It would be interesting to trace to their origin the liberal, but to Americans then unfamiliar, notions of Jefferson, President Nott, Francis Wayland, Joseph Story, Prof. Ticknor, and others, touching this movement. It has a tendency to lead one into a kind of hero-worship to know how large a place the ideas of a few men have filled in the educational history of this country, until it is found that the few men

---

* Dr. Chase, "Liberal Education," address at the opening of Bryn Mawr College, 1885.

were exponents of a common sentiment, in whose minds the general impulse took shape, and who so became public spokesmen.

The early efforts to establish mechanics' and manual labor institutes are interesting as marking a reaction against the dominance of language and metaphysics, and an ingenuous appeal for a larger recognition of the physical sciences. The University of the City of New York, in 1830, organized with sixteen departments, one half of which were of science and the modern languages. Union college, under Dr. Eliphalet Nott, established and maintained for many years both classical and non-classical courses; the latter substituting German and an increased amount of mathematics in place of the classics, and both admitting a limited choice within the courses.

Harvard also was early led to consider the "fitness of the course of instruction," possibly at the suggestion, certainly with the support, of Judge Story, and in the year 1824 provided, through the corporation and overseers, and against the judgment of the faculty, "for the consideration, to a limited extent, of the desires of students in the arrangement of their studies." Under this provision, French and Spanish were offered as "voluntaries" by Prof. Ticknor, and with minor interruptions continued so throughout his own, and Prof. Longfellow's connection with the institution, for twenty years. Further than this, with the exception that juniors might choose a substitute for one term of Hebrew, and seniors between chemistry and fluxions, all the studies of the college were required, as they had been for two centuries.

B. THE UNIVERSITY OF VIRGINIA.

One of the most interesting of American university foundations is that of the University of Virginia. Its constitution and management are full of instruction to institutions both older and younger. Fortunate in wise direction, its comprehensive organization has been more or less copied by institutions of even greater pretensions.

18

He who would know the origin and inauguration, and
from them learn of the inner spirit, of the University of Virginia, must read the life and study the correspondence of
Thomas Jefferson. He was the controlling spirit in the enterprise from its inception till his death. His letters to Cabell and Dr. Priestley and Thomas Cooper and John Adams
are full of interrogation and suggestion and plan concerning a " real university."

As early as 1779, while yet the " Old Dominion " with her
sister States was embroiled in a doubtful war; and again in
1814, after numerous defeats and constant opposition from
the already established William and Mary College, from the
Protestant churches, and from most of the political leaders
of the time, Mr. Jefferson and his friends sought to provide
for the State, along with a general system of education, a
university, in which should be taught in the highest degree,
" every branch of knowledge, whether calculated to enrich,
stimulate, and adorn the understanding, or to be useful in
the arts and practical business of life." Five years later
(1819) an act of the Assembly was obtained establishing
the University of Virginia. When six years later it was
opened, after a wide acquaintance and careful study of the
most progressive institutions in the United States, it was
found that in discipline and instruction, in constitution and
means, it very materially differed from them all. In Mr.
Jefferson's words publishing his plan it was said: " There is
one practice from which we shall certainly vary, although
it has been copied by nearly every college and academy in
the United States. That is the holding of the students all to
one prescribed course of reading, and disallowing exclusive
application to those branches only which are to qualify
them for the particular vocation to which they are destined.
We shall, on the contrary, allow them uncontrolled choice
in the lectures they shall choose to attend, and require elementary qualifications only, and sufficient age." *

---

* Letters to Prof. George Ticknor. See also Jefferson's " Works," vol.

Substantially this policy has been in operation ever since, now (1889), sixty-four years. There is no curriculum of studies as in most institutions of like grade. Each distinct branch of knowledge is assigned to, and presented by a separate "School," under the exclusive charge of its own professors, and conferring its own certificate. The eight schools with which the university opened, have expanded to nineteen—twelve academic and seven professional. The academic schools are of two classes, the literary and the scientific. The former (literary) comprise Latin, Greek, modern languages, English language and literature, historical science, and moral philosophy; the latter (scientific schools), mathematics, natural philosophy, general chemistry, analytic and agricultural chemistry, natural history and geology, and practical astronomy.

The professional schools are of four classes, the medical department, three schools; the law department, two schools; the engineering and agricultural departments, one school each. Each of these nineteen schools is independent of every other, both as to subjects included and internal control. This is the "freedom of teaching," widely known as one of the cardinal principles of the German university system; and is the correlative of that (to them) equally fundamental "freedom of learning" which in this country has come to be known as the "open system," * or elective principle.

C. HARVARD UNIVERSITY.

In view of its historical development, the most valuable information concerning optional courses comes from Harvard. The official reports for years have been suggestive upon many points of interest to college-men, and especially

---

viii, p. 300. Also "Thomas Jefferson and the University of Virginia," by H. B. Adams.

* This, as it appears in the University of Virginia, is very clearly set forth by Prof. J. M. Garnett in "The Andover Review," April, 1886, under the title " The Elective System of the University of Virginia."

upon this. Harvard is distinguished as not only foremost
among the institutions of the country, but forward in the
effort to adapt the resources of the university to the modern
conditions, and the current demands of highest culture. In
a generous way it has been recognized by general, official,
and special reports, and in frequent public discussion that,
"the experience of Harvard, during the long transition from
a uniform required curriculum to a regulated freedom in
choice of studies," might be helpful to other institutions.
And from the records preserved, for more than fifty years,
the steps of advance and occasional retrogression can be
studied for Harvard as for almost no other institution in
this country.

After the first liberal impulse under the influence of Judge
Story (1824), little more was done for many years than to
work over and revise the original plan. Within eight years,
however, half the students in modern languages were taking
the study as an extra, or a substitute; as a result of which
success, a like concession for a time was made to mathematics, Greek, Latin, theology, philosophy, logic, and rhetoric.
Having little encouragement, outside the department of
French, less was accomplished. Really, the extension was
discouraged, extras in most of these subjects being paid for
in students' fees.

In 1841, however, there was adopted a course, which
President Eliot describes as "by far the broadest plan enacted up to that time." For the freshman year all the
work was still prescribed ; for the sophomore year, only
five subjects ; for the junior, eight ; and the senior, eight ;
while students of these three years might, so far as their
time would allow, and the means of such instruction
"were within the resources of the university," elect from the
following subjects : mathematics, chemistry, Greek, Latin,
natural history, geology, geography, the use of the globes,
and any modern language. It was a large concession, and
had a permanent influence upon the course.

A condition of no less interest was found in the fact that

certain studies, once altogether excluded from the course were occasionally regarded as essential to a liberal discipline. For three years, under Prof. Longfellow, French was a required study (1839-'42), and even natural history was prescribed in 1846, along with the classics, as were chemistry and psychology. Twenty years later German was required for a time, of sophomores, though it was elective for juniors. But there was no system. The published electives one year were required the next, and might become extras the year following. There was no settled policy, the argument for change in particular cases being frequently convenience or expediency. French, for example, was three times an elective in forty years, twice prescribed, and twice extra. Chemistry was repeatedly shifted, until 1851, when it became fixed as a part of the prescribed course.

It should be remembered that, during all these years, there was still maintained a uniform four years' course, and the extras and electives, for which students were given no credit on the rank lists were so much additional instruction imposed upon an already burdened faculty. Besides, Presidents Everett and Sparks were pronounced opponents of the whole elective system. Changes were made slowly and with little foresight; with the administration of Dr. Walker, however (1853), and later, of President Felton and Dr. Thomas Hill, the tendency was strengthened and the policy became fairly established. With increased attendance, there were larger resources, leading to an enlargement of the faculty, to added electives, and more generous privileges granted to students. Slowly, sometimes with limitations, but on the whole forward, the amount of prescribed work has been reduced, and the proportion of options correspondingly increased.

In the year 1867 a committee of the faculty, of which the President (Dr. Thomas Hill) was chairman, reported the following scheme of studies, which was adopted.

It is given in full, as being, first, a step in the development of the Harvard instruction ; and, second, as an interesting attempt to distinguish between fundamental and desirable studies in a liberal schooling :

HARVARD CURRICULUM OF 1867.

Freshman year :
> Mathematics, Latin, Greek—each four hours a week ; Greek history, French, ethics—each two hours a week ; elocution—once a week.

Sophomore year :
> *Required Studies.* — Chemistry, German — each two hours a week; Roman history, psychology and rhetoric—two hours a week, for half the year.
>
> *Elective Studies.*—Latin, Greek, mathematics, pure and applied—each three hours a week. Each student required to take two.

Junior year :
> *Required Studies.*—Physics—three hours a week; logic and metaphysics—each two hours a week, for half the year.
>
> *Elective Studies.*—Latin, Greek, ancient history, mathematics, chemistry, natural history, German, English—each three hours a week. Each student must take two, may take three. Italian and Spanish as extras.

Senior year :
> *Required Studies.* — Political economy, philosophy — each two hours a week, for half the year ; history— three hours a week ; ethics—once a week for half the year.
>
> *Elective Studies.*—Latin, Greek, mathematics, physics, chemical physics, history, modern languages (for advanced students only)—each three hours a week. Each student must take two, and may take three, or give the time of three to two.

It will be noticed that neither Greek, Latin, nor mathematics is required after the freshman year ; but instead, philosophy in some form, psychology or ethics. The only physical sciences prescribed were physics and chemistry ; and they were only half studies in the sophomore and junior years.

Five years later all required studies had dropped from the senior work ; in 1879, from the junior; and in 1884, from the sophomore. The only present prescribed work for the degree of Bachelor of Arts is a weekly lecture for.half the year in physics and chemistry each ; rhetoric and English composition, including themes, throughout the four years, and either German or French in the freshman year. About the time of the last regulation, what is of not less importance and not less revolutionary, it was granted that seniors might take their elementary German with juniors—a step toward the abolition of class distinctions, one of the characteristics of the elective system.

D. MICHIGAN UNIVERSITY.

In Michigan the first change was made under the administration of President Tappan, in the adoption of, and the right of choice between, classical and scientific courses. Dr. Tappan brought to his new position as first president of the first great university of the West, not only ability and scholarship, but a large acquaintance with the best contemporary thought on university training. Moreover, he was an enthusiast in higher education, whose problems and management he had studied at home and abroad.

The liberal policy of the State under Superintendent Pierce was accepted and enlarged. The scientific course was arranged to cover four years, with students classed as in the usual course, but graduating as Bachelors of Science. These parallel courses did for Michigan what Harvard and Yale but a few years before had attempted to accomplish in the establishment of separate scientific schools. This intimate connection and common dependence of all departments in the Western and newer institutions is by no means the smallest factor in their easier and more rapid readjustment of the curriculum, and their reorganization of faculties. The past is always a teacher; to the older colleges it has sometimes been a burden.

In addition to this double course in Michigan, students were allowed " to pursue special courses, and receive at their departure certificates of proficiency." The sentiment was growing that in some way a college of means, and the appliances of highest culture available, should minister also to the more popular demand for a share in the learning and the privileges once accorded to the few; that, in a word, as Prof. Ticknor said, fifty years in advance of his surroundings, " it should extend effectual instruction to portions of society that now never resort to it." The sentiment, whether well or ill founded, as respects the true university, had become, by the war decade, a mastering force, reshaping the control and enlarging the functions of college and school, setting new limits to instruction, and giving direction to new interests.

E. CORNELL UNIVERSITY.

Cornell opened in 1868, dominated by this idea, that while providing opportunities for the highest learning, it should be a place the farthest removed from all exclusiveness; a place " where any person may find instruction in any subject." Though throwing out inducements to higher special studies, its doors should be closed to no one seeking even its temporary privileges. The institution was organized with five collegiate courses, of equal rank and scope; fifteen special courses, seven of which, chiefly science, led to no degree; and nine graduate courses. Of the first there were offered—1. A course in literature, with Latin but no Greek (B. L.). 2. A course in philosophy, also requiring Latin but no Greek (Ph. B.). 3. A course in science, including neither Latin nor Greek (B. S.). 4. A course in science and literature, with neither Latin nor Greek (B. S.). 5. A course in arts, the common academic course (B. A.). The fifteen special courses have been changed to twelve, and the nine graduate courses expanded to seventeen. Including the medical preparatory, then, Cornell offers thirty optional courses, and confers nine different degrees. Liberty in the choice of studies is regarded as fundamental.

F. COLUMBIA COLLEGE.

Columbia as early as 1830 provided and for seven years maintained two courses of study; in 1857 made German voluntary, and a few years later allowed seniors a choice between the classics and higher mathematics. Since 1880, except two hours per week of modern languages required of freshmen and sophomores; history, English, and Anglo-Saxon of juniors; and English and Anglo-Saxon of seniors. all the studies are elective. Three degrees are conferred, Bachelor of Letters, Bachelor of Science, and Bachelor of Arts, according to the predominant character of the studies.

G. YALE UNIVERSITY.

Even Yale, which has been generally and very properly regarded as the conservator of the principle of authority in college instruction, has granted large liberty in a quarter of a century. The institution was prosperous, new subjects were yearly added to the curriculum, and the number of departments increased. Within fifteen years from the election of President Woolsey (1846), six new chairs had been added to the faculty, and eight new subjects to the course. The two professorships in chemistry soon grew into the "Department of Philosophy and Art," in which chairs were instituted in metallurgy, industrial mechanics and physics, physical and political geography, agriculture, botany and zoölogy. The section came to be known as the Sheffield Scientific School, and before 1870 had already developed into seven full courses, besides certain "select studies," preparatory to minor pursuits, business, etc.

Along with this extension and enrichment of the course, had been necessarily exercised the principle of selection. From such a wealth of subjects, not all could be taken by each. What should be omitted? Clearly the individual preference must be a factor. For some years, therefore, as early as President Woolsey's administration (1846–1871), the elective system had obtained, in a guarded way, in the later years of the course. In 1868 Bancroft's "History of the United States" was elective; while in the next decade options in the modern languages were greatly increased, as also in natural science. Some choice, too, was admitted in entrance examinations. Toward the close of President Woolsey's administration, and in the ten years following, so rapidly had the course enlarged, and so numerous were the concessions, that "nearly one half the work of the last two years," says Prof. Dexter, "was left to be determined by each student for himself." At present juniors elect about sixty per cent of their work, and seniors more than eighty per cent.

From the standpoint of the ancient, or even of a scholar of the Revolutionary period, the change would seem to be ruinous. And yet, in the most pronounced departure of reputable institutions, there has been no revolution, no disorganization. The transition is a hazardous one, and has need of calm judgment and wise foresight. But no one longer denies either the necessity or the wisdom of the elective principle. "To permit choice," says Prof. Palmer, "is dangerous; not to permit it is more dangerous." Only so can superficiality, on the one side, be avoided, or, on the other, cramping of minds. Yale offers ninety-one courses; the Universities of Kansas, Indiana, and California, more than one hundred each; Harvard two hundred, and Michigan two hundred and sixty-nine. Cornell, Columbia, Wisconsin, Illinois, and Pennsylvania Universities offer long lists of subjects. And yet, with no greatly heterogeneous conditions, there is no common ground of agreement, or control at least, among college authorities, as to this question. Harvard and Columbia make the whole course practically elective, and the University of Kansas largely so, after the freshman year. In the University of Texas it is one half elective from the first. The University of Minnesota, Dartmouth, and Princeton, average about one half elective after the sophomore year. To this the Universities of California, Brown, and Bowdoin, add as elective one fourth of the sophomore work. In Williams College the electives constitute from one half to three fourths of the work of the last two years, and in Amherst almost four fifths of the work from the middle of the sophomore. In Swarthmore, but about one fifth of the course is elective after the freshman year; and in Boston University, the order of subjects only. With a few institutions the choice is between courses alone; as in Lehigh University, the University of Georgia, and the Tulane University, in the last of which there are six courses, two including something of the classics, but each leading to the degree B. A.

H. THE GROUP SYSTEM OF STUDIES.

In the attempt of educators to give a rational answer to the question how the elective principle may be applied to university work, without doing violence to the demands of liberal culture, the "group system" is historically significant. This assumes that there are certain studies which must be held indispensable to a liberal education. These form the groundwork of all the courses, whose additional branches give specific character to each. The Johns Hopkins University (opened 1876) is a representative of this class of institutions. The "essential studies" are logic, ethics, psychology, German, French, English, science (chemistry, physics, or biology), physical geography, and history (Greek and Roman, or modern European). Upon this foundation seven groups of studies are constituted, called respectively: 1. Classical. 2. Mathematical-physical. 3. Chemical-biological. 4. Physical-chemical. 5. Latin-mathematical. 6. Historical-political. 7. Modern languages. The several courses lead equally to the degree of Bachelor of Arts. Just here, institutions which insist upon a more or less close following of the traditional course (mathematics, philosophy, and the classics), as entitling the graduate to the degree B. A., would break with the Johns Hopkins control in the plan proposed.

The question is not, they say: Shall a degree be given where the classics have been omitted ? but: Shall the B. A. be conferred without them ? Johns Hopkins, in Groups II, III, IV, and VI, says Yes.

The curriculum of the recently founded college for women, Bryn Mawr, near Philadelphia, is the group system, as are those of Indiana University, Washington and Lee, and Tulane Universities, substantially. Graduate work for advanced degrees in the University of California, and a few others, is also set off into groups upon the same principle.

6. Graduate Courses.

As an outgrowth of the larger personal interest, and the less insistence upon a uniform curriculum, certain colleges have developed an amount of advanced and original work in various lines hinting at a true university spirit.

The admission of unmatriculated students to select courses, or to lectures in particular lines only, has thrown open the majority of higher institutions to a larger general and popular patronage. For the academic year 1885–'86, out of a total of three hundred and forty-six institutions, one hundred and fifty-four reported four thousand six hundred and five * students pursuing these special courses. These are frequently undergraduates, studying for no degree, and represent more or less incomplete and desultory work. That this is not an unmixed evil might be shown; but among the special students are some who have already taken their first degrees, and whose work is therefore advanced, and special only in the sense of looking to mastery in particular fields of learning. Historically, in this country, graduate study was sequent to elective courses. Both were phases of the same general impulse to adapt the instruction of the college, by selection within, or by extension beyond the course, to pronounced tastes and individual wants. It is not meant by this that there were not instances of prolonged and special

---

* Nearly ten per cent of the total attendance (48,485).

disciplines under the former system; but they were rather individual than part of the plan, though frequent and worthy.

As early as 1832 Harvard had provided for additional instruction in the modern languages and philology, and Yale ten years later in Arabic and Sanskrit, as also occasional terms in chemistry under Prof. Silliman. General philosophy soon followed in offering graduate instruction. Early in President Tappan's administration, the University of Michigan outlined a " university course," * in which lectures were given in most of the departments, and which were open to such students only as had already obtained the degree of Bachelor of Science or of Arts. Such student, by pursuing two courses during each semester of one year, sustaining an examination upon three of the courses, and presenting a satisfactory thesis, was given the degree of " Master of Arts or of Science."

Columbia College also, about 1840, opened a " post-graduate " course, in which Prof. Arnold Guyot delivered his celebrated lectures on " Comparative Physical Geography, in Relation to History and Modern Civilization "; and Mr. George P. Marsh a course upon the English language.† These were not continued after the one year, though reappearing in the broadly elective system and formal provision for graduate instruction in 1880.

Reference has already been made to the nine graduate courses of Cornell, established at its opening, and the nineteen at Johns Hopkins, seven years later.

The graduate department at Harvard was instituted in 1872. Upon the extension of the elective principle in 1882, the lines of class distinction were obliterated, and all courses thrown open alike to graduate and undergraduate—advanced courses in mathematics, physics, chemistry, philosophy, and classical philology being most frequently pursued for higher degrees.

---

* " Farrand's History of the University of Michigan," p. 113.
† " Historical Sketch of Columbia College," 1884.

Altogether, eighty-three institutions in the United States, having advanced courses, report eight hundred and eighty graduate students. In Princeton the class forms seventeen per cent of the entire enrollment ; in Columbia, four per cent ; Harvard, seven per cent ; Cornell, five per cent ; University of Notre Dame, Indiana, fourteen per cent ; South Carolina College, ten per cent ; and Johns Hopkins University, an average of sixty per cent for twelve years.

B. UNIVERSITY ORGANIZATION.

In a recent characterization of the American university, Dr. Gilman notes * four types as determined by their foundations. These he denominates : 1. The College University; 2. The State University ; 3. The privately endowed University ; 4. The Supervisory University.

The first has already been described in the sketch of the colonial and Revolutionary colleges. Their object was a rich and severe culture, classical in scope, and religious in aim. Except for the theological bias, they betrayed no impulse toward specialization. They were academic institutions, collegiate in method, and universities only *in potentia*. In general the first American schools were of this type, including all the colonial colleges, except perhaps the University of Pennsyvania, which was a State institution. William and Mary College, Virginia, and Columbia College, New York, were established under the support and protection of royal charters, but were in all other respects of the "college university " type.

The fourth class has, in this country, but one representative, the University of the State of New York. It is an organization including all the incorporated colleges and academies of the State, and certain academical departments of the public schools. The governing body is vested in a board whose corporate title is " The Regents of the Univer-

---

* " Cyclopædia of Political Science," article " Universities."

sity of the State of New York," and whose functions include general control and inspection, but not instruction.

Looked at from the present century, then—that is, descriptively and not historically—the second and third classes only remain. To these should be added the purely denominational institutions, to which class belong about seventy-five per cent of the colleges of the country.

1. State-established Colleges.

The State university had its inception within, and its control more or less determined by, the civil authorities, and the foundation of its support in the public revenue, either national or local, or both. Its instruction is non-sectarian and free, or with nominal tuition only. As a State agency, its principal object is general training. It belongs practically to the present century, only four institutions antedating 1800. These were the college in Philadelphia, which at the close of the Revolutionary war became merged in the University of Pennsylvania; the University of North Carolina, 1789; University of Vermont, 1791; and the University of Tennessee, 1794. The last received national as well as State aid.

From this time, excepting the Universities of Georgia and South Carolina, both established in 1801, and Ohio, in 1804, no other State institutions were founded for a generation. The Ohio University * was the first in the Northwest, and was established on a grant of the Ohio purchase. After Virginia (1825) came Indiana in 1828, Alabama in 1831, and others in rapid succession, so that by the middle of the century seventeen of the twenty-four States then existing had made public provision for university training. There are now thirty State universities. Of the thirteen original States, six only have such provision.

---

* Dr. Manassah Cutler, who was the author of the public policy of reserving Government lands for the support of education, also drew the articles of incorporation, arranged the course of study, and selected the teachers for the Ohio University.

The table shows not only the State institutions, but the time and order of their founding:

State-established Colleges.

States.	Date.	States.	Date.
1. Pennsylvania	1755	18. Kentucky	1858
2. North Carolina	1789	19. Kansas	1861
3. Vermont	1791	20. West Virginia	1867
4. Tennessee	1794	21. Illinois	1868
5. Georgia	1801	22. Arkansas	1868
6. South Carolina	1801	23. Minnesota	1868
7. Ohio	1804	24. California	1869
8. Virginia	1825	25. Nebraska	1869
9. Indiana	1828	26. Nevada	1874
10. Alabama	1831	27. Colorado	1875
11. Delaware	1833	28. Oregon	1876
12. Michigan	1837	29. Texas	1881
13. Missouri	1839	30. Florida	1883
14. Iowa	1847		
15. Mississippi	1848	1. Washington Territory	1861
16. Wisconsin	1848	2. Dakota "	1883
17. Louisiana	1853	3. Montana "	1884

2. Privately Endowed Institutions.

These perpetuate the name of the donor, and comprise some of the best-equipped and most efficient institutions; but, far more and better, they point to a wide-spread individual interest in the highest education. Bishop Fraser, twenty years ago, condemned unsparingly the needless multiplication of universities in this country, but commended as warmly the instances and the spirit of "individual munificence so common in America, so rare in England, as among the not unhealthy signs of the times."

The institutions of this class are far too numerous for more than representative mention. They are among the wealthiest, and, in larger or smaller gifts, include more than three hundred of the colleges. Among those founded by private means are Cornell University, Johns Hopkins, Lehigh, Wellesley, Tulane, Vanderbilt, Bryn Mawr, Boston University, Leland Stanford, Jr., University (California),

Vassar College, and the Clark University (Worcester, Massachusetts)—ten institutions, not to name others, representing a productive endowment, exclusive of buildings and other properties, of twenty-five million dollars.

But, besides the privately founded and endowed institutions, some of the State schools and most of the denominational are more or less dependent for their endowments and after-prosperity upon private means. Of this class are Harvard, Yale, Princeton, Brown, Dartmouth, the Northwestern (at Chicago), De Pauw University (Indiana), Amherst, etc., representing more than ten million dollars, most of which has come from private beneficence.

Naturally the aggregate of such benefactions can only be approximately estimated. The following table, made from information collected chiefly from the reports of the United States Commissioner of Education, and excluding gifts for secondary or professional schools, may be taken as fairly representing the annual and aggregate amounts contributed to colleges and universities alone, in the years for which reports are had since 1871:

Private Endowment of Colleges by Years.

YEAR.	Total endowments.	To colleges for women.	YEAR.	Total endowments.	To colleges for women.
1872	$6,282,461	$689,993	1881.....	$4,601,069	$214,529
1873	8,238,141	242,295	1882.....		
1874	1,845,354	26,035	1883.....	3,522,467	81,604
1875	2,703,650		1884.....	5,688,043	310,506
1876			1885.. ..	5,134,460	322,813
1877	1,273,991·	79,128	1886.....	2,530,948	266,285
1878	1,389,633	241,820	1887.....		
1879	3,878,648	62,815			
1880	2,666,571	399,987		$49,755,436	$2,937,810

Supplementary to the table just given is the following, showing a few of the large benefactions and their recipients. But it should not be forgotten that beyond the forty millions which these few names represent, the most hopeful mark of educational vigor is the large number of relatively small gifts

14

from hundreds of donors. This, too, it has been already said, includes only the moneys for colleges and universities, excluding secondary schools, medical and theological schools, special large benefactions to the South, etc. :

Table of Benefactions.*

1. Asa Packer........Lehigh University, Pa................	$3,500,000
2. Johns Hopkins ....Johns Hopkins University, Md........	3,500,000
3. Isaac Rich.........Boston University, Mass..............	2,000,000
4. Leonard Case......School of Applied Science, Ohio........	1,200,000
5. James Lick........University of California...............	1,650,000
6. Peter Cooper......Cooper Union, N. Y...................	1,200,000
7. Ezra Cornell.......Cornell University, N. Y..............	1,000,000
8. The Vanderbilts...Vanderbilt University, Tenn...........	1,775,000
9. Paul Tulane.......Tulane University, La.................	2,500,000
10. W. C. De Pauw ...De Pauw University, Ind..............	1,500,000
11. Leland Stanford ...Leland Stanford, Jr., University, Cal...	5,000,000
12. S. W. Phœnix.....Columbia College, N. Y..............	650,000
13. Amasa Stone......Adelbert College, Ohio...............	600,000
14. John C. Green.....Princeton College, N. J..............	1,500,000
15. Mathew Vassar....Vassar College, N. Y.................	908,000
16. George I. Seney....Wesleyan University, Conn...........	700,000
17. Ario Pardee.......Lafayette College, Pa.................	500,000
18. Benjamin Bussey ..Harvard College, Mass...............	500,000
19. Joseph W. Taylor .Bryn Mawr College, Pa..............	450,000
20. Joseph Sheffield ...Yale College, Conn..................	500,000
21. Henry W. Sage....Cornell University, N. Y.............	342,000
22. E. P. Greenleaf....Harvard University	630,000
23. J. P. Jones........Haverford College....................	500,000
24. Stephen Girard....Girard College, Pa...................	8,000,000
25. Jonas G. Clark.....Clark University, Mass..............	2,000,000

Without elaborating, it may be noted that there is an evident tendency, both in the older institutions and the later founded, toward non-sectarian education; this, in face of the fact that two hundred and fifty-nine of the three hundred and forty-six colleges are denominational, and that four fifths of those founded since 1850 are more or less under the control of church organizations. Within the last twenty

---

* Of course many millions have been given for secondary education also, attention being called here to superior institutions only.

years, church enterprise has been especially active in the introduction of higher education into parts of the West, and into the reconstructing States of the South; nearly three fourths of the denominational colleges founded in the period, being in the South, and in the States bordering upon the Mississippi River. Beside this is put the fact that, while seven of the thirteen original States have no State-maintained colleges, every State admitted since 1790 has assumed the responsibility of providing collegiate training along with elementary.

Out of a total attendance of less than fifty thousand in superior institutions, those supported by the State enroll about ten thousand; or eight per cent of the institutions (State) instruct twenty per cent of the students. In West Virginia the proportion is sixty per cent, Colorado twenty-nine per cent, Michigan twenty-five per cent, Nebraska twenty-two per cent.

The table appended exhibits the relative endowments of representative institutions of the three classes, private, ecclesiastical, and State foundations. There are a few State institutions that rank well with the majority of those from other classes—a fact which will appear more to their credit when the comparatively recent foundation of most of the former is noted:

Table of University Endowments.

INSTITUTIONS.	Property.	Endowment.	Total.
Ecclesiastical Institutions :			
Harvard.................................	....	$5,190,772	$5,190,772
Yale......................................	509,600	657,680	1,167,280
Princeton................................	750,000	1,400,000	2,150,000
Northwestern University.......	1,615,000	812,000	2,427,000
Wesleyan (Connecticut)........	509,000	667,000	1,176,000
Brown University..............	600,000	767,000	1,367,000
Tufts	200,000	700,000	900,000
Amherst......................	500,000	650,000	1,150,000
Hamilton.....................	400,000	277,000	677,000
Madison	200,000	550,000	750,000
	$5,283,600	$11,671,452	$16,955,052

INSTITUTIONS.	Property.	Endowment.	Total.
State Institutions:			
Michigan..................	$1,333,000	$981,000	$2,314,000
Minnesota.................	650,000	800,000	1,450,000
Wisconsin.................	790,000	800,000	1,590,000
Virginia..................	1,370,000	672,000	2,042,000
California............. ...	1,000,000	1,680,000	2,680,000
Missouri..................	1,050,000	582,000	1,632,000
Ohio......................	600,000	540,000	1,140,000
Texas.....................	482,000	860,000	1,342,000
Illinois..................	450,000	400,000	850,000
Pennsylvania..............	1,550,000	1,100,000	2,650,000
	$9,275,000	$8,415,000	$17,690,0.0
Privately Endowed Institutions:			
Cornell...................	$1,300,000	$5,000,000	$6,300,000
Boston....................	....	....	1,200,000
Tulane....................	225,000	1,038,657	1,264,000
Vanderbilt................	500,000	900,000	1,400,000
Bryn Mawr	350,000	750,000	1,100,000
Wellesley.................	2,000,000	225,000	2,225,000
Vassar....................	723,000	444,000	1,167,000
Johns Hopkins.............	650,000	3,000,000	3,650,000
De Pauw...................	250,000	300,000	550,000
Lehigh....................	1,000,000	2,000,000	3,000,000
	$6,998,000	$13,658,000	$21,856,000
Grand totals.............	$21,557,000	$33,744,000	$56,501,000

Bibliography.

The current literature on this section is very extensive, and the following selections are made more because they are generally available, than that others are inferior. In general, consult: " The College of To-day," by R. R. Bowker, " Princeton Review," 1884, p. 89 ; " Our Colleges before the Country," by W. G. Sumner, " Princeton Review," 1884, p. 127 ; " Aspects of College Training," D. C. Gilman, " North American Review," 1883 ; " The True Ideal of an American University," J. Dwight, 1871 ; " What an American University should be," James Mc-Cosh, " Education," vol. vi, p. 35 ; the " University of the Future," Hiram Corson, 1875. Also, " Student Freedom in Colleges," Presidents Eliot and McCosh, before the Nineteenth Century Club, New York, February, 1885, and the discussion of this by Dr. F. Patton, " Presbyterian Review," April, 1885 ; the " Elective System in Harvard College," Samuel Brearly, 1886 ; " Electives," " Education," vol. v, p. 473 ; " Elective System in Education," " Our Continent," February 22, 1882 ; the " Early History of the University of Virginia," Jefferson and Cabell, 1860; "Academic Freedom in Germany," H. W. Farnam, "Yale Review," January, 1887; Discussion of President Eliot's "Annual Report" for 1884–'85, in "New York Independent," May 6 and 13, 1886; "Should Colleges give the B. A. where Greek is omitted?" "New York University Convocation," 1886, p. 105; "Post-Graduate Degrees," "Proceedings of the University Convocation," 1884, p. 251; the "Place of Original Research in College Education," J. H. Wright, "Proceedings of the National Educational Association," 1882 (includes an exposition of the German seminary idea); "Original Research as a Means of Education," H. E. Roscoe, 1884; "Handbook of Requirements for admission to American Colleges," A. F. Nightingale, 1879; the "Question of a Division of the Philosophical Faculty," A. W. Hoffman, 1882; the "Organization of University Education," in Conference on Education ("International Health Exhibition Literature," vol. xv.); "University Corporations," J. L. Diman, 1882; "College Endowments," Rossiter Johnson, "North American Review," May, 1883.

CHAPTER XII.

THE PROFESSIONS.

NEXT to the universities, both in time and in importance, are those institutions providing for what are known as the learned professions—theology, law, and medicine. Among every civilized people these professions have been recognized as the conservators of learning, and the most efficient connecting links between school and life. Whatever their limitations, their dogmatism and pedantry and quackery, they have been from early history the best representatives in society of the culture of the university. Until recent years, for them were taught science, history, and philosophy. Their attitude has determined courses of study, and fields of investigation, and schools of literature, historical interpretations and standards of culture. That they have lost much of this almost absolute control over the means and standards of general culture, neither detracts from their historical signifi-

cance, nor depreciates their present eminent social importance, or their contributions to the general welfare.

1. Theological Education.

From the nature of American institutions, theological education, of course, has no organic connection with the general
system.   No State institution supports such a department;
though Straight University, Louisiana (founded by the Congregationalists), Livingstone College, North Carolina (of the
African Methodist Episcopal Zion's Church), Howard University, District of Columbia, Harvard, and Yale, all claiming
to be non-sectarian, maintain theological courses.   With
these exceptions the current education of the profession is
denominational, though variously liberal as to sectarianism.

The Roman Catholic Theological Seminary of St. Sulpice and St. Mary's University, Baltimore (1791) has been
claimed as the oldest institution of the kind in the United
States, though it seems that the Reformed (Dutch) Church
had established one at New Brunswick, New Jersey, seven
years before.   The only other school of the kind belonging
to the last century is the United Presbyterian Theological
Seminary of Xenia, Ohio, founded in 1794.

Among the colleges, Harvard was first to establish a
separate department of theology (1817), Yale following after
ten years.   The instruction in both of them, as well as in
William and Mary College, had been given since their foundation with more or less of ecclesiastical bias.   In Yale it is
said, under Dr. Dwight (1795–1817), students received in the
Sunday sermons a somewhat complete course in divinity ;
so that graduates frequently went at once into the pulpit
without further special studies.

Even before this the Moravians had opened a seminary
at Bethlehem, Pennsylvania (1807) ; the Congregationalists,
at Andover (1808), and Bangor, Maine (1816); the Presbyterians, at Princeton (1812) ; and the Lutherans, Hartwick
Seminary, New York (1815).   Besides those named, there
were established twenty-eight schools before the middle of

the century. In less than forty years since, more than one hundred seminaries have started. These one hundred and forty-two institutions, representing twenty-seven denominations, are found in twenty-eight States, the District of Columbia, and Indian Territory (this last is a Baptist Seminary, maintained by the Indians themselves, having six in the faculty, and seventy students). The Jews support one—the Hebrew Union College—at Cincinnati. Ten States—Arkansas, Delaware, Florida, Kansas, Nevada, New Hampshire, Rhode Island, Vermont, and West Virginia—report none.

The total number of students in these seminaries is six thousand five hundred, less than one fourth of whom are graduates with literary or scientific degrees; fifteen years ago the proportion was nearly one third. In the seminaries of four States—New York, Pennsylvania, Massachusetts, and Connecticut—at present the percentage of college-bred students is about forty-two; fifteen years ago it was fifty-five per cent. In some sections the standard of required entrance scholarship is very low. In one State, with two hundred and thirty theological students, but five had taken degrees; and less than half of them had more than a high-school training. In another, among one hundred and seventy-nine students, the showing was yet worse.

It would seem that there is a strong tendency in theology as in trade to rush into the work with a constantly decreasing general preparation. The average length of course of one hundred and nineteen institutions is a fraction over three years. In its character, as in that of the college of liberal arts, modern thought has forced some noticeable modifications. Modern theology, modern theism, and anti-theistic theories, occupy a large place, with something of the philosophic relations of Christianity to science and comparative cosmogonies. The course in Harvard includes the history, methods, and principles of biblical interpretation; comparative studies in Vedic religions, Hindoo philosophies, Buddhism, Mazdaism, and Chinese religions; the psychological basis of religious faith and its content; and ethics, in a study of such social questions as public charity, labor, prisons, temperance, divorce, and the treatment of the Indians. And yet there are fields of investigation and discovery in pagan experience, and pagan cosmogonies, and pagan myths; plant and animal worship ; blood covenants and the vicarious sacrifices of primitive peoples, with large possibilities in the newer development of anthropological and contemporary social science, which would seem to contribute to any rational study of the Christian religion, but which are usually omitted from the professional preparation.

2. Legal Education.

If a fairly comprehensive elementary education, generally diffused, is fundamental to a free people, not less material is it that there be generous provision for the profoundest and freest discipline in law and government. Failure in this is suicidal. The profession is large and increasing. Its members have been a ruling factor in shaping both constitution and law. From the presidential office, through both Houses of Congress, the Cabinet, State Legislatures, and administrative departments, State and Federal, a majority of the incumbents have been of this class. For the safe exercise of such function is demanded a broad and liberal preparation. Questions of government are to be studied at first hand; institutions in their genesis; social law and custom; historical and comparative studies in legislation and judicature. Familiarity with economic forces and political questions—the conditions and interests in concrete, which underlie all legislation and administration as well, is indispensable. But all this is needed for the lawyer as such. Whatever culture makes him wiser to frame laws, rationalizes his practice as a jurist and at the bar.

Here as elsewhere the sphere of interest has been greatly enlarged in fifty years. Anthropology and institutional history and ethics can not be ignored. In a recent address before the Yale Law Club, David Dudley Field, after insisting that there is something more for a lawyer to do than to

learn what is contained in Kent's "Commentaries," said:*
"Population increases; the wants and industries of the people increase also; developments occur on all sides, more
often in the right direction, sometimes in the wrong; and
we who are affected by them have to see to it that we forward and guide the one, while we hinder or arrest the other;
I say we have to see to it. We, all of us, the lawyer in his
sphere, the citizen who is not a lawyer in his."

It would be satisfying to know that the average formal
training of the lawyer covered so large a field. That it does
not, requires no special training to see. The profession has
not wholly lost the "scholastic fondness for verbal subtleties,
puerilities, and refinements which obscure sound reasoning."

Of the highest ideas of "fitting for the bar," current at
successive periods, the data are wanting for any connected
study. Enough, however, is known to indicate the line of
development. In the United States two courses have been
open to the prospective lawyer. These correspond to the
apprentice and technical methods of learning a trade. The
one belongs to the office, the other to the school. The one
emphasizes the practice, the other the principle. Against
the thought is too often set the form. The office service,
viewed pedagogically, is not without its advantages. It involves the principle, so familiar to teachers, of "learning by
doing." Besides there is a wholesome economy in seeing
half-understood theory put into daily practice by a master.
To have grown into a knowledge of law, under no formal
lessons, but in daily contact with Kent or Story or Marshall,
were better than four years at Harvard or Columbia. But
not every lawyer is a jurist, and many offices are shops. To
know the practice only is scarcely professional. Ability to
reproduce legal forms—though necessary—is a small part of
legal knowledge.

From an early day in our national history, there were not

* Quoted with comments in the "American Law Review," February,
1888, p. 58.

wanting those who saw the need of a better preparation than
is possible to an apprentice or lawyer's clerk. Chancellor
Kent, the distinguished jurist, and professor in Columbia
College, delivered successive courses of lectures as early as
1796; and Judge Wilson, in the College of Philadelphia, six
years earlier (1790–'91). A kind of private school, at which
lectures were given by one Timothy Reeves, had been opened
at Litchfield, Connecticut, 1784. The lectures however, were
few, desultory, with no attempt at a logical treatment, and
very inadequate. Later (1798), Judge Gould became associated with him, and the school is said to have been continued
for more than thirty years, and to have been the first successful one in the United States. In the first years following
the Revolution, the ranks of lawyers were rapidly filled and
extended. A generation before, ambitious young men had
prosecuted their legal studies in England. Independence
once established, intercourse with Europe was less frequent.
An English work of 1790 affirms that there were three hundred practicing lawyers in Connecticut; and that in New
York State and the North "lawyers swarmed." Burke had
said, fifteen years before, that "nearly as many of Blackstone's 'Commentaries' had been sold in America as in
England." Office pupilage, and a year in Blackstone, were
the order of the day.

The first school inaugurated after the beginning of the
century, and the earliest of those still in existence, was that
of the University of Maryland, founded 1812. (At this time
there were seven medical schools in the States, one of which
had been in existence nearly half a century.) The Maryland experiment was followed (1815) by a professorship at
Harvard, which two years later was dignified by the name,
if not the appointments, of a "school." Private enterprise
in a Yale graduate had maintained, for a quarter of a century, a law-school in New Haven, to which students came
from the adjoining States; and which, in the year 1824, at
the instance of President Dwight, was recognized and incorporated as a part of Yale College.

The particular achievement, though, with which the present consideration is concerned, coming within the first half of the century, is the founding of the University of Virginia. It opened (1825) with eight independent schools, in which law was co-ordinated with medicine, philosophy, science, the languages, and mathematics. This was the most progressive step of the period, and did much throughout the States to confer upon the profession its rightful dignity. Of others in the same period there were the Law School of Cincinnati College (1833), and departments in Emory College, Georgia, (1837), Indiana University (1840), Cumberland University, Tennessee (1847), and the University of Mississippi (1848); perhaps a dozen institutions in all, with an aggregate of four hundred students. There were even fewer colleges giving serious attention to history or political science, and none, if the work of Lieber be excepted, to the constitution and functions of government, and the nature of civil rights, as the basis of legal study. And yet the period was rich in the seeds sown for the generations. Story was in Harvard, and Thomas R. Dew in William and Mary. The "Commentaries" of Kent had been published, and, scarcely less important in their legal aspect, the "Hermeneutics" of Lieber, his "Political Ethics," and "Civil Liberty and Self-Government."

Within the next ten years the number of institutions was almost doubled: in 1872 there were thirty schools, reporting two thousand students. One impulse to this larger activity is to be found in the establishment of more thorough courses in Columbia College and Michigan University, both in the same year (1858), and both regenerative, if not revolutionary. This may be taken as the beginning of the more systematic and comprehensive and scientific study of law in the United States. The stand then taken by these two institutions has given them an enviable record, and commends the severer standards of legal fitness. Their prosperity has been constant, the two schools including at present nearly twenty-five per cent of all the law students in the United States.*

Concerning the legal profession as a representative of a liberal culture, a study of the records of forty-five schools reveals certain unwelcome truths. Very few institutions impose any scholastic conditions for entrance; fewer yet provide a graded course of instruction—either lectures or reading—or, even indirectly, give any marked encouragement to graduate study in the profession.

Of the first of these points, a recent correspondent in the "American Law Register" says that, of twenty-three law-schools interrogated, " eleven do have some sort of entrance examinations." Most of them, however, must be very meager. To the Law School of Columbia College candidates for a degree may—(1) present diplomas of graduation from some reputable college, and be admitted without examination; (2) present a certificate of having satisfactorily passed the regents' examination; or (3) take the formal entrance examination, which includes (a) history—Greek, Roman, English, and United States; (b) grammar, rhetoric, and composition; (c) Latin—Cæsar's Gallic War entire, six books of Virgil's Æneid, and six orations of Cicero. Michigan has similar requirements, and Iowa since 1885. Harvard imposed an entrance examination in 1877 ; an act which had the effect, says President Eliot, "to increase the proportion of college graduates." Yale had examined for admission, two years before. Other institutions, as the University of Kansas, recommend candidates to take a course of general culture, but have no established conditions for entrance. Of the students in the Harvard Law School from sixty-five to seventy per cent have taken academic degrees, in the University of Georgia sixty-six per cent. Columbia fifty-three per cent, Boston University forty-four per cent, and Albany Law School forty per cent. But these are supe-

---

* Seven hundred and thirty-seven, out of an aggregate of three thousand one hundred and eighty-five, reported to the Bureau of Education.

rior—the average for 1886-'87, of fifty institutions, was but
twenty-one per cent.

Referring again to the statistical article in the "Law Register," it was claimed that nineteen institutions have made
some attempt at grading the courses of study—requiring certain subjects to be taken in course and before others specified.
In no other class of professional or academic work has so
little effort been made to co-ordinate the parts, or arrange
and present them with an eye to their logical or economic
sequence. In the last decade, however, something has been
accomplished. Harvard since 1877 has had a three years'
course, the first two years of which are elective, and Michigan University a full graded and prescribed course since 1886.
In both the last and at Columbia the work covers two years;
but at the latter each year is complete in itself, and recognizes
almost no necessary sequence of subjects.

3. Medical Education.

In its relation to general knowledge, the attitude of
medicine is unique. As a profession it is pre-eminently the
scientific one ; it stands close to physical Nature, and concerns the material interests of man. It is one of the oldest,
and yet, of all the professions, its practice is most empirical.
Few callings have wider contributing fields of thought, or
are richer in the conclusions of modern inquiry. That the
profession has vastly profited by the general advance, is evident upon a superficial investigation only—how much less
than it should, appears from the insufficient and hasty
courses in its schools.

As the earliest practice of medicine was non-professional, so
the first instruction was private. In this, as in colonial times,
theology, and in law even yet, the apprenticeship system has
been widely prevalent. With few physicians, no schools,
an undeveloped chemistry, and biology unknown, medicine
was chiefly a practice, and but imperfectly either a science
or a profession. Successful practitioners everywhere drew
about them would-be doctors. Pupilage was common. Emi-

nent men sometimes had students from the adjacent colonies. These provisional courses of reading were followed by a certificate, and so the ranks of the profession recruited and enlarged. Sometimes, also, formal indentures were practiced, the English period of seven years being served.

As early as the year 1745 one Dr. Thomas Cadwallader, of Philadelphia, gave his students, and a few others who joined them, more formal and systematic and complete instruction in anatomy than was usual. A few years later, similar training was to be had in Newport, Rhode Island, and just prior to the Revolution, in a dozen or more colonial towns and cities. By the middle of the century, also, dissection as a means of instruction was employed in New York city. All this, of course, was only a temporary expedient. It was individual and local. Text-book anatomy, with rare exceptions, the compounding of medicines and an occasional attendance at the treatment of a " special case," comprised the whole education of many early physicians. It is not strange that the thoughts of the best practitioners were soon turned to some more efficient means of professional training. The problem was not a simple one.

The University of Pennsylvania, founded in 1749, and chartered a few years later, was already in a prosperous condition. In the year 1765, five of the twenty-four trustees being themselves physicians, the growing demand for medical instruction was warmly approved by the board, and in that year was elected the first medical professor to fill the new chair, " The Theory and Practice of Physic." This, it should be remembered, was twenty years before the first theological seminary, and almost half a century before the oldest of existing law-schools. There was neither time for specialization nor means ; and the department covered the subjects now requiring, in the same institution, fifty professors. The first permanent hospital for the sick had been opened some years before, in the same city ; and in 1768 King's College founded a medical " school," which had a half-century's doubtful success, and closed. Harvard organized a similar department in 1783 (a generation before the other professional courses) ; Dartmouth in 1797 ; and the University of Maryland three years later. During the same year also (1800) was established the first pronounced special· ization, and the only institution of the period, with specific provision for instruction in surgery—" The College of Physicians and Surgeons of New York City." It initiated a new period in medical training.

With the opening of the year 1811, the department of Columbia College being discontinued, there remained, as the net result of almost fifty years' experience, five institutions, with an aggregate attendance of six hundred and fifty students, two thirds of whom were in the University of Pennsylvania. The population of the country was about seven millions. From all these institutions, six hundred applicants had received the degree and been admitted to practice. Prior to the Revolution, it has been estimated that there were four hundred physicians, not more than fifty of whom had the sanction of colonial schools, and fewer still of English training. The improvement was very great, and had been almost wholly accomplished in a single generation.

In the next quarter of a century, five other colleges, including Yale, established departments, and in six States independent medical colleges were founded. The spirit of expansion and reorganization was upon this as upon all other phases of education. In the seventeen years from 1837 to 1853, twenty-five new schools were set on foot ; and, in the period since, the multiplication has been almost fourfold. There are now one hundred and seventy-five institutions (including dentistry and pharmacy) out of two hundred that have been attempted, representing thirty-two States (Delaware, Nevada, New Jersey, Rhode Island, Texas, and West Virgina reporting none). More than one third of the institutions are in the four States of New York, Ohio, Illinois, and Pennsylvania; one fourth of them are in the South. The ten cities—Baltimore, Boston, Chicago, Cincinnati, Louisville, New York, Philadelphia, St. Louis, San Francisco, and Washington—contain half of them.

The specializations also mark another significant change. The one all-inclusive professorship of 1765 has developed into dental, pharmaceutical, and veterinary courses, besides the schools of medicine and surgery; the latter appearing as allopathic, homœopathic, eclectic, and physio-medical—half of all the schools and sixty-three per cent of the students being "regulars."

Concerning the course of study, almost no uniformity exists, either of opinion or practice. In length it varies from two to six years, of from sixteen to forty weeks each. Eighteen institutions report one course only, and one hundred and twenty-nine but two courses.

The conditions for admission are not more encouraging. It can scarcely be regarded as a "learned profession," in the sense of being founded upon a liberal general scholarship. Less than eight per cent of the more than sixteen thousand medical students have previously taken any academic degree. In respect to this, it stands lowest among the professions; and it is a change earnestly to be desired that the efforts of Michigan and Harvard, and certain other institutions in Philadelphia and New York, to increase the requirements, should be successful. Within the last quarter of a century, also, something has been done toward grading the medical course, by Northwestern University at Chicago, Michigan, and elsewhere. That medical instruction should follow some systematic plan, such as governs in all other study, need scarcely be urged. The steady, vigorous growth and popularity of institutions that have such requirements would seem to recommend its more general adoption.

But the most important changes are those taking place in the subject-matter of the course itself—in the occasional introduction of certain correlative branches. Primarily, more attention is being given to the history of medicine, both its practice and philosophy. Small beginnings have been made in psycho-physical studies also, and the pathology of mind and general biology; and it appears as if, along with abundant clinical advantages, and a well-used dissecting-room, the medical college of the future will require large general and special laboratory facilities.

Post-graduate and polyclinic schools also mark an advance on previous years. Seven such schools are reported—two each in Chicago, New York, and Philadelphia, and one in St. Louis—where opportunities are afforded for advanced and special study. In this department the University of Pennsylvania offers thirteen courses.

Bibliography.

"On the Education of Ministers," Dr. F. L. Patton, "Princeton Review," May, 1883; "Ministerial Education in the Methodist Episcopal Church," S. M. Vail, 1883; "Medical Education," "Proceedings of the New York University Convocation," 1885, p. 291; "Medical Education," "Science," March, 1888, p. 103; "Medical Education and Medical Colleges in the United States and Canada" (1765–1885), "Report of the Illinois State Board of Health," 1885; the "Physician of To-day and of the Future," "Yale Review," December, 1887; the "History of Medical Education in the United States," N. S. Davis, 1876; "Legal Education, its Aim and Method" (pamphlet), G. B. Finch, 1885; "A Century of Law in America," G. T. Bispham, "North American Review," 1876; the "Learned Professions in America," "Chambers's Journal," vol. xli, p. 6.

CHAPTER XIII.

TECHNOLOGICAL EDUCATION.

THE three professions named, it has been said, were called "liberal" because "they require the utmost perfection of character in their members; and because, as devotees of religion, law, and medicine, they have in all ages pursued them as freemen, with hands unfettered and tongue untied, subject to no bonds except those of truth." Whether this be true, it

15

expresses a common sentiment, and the idea does not seem to have occurred to most minds that "there is a score of occupations, professional in the fullest, and practical in the most literal sense outside of those called learned, in which a careful scientific education opens the door to the highest usefulness and success." *   Technological instruction, regarded in its general scope, is not more practical than professional. Viewed from the standpoint of society, its organic laws studied, and looked at in its civic and State conservative relations, the technology of industry becomes more than a trade. From the standpoint of the individual, its pursuit requires all the perfection of character, all the devotion to truth, and freedom from restraint and bias, ascribed to students and practitioners in law, medicine, and theology. Both in influence and dignity it has vastly appreciated in a generation. It is assuming the professional aspect.

The nomenclature of industrial education is not a little confusing. "Technology," says a standard and recently revised "Cyclopædia of Science," "is a term invented to express a treatise on grammar." In the "American Cyclopædia" it is made to include the "principles of science as applied or related to the industrial arts." The term "industrial" itself is no less obscure. Now it is referred to manual-labor schools; again, to trades. A recent magazine article confines the term to shop-schools. It is not unfrequently made coextensive with agriculture. According to the "Cyclopædia of Education," it includes any course in which are taught one or several branches of industry. It is a matter of history that industrial schools were formerly, in England, institutions founded and supported by the Government, as "reformatory agencies for young offenders." Sixteen contemporary reformatory institutions in the United States. bear the same name. In a recent most admirable article, "Industrial Art Education" is used to comprise every sort of school subor-

---

* S. T. Wallis, in "Johns Hopkins University in its Relation to Baltimore."

dinating science to art or industry, from veterinary colleges and schools of commerce and forestry to schools of textile design, metal-working, and invention. Art itself means to one, skill ; to another, industrial achievement ; to a third, invention; to a fourth, painting or sculpture. The earliest manual-labor institutes were farms; now they may include any work but farming. The few exceptions are of an earlier foundation, and only serve to confirm the statement.

At the bottom of technical training is a mastery of the principles of science in their relation to productive and administrative art. Mr. J. Scott Russell, from the standpoint of his own countrymen, has phrased it as "that which shall render an English artilleryman a better artilleryman than a Frenchman; an English soldier a better soldier than a Prussian; an English locomotive-builder better than a German; an English ship-builder better than an American; an English silk-manufacturer better than a Lyons silk-manufacturer; and an English ribbon-maker superior to a Swiss ribbon-maker." It is the perfecting of man on the creative side. And in so far as this spirit takes on the character of universality, technology becomes professional.

In a historical treatment of the subject, much appears that is in no sense professional, is local and transient; but which belongs to the development of the impulse, and explains the current interest. It was antecedent to, because the logical ground of, the more scientific study of recent years.

1. The Beginnings of Industrial Training.

One of the first manifestations of the new industrialism in the first half of the present century was the inauguration of the manual-labor seminaries. Among these were the Rensselaer School, New York (1824), and the Fellenberg Institute, at Windsor, Connecticut. Within ten years the experiment had been tried in a dozen States. It was proposed to combine literary instruction with manual labor, sharing the day between them, and afford students the means of

wholly or partially meeting their expenses. Of this character were the Oneida Institute, the Genesee Manual Labor
School, and the Yates Polytechnic, of New York, all founded
before 1830, and a dozen or more in Illinois, out of one of
which Knox College took its rise. Franklin College, Indiana, was first a manual-labor organization, as were others in
Michigan and adjoining States. Though many of these
efforts to promote industry in connection with literary institutions failed, and most of the schools were closed or reorganized as academies, they served a double and worthy
purpose: the function of intelligent labor was magnified,
and the seed sown for a more fruitful harvest. For how
much of the idea of technical education in agriculture and
the mechanic arts the present is indebted to these institutions, can not perhaps be determined. Enough is known to
suggest that the obligation must be large.

The Rensselaer School (1824) had, for that day extensive
laboratory advantages in chemistry and physics, and taught
the analysis of soils, fertilizers, minerals, and animal and
vegetable matter, with their applications to agriculture, domestic economy, and the arts; and as early as 1835 had a
department for instruction in engineering and technology.
Its influence throughout has been bracing and intelligent,
and it deserves abundant honor as the pioneer in the United
States in a much-needed culture. Among its hundreds of
alumni, to name only two, are S. Edward Warren, of the
Massachusetts Institute of Technology, and the late Washington A. Roebling, chief-engineer of the great East River
(New York) suspension-bridge.

Next to the institutions named, and generally of a more
technical character, were the three or four military academies of forty to sixty years ago. The United States Military
and Naval Schools, the Military Institute of Virginia, and
the South Carolina Military Academy, all founded before
1846, offered even then the best training for ordinary engineering and mechanical pursuits to be had in this country.
Indeed, the only other institutions of the period, pretending

to give such instruction, were the University of Virginia, whose course in science, however, for twenty years after its founding meant little more than chemistry; Norwich University, Vermont; and the Franklin Institute, Philadelphia. To these should be added, perhaps, the school of civil engineering first established (1846) at Union College, under Prof. W. M. Gillespie.

In the fifteen years following, and covering the period up to the national land grant of 1861, twelve other institutions were founded having pronounced scientific aims. Six of these were special schools, independent organizations of well-defined purpose, and the first considerable approach to the true technical institution. These were the Spring Garden Institute, the Wagner Free Institute, and the School of Design for Women, all of Philadelphia; and the O'Fallon Polytechnic Institute, established ten years later in connection with Washington University, St. Louis.

Supplementing these special schools or technological institutions, perhaps logically antecedent to and sometimes chronologically antedating them, are the fixed and more or less independent scientific departments of the older and better endowed collegiate schools. It has been seen that the university curriculum in a century has greatly changed. From the single classical course of the colonial school to the present aggregation of studies the steps have been both many and slow. It took Harvard half a century to accept a chair of Chemistry, the Erving professorship (1783) being the first formal recognition by an American college of the broad field of natural science. Yale (1802) appointed Prof. Benjamin Silliman to a like position. The Massachusetts professorship of Natural History was added to Harvard about the same time, and the Rumford chair of the "Application of Science to the Useful Arts," ten years later, marking the only advance for a quarter of a century. The impulse, however, was being felt for a more generous recognition of science. Silliman and Prof. Olmsted, in Yale, Prof. Amos Eaton in the Rensselaer school, the Connecticut and American Academies of

Arts and Sciences, and the Philadelphia Academy of Natural Science, were all so many agencies to magnify the importance and service of acquaintance with natural phenomena and their laws.

In 1846 Yale instituted two new professorships, one in agricultural chemistry, and the other in practical or applied chemistry; and the year following the corporation of Harvard voted to establish in the university an advanced school of instruction in theoretical and applied science, and in the other usual branches of academic learning, to be called the "Scientific School of the University of Cambridge." The two developed into the Sheffield and Lawrence Scientific Schools of Yale and Harvard respectively.

Union College (since 1873, Union University), New York, chartered (1795), has for more than forty years maintained a course called the " School of Civil Engineering." Except the Rensselaer Polytechnic, this was apparently the only institution providing instruction in civil engineering, until the Lehigh University, founded and generously endowed by Asa Packer in 1868. The "School of Mines," Columbia College, established four years before, perhaps included civil engineering as one of its subordinate courses. Besides these, the University of Missouri (1871), Ohio University (1879), and the University of Wisconsin (1881), provided instruction in mining and metallurgy. Kindred courses or departments are sustained in a number of the agricultural and mechanical colleges, the Colorado School of Mines, etc.

The Chandler Scientific School of Dartmouth College grew out of a bequest of fifty thousand dollars (1851) for the establishment of a school of instruction in the college " in the practical and useful arts of life." It includes mechanical and civil engineering, and provides that " no other or higher preparatory studies shall be required for entrance than are pursued in the common schools of New England." This aims to turn out intelligent workmen. On the contrary, the School of Technology of Lehigh University has a five years' course, has chemical laboratories said to be unsurpassed in this country, and sets forth as its object the fitting of foremen and superintendents, rather than workmen of manual dexterity and skill in the use of tools. The Towne Scientific School (1872) of the University of Pennsylvania, similar to others in general, differs in the recent provisions made for instruction in "marine engineering and naval architecture." The Pardee Scientific Department of Lafayette College, Pennsylvania, the Scientific School of the University of California, and the John C. Greene School of Science in Princeton, all deserve mention, both for their excellent work and their contributions to the solution of current technologico-industrial problems.

The Case School of applied Science (1877), Cleveland, Ohio, and the Sibley School of Cornell University, are excellent examples of the two classes of technological agencies — independent schools and university departments, well endowed, and with a purpose to fit for the highest service in science and the arts.

2. The Curriculum.

Though homogeneous in the scientific principles involved, the instruction as to its applications is very diverse. Upon this fact rests the most hopeful promise of the present tendency. A few things well taught, a grounding in the principles of abstract science, knowledge of and skill in the most comprehensive applications, open the way for indefinite developments.

Without attempting an exhaustive, or a strictly logical classification, it may be said that technical training, as represented in the institutions of the United States, appears as agriculture in forty-seven of them ; mechanical art in fifty-six ; architecture, including naval and military, in sixteen ; metallurgy specified in seventeen; and engineering, eighty-nine (civil, fifty-four ; mining, thirty ; electrical, five).

Of the eighty-six institutions prominently identified with advanced technological work, twenty-eight, or about one third, are provided with shops for instruction in practical mechanics. The great significance of this fact appears in the statement that two thirds of these (twenty-eight) institutions have been founded within the last twenty years, and most of the practice schools even later.

Supplementary, also, to these courses are thirty-seven schools of instruction in art and design ; a dozen or more manual training schools ; either public and free, as in Toledo, Baltimore, Boston, New York, and Philadelphia ; endowed, as the Miller Manual Labor School, Crozet, Virginia, and the Manual Training School of Washington University, St. Louis ; or private and maintained by tuition, as in Chicago, Cincinnati, and Cleveland ; several industrial organizations (forty to fifty), of the nature of " homes," " reformatories," " orphanages," " Indian schools," etc. ; besides more or less of like work in the elementary grades of public schools in the larger cities,* and a very satisfactory introduction to it all in the constructive habit born of the Kindergarten.

Most of the schools include two or more of the courses named. Delaware College ; Cornwallis College, Oregon; four of the six institutions in Georgia ; the Storrs Agricultural School, Mansfield, Connecticut; the Agricultural College, Brookings, South Dakota; and the Massachusetts School at Amherst, are almost wholly given to agriculture and immediately related subjects. Colorado has a special school of mines, and the technological instruction of the Western University of Pennsylvania, of Syracuse University, the University of the City of New York, and Union College, is practically confined to civil engineering. A few schools are really polytechnic : such as the Massachusetts Institute of Technology, the Worcester Polytechnic School, the O'Fallon Institute of St. Louis, the School of Technology, Lehigh University, the Cornell College of Agriculture and Mechanic

---

* Jamestown, New York, is a good illustration of what may be accomplished in this direction in any town if sensibly undertaken. The manual of Superintendent Love is suggestive of thoughtful training.

Arts, and Rose Polytechnic Institute, Indiana. The Columbia College School of Mines, the John C. Greene School of Science, and the Universities of Wisconsin and Minnesota, comprehend most forms of engineering. Cornell and Yale, the Industrial University of Illinois, and the State Agricultural Colleges of Indiana, Kansas, Kentucky, Minnesota, Missouri, Ohio, and Oregon, have more or less complete courses in forestry ; and by a few institutions are taught veterinary science, domestic economy, telegraphy, printing, etc.

Of the thirty-seven schools of design, one half have for their leading purpose the promotion of the industrial arts, as architecture, engineering and manufactures; most of them include something of the fine arts, a dozen of them such instruction only. The Massachusetts Art Normal School is a training-school for teachers of industrial drawing. This was founded under the direction of Prof. Walter Smith, than whom it is safe to say no individual has done more for the higher industrial interests of the country ; and was doubtless inspired by the profound conviction, then becoming general, that at the bottom of all this work—the alphabet of technical training—is thorough instruction in drawing, fixing habits of invention and construction. The Massachusetts law of 1869, authorizing free instruction in mechanical drawing in the cities and large towns, the employment of Prof. Smith as Superintendent of Drawing in Boston the year following, its introduction into twenty-two other cities almost immediately, Prof. Smith's State directorship, and the establishment of the State Normal Art School (Boston, 1875), mark the beginning of an intelligent interest in drawing in the United States. It had already (1869) been put into the public schools of Cincinnati and Syracuse, and within ten years appeared on most of the programmes in the larger cities of the country. In a recent report on drawing made to the National Educational Association (1884), of seventy cities giving information, sixty-seven make it compulsory along with other branches. About half of them have special supervision, the work graded and extended into the high-school. It forms a part of the regular course of instruction, also, in one hundred and eleven of the one hundred and twenty-four public normal schools of the country.

Concerning the manual-training school there are two widely different views. The one insists that it shall teach no trade, but the rudiments of all of them; the other that the particular industries may properly be held to maintain schools to recruit their own ranks. The first would teach the use of the axe, the saw, the plane, the hammer, the square, the chisel, and the file; claiming that " the graduate from such a course at the end of three years is within from one to three months of knowing quite as thoroughly as an apprentice who had served seven years any one of the twenty trades to which he may choose to turn." Of this class are, besides most of those already named, the Haish Manual Training School of Denver; that of Tulane University, New Orleans; the Felix Adler's Workingman's School, of New York City; and the School of Manual Technology, Vanderbilt University, Nashville.

Among schools of the second class are some interesting institutions. They include the numerous general and special trade-schools for boys, instruction in the manifold phases of domestic economy for girls, and the yet small but rapidly growing class of industries open alike to both.

Sewing is taught in public or private schools in Baltimore, Boston, Cincinnati, Chicago, New York, Philadelphia, Providence, St. Louis, and about a dozen other cities, besides in a number of special institutions.

Cooking-schools are no longer a novelty in half as many of the larger cities, since their introduction into New York city in 1876. Printing may be learned in the Kansas Agricultural College ; Cooper Union, New York ; Girard College, Philadelphia, and elsewhere. Telegraphy, stenography, wood-engraving, various kinds of smithing, and carpentry, have, especially the last two, numerous representatives. The

New York Kitchen Garden, for the instruction of children
in the work of the household, is an interesting modification
of the Kindergarten along the industrial line. For young
ladies, the Elizabeth Aull Seminary, Lexington, Missouri, is
a school of home-work, in which "are practically taught
the mysteries of the kitchen and laundry," and upon whose
graduates is conferred the degree of "Mistress of Home-
Work." The Lasell Seminary at Auburndale, Massachusetts,
also has recently (1885) undertaken a similar but more comprehensive experiment, including lessons and lectures in
anatomy and physiology, with hygiene and sanitation, the
principles of common law by an eminent attorney, instruction and practice in the arts of domestic life, the principles
of dress, artistic house-furnishing, healthy homes, and
cooking.

Of training-schools for nurses there are thirty-one, distributed through twelve States and the District of Columbia.
New York has eleven ; Massachusetts, five ; Pennsylvania,
three; Connecticut and New Jersey, each two; and Illinois,
Indiana, Minnesota, Missouri, Rhode Island, South Carolina, Vermont, and the District of Columbia, one each.

Of schools of a different character still, there have been
or are the Carriage-Builders' Apprenticeship School, New
York; those of Hoe & Co., printing-press manufacturers; and
Tiffany & Co., jewelers ; and the Tailors' "Trades School "
recently established and flourishing in Baltimore, besides the
Pennsylvania Railroad novitiate system, at Altoona ; in
which particular trades or guilds or corporations have
sought to provide themselves with a distinct and specially
trained class of artisans.   The latest and in some respects the
most interesting experiment of the kind is that of the "Baltimore and Ohio Railroad service " at Mt. Clare, Baltimore.
It was inaugurated in 1885, apprentices being selected from
applicants by competitive examination.

It was a technological school, whose instruction primarily comprised the various phases of railroading, but was prepared for, and supplemented by, drill in geometry, algebra,

physics, locomotive - engineering, mechanics, mechanical drawing, free-hand drawing, geometrical drawing, English, and history.

3. Agricultural Education.

Of all the institutions for investigating and realizing the applications of science to the arts, the most prominent in recent years have been the agricultural schools founded under the congressional Land Grant Act of 1862.

The Legislature of Michigan in 1850 instructed their delegates to Congress to ask three hundred and fifty thousand acres of land for the establishment of agricultural schools in their State. In a generation twelve new States had been formed; and the center of population had moved westward one hundred and fifty miles. Large developments in industry were taking place in the Mississippi Valley. The section was predominantly agricultural. Wealth lay in the right tilling of the soil. This great and newly recognized need of the country for intelligence in farming soon became matter of common discussion. It was an era of farmers' societies, agricultural conventions, etc. Following the legislative and general interest in Michigan,* Illinois the next year held at Granville an "Industrial Convention," inviting those engaged in agricultural and mechanical pursuits. The burden of discussion was the lack and need of industrial education; and a resolution was passed urging the "immediate establishment of a university to meet the wants of the industrial classes." A second convention was held in June of the following year at Springfield, and a third at Chicago a few months later, at which the nature and organization of such institution were discussed. one committee appointed to digest a plan, and another to petition Congress, through the State

---

* A comprehensive discussion of the value of agricultural colleges, as seen at that early day, and valuable bits of history, both of the Michigan institutions and of the attempts made in other States, may be had in the "Reports of the Michigan Schools," under Superintendent Ira Mayhew, 1885-'88.

Legislature, for the needed lands "*for the establishment of an industrial institution in each State*, to co-operate with the Smithsonian Institution at Washington, for the more liberal and practical education of our industrial classes and their teachers."

As a result of these and similar efforts, East and West, an act of Congress was passed in 1860 appropriating certain lands for such purposes, but it was vetoed by President Buchanan.   Two years later substantially the same act was passed, which, with the sanction of President Lincoln, provided for the appropriation of lands, thirty thousand acres for each senator and representative in Congress, according to the representation of 1860.   From the privileges under this act, mineral lands were excluded ; not more than a million acres might be located in any one State ; and a share in its benefits should accrue only to those States accepting within three years after its passage, i. e., prior to July 2, 1865, or to new States within three years of their admission as States. The act further provided that all moneys derived from the sale of apportioned lands should constitute a perpetual fund, the interest only of which might be appropriated " to the endowment, support, and maintenance of at least one college " in each State, where " the leading object should be, without excluding other scientific and classical studies, and including military tactics, to teach such branches of learning as are related to agriculture and the mechanic arts, in such manner as the Legislatures of the States may respectively prescribe, in order to promote the liberal and practical education of the industrial classes, in their several pursuits and professions in life."

In course of time every State accepted the congressional offer.   Seventeen had opened institutions before 1870.   Rhode Island, Kansas, Massachusetts (in part), New Jersey, and Vermont, very early ; * Mississippi, South Carolina, and

---

* A very full report of the establishment of these first institutions may be found in the first " Report of the United States Commissioner of Education," Hon. Henry Barnard, 1867-'68, pp. 133-309.

Georgia (in part), since 1880. There are now forty-eight schools operating under the act. In most of the States South, the institutions founded have been opened since 1870 ; Tennessee, Virginia (at Hampton), and Kentucky only, beginning before that time. Massachusetts, Mississippi, Missouri, Virginia, and South Carolina, have each two schools. In Georgia the fund was divided among six institutions. In twenty-two States the instruction required is provided by State colleges or universities. The other institutions are independent schools of science. Twenty-four of the forty-eight institutions admit women on equal terms with men.

The whole area of land appropriated was nine million six hundred thousand acres. Not all of it has been sold, but the amounts realized aggregate something over seven million dollars, an average endowment to each State of nearly two hundred thousand dollars. Almost as much, however, has been received from other sources ; about six million dollars from individual benefactions. Two thirds of the schools have experimental farms,* averaging about three hundred acres each.

Mr. Scott Russell concludes that the complete agricultural school should teach technically the following subjects and their immediate applications to the business of farming, in both its fixed and commercial aspects : 1. Surface geology; 2. Anatomical botany ; 3. Physiology ; 4. Agricultural chemistry ; 5. Comparative anatomy ; 6. Animal physiology ; 7. Veterinary medicine and surgery ; 8. Land-surveying ; 9. Leveling ; 10. Practical mechanics ; 11. Agricultural economy and plans ; 12. Agricultural geography; 13. Theoretical mechanics ; 14. Elements of mechanism ; 15. Technical botany. Alongside of this ideal and admirable course are presented two actual courses as they are

---

* An act of Congress approved March, 1887, provides for an annual appropriation " to establish agriculture experiment stations in connection with the colleges " established under the above-named act.

followed in Massachusetts and Colorado. These are fairly representative of their respective sections, and illustrate the work under widely differing conditions.

Massachusetts.	*Colorado.*
Freshman year :	Freshman year :
Chemistry.	
Human physiology.	
Botany.	Botany.
Agriculture.	
Algebra.	Algebra.
Geometry.	Geometry.
Drawing.	Drawing.
English.	English.
French.	
	Book-keeping.
	History.
Sophomore year :	Sophomore year :
Geology.	
Zoölogy.	Zoölogy.
Botany.	Horticulture.
Agriculture.	Agriculture.
Surveys and leveling.	Surveys and leveling.
Geometry.	Geometry.
Trigonometry.	Trigonometry.
Drawing.	Drawing.
History.	History.
English.	English.
French.	
	Chemistry.
	Physics.
	Mechanics.
Junior year :	Junior year :
Practical chemistry.	Agricultural chemistry.
Entomology.	Entomology.

Junior year :

Physics.
Horticulture and gardening.
Stock and dairy.
Mechanics.
Astronomy.
Drawing.
Roads and railroads.
Agricultural debate.
German.

Junior year :

Physics.
Horticulture.

English.

Physiology.
Meteorology.

Senior year :

Practical chemistry.
Microscopy.
Botany.
Agriculture.
Landscape-gardening.
Veterinary science.
Roads and railroads.
Rural law.
Book-keeping.
History.

English.
Mental science.

Senior year :

Botany.

Landscape-gardening.
Veterinary science.

United States Constitution,
and political economy.

Mental science; logic; ethics.
Stock-breeding.
Shop mechanics.
Astronomy.
Domestic economy.

With a general correspondence, especially in the first
two years, there is considerable divergence, growing out of
the different social and commerical and physical surroundings, very natural from a pedagogical point of view, and
suggestive of intelligent control.

4. Military and Naval Education.

The need for trained soldiers and seamen was early felt in this country. The War for Independence had been a school of tactics. Its heroes were the country's teachers. The war closed, their influence was still held for the maintenance of some school which, in the words of Washington, should keep the nation " supplied with an adequate stock of military knowledge."

Although the Military Academy was formally instituted at West Point, in 1802, the idea was poorly appreciated. It was a school in name only, and scarcely military. It had little system, because no purpose. Following the second war with England, it was reorganized, a course of study devised, and its discipline prescribed much as it remains to-day. The conditions of admission which then required only that the candidate be " well versed in reading, writing, and arithmetic," now include in addition a knowledge of the elements of English grammar, descriptive geography, particularly of our own country, and the history of the United States. The new course of study, besides English grammar, geography, and history, each occupying one year, was made to include also two years of French, algebra, geometry and logarithms, geometrical constructions, mensuration, plane and spherical trigonometry, conic sections, natural and experimental philosophy, astronomy, engineering, and ethics. As will be seen, it furnished a substantial mathematical drill, and one of the earliest expansions of the curriculum on the side of science to be found in this country. It was still, however, chiefly academic, and only indirectly or secondarily contributed to the fixing of a military science. The present curriculum is more specialized, and, while affording an admirable general discipline, has a decided scientific and technological bias, and particular functions. As set forth in the official regulations (1883) it embraces :

1. Infantry, artillery, and cavalry tactics; target-practice;

16

military police and discipline; use of the sword, bayonet, and gymnastics.

2. Mathematics.

3. English, French, and Spanish languages.

4. Chemistry, chemical physics, mineralogy, geology.

5. Natural and experimental philosophy.

6. History, geography, and ethics.

7. National, international, and military law.

8. Ordnance, gunnery, and the duties of a military laboratory.

9. Practical military engineering.

10. Civil and military engineering and the science of war.

The courses in mathematics and physics are comprehensive, and, in forming the general merit roll, rank in relative value, with civil and military engineering and the science of war, the highest in the course. The subjects and their order are prescribed, and the discipline is founded upon an absolute authority. Election has no place in the four years academic or military training. The instruction from a technological standpoint, is of a high order, and commands general confidence. It was recently said by General Hazen, "After seeing much of European armies, I believe that, at the opening of our civil war, our little regular army was officered by better technical soldiers than any other army in the world—due, I believe to West Point."

The object of the institution is not civil but martial life. It is "neither metaphysical discussion nor hair-splitting argument on the law, in which the young men are expected to excel. They are to have the sterner arguments of the battle-field; to arrange squadrons for the hardy fight; to acquire that profound knowledge of the science and materials of nature, which should fit them for the complicated art of war; to defend and attack cities; to bridge rivers; to make roads; to provide armaments; to arrange munitions; to understand the topography of countries; and to foresee and provide all the resources necessary to national defense."

The number of cadets is prescribed by law, as follows:

1. One for each congressional district.
2. One for each Territory.
3. One for the District of Columbia.
4. Forty whom the President may appoint, ten each year, from the country at large. The selection is by competitive examination, and includes both physical and intellectual capacity.

After the manner of the United States Military Academy were soon established similar institutions elsewhere, under State or local or private control. The first of these was the "American Literary, Scientific, and Military Academy" at Norwich, Vermont, in 1820. Fifteen years later, two were opened at Portsmouth and Lexington, Virginia, the latter of which became the Virginia Military Institute,* is still in existence, and, next to the West Point school, the largest, and most flourishing military institution in the United States, and besides ranks high as an engineering school. In the years before the war, also, were founded the South Carolina Military Academy (1842), the Kentucky Military Institute (1845), and the Louisiana State University, which had been established upon a military basis (1860), and of which, at the breaking out of the war, General W. T. Sherman was president.

Since the last, Pennsylvania and Michigan have organized academies; and the national Government an "Artillery School" at Fortress Monroe, Virginia (1867), an "Infantry and Cavalry School" at Fort Leavenworth, Kansas (1882), and the "Artillery School" at Fort Riley, Kansas (1886). The curriculum of the last covers two years, and includes, besides literary studies, the construction and service of artillery and material, gunnery, and mathematics as applied in the artillery service, and lectures upon the organization, use, and application of artillery; the duties of artillery troops in cam-

---

* "Stonewall" Jackson was for some years a professor in this institution.

paigns and sieges; the construction of guns, carriage and other material; and upon military law and military history.*

Reference has already been made to the Morrill Land Grant Act (1862), one of whose provisions was for instruction in military tactics. The original act was amended four years later, providing for a special detail of officers of the army to give instruction in drill and tactics in the higher literary and other educational institutions of the country. Under the provisions of this act more than one hundred and fifty officers have been reported as giving instruction for longer or shorter periods in colleges in two thirds of the States.

But nautical training in the mean time has not been ignored. In this modern day of commerce and the brotherhood of races, no people can be national without being at the same time maritime. Other things equal, the strength of a people is the strength of its bond with other people. A mastery of the seas means not only power abroad, but vigor at home. If, then, domestic industry and social and professional life demand a preparation, not less a life on the sea and commerce with nations.

The United States was fifty-six years old before the first formal instruction of her seamen. The department of the navy had been created in 1798, and, in imitation of the English custom, chaplains of the ships were required to act as schoolmasters. Fifteen years after, it was ordered that each of a number of new ships should carry an instructor; but he was merely a chaplain worked over, with only a chance fitness for his position, and in no wise supported in his teaching.

Better provision was recommended (1814) by President

---

* The Government also provides instruction in the branches usually taught in the common schools, at nearly every one of the one hundred and twenty military posts in the United States. The day-school is open to all the children at the station. A night-school is usually maintained for such enlisted men as desire to attend. The teachers also are enlisted men, who are detailed for the purpose, with extra pay. (From a private letter by Chaplain George Robinson, in charge of education in the United States Army.)

Madison, as it had been before, and was afterward by others, but "the United States had not yet learned the fact," says Prof. Saley, "that a nation with a large commerce is bound to do its part in maintaining the police of the ocean." Instruction was, of course, given all these years and long after at the navy-yards or on board cruising ships. The former were at New York, Philadelphia, and Norfolk. In 1835 there were three ships which, seven years later, had thirteen instructors of mathematics alone. At the navy-yards there were twice as many. At this time Prof. Chauvenet was in charge at Philadelphia, and was a man in a thousand. He was a master, both as teacher and scholar. In 1845 George Bancroft became Secretary of the Navy. After years of compromises, the Government had found a man who was equal to the situation. He asked for no legislation. He only proposed to use the power he had and make the most of it. A school on shore was projected, whose instruction should include both theory and practice, and embrace besides academic studies, the law of commerce, marine surveying, ordnance, gunnery, and the use of steam. A half-dozen of the most efficient of his force were selected, the rest were retired, and there was opened at Annapolis, Maryland, in 1845, a school which became, under Chauvenet and others, five years later, the United States Naval Academy.

The present course includes:

1. Naval tactics and practice in seamanship.

2. Mathematics, navigation, astronomy, land and nautical surveying, and drawing.

3. Natural and experimental philosophy, mechanics, the construction and management of the steam-engine.

4. Chemistry, mineralogy, and geology.

5. Gunnery and infantry tactics.

6. Modern languages.

7. Ethics.

Besides the instruction afforded at the Naval Academy, there is also the Nautical School on board the St. Mary's vessel at Brooklyn, seventy per cent of whose five hundred graduates have become seamen, and that on the California training-ship Jamestown. The University of Michigan gives annually a course of lectures on naval architecture in which are discussed the resistance of ships, speed, buoyancy, stability, wave-motion, etc. In Massachusetts, towns are authorized by law to establish schools for training young men in nautical duties.

The Naval War College at Newport, Rhode Island, is a school of graduate instruction for officers of the navy. It was opened in 1884, with a greatly specialized but withal a comprehensive course of technical instruction in military and naval science. It embraces (1) the science and art of war; (2) law,and history. Under the first are taught (a) strategy and tactics; (b) military campaigns, (c) joint military and naval operations, (d) the management of seamen in military operations, and (e) elements of fortification and intrenchment—all from the military point of view; supplemented by (f) naval strategy and tactics, (g) naval campaigns, and (h) joint military and naval operations, from the naval standpoint. Under the second are embraced, (a) international law, (b) treaties of the United States, (c) rules of evidence, (d) general naval history, and (e) modern political history.

Bibliography.

"Scientific Schools in Europe, considered with reference to their Adaptation to America," Dr. D. C. Gilman, Barnard's "American Journal of Education," vol. ii ; "Art Education—Scholastic and Industrial," Walter Smith,1873 ; "Report on Industrial Education," Senate document, 1883 ; "Report on Technical Education in the United States and Canada," by the English Commission, 1884 ; " A New Principle in Education—Development of the Constructive Faculty," Felix Adler, "Princeton Review," 1883 ; the same reviewed and criticised in the "Presbyterian Review," January, 1884 ; "Education in its Relation to Industry," Arthur McArthur, 1884 ; "Industrial Education, a Pedagogical and Social Necessity," P. Seidel, 1887 ; "Industrial Training," "Forum," April, 1887 ; the "Progress of Industrial Education," P. C. Garrett, 1883 ; "The Modern Polytechnic School," inaugural address of Dr. C. O. Thompson, of

Rose Polytechnic Institute, 1883 ; "Technical Instruction in America," J. H. Rigg, "Contemporary Review," August, 1884 ; "Technology and Public Education," C. O. Thompson, before Michigan State Teachers' Association, 1884; "Manual Training," Charles Ham, 1886 ; "Manual Training," C. M. Woodward, 1887 ; "Manual Training," by Colonel Augustus Jacobson, "Proceedings of the National Educational Association," 1884, p. 293 ; "Manual Training," Felix Adler, ibid., p. 308 ; the "New York Trade School"; "Report of Massachusetts Board of Education, 1884 ; "Naval Education," D. D. Porter, the "United Service Magazine," July, 1879.

CHAPTER XIV.

EDUCATION OF UNFORTUNATES AND CRIMINAL CLASSES.

THE idea of education in its economic aspect, as a means of reforming the offending classes, while not new, has a larger field, and, in the different ethical standards of the time, more favorable conditions for its growth.   No intelligent person supposes that a limited education is a sure cure or prevention of crime, but that, other things equal, the advance in general intelligence means higher measures in conduct ; and the frequent reform of the viciously inclined, if taken early, may be proved by history for a hundred years.   The idea itself is not recent ; but faith in the principle such as seeks to make the regenerative influences of a right education common to all the class is altogether modern.

So also it may be said that care for the dependent classes, as charity to the unfortunate and needy, is a characteristic of recent civilization.   But other than this and indefinitely superior is the attempt to enlarge their intellectual horizon. Brotherly kindness has fed and clothed, sheltered and protected them in all ages of civilization.   But provisions for their education, not only as mental improvement, but training them to self-support, and as lifting them out of the pauper class, point to a higher and more recent interest. The blind, deaf-mutes, minor orphans, imbeciles, the insane, vagrants, and young and uncared-for offenders against society, all, speaking broadly, belong to the same non-productive class, a drain upon society, except they be given possession of their remaining powers, and a mastery of nature by patient, intelligent training.

In this class, also, are to be considered the Indians in large part, and their education in learning, industry, and the ways of civilized life.

1. Deaf-Mute Education.

Even the oldest records of teaching the deaf are recent. Among the ancients, regarded as under a curse, or idiotic, or at best so deficient in intellect as to be irresponsible, they were debarred from all civil rights. Even Blackstone held * that a man who is born deaf, dumb, and blind is to be regarded " in the same state with an idiot."

The first systematic attempt to instruct them was by Pedro Ponce de Leon, in Spain, in 1550. Seventy years after, was published a simple alphabet. By the middle of the century the system was introduced into England ; lipreading was described by a Hollander about the same time, and before 1700 the two-hand alphabet was invented. But for two centuries from the time of Ponce de Leon, the interest was wholly benevolent and individual. In 1774, at Leipsic, was opened a government school. Such American deaf-mutes as received any instruction were sent to England. In the year 1815, however, Rev. T. H. Gallaudet, a recently ordained minister in Connecticut, interested in the deaf-mute child of his neighbor, undertook her instruction. The attention of others gained, steps were taken to found an institution. Mr. Gallaudet was made director. He at once visited the schools of England and Scotland, and spent three months with Sicard in Paris. Immediately upon his return there

---

* " Commentaries," Book I, chapter viii.

was opened at Hartford "The Connecticut Asylum for the Education of Deaf and Dumb Persons." The State Legislature appropriated five thousand dollars. Private means did most. Later, Congress granted the institution twenty-three thousand acres of land, whose proceeds form a part of the present endowment, and, upon the assumption that the one institution would be sufficient to accommodate the deaf-mutes of the country at large, the name was changed to the "American Asylum for Deaf-Mutes at Hartford." But many children were found so affected, and in 1818 the New York Institution was opened as a day-school, and for several years was under the direction of the State Superintendent, as were other public shools.

Following these were established similar asylums in Pennsylvania (1821), Kentucky (1823), Ohio (1827), Illinois (1837), Virginia (1839), Indiana and Tennessee (1847), North Carolina and Georgia (1845), and South Carolina (1849)— twelve in all, in as many States, in thirty years.

There are now sixty-one institutions in thirty-five States (Delaware, Louisiana, Nevada, New Hampshire, and Vermont, arranging for the education of their deaf in adjoining States), two Territories—New Mexico, and Utah, and the District of Columbia. Eleven States have two or more each; New York has six, and Missouri four. These schools enroll in the aggregate nearly eight thousand pupils, and represent an expenditure of a million and a half of dollars. More than half of them are public institutions, and all, with perhaps half a dozen exceptions, receive State (or municipal) aid. Yet a large majority of them require tuition fees, and are so made exclusive or pauper establishments.

In deaf-mute instruction two methods are chiefly used; that of De l'Épée, the sign method, introduced by Gallaudet, and in exclusive use in this country for fifty years. It includes writing, and teaches by means of objects, gestures, and arbitrary symbols. The other is the German or articulation method, and involves lip-reading. This begins with the voicing of simple sounds, slowly and distinctly by the instructor, whose motions are carefully watched by the pupil, and afterward imitated. Other sounds follow in the inverse order of their difficulty. The method was first introduced into the United States by the Clarke Institution, Northampton, Massachusetts, in 1867. Since its successful use there it has been introduced elsewhere, noticeably, and with equal results, by the "New York School for Improved Instruction," founded soon after, by the Boston Day-School, and others.

Besides these establishments for elementary instruction, there was chartered in 1857, and opened seven years later, at Washington, in connection with the Columbian University the "National Deaf-Mute College" for advanced instruction. It offers the usual college course, and uses the same textbooks. The Iowa school also, besides the usual elementary graded courses, has advanced academic, art, and industrial departments.

Concerning industrial training it need only be said that all schools provide it in some form, and there are few positions in life which the well-taught individuals of this class may not fill to public profit as well as personal credit. The industrial exhibits of deaf-mutes at recent expositions are a monument to their skill and intelligence.*

2. Education of the Blind.

There are estimated to be about thirty thousand blind in the United States; of these, less than three thousand are reported as receiving any formal instruction. The attempt to provide for their education, while older than that of the deaf in Europe, was introduced into the United States fifteen years later. The "Hospital for the Three Hundred," founded in Paris in 1260, was only an asylum, no attempt being made at systematic mental training prior to Valentine Haüy, the "Apostle of the Blind," who in 1786 published a relief print,

---

* At New Orleans (1885) eighteen institutions made exhibits of both literary and industrial products, the latter including needlework, printing, shoemaking, carpentry, photography, drawings, and fine art.

and five years later opened a school for the blind. This, receiving the king's sanction and favor, became afterward the "Royal Institution of France," and has been followed by many others in the intervening century: first in Germany, then in Russia, England, Scotland, and the United States. To Dr. S. G. Howe—educator and philanthropist, whose name is inseparably associated with the work in the United States—belongs also the honor of its introduction. The Perkins Institution in Boston (1832) did for the blind of New England and the East what the American Asylum at Hartford acomplished for deaf-mutes. Others were immediately founded, one in New York the same year, and another in Philadelphia the year following. By the middle of the century, there were eleven. There are now thirty-two such institutions in thirty States; the blind of Connecticut, Delaware, Maine, Nevada, New Hampshire, New Jersey, Rhode Island, and Vermont, being accommodated in neighboring schools; and New York and Maryland having two institutions each.

All reputable schools of this class afford instruction in most subjects of the average curriculum of secondary institutions, including a full course in mathematics, the languages, and history, the philosophical studies, and something of natural science. To this are generally added some form of industrial training and always music. The one is given as part of the general culture which every child needs, not less than as a means to intellectual growth; the other as satisfying the peculiar need incidental to blindness.

That the industrial training called for is neither insignificant in character nor seriously restricted in variety, appears from the occupations of the educated blind.* In a late report of the United States Commissioner of Education, the following statistics are given; and, while it is not supposed that

---

* At the New Orleans Exposition the exhibit of the blind was quite remarkable. A dozen institutions in this country were represented, and twice as many forms of industry—all from children.

the list is complete in any particular, it is suggestive of the industrial importance of the class:

Occupations of the Blind.

Superintendents of institutions..	*16	Piano-tuners	125
Teachers in schools not for the		Composers and publishers of mu-	
blind	62	sic	14
Teachers of the blind	†135	Graduates from colleges	17
Ministers	36	Manufacturing	305
Studying or practicing law	5	Handicraftsmen	702
Authors	17	Merchants	269
Publishers	8	Farmers	59
Agents and lecturers	70	Newsdealers	7
General teachers of music	463	Dealers in instruments	6
Church organists	88	Horse-dealers	9

It appears that about seven hundred, or nearly one third of the whole, have to do with music—next to handicraft, the largest single interest. Education along this line is of paramount importance. It is on the side of culture and refinement and the growth of the gentler feelings, and very properly forms a part of every course.

Fundamentally, all literary training rests upon the ability to read. Two principal alphabets have been designed, both employing the fingers. In the one are used raised letters, either in the common or some slightly modified form. The other makes use of dots or points, raised also, but not resembling the letter in any way. A modification of the latter—a system of point-writing and printing—is the one generally in use in the United States. In 1856 it was said there were but forty-six books for the blind published in English; now there are three large publishing-houses in this country alone. The point-system has also been applied to musical notation.

No study of the blind in this country, their education, the means employed, and their success, would be in any sense complete that failed to include the case of Laura

---

* This includes half of all the schools for the blind in the United States.
† One fourth of all the teachers employed.

Bridgman. A deaf-mute, and blind, and her other senses impaired, the limitations of her life have scarcely been equaled in the world's experience, much less the marvelous results of her education. The case has been repeatedly and admirably described, but must remain of perennial interest.* What she became, one is tempted to say, Dr. Howe made her. The story of her training should be familiar to every teacher. "His work," says Prof. Hall (referring to Dr. Howe), "was so ingenious and successful that it remains one of the greatest triumphs of pedagogical skill; and his studies of his pupil during the most interesting period of her education may be called almost classical for the psychologist."

3. Education of the Feeble-Minded.

Fifteen States † have made permanent provision for the respectable maintenance, education, and training of those of feeble minds. In these States are nineteen schools and homes, with nearly four thousand inmates, all of whom, with one exception (the New York State Custodial Asylum for Feeble-Minded Women), are children.

These schools are provided with over four hundred teachers and a course of training which, while chiefly industrial, usually comprises, according to the capacity of the children, something of language, calculation, and the use of the pencil. Though this must be meager, the importance of systematic and persistent and uniform intellectual exercise, simple as may be, but with an intelligent purpose, can not be overestimated. Next to this, possibly first in importance, because more available is the industrial training, the ability

---

* A second case, promising to be of scarcely less interest, is that of Helen Keller, of Alabama—a second Laura Bridgman—a report of whose condition and intellectual beginnings may be found in the "Annual Report of the Perkins Institution," Boston, for 1887. A notice appears in "Science," also, February 24, 1888.

† California, Connecticut, Illinois, Indiana, Iowa, Kansas, Kentucky, Maryland, Massachusetts, Michigan, Minnesota, Nebraska, New York, Ohio, and Pennsylvania.

to use the organs of the body, to subordinate them to the simple purposes of the mind, the use of tools and implements, and a knowledge of things.

In the Illinois Institution and a few other schools Kinder-garten exercises have been tried with the most marked and satisfactory results.

4. Reformatories.

It has been said that institutions for reformatory educa-- tion began in this country as "Houses of Refuge"; that, later, they were called "Reform Schools," both names being discarded in the more recently established institutions of like functions—"Industrial Schools." In its unqualified form the statement is misleading, though true to the spirit of progress. The significance attaching to it seems to be that the institutions described are coming to be more and more educative, and so regenerative, rather than merely cor-rectional and retributive. Discipline through growth is su-perior to any coercion. Besides, not all institutions so called are for the vicious and law-breaking. The system includes as well the unfortunate, the homeless, the evilly-surrounded, the idle and vagrant, the needy. And, wheth-er the term used be "Houses of Correction" or "Indus-trial Schools," "Orphans' Homes" or "Houses of Deten-tion," "Farm-Schools," "Reformatories," or, as in France, "Correctional Colonies," or "Ragged Schools," as in Eng-land and Scotland, or by whatever name, they concern a body of necessitous youth of both sexes, not always nor usually of the criminal class, but numerous and danger-ous, except their impetuous energies be directed into whole-some service.

The contemporary reformatory institution in this coun-try dates from the year 1820, in the founding of the New York House of Refuge, on Randall's Island. This does not imply that no previous care had been had and ex-ercised in behalf of wayward youth. Plymouth Colony, in 1658, had "joyned to the prison a House of Correction," * and other communities and States, and every generation, perhaps, had felt the danger and sought to stay it; but action was local and temporary. The Plymouth experiment bore no fruit in similar institutions, and was itself soon abandoned. The New York "House" originated in the efforts of Edward Livingston and others, and was purely philanthropic.

The Boston House of Reformation was established in 1826, and one in Philadelphia two years later. For almost twenty years these seem to have been regarded as local experiments, and not generally understood. Then came the "Isaac T. Hopper Home" and "Western House of Refuge," both in New York, and an institution for boys at New Orleans. All these, it should not be lost sight of, had been instituted by individual beneficence and philanthropy, and, though receiving occasional aid from the State, they were yet private institutions, or privately founded and managed by corporations. In the year 1848 was established at Westborough, Massachusetts, a State Reformatory, and that it was the right and policy of the State to care for this class soon came to be common sentiment. Similar institutions were directly opened in Pennsylvania, Maine, Connecticut, New Hampshire, and Ohio, followed since by other States both West and South.

Of Reform Schools proper there are sixty in twenty-five States. These have approximately fifteen thousand inmates, supported at an annual cost to the public of two million dollars. Besides these, there are from four to five hundred "Homes" and asylums for orphans, dependent and vagrant children, which, since the Charleston (South Carolina) "Home," 1790, have housed and reared and educated half a million children. Of the Industrial Reform Schools, eighty-three per cent are State or municipal. The former are chiefly public ; of the latter more than half are denominational. The establishment, following the war, of homes for

* " Plymouth Colony Records," vol. iii, p. 137.

soldiers' orphans, and the recent provision of some of the Western States to furnish separate care for almshouse children, have greatly increased the enrollment in these institutions.

In all of them, whether reformatory or preventive only three phases of training seem not only desirable but necessary. The nature of the instruction here, also, must be determined by the class want.

First, there are needed habits of industry. This is universally admitted, and has led everywhere to the introduction and pursuit of farm and shop and household exercises—exercises in the practice of which may be taught, if not trades and special businesses, at least the principles of industry and the busy habit. These are great conservers of purity, and, from pedagogical motives only, to have fixed these tendencies is so much fundamental gain. A few of these schools have farms, thirty institutions reporting somewhat of agriculture and more of gardening. In most of the institutions for girls, house-work is required ; laundry and tailoring in twenty-four, and in these and others shoemaking, cane-seating, carpentry, smithing, etc.

To furnish a second kind of training, as the basis of all other instruction, and as a means of literary and academic drill, the common branches are taught, of which, besides reading and arithmetic, history and drawing and music, for obvious reasons, are emphasized. The schools report in the aggregate fifty thousand volumes in their libraries, which, well selected and used under intelligent guidance, are an important factor in their education.

As a third function of these schools, if anything be accomplished, they are called to establish right ethical sentiments, and develop standards of conduct. This is effected slowly, if at all, and only by virtue of the wisest foresight and patience. Toward the fixing of such moral and restraining influences, transferring authority from without to within, perhaps nothing has been more generally efficient than the school-room discipline : the habit of regular and instant obedience ; subordination to authority for a common interest ; the general spirit of co-operation ; the growth of a class sympathy ; the frequent self-sacrifice, and the rendering of services to companions and teachers ; and the constant familiarity with the moderation of impulses and frankness of demeanor which the well-regulated school-room uniformly teaches.

Altogether, the right management and discipline of these classes—almost one hundred thousand of them in the schools, and a larger number yet without—constitute one of the most serious economic and educational problems of the day.

5. Indian Education.

A. THE COLONIAL PERIOD.

Outside of New England and the other Atlantic colonies, the earliest attempts to educate the Indian were by the Catholics. Father Juan Roger in Carolina, in 1568, and Benavides, among the Pueblos of the Southwest, half a century later, began the work of teaching the savage reading and the productive arts of life. In the early part of the last century Spanish missions were established among the Indians of southern California, whose descendants are known as "Mission Indians." * The first colonies on the Eastern coast were founded upon land-grants in which care for the Indian was one of the stipulations. The charter of the Virginia Company, and, fifteen years later, the supplementary acts of the Colonial Assembly, specified as one of their functions, "the enlargement of God's kingdom among the heathen people." "That the Christian faith may be propagated among the Western Indians," was one of the reasons assigned for the founding of the College of William and Mary ; and for a hundred years the organization of the college included an Indian school. For many years also prior to the Revolution

---

* See Helen Hunt Jackson's "A Century of Dishonor," and "Romona" ; also, report by Mrs. Jackson to the United States Indian Commissioner, 1883, and one by Prof. C. C. Painter, 1887.

17

William and Mary shared with Harvard a bequest of Hon. Robert Boyle* "for maintaining and educating Indian scholars."

Soon after the founding of Harvard, the General Court of Massachusetts ordered "that the county courts in their jurisdiction take care that the Indians of the several shires be civilized," and about the same time was begun the great work of John Eliot, teaching them, learning their language, translating the Bible, and setting them off into towns.† "They must be civilized," he said, "as well as, if not in order to their being, Christianized." The mantle of Eliot seems to have fallen upon Eleazer Wheelock, who in 1743 opened in his own house a school, which for many years he maintained at his own expense, feeding, clothing, and schooling Indian children from the neighborhood. This was followed ten years later by Moore's Indian Charity School, enrolling fifty to sixty children annually until about 1770, when it was merged into and became the nucleus of the newly founded Dartmouth College. Hamilton College, New York, had a similar origin (1812).

Up to this time the effort to educate the Indians had been almost wholly individual, much scattered, and entirely without concert or plan. Next to Eliot's labors and Moore's Charity School the work with the Oneidas in New York through and after the Revolution was probably most efficient. The descendants of this tribe in New York and Wisconsin are said to be practically self-supporting, having their own churches and schools, owning their lands, and being fairly industrious. Following the Catholic missions, Protestant churches sought and found numerous fields for both religious and secular service. The Moravians early in the eighteenth century and the Quakers near the close, Episco-

---

* Died 1691.

† Whatever may be thought of the wisdom of Eliot's methods, these fourteen "praying towns" have an historic interest wholly apart from their religious aim.

palians, Methodists, Baptists, Presbyterians, and numerous union and Indian missionary associations, have many fold increased the efforts to serve the Indian. Sometimes the service has added to his knowledge and happiness, sometimes to his knowledge only. The best meant offices have not unfrequently been the most short-sighted and irrational. All that had been accomplished at the opening of the century was to show that the average Indian was not lacking either in ability (intellectual) or skill. It remained to be seen whether he have the requisite flexibility of temper, the adaptability to take on the co-operative and confiding habit of civilized life.

B. GOVERNMENT CONTROL.

For half a century the almost uniform attitude of the Government toward the red man was one of military dominion. Nominally the administration has been by civilians; but the policy has not generally been a civilizing one. Coercion and treachery and neglect have sometimes taken the place of nurture and fidelity and the wise forbearance that mark true teaching.*

From the first, Congress was supposed to exercise a sort of supervision over the race, neither knowing how nor seeking, however, to establish fixed relations of comity or helpfulness. About 1820 was made an appropriation of ten thousand dollars called the civilization fund, which was for many years the only Government aid to Indian education. The Indian Bureau, at present belonging to the Department of the Interior, was created in 1833. Not, however, till the so-called "peace policy" of President Grant's Administration was any particular emphasis placed upon education. The positive course of Government then and subsequently, and the co-

---

* An Indian visiting Washington in 1880, being called upon, made the following speech to official listeners : " Four years ago the American people promised to be friends with us. They lied. That is all."—" Report of the Bureau of Ethnology," 1879-'80, p. 526.

operation with existing agencies, mark the beginning of Indian education as now known.

In order to understand the present conditions it is necessary to recall certain administrative facts. Prof. Painter summarizes the Government Indian policy under three heads: "treaties, the reservation and agency systems, and the administrative and judicial departments at Washington."

Of the first, General Sherman is quoted as saying, "We have made more than a thousand treaties with various Indian tribes, and have not kept one of them." *

Growing out of the treaty system, and as a part of the inevitable accompanying compromises, are the "reservations." These amount in the aggregate to more than 212,-000 square miles.† Of this policy the almost uniform testimony is that it is irredeemably vicious. " The reservation line is a wall that fences out law, civil institutions, and social order, and admits only despotism, greed, and lawlessness."

Supplementing this treaty-reservation policy is the agency system, whereby each reservation is provided with a Government representative, resident and supreme. That almost unlimited power held as a political reward easily degenerates into a source of abuses must be expected.

So general had become the impression that the first of these was a mistake, that Congress in 1871 enacted that thereafter " no Indian nation or tribe within the territory of the United States shall be acknowledged or recognized as an independent nation, or tribe, or power, with whom the United States may contract by treaty." And seven years later, equally persuaded of the viciousness and general unfairness of the reservation policy, Congress passed the " General Land in Severalty Bill," authorizing the President of the United States, according to his judgment, to allot the land in any reservation to the Indians located thereon.

---

* Address of Prof. C. C. Painter, Mohawk Lake Conference, 1886.

† The one single reservation of the Indian Territory is larger than all New England.

So much has been said the better to exhibit the little that is known of the purely educational work being done among the Indians. The problem is a complex one and far from present settlement. Abused confidence among them, the disorders growing out of a common ownership in land, the evils of a machine-made agency, a large enforced idleness, and the dissipation incident to unaccustomed modes of life, negative the best results. It is not too much to say that for no single year in the history of this question has the full civilizing force of the simplest education had room to be felt. Further, the elevation of a people from a wandering hunter's life to a settled industrial one is a matter not of a year or years, but of generations. In such a process education requires more than books and forms. Even the restraints of an agricultural life may be too exacting. The nearest industry that suits his taste, lying on the side toward civilization is, pedagogically speaking, the lesson next to be learned. But the conventionalities of the new life must also be learned. As one of the conditions of any general co-operation the language of their surroundings must be known, means of intercourse and record adopted, new attitudes of mind and desire; and the part of education most essential is "making one understand what kind of place this world is, what one's relations to it are, and consequently his rights, duties, and responsibilities." *

That this is the kind of education the Indians are everywhere getting nobody supposes. That individual schools, and individual pupils in many schools, are getting it, can scarcely be denied. And it is by the elevation of individuals that races are civilized.

C. CONTEMPORARY INDIAN SCHOOLING.

Since 1882 there has been a special "Education Division" in the Indian Bureau. The first superintendent was Mr. J. M. Haworth, who at his death (1885) was succeeded by the

---

* W. G. Sumner, "The Forum," May, 1887, p. 260.

present incumbent, Hon. J. B. Riley. Besides reservation Indians and the five civilized tribes in the Indian Territory —two classes with which the present consideration is chiefly concerned—there are the remnants of the Six Nations in New York, scattering settlements in half a dozen other States east of the Mississippi River, and those in tribal relations, no account of which will be here taken.

The Indian school-population aggregates nearly thirty-nine thousand, scattered over nineteen States and Territories, with a school enrollment of about sixteen thousand, and a daily attendance of thirty-four per cent. When it is considered that but forty-one per cent of the school census of cities throughout the United States are daily in school, the success among Indian children seems surprisingly great. If the centers of civilization, with from fifty years to two centuries of school experience, and resting upon a civilization reaching back to Alfred the Great, may take pride in so little, what hope may not be cherished of the future of the Indian ?

As appears from the table, Indian schools are : 1. Those under the immediate charge of the Indian Office, about seventy per cent of all. 2. Those for whose support special appropriations are regularly made, but which are not managed directly by the Bureau. 3. A class of schools chiefly maintained by missionary or church organizations, or under private endowment, but schooling a definite number of Indian children by agreement with the Department. These are the " Contract Schools "—item three in the table. 4. The schools of the Indian Territory. Besides these there are a few schools in the far West, chiefly maintained by societies or individuals, with uncertain support, and from which only imperfect statistics are to be had.

(1) Bureau Schools.

The first class are under the general management of Superintendent Riley. They comprise boarding, day, and industrial training schools—numbering one hundred and

sixty-three. The boarding-schools have about half of all
the pupils. In the industrial schools, and in the boarding-
schools, indeed, are taught the common processes of farming
and related tasks—dairying, stock-raising, fencing, building,
ditching, and domestic management and service ; in some
of them blacksmithing, carpentry, etc. At Standing Rock,
Dakota, there is an Agricultural School, having a farm with
one hundred and fifty acres under cultivation, and about
sixty pupils ; and an industrial boarding-school with twice
the enrollment. The Normal and Training School at Santee
Agency, Nebraska, is particularly worthy of note. It was
organized in 1870, and gives instruction in reading, writing,
drawing, arithmetic, English composition, geography, history, physiology, and music. From this, and from the Hampton and Carlisle schools, have been furnished a large number
of Indian young men and women as teachers to other agencies. A graduate of the Hampton school is principal of
the Shawnee boarding-school, another at Pawnee, etc. At
Chilocco, two educated Kiowa girls and a Comanche Indian man have the local management. The normal school
referred to accommodates both sexes. It has an industrial
department, with thirteen instructors, and provides training in carpentry, smithing, shoemaking, brick-making, and
farming for the boys, and housekeeping and related tasks
for the girls. It has thirteen teachers in the academic
school, uses eighteen buildings, and enrolls over two hundred students.

Both the Pine Ridge Indians and the Osages have compulsory education laws of their own construction and enforcement, pronounced the " best ever devised." A child's
absence from school, except for good reasons, cuts off the
rations for the whole family. The Osages, a rich tribe, with
landed possessions and large money annuities, in their own
Council (1883), and not directly influenced by the United
States authorities, provided for an attendance of not less
than six months yearly. The school age is generally from
six to sixteen years.

Indian Schools.

KIND OF INDIAN SCHOOLS.	No. of schools.	Capacity.	No. enrolled.	Attendance.	Cost.
1. In charge of Indian Bureau :					
a. Boarding-schools....................	68	5,050	5,484	4,111	$548.787 65
b. Day-schools.......................	90	3,135	3,115	1,896	59,678 80
c. Industrial training-schools..........	5	1,455	1,573	1,342	243,089 12
Total Bureau schools..............	163	9,640	10,172	7,349	$851,555 57
2. Special schools :					
a. Carlisle Training, Carlisle, Pa........	....	500	617	547	$81,000 00
b. Chilocco Training, Chilocco, Ind.Ter.	....	180	197	166	28,544 64
c. Genoa Training, Genoa, Neb.........	....	175	215	171	31,264 77
d. Hampton Institute, Hampton, Va....	....	150	160	116	19,382 79
e. Haskell Institute, Lawrence, Kan....	....	350	339	273	61,532 00
f. Lincoln Institution, Philadelphia, Pa.	....	200	218	200	33,364 10
g. Salem Training, Chemawa, Or........	....	250	205	185	40,747 71
h. St. Ignatius Mission, Flathead Res., Mont...............................	....	200	186	170	22,500 00
Total special schools..............	8	2,005	2,137	1,828	$318,336 01
3. Under contract with the Indian Bureau:					
a. Boarding-schools....................	41	2,733	2,553	2,081	$228,445 58
b. Day-schools.......................	20	843	1,044	604	10,777 53
Total contract schools.............	61	3,576	3,597	2,685	$239,223 11
Total Indian schools.............	232	15,221	15,906	11,862	$1,409,114 69

(2.) Special Schools.

Of special institutions belonging to the second class named, there are four training-schools—at Carlisle, Pennsylvania, Chilocco, Indian Territory, Genoa, Nebraska, and Chemawa, Oregon—the Hampton Institute, Virginia, and the Haskell Institute, Lawrence, Kansas; the Lincoln Institution, Philadelphia; and the St. Ignatius Mission, on the Flathead Reservation, Montana. The first of all these so recognized was that at Carlisle, Pennsylvania. Captain R. H. Pratt, being put in possession of seventy-four Indian prisoners at St. Augustine (1875), undertook their education. At first chiefly industrial, upon the removal of the school in 1879 to Carlisle, formal instruction was begun in literary branches as well, and with the number more than doubled. They are taught, besides books, carpentry, harness-making, shoemaking, blacksmithing, carriage-making, tinsmithing, baking, sewing, laundrying, and farming. The course at

Hampton and the Western schools is much the same. At Carlisle has been recently introduced a device, possibly adopted elsewhere, for acquainting Indian youth with the ways and insights and conventionalities of civilized life. It is known as "outing," and consists in putting into farmers' families boys and girls who have had a partial training in the school. They remain on the farm from a few months to a year, receive nominal wages, are admitted to the family, and not unfrequently attend the district school of the neighborhood. Of nearly six hundred in attendance, more than half have been so accommodated. At Hampton Normal and Agricultural Institute about one fifth of the six hundred students are Indians, the others negrões. All receive pay for work, at the rate of five to eight cents an hour.

(3.) Contract Schools.

Two thirds of the schools of this class are boarding-schools, well represented in the White's Institutes, at Wabash, Indiana, and Mount Hamill, Iowa. Both have large farms and shops, and accommodate each from fifty to seventy-five Indian children, besides a small number of whites.

The former are received from various reservations and tribes, and educated for a definite period at a stipulated price under contract with the Government Bureau. They include pupils from the Sioux, Wyandottes, Senecas, Modocs, Peorias, Miamis, Comanches, and perhaps a dozen others, of both sexes, and varying in age from eight to eighteen years.

(4.) Education in Indian Territory.

The civilized tribes of the Territory embrace the Cherokees, Choctaws, Chickasaws, Creeks, and Seminoles. Each has an independent school system, both of common and secondary instruction, and in the English language only. Most of the teachers are educated Indians. There are sustained boards of education, directors, superintendents of public schools, and an annual teachers' institute for each nation.

In the management the local neighborhood provides the house and furniture; the nation, the books and teachers.

In the elementary schools, the Five Nations enroll over eight thousand pupils; in the secondary schools, fifteen hundred. The Cherokees and Chickasaws each maintain an orphan school and asylum, that of the former having one hundred and fifty inmates. The Creeks and Cherokees, as a part of their system, support separate schools for the four hundred to six hundred negro children among them. Co-education of the races, while the exception, is not uncommon. The Choctaws and Creeks have maintained regularly from forty to fifty of their youth at colleges in the States; and Dr. T. A. Bland is authority for the statement that "there is not in the Cherokee nation an Indian man, woman, or child of sound mind, fifteen years of age or over, who can not read and write."

Out of a school population of fifteen thousand the Five Nations provide regular instruction for more than nine thousand, or sixty-two per cent. This is a more general participation in the benefits of the public schools than was enjoyed in the States of Alabama, Arkansas, California, Florida, Kentucky, Louisiana, Maryland, New Jersey, New York, North Carolina, or Virginia, for the same year.

6. Education in Alaska.

Alaska is so far away from most of the States, so little is known of its people, so habitually do we associate them in our thoughts with the American Indians, that the education of the Territory is scarcely regarded even by school-men as belonging to our system. And yet there are towns whose adult illiteracy can be in many cases paralleled in large sections east of the Mississippi River, and whose schools have developed a skill that strongly hints at Yankee competition. For half a century before its purchase by the United States there were maintained by the Russians boarding and day schools, elementary and advanced for both sexes; academies which taught, besides the usual branches, the Slavonian and

English languages, higher mathematics, navigation, and astronomy; and a theological seminary.

The natives, especially the Aleuts, are represented as superior intellectually to the Indians, belong to the Russo-Greek Church, live in good houses, dress in American garments, and use the tools, utensils, and means of culture of a civilized home.

Two hundred and fifty miles to the northwest of Unimak Island are the Pribylov Islands. In 1870 these were leased for twenty years to the Alaska Commercial Company for seal-fishing, one of the conditions of which contract was that a school for the natives should be maintained on each island, at the expense of the company, and for at least eight months each year. From a recent report it appears that out of a total population of less than four hundred there were enrolled in the two schools seventy-five children, or ninety-five per cent of the minors. The first successful school organized and maintained by the Government was established at Sitka in 1880. A system of compulsory education was inaugurated and enforced, and within a year the school had two hundred and fifty pupils. A boarding-school for girls opened at Fort Wrangel about the same time, being removed to Sitka, was united with the former, under the organization of a Government Industrial and Training School. The school population numbers between five and six thousand, of whom twelve hundred are enrolled in thirteen schools. A number of these are denominational or missionary enterprises. In 1885 there was created the office of "General Agent of Education in Alaska," and Mr. Sheldon Jackson appointed to the position.

Bibliography.

See "Visible Speech," by Alexander Melville Bell, 1867; "Education of the Blind—History of its Origin, Rise, and Progress," by M. Anagnos, 1882; "Life and Education of Laura Dewey Bridgman," by Mary Lamson (for three years her special teacher), 1878; "Laura Bridgman," by G. Stanley Hall, in "Aspects of German Culture," 1881. See also sketch of the Perkins Institution for the Blind, and notice of Laura Bridgman, in Dickens's "American Notes," chap. iii. See "The Jukes," by R. L. Dugdale, 1877; and "Dangerous Classes of New York," by C. L. Brace, 1872; "Indian Education," "Proceedings of National Education Association," 1884, p. 177; "Latest Studies on Indian Reservations," by J. B. Harrison, 1887; "Education in Alaska," by Sheldon Jackson.

CHAPTER XV.

SUPPLEMENTARY INSTITUTIONS.

1. Private Schools.

IN a sketch of public education in a new country private schools might fill a large chapter, for it is almost without exception true that the one grew out of the other. In most localities before public education by the State was tolerated or encouraged its benignant influence was suggested, and its right to general recognition justified, by public-spirited men and women, who did what the community as a whole would not undertake.

Private enterprise has commonly been the genesis of the public institution. Every reform, every adoption of the new and promising was once personal opinion. The wholesome conservatism of government throws the burden of proving a thing good upon individuals and societies. The first manual training, the first Kindergartens, the first emphasis of science, were born of personal conviction, grew alone or in contracted circles, and were forced to wait for public recognition. The first art schools and galleries, and museums and libraries and reading-rooms ; the earliest surveys and explorations ; the first study and instruction in agriculture ; the first Indian, negro, and Alaskan schools— were all the product of individual effort or private co-operation. So the beginnings of primary schooling, the instruction of girls and the higher education of women, were even less honored than the "annex." And, equally so, the common school had its birth in the abounding individual enterprise of colonial New England and New York and the South.

Danyell Maude, the first private schoolmaster of New England, was the contemporary of "Brother Philemon Purmont." Father Channing, in his "Early Recollections of Rhode Island," says that "prior to 1770 private schools were the only ones that were continuous, even for Providence and Newport." In New York, throughout the State, and into the present century, the supplementary services of individuals were the impulse that, through Governor Clinton and Gideon Hawley, eventually brought about the present public-school system.

Moreover, in many States, both East and West, even after the public schools were begun, the private schools were these public schools continued by subscription. The average length of the school year, in thirty-six States reporting, is a fraction over six months, Excluding the six States—Maryland, Massachusetts, Connecticut, New York, New Jersey, and Rhode Island, having the longest terms (nine and a half months)—the average length for the remaining States is barely five months. In these States, the private school comes in as a valuable supplemental agency extending the school term ; not unfrequently continuing the same teacher, and by common consent, if not by law, more or less of the same supervision and the established course. Besides these also there is a class of secondary schools similar in grade to the public high-school. In cities these take the form of ladies' seminaries, or boys' classical schools, numbers of which may yet be found, especially in the South and East.

A secondary school of somewhat different character is the so-called business college.* There is unquestionably a

---

* The Bryant and Stratton "International Chain of Commercial Colleges," begun a quarter of a century ago, many of which remain in the larger cities, is an interesting development in American education.

sufficient reason for its existence. General Garfield insisted that "business schools were an attempt to answer the public demand for a practical education "—a kind of materialized protest of the provident mind against the too common unpractical education of the elementary schools. The public asks a really available culture.

Out of environing conditions, and the constitutional impatience of a long preparation, have been evolved the trade school, the business institute, commercial college, etc. Setting themselves up in recent years as professional schools, now chartered and authorized to issue diplomas and confer degrees, and now, in the fullness of unlicensed Philistinism, without established curriculum, but assuming to include the circle of practical knowledge—to book-keeping, penmanship, and arithmetic they have added political science and economics, commercial law, modern languages, phonography, telegraphy, etc. There are two hundred schools of the class, with almost fifty thousand pupils.

2. Denominational Schools.

As has been seen, the earliest approaches to the public school in this country were among a people who strongly dissented from established ecclesiastical authority, and, in more or less independent religious bodies, sought the freedom of worship and intellectual intercourse that they were elsewhere denied. This independent, protesting spirit, an unwillingness to submit to anything like a hierarchal authority, has everywhere been favorable to the most widely diffused education. Every phase of literary and professional and technical institution has been, in turn and co-operation, made to contribute to the general intelligence. In the line of this current, co-operating more or less with State and private agencies, and more often supplementing them, the Church has claimed and been granted a place. Most Protestants use the public schools for elementary instruction, but sustain more or less generally their own institutions for superior and sometimes secondary training.

Among the oldest of existing denominations, the Methodists have for nearly a century supported church-schools. Their first permanent college* was the now venerable Wesleyan University at Middletown, Connecticut, founded in 1831. They have now similar institutions in every section of the country, and for a decade have been especially active in the West and South. These comprise ten theological schools, prominent among which are the Boston University School of Theology and the Drew Theological Seminary ; forty-five colleges and sixty-one classical seminaries, besides eight female colleges.

Forty years before the Methodist Cokesbury School in Maryland, the Presbyterians had founded the College of New Jersey in Princeton—not only one of the oldest, but now one of the solid institutions of the United States. Besides thirty-six colleges, Presbyterianism supports and is supported by thirteen theological schools, well represented in Princeton, Lane Theological Seminary, Cincinnati, and the Theological Seminary of the Northwest at Chicago.

Among the Baptists are thirty-four colleges, seven theological schools, and forty to fifty academies for secondary instruction, chiefly in the South.

As the school system started among the Congregationalists, so it has had their constant and generous support. Among both colleges and academies they have a large representation. Of the former, are : Harvard, in its founding ; Yale, Dartmouth, Williams, Bowdoin, Amherst, Oberlin, and the later Fiske; of the latter, Andover (theological seminary), and Phillips Academies at Andover and Exeter ; besides Mount Holyoke and Wellesley.

But all other denominational service in education is partial and irregular compared with the comprehensive grasp of the Catholic Church. Their aim is all-inclusive, and assumes no other agency. Ignoring the public school, their

---

* Cokesbury College, at Abingdon, Maryland, founded 1787, being twice burned, was not afterward rebuilt.

plan is coextensive with their membership. With one fifth of all the theological seminaries, and one third of all their students ; with one fourth of the colleges, nearly six hundred academies, and twenty-six hundred parochial (elementary) schools, instructing more than half a million children, the church is seen to be a force which, educationally considered, is equaled by no other single agency but the Government itself.* The twelve Catholic provinces—Baltimore, Boston, Chicago, Cincinnati, Milwaukee, New Orleans, New York, Oregon, Philadelphia, St. Louis, San Francisco, and Santa Fé—are subdivided into seventy-nine dioceses. The latter average from thirty-five to forty parishes, each of which is supposed to have a school for the elementary training of their children. As a matter of fact, ninety-three per cent of them do maintain parochial schools, in which are educated, generally by the priesthood, rarely by laymen (except in the teaching congregations), the 511,063 pupils. In addition to these are 588 academies, usually for girls, and 91 colleges.†

The Theological Seminary of St. Sulpice, Baltimore (recently raised to the rank of a university, and authorized to confer degrees), is, according to the "Catholic Year-book," the oldest organization for theological instruction in this country, dating from 1791. To the Catholics, also, belong several industrial and reform schools, orphans' homes, and normal schools.

---

* For a statement of the work of the "Brothers of the Christian Schools" see "Education," November, December, 1885 ; also "Government Report of the Educational Exhibits and Conferences at the New Orleans Exposition," 1885.

† The corner-stone of a Catholic University was laid in May, 1888, near Washington, District of Columbia. It is to receive its students from the Catholic colleges, and to have a full university organization. The enterprise was started by a gift of three hundred thousand dollars from a Miss Caldwell, of New York. (See the announcement in "American Catholic Quarterly Review," April, 1885.)

3. Evening Schools.

The evening school, as found in our large cities, is a very natural product of the conditions. There are two classes in whose interest it exists : 1. For children who can not be brought into the system of day-schools ; and, 2. For (a) men and women of limited education, employed during the day, but ambitious for intellectual and industrial improvement, or (b) recent immigrants who wish to know the national language, the forms of business, and means of industry. Evening or night schools, like elementary industrial schools, and nautical or floating schools, are illustrative of the attempt constantly making to adjust the public-school forces to the public needs. How well it has been accomplished can only be suggested.

The first evening schools were probably due to the evils of vagrancy, and to the truancy of children, and those of school age. Again, they were demanded in manufacturing towns, and, generally, in cities for messengers, clerks, and servants. They were tried in New York city in 1834, but failed for want of teachers. Fourteen years later they were successfully established by the Public School Society, which within two years had fifteen schools and eight thousand pupils. They were introduced into Boston through a charitable organization, and legalized in 1857. The recent growth of the system has been rapid. The Chicago enrollment has more than trebled in five years ; and those of New York and Philadelphia doubled.

For the most part, the night-schools in the United States are provided for, and used by, the maturer classes of the young. Indeed, in some cities they are opened to men and women only, or to children beyond the compulsory school age, employed during the day. The abundant material resources of the country, the open avenues to industry, the power implied in wealth and property, drive youth into business before manhood even ; and, under the most guarded systems, the education is often meager and unsatisfactory.

18

To give these the opportunity of continuing their studies is both politic and beneficent. New York maintains a large system of night-schools for this class chiefly. With an enrollment of twenty thousand, one half of them are between eighteen and twenty-one years of age.

For the classes described the studies are chiefly elementary. They include, primarily, writing and calculation (including book-keeping), grammar and physiology, sometimes history, and always drawing. Occasionally there are introduced the elements of geometry and algebra; and in Cincinnati general history and elocution, both of which are excluded from the Boston course. Perhaps the most profitable parts of the instruction are book-keeping and drawing. For certain classes, industrial training is fundamental. It should be borne in mind that, in these schools, is no hard and fast course of study to which all are held, and the completion of which counts for advanced standing. Boston only, so far as appears, has made any successful attempt to establish a grade. Usually, upon entrance, each applicant chooses his work—it is rarely chosen for him, even by advice. Few take all that is offered. That it seems necessarily so is the misfortune of, not so much the school, as the social conditions.

Not all night instruction, however, is elementary. Of sixteen of the larger cities making returns (1884), five report one evening high-school each, and Brooklyn two. The attendance upon these seven schools alone aggregates about three thousand students, representing more than a hundred trades, and justifying the agency beyond criticism. One educator has said, "There is no argument for the regular high - school that does not apply with equal force to the evening class of like grade." And, as might have been predicted, this night high-school is far more efficient, securing more certain good results than the elementary evening school. Attendance is more regular, and study more to the purpose. New York, Boston, Paterson, Cincinnati, and Brooklyn, all sustain elaborate courses of study, or rather long lists of subjects offered, from which applicants may choose. Philadelphia has among the secondary classes one German-English school and one Italian-English; Louisville teaches German; San Francisco, Spanish; Boston, whatever foreign languages the demand justifies.

The last-named city requires examination for admission to the high-school, as in other parts of the system ; the examination including reading, writing, arithmetic, and geography. A half-dozen cities give certificates of proficiency for completed work.

Among evening schools also which offer advanced and higher technical instruction are those of the Maryland Institute, Baltimore, and Cooper Union, New York.

Peter Cooper was born in New York city, February 12, 1791, where he died in 1883. He had but a single year of schooling, yet in his manhood he took a man's interest in all that concerns the public or individual welfare. He was prominent in the development of public-school education in his native city. He was a trustee and officer of the Public School Society; later, a school commissioner, and throughout his life identified with the schools. The high opinion he held of the value of education, both from a business point of view and in its moral aspect, led him early to consider how he might contribute to the better enlightenment of those whom the schools did not reach. " I determined," he says, " if ever I could acquire the means I would build such an institution as would open its doors at night, with a full course of instruction, calculated to enable mechanics to understand both the theory and the most skillful practice of their several trades ; so that they could not only apply their labor to the best possible advantage, but enjoy the happiness of acquiring useful knowledge—the purest and the most innocent of all sources of enjoyment."

Cooper Union was incorporated in 1857. As provided by the will of the founder, the institution, among other advantages, maintains a course of academic instruction, and a School of Art, both at night. It has a library of twenty thousand volumes, and a reading-room furnished with four hundred and fifty periodicals. The course of instruction has industrial bearings, wholly apart from humanistic or disciplinary studies. It includes algebra, geometry, trigonometry, calculus, physics, elementary and analytical chemistry, astronomy, engineering, descriptive geography, mechanics, and mechanical drawing. It is meant to cover the elementary principles of science, and their application to the practical business of life. The School of Art furnishes instruction in perspective, mechanical, and architectural drawing ; wood-engraving, photography, and telegraphy. In full, the regular course covers five years, whose completion is marked by a diploma and the medal of the Cooper Union. The institution enrolls over four thousand students, one half of whom are clerks and mechanics.

4. Museums of Art and Science.

The rapid development of science and the consequent turning of the public attention to the study of Nature, physical investigation, and observation generally, has emphasized the great importance of collections of objects of study, including also works of art. Except a half-dozen of them the museums of the present are the product of the last forty years. This is especially true of art collections, though the Pennsylvania Academy of Fine Arts was founded 1805 and the Boston Athenæum two years after.

The National Academy of Design, New York, was established in 1826, and four years later was begun that rare collection of coins, gems, and specimens of printing by the Historical Society of Pennsylvania. If to these be added the Museum and Gallery of Art of the New York Historical Society (1804) and the Museum of the Maryland Historical Society (1844), the Wadsworth Athenæum, Hartford (1842), the Yale School of Fine Arts (1825), and the fine arts department of the Essex Institute, Salem, Mass. (1848), all have been named that were founded prior to 1850. These museums number in the aggregate about thirty in two thirds as many cities. A dozen of them belong to colleges and four to libraries. Of the last are the Peabody Institute, Baltimore, and the Boston Athenæum, Lenox, and Redwood Libraries. Among the most notable galleries of art is the Corcoran Institution, Washington. Founded in 1869 and generously endowed by W. W. Corcoran with an annual income of seventy thousand dollars and its already choice collection, its growth and wholesome influence are assured. The principal collections of the old masters are to be found in the Metropolitan Museum of Art of New York (1870), the Bryan Gallery of the New York Historical Society, the Jarvis collection in Yale, and in the Pennsylvania Academy. The most notable institutions in the West are the Art Gallery of the Illinois Industrial University, the Museum of Art and History in the University of Michigan, the Crow Museum of Fine Arts, Washington University, St. Louis, and the Museum of the Western Reserve Historical Society, Cleveland, Ohio. To half of them there is unrestricted admission by the public, and by nearly the same number regular lectures are sustained.

Of museums of science that of the Philadelphia Academy of Natural Science is perhaps the oldest, dating from 1812. Like most others it is general in its character. Besides these, rapid developments in particular fields of science have here and there built up special collections for their illustration and verification, giving rise to museums of zoölogy like that at Harvard ; and botany, as the Agricultural Museum at Washington; of geology and mineralogy, as at Rochester University; of entomology and ornithology, as the Cuttings Museum, Vermont; and of medicine, as at the Army Medical Museum, Washington, and that in Yale College. Of the first class, the State Museum of New York is an admirable example. It had its origin in the specimens gathered in the progress of the State Geological Survey, begun in 1836. It comprises a library, a laboratory of analytical chemistry, and collections of seeds and zoölogical and mineralogical specimens, and is maintained by State grants. Having many duplicate specimens, it has been a part of its policy to encourage the establishment of museums, and has in ten years distributed to normal schools, colleges, and academies in the State more than twenty thousand labeled and classified specimens. The enterprise is unique and of incalculable benefit. A similar but more specific service has been rendered the teachers of New York city by Dr. Bickmore, in charge of the American Museum of Natural History in Central Park. The plan includes a course of lectures at the museum rooms, primarily for teachers, covering in a period of years the various phases of natural science, including ethnology and special anthropological studies. It was initiated in 1884.

The Museum of Comparative Zoölogy at Harvard had its origin in the collections made by Prof. Louis Agassiz. By the year 1858 a vast amount of material had been gathered, and specimens were being received—thousands annually— from all quarters of the globe. In the year named there came a generous bequest of fifty thousand dollars to found a " national museum." Friends of the institution contributed seventy-five thousand dollars, and the State Legislature one hundred thousand dollars more. The museum management is independent of the university control, though co-operating with and supplementing its departments.

The one great museum, however, both in fact and in making, is that of the Smithsonian Institution at Washington. It has numerous departments, the more important of which are : 1. Anthropology; 2. Archæology; 3. Natural resources ; 4. Exploitive industries ; 5. Elaborative industries; 6. Ultimate products; and, 7. Social relations. The Ethnological Bureau has made large collections in recent years.

Of a more specific function are the Pedagogical Museum of the Bureau of Education at Washington, and that of the State Educational Department of New York, recently begun at Albany.

In this connection, also, should be included—though deserving a larger place—industrial and other expositions as educational agencies. The interdependence of nations, the kinship of interests, the diversity of conditions, and the abundance of skill in the world of our neighbors, have been brought out by these schools of competition. Even the local exhibits of limited sections of our own country, of single States or cities, or particular industries, constitute a feature of great educational value. New industries have been created, new resources discovered, new tools put into shops, new implements into fields, new machinery into factories, new apparatus into laboratories; millions of capital have been re-invested, and the centers of population shifted, as a result of their suggestions. They represent something of the universal spirit brought to the merchant's and farmer's and shopman's doors. They furnish the much-needed occasions for comparative study within the limits of local experience. It is a wholesome club-life on a large scale, where friction of mind brings sharpness of thinking.

" From whatever point of view we look at them," it has been said, " whether material, intellectual, politico-economical, or merely commercial or industrial, expositions exert a decided influence on the welfare of nations. They are the milestones of progress ; its measures of the dimensions of the productive activity of the human race. They make people acquainted with the market, they cultivate taste, and afford material for valuable comparisons. They bring nations closer to one another, and so promote civilization." *

5. Clubs and Circles.

In its social significance, the distribution of culture is the great educational desideratum. How to make the technical and particular knowledge of the few the common experience of the many, this fixes the direction of all systems of education. Yesterday's doctrine of a class is the wide rule of conduct to-day. To extend the boundaries of knowledge and obedience, and man's mastery of nature, is the function of

---

* J. D. Blanqui, in " Cyclopædia of Political Science " : " Expositions."

universities and societies, of laboratories and endowed research. To the college and secondary school, the Church,
the lecture, and the press are left the diffusion of this knowledge, and making more wide-spread this obedience and mastery. Looked at from the social standpoint, the latter is
fundamental. The success of the undertaking conditions the
health of the social body and the perpetuity of government.
In homogeneity of culture are political and civil strength.
"There is no future for a stratified civilization"; hence the
need for every possible local agency for the exchange and
circulation of the maturest and most saving experience. It
is of less importance even that much intelligence exist than
that the data of intelligence shall under wise direction be
brought within easy reach of all. It is a law of life not less
sociological than biological that vigor and fruitfulness are
promoted by adaptation and correspondence among the parts.
Personal culture and special knowledge, and individual invention and local intelligence, must somehow be worked
down into communities, crystallized into form, talked about
around hearthstones, shaped into customs, and so erected into
institutions. And to this end, born of the need and fed by
the spirit of local self-interest, have sprung up more or less
general, less or more formally organized societies. They are
variously named, and even more diverse in constitution and
aim ; but, taken as a class, they are of greater importance as
educational means than appears from a casual view.

Under the guise of clubs for intellectual and social advantage have been formed philosophical and scientific organizations, less pretentious than the learned societies ; literary bodies for the study of the masters ; and historical
unions, with no official countenance from the large associations, but gathering up into permanent records the delicate
and far-reaching but fast-wasting threads of a rich local life.
Then there is the modern reading circle, including societies
for home study, correspondence schools, the Chautauqua, and
Agassiz Associations, etc. These can not be regarded with
indifference when it is considered that they enroll nearly

twice as many students as all the colleges of the United States combined, for both men and women, and as many as all the secondary institutions * taken together.

A. SOCIAL CLUBS.

The " Junto," of Philadelphia, was one of the earliest social clubs whose history is left us, and more or less closely the model of this class. It was a " club for mutual improvement," and enrolled Franklin and his few thoughtful ac· quaintances. It had weekly meetings, and was called by Franklin the best school of philosophy, morality, and politics then (1727) existing in the province. About the same time was a similar organization at New Haven, under the lead of Bishop Berkeley; another in Charleston, South Carolina. In the Revolutionary period there were many of them. The last half of the nineteenth century has no monopoly of this means of culture, but in every generation it has been a natural outgrowth of thoughtful intercourse.

Contemporary clubs cover every possible field of inquiry, from theology and metaphysical speculation to politics and agriculture, and concern every city, besides many of the large and smaller towns. Boston, Philadelphia, St. Louis, Cincinnati, and New York, have been forward in encouraging the former. The Cincinnati " Literary Club " has been in existence since 1849, and been honored with the membership of such men as A. R. Spofford, the founder, Justice Stanley Matthews, T. Buchanan Read, Salmon P. Chase, Oliver P. Morton, George B. McClellan, ex-President R. B. Hayes, J. J. Piatt, and others. The membership is limited to one hundred. Among numerous other clubs in the same city, the "Unity Club," the "Historical Society," and the "Cuvier Club" are deservedly prominent.

The Philosophical Club of St. Louis is particularly worthy of note as the center of one of the most pronounced

---

* These include high-schools, academies, and seminaries, college preparatories, and normal schools.

philosophical movements of this country. It was formed in 1862, under the influence of ex-Governor Brockmeyer, of Missouri, and Dr. William T. Harris, who drew about them a coterie of men and women interested in and intelligently alive to the problems that have attracted the philosophic minds of all the ages. In the atmosphere of its influence was begun (1867) and is yet published the "Journal of Speculative Philosophy," edited by Dr. Harris, and which, for profundity of learning and for comprehensiveness of philosophical discussion has not its equal in this country.

The Concord School of Philosophy is itself * an organized club, with annual meetings, at which Dr. Harris, Julia Ward Howe, Dr. Hiram K. Jones, F. B. Sanborn, Rev. C. A. Bartol, and, in their time, Emerson and Alcott, have elaborated their philosophies. Its first session was held in the summer of 1879, with a programme of lectures and conversations that covered five weeks. In addition to some unrelated courses of lectures, incident to the association of teachers of more or less diverse views, one season each has been devoted to Goethe, Emerson, and Aristotle, and repeated and comprehensive courses upon Plato and Hegel and their philosophical implications. Milwaukee has, for some years, maintained a society of like general aims, though of less formal and permanent organization. Indianapolis, for nearly twenty years, has had among the residents of one quarter of the city a "College Corner Club," spending three years at one time upon Shakespeare, and nearly as much upon Browning, besides studies in Goethe, and other literatures and philosophies. It is estimated that there are over one hundred Browning clubs in the United States, and others for the consideration of special philosophies, histories of particular periods or events, or for definite scientific investigation. In Jacksonville (Illinois), as a center, was formed a philosophical club called "The Akademe," which enrolled members from all parts of the country. It

---

* See "International Review," vol. ix, p. 459.

held regular monthly sessions, and for several years published its proceedings (including papers read) in a monthly journal. Dr. H. K. Jones, a distinguished Platonist, was the founder of the movement.

Of a less general and more technical character were the discussions of the "Round Table," maintained years ago in the West among the city school superintendents of St. Louis, Chicago, Cincinnati, Cleveland, Indianapolis, Detroit, Dayton, and two or three other cities, than which no single influence, perhaps, did more to rationalize and unify and perfect the organization and instruction of Western school systems. The Michigan "Schoolmasters' Club" and one of the same name in Boston (1881) represent the contemporary high-class teachers' society, and the highest authority upon questions of education and civilization.

B. THE "OLD SOUTH" MOVEMENT.

Of a different kind, but eminently helpful, are the historical lecture courses that, in ten years, have been formed after the manner of those of the "Old South Church," Boston.

During the winter of 1878–'79, Miss Alice Baker gave to the young people of the city a series of talks on "Early American Times," and the year following, Prof. Fiske a course of lectures on the "Discovery and Colonization of America." Out of these two have developed the successive annual courses since 1883. These lectures are for young people, not for children; are historical, and designed to promote studies in American history among the youth of Boston. At each lecture are distributed "Old South Leaflets," generally a republication of matter pertinent to the topic discussed. Historical courses of the same kind are maintained at Indianapolis (1885), Madison, Wisconsin (1886), Chicago and Bloomington, Illinois, Milwaukee, Wisconsin, and perhaps elsewhere.

C. READING CIRCLES.

The idea of the organized reading circle—providing assistance and encouragement for home study—seems to have been brought to this country from London about fifteen years ago. There was doubtless similar co-operation long before, but it was chiefly local and occasional, with results correspondingly individual. In fifteen years the impulse has become a force involving the concert of communities, and looks to an immediate general good. In this sense the institution is modern.

(1.) General Organizations.

Miss Anna E. Ticknor, of Boston, learning of the English society, invited the co-operation of some friends in the organization of extra-school study in New England, which effort resulted (1873) in the "Society to encourage Studies at Home." The purpose, as then formulated and still held, is " to induce among ladies the habit of devoting some part of every day to study of a systematic and thorough kind." Instruction is entirely by correspondence, and is given in six departments—History, Science, Art, Literature, German, and French—representing twenty-four subjects ; of which history, science, and English are most prominent among courses taken. The staff of six, having in charge the forty-five readers of the first year, has been enlarged to one hundred and ninety-one correspondents, with over five hundred members. These represent thirty-seven States and one Territory, and all classes and conditions of society. A very important factor in carrying on the work of the society is the "Lending Library." Members may, if they choose, borrow from the society their books, paying carriage one way and one half cent a day for their use. The privilege is used by about two thirds of the membership.

Similar to the last in aim and organization, though of more recent date, is the "Society for Home Culture," started in Philadelphia in 1880, by members of the Society of Friends. Instruction is given in Grecian and Roman history, church and mediæval history, modern European history, American history, English history, travels and descriptions of nations, physical geography, geology and mineralogy, botany, astronomy, literature and language, political science, and education.

The Chautauqua Literary and Scientific Circle, instituted in the summer of 1878, prescribed a definite course of reading and study covering the principal subjects of a college curriculum, though "omitting of necessity the thorough drill in mathematics and the languages." The peculiar Chautauqua idea is the plan of simultaneous study by all classes— the work of each year being complete in itself. In addition to the regular course of four years, are special courses in Roman history and literature, English history and literature, astronomy, political science, microscopy, botany, chemistry, psychology, philology, art, temperance, missions, agriculture. The circle enrolls seventy-five thousand members—from every State in the Union, from the Dominion of Canada, Alaska, the Sandwich Islands, Great Britain, several of the European states, India, Japan, South Africa, and the isles of the sea. The local club idea is admirably exemplified in the separate Chautauqua circles, of which there are many thousands. Besides these are the local unions, embracing the circles of a given section—as the New England Chautauqua Association, the Northern Illinois Union, the United Circle of Philadelphia, the Brooklyn Assembly, and the North Carolina Chautauqua. The C. L. S. C. (as it is known) is but part of a plan which, taking more definite shape, was organized (1883) into, and incorporated as, the "Chautauqua University." To the original function have been added the College of Liberal Arts and the School of Theology. Six courses are offered in the former, two each, leading to the degrees of A. B., Ph. B., and B. S.

Similar in general scope and workings to the last is the "Correspondence University," organized the same year at Ithaca, New York. It has regularly sustained classes in physical science, languages (including Hebrew), philosophy, history and political science, and law.

Out of these experiments developed the idea of providing special courses for particular classes. It was not entirely new, though the application was. The Mechanics' Institutes and Libraries, and Apprentices' Societies of cities had been more or less common for a century. Very early, also, both East and West, especially in Pennsylvania and Ohio, were teachers' libraries, circulating, limited in books, and more restricted in variety, but designed to provide all the teachers of a neighborhood with a somewhat uniform course of reading. Later, the organizations noticed in the preceding section were doing something for teachers; but the influence was general and quite as serviceable to the clergyman, the farmer, or the school-girl, as to the teacher. The Boston society was exclusive and had a limited membership, while others were specialized in subjects foreign to the profession, and so were missed by the teacher.

In the winter of 1883 Ohio organized a "State Reading Circle" for teachers, and published a suggestive list of books in literature, history, science, and pedagogy, with directions for reading and organizing into local circles. No course was prescribed, the multitude of books recommended left teachers, as before, in doubt as to what to read, and with little of joint action. Besides, it also suggested much of general culture, and little of professional. It soon came to be recognized, in Ohio and the neighboring States, that if the name and the idea have any significance, the "Teachers' Reading Circle" must be chiefly professional. There is much to be mastered : familiarity with professional literature, the historic systems and reformers of education, something of philosophical doctrine as a basis for one's theories, current systems and contemporary school interests, the constitution and functions of the child and the teacher, the State and society in which he finds his labor. This does not mean that one shall be less a man or woman, less cultured and scholarly, but more a teacher.

Toward this idea Ohio had pioneered the way. With this thought before them, the year following teachers in Indiana organized a circle. It is a State institution, the control vested in a board of nine members elected by the State Teachers' Association, the State Superintendent of Public Instruction being a member *ex officio*. It has a prescribed course of reading, after published outlines, with directions and bibliographical references, an official department in the "State School Journal," and a system of certificates and diplomas for completed work. The course extends over four years, and is made to include three lines of study, two of which are professional and one general culture. As a result of the four years of experiment in Indiana—for it was an experiment—the last year reported a membership of over seven thousand, with all the counties in the State represented, and enrolling in some counties every teacher.

Reading circles now in some form are parts of half the State systems and they are found in many cities. The year following the movement in Indiana similar organizations were effected in Illinois, Iowa, Michigan, Minnesota, Wisconsin, Kansas, Nebraska, Texas, Kentucky, Tennessee, Dakota, Alabama, and North Carolina. Something has been done in Rhode Island, also in New York, Missouri, Pennsylvania, Maine, Georgia, Louisiana, Mississippi, New Jersey, and Arkansas—twenty-five States in all. The organizations, as might be supposed, vary greatly in plan, in management, in comprehensiveness and efficiency. Illinois reports 2,341 members in the first two years, and 738 who finished and passed upon the work prescribed. Two courses were maintained—an elementary course of two years and an advanced one of three. Similarly the Missouri organization, while contemplating a four years' course, makes the first two years complete in themselves and elementary. The New Jersey Circle opened in 1887 with flattering prospects, city and town teachers joining with those from rural districts, and the enrollment as to numbers being out of all proportion to the number of teachers in the State. Of the Rhode Island

Circle the membership is coextensive with that of the State Institute of Instruction, and without further fees. The subjects offered are pedagogy, history, literature, language, geography, and science. The work is voluntary and elective. In Michigan the general course is three years, though the State Council offers additional subjects for advanced study. The "Chautauqua Teachers' Reading Union," organized in 1885, is part of the general Chautauqua plan, and so more national than State. It has nine courses of study, elective, and extending over three years. The "Teachers' National Reading Circle," instituted the year following, has a like organization and similar course.

Two States—Indiana and Illinois—have projected "Children's Reading Circles," to suggest appropriate books and, working through local teachers, encourage the better selection of books, and their more thoughtful reading by the young. The management otherwise is the same, and under the same board of control as is the "Teachers' Reading Circle."

The Agassiz Association is an organization of several hundred local societies banded together for the elementary study of nature. Primarily for children and young people, its membership has come to include all who wish to do, or use it to induce others to do, original work in science. The parent society was that of Pittsfield, Massachusetts, organized in 1876, from which and under whose direction others have taken their plan and inspiration. The clubs number nearly one thousand, with fifteen thousand members, and are found in every State, Canada, England, and Japan. They study botany, entomology, geology, anatomy, physiology, etc. The official organ is "The Swiss Cross."

Bibliography.

"Sectarian *vs.* Public Schools," "The New-Englander," vol. vi, pp. 230, 299; "Defects in Political Institutions," Cardinal Gibbons, "North American Review," October, 1887; "The Proposed American Catholic University," "American Catholic Quarterly Review," April, 1885; "Peter

Cooper," "The Chautauquan," vol. iv, No. 7, p. 398; "On the Educational Uses of Museums," "Proceedings of the New York University Convocation," 1887, p. 208; "How to spread Information," "National Educational Association," 1887, p. 238; "The Chautauqua Movement," by J. H. Vincent, 1886; and "Expositions," in "Education," vol. vi, pp. 62, 178, 272; "History of the Agassiz Association," by H. H. Ballard, "Science," vol. ix, p. 93.

CHAPTER XVI.

LEARNED SOCIETIES AND LIBRARIES.

1. General Societies.

"AN inventory of the means of general intelligence," said Horace Mann, "which did not include these institutions —the lecture, mechanics' institutes, and scientific and general societies—would justly be regarded as incomplete."

Less formal in its organization but more spontaneous in its results than the school, the free association of students and investigators has led to some of the most valuable conclusions of modern science. The individual bias corrected and the personal enthusiasm tempered by the combined judgment and diverse views of one's fellows, knowledge takes on the form of universality, and so becomes true science. This friction works out a revision which otherwise must come from the slow process of the unskilled criticism of the general public. The scientific academy has a field as definitely marked as the college or university, and has been described * as "the most potent agency which our civilization possesses for the discovery of truth."

While the Smithsonian Institution combines in itself the two functions of increasing and diffusing knowledge, about

---

* By President Gilman, "Proceedings of the American Philosophical Society," vol. xviii (1880), p. 538.

equally emphasizing both, "the prime function of the university is education, its secondary object research. The converse is true of the academy." This aims at investigation, experiment, observation, and only incidentally instructs. It looks to the enlargement of the field of knowledge, and yet the academy as an organization finds its chief service in the stimulation it affords the individual, the suggestion and criticism, the direction of thought and broadening of views. The association is the occasion only for a sharpening of insight and a multiplication of data whereby right comparisons are possible.

A. SCIENTIFIC SOCIETIES.

Such academies are, first, scientific, and find their type in the American Philosophical Society, established by Franklin and his companions in 1743. This, besides the American Society of Philadelphia and the Berkeley Society of Newport, Rhode Island, fifteen years before, both of which were short-lived, was the only organization of the kind for half a century.* At the close of the century the Connecticut Academy of Arts and Sciences was founded (1799), and twelve years later the Academy of Natural Sciences, Philadelphia, and a similar body in New York (1818). If, then, the Linnæan Society (1807) and half a dozen literary and semi-historical associations be excepted, the development of the academy belongs to the last fifty years. This enlargement was a part of the new spirit of the period, which took shape in the American Ethnological Society (1842), the American Association for the Advancement of Science (1848), and the American Geographical Society, all typical of manifold new interests. So also may be named, not excluding others of equal merit per-

---

* It is told (see " Proceedings of Washington Biological Society," February 6, 1886) that, before the middle of the seventeenth century, Bishop Wilkins, of London, Mr. Boyle, and other scholars, purposed leaving England to establish in America a "scientific society" or community and organization for research, hearing which Charles II provided for the establishment of the "Royal Society" instead.

haps, the American Philological and Modern Language Associations, the Oriental Society, the Archæological Institute, the American Society of Microscopists, the Ornithologists' Union, etc., all of which, national in their field and so general, are yet special in their inquiry.

Further, there are local organizations also for special research, as the science clubs, most State societies, the Tyndall Association, and, in certain colleges, seminaries of mathematics, engineering, the natural sciences, psychology, economics, or of particular phases of these.

(1.) The American Philosophical Society.

An account of the American Philosophical Society, the oldest of these organizations, and the type in form and conduct of many, will suggest the constitution of most others.

The society began with eight members besides the founder (Benjamin Franklin), including a physician, a botanist, a mathematician, a mechanician, a geographer, and a natural philosopher. It was chartered (1780) as the "American Philosophical Society held at Philadelphia for promoting Useful Knowledge." For many years its work was done in the five sections: 1. Medicine and anatomy; 2. Natural history and chemistry; 3. Trade and commerce; 4. Mechanics and architecture; 5. Husbandry and American improvement. Put beside the better of the more recent societies, this seems very general and ill-defined. A section was added about 1790 on "history, moral science, and general literature," * and a few others later, specialized from the first. Franklin was for many years the society's secretary and the first president of the incorporated organization (1780-'90). At his death he was succeeded in office by David Rittenhouse, of whom Jefferson (himself a member for forty-six years) †

---

* The genesis of the Pennsylvania Historical Society.

† Mr. Jefferson was much interested in all scientific and philosophical questions. It is related of his horseback-ride to his inauguration as President of the United States that he carried with him a saddle-bag of strange

said, "Genius, science, modesty, purity of morals, and simplicity of manners, marked him one of Nature's best samples of the perfection she can cover under the human form."

The membership has included, besides those already named, men of such eminence as Benjamin Rush, A. D. Bache, Bertram the botanist, Alexander Hamilton, John Randolph, Benjamin Silliman, and Robert Fulton; and of foreign gentlemen, Priestley, Erasmus Darwin, Dr. Jenner, and Sir Humphry Davy—seeming to justify the contemporary comment that the "Philosophical Society of Philadelphia comprehended within itself whatever the American world had of distinction in philosophy and science in general." In its meetings were first discussed and revised many of the theories and discoveries in physics, chemistry, meteorology, and economics, which have played so large a part in modern science and progress. The orrery of Rittenhouse, the Delaware Canal, American silk-culture, the use of fertilizers, and the revision and enlargement of the census, all took their impulse from its deliberations.

(2.) The Boston Academy of Sciences.

As representative of a comprehensive organization that of the Boston Academy of Sciences is presented. It consists of fellows and honorary members assigned to three classes, with the minor sections as follows:

CLASS I. The mathematical and physical sciences:
    1. Mathematics.
    2. Practical astronomy and geodesy.
    3. Physics and chemistry.
    4. Technology and engineering.
CLASS II. The natural and physiological sciences:
    1. Geology, mineralogy, and the physics of the globe.

---

fossils, whose description he had attempted, and concerning which he sought scientific authority.

2. Botany.
3. Zoölogy and physiology.
4. Medicine and surgery.
CLASS III. The moral and political sciences:
1. Philosophy and jurisprudence.
2. Philology and archæology.
3. Political economy and history.
4. Literature and the fine arts.

(3.) The Philadelphia Academy of Natural Sciences.

Early in the century natural history had received a strong popular as well as scientific impulse in the publication of Wilson's "American Ornithology," and certain developments in botany, under Dr. Muhlenberg and his school. The study of the general phenomena of life, in France and England, was claiming scientific attention, in which Americans participated. The Philadelphia Academy of Natural Sciences took its origin about 1812, with the versatile scientist Mr. Thomas Say and his companions, and, very early, under the prevailing scientific interest, became specialized toward biological investigations. This was in contrast with other societies, as appears from the organization. The eight sections comprise: 1. Biology and microscopy. 2. Conchology. 3. Entomology.* 4. Botany. 5. Mineralogy and geology. 6. Invertebrate paleontology. 7. Invertebrate zoölogy. 8. Ethnology and archæology. Its library is said to be one of the most complete and reliable collections of works upon natural history in the United States.

B. TECHNOLOGICAL SOCIETIES.

The Franklin Institute, Philadelphia, is representative of a large class of organizations whose function is to point out and enforce the applications of science to the industrial interests of society. It includes mechanics' institutes, dating from the last century; industrial associations of the more

---

* This constitutes the American Entomological Society.

modern type, to which the public is largely indebted for a revival of handicraft training, the promotion of art, and the constructive habit, so important to an industrial people; and the more formal trade and technological organizations. Of the latter are the "Society of Arts," of the Massachusetts Institute of Technology, and the "Associates of Cooper Union." In a general way, also, the National Academy of Sciences, which was formed during the civil war, and which grew out of the exigencies of the period, has a like constitution.

(1.) Cooper Union.

In the act of incorporation of Cooper Union it was provided that the trustees of the corporation might associate with themselves such persons as they should see fit, whose united organization should be known as the "Society of the Associates of Cooper Union for the Advancement of Science and Art." Its objects are stated to be "the encouragement of science, arts, manufactures, and commerce; the bestowal of rewards for such productions, inventions, and improvements as tend to the useful employment of the poor, the increase of trade, and the riches and honor of the country; for meritorious works in the various departments of fine arts; for discoveries, inventions, and improvements; and, generally, by lectures, papers, and discussions thereon, and other suitable means, to assist in the advancement, development, and practical application of every department of science in connection with the arts, manufactures, and commerce of the country." Investigations are carried on in fourteen sections, comprising both technological and economic inquiries.

(2.) Society of Arts.

In conformity with the original plan of the Massachusetts Institute of Technology, the Society of Arts was established in 1861. It looks to the advancement of the practical sciences in connection with arts, agriculture, manufactures, and commerce. An idea of the society's function may be gathered from the following list of topics discussed in one year (1886–'87): "Steel for Warfare," "Railroad Engineering Education," "Incandescent Lighting," "Electric Welding," "Stellar Photography," "Evolution of the Modern Yacht," "The Freezing Process in Excavations," "Water-Power of the United States," "Bessemerizing of Copper," "Coal-Min ing," "Sources of Business Profits," "Railway-Tracks," "Automatic Fire-Alarms," "Submarine Signals."

C. HISTORICAL AND ECONOMIC SOCIETIES.

Of a different character are the general historical associations for the collection and preservation of records, eminent biographies, State and administrative papers, and whatever adds permanence and completeness to the traces of institutional life.

The Massachusetts Historical Society (1791) is the parent of all this large class. Among other active organizations are the New England Historico-Genealogical Society, the American Antiquarian Society, the Pilgrim Society (Plymouth), the American Historical Association, of somewhat general interest, the Newport (Rhode Island) Historical Society, and the Albany Institute, in the East; the Maryland, South Carolina, Kentucky, and Missouri, and Southern (Virginia) Historical Societies, in the South; State pioneer associations in California, Michigan, Ohio, and Wisconsin, and numerous historical societies throughout the West belonging to this class. Besides these, there are the more recent economic organizations, represented in the American Social Science Association, the Institute of Civics, etc.

Such organizations are to be found in every State and most of the Territories—more than one hundred in all—besides a number of others that, including more or less of philosophical and scientific inquiry, or connected with libraries and museums, have a similar character.

D. SOCIETY PUBLICATIONS.

One of the most helpful services of these general societies of whatever aim is the publication of their proceedings and

contributions.   In the aggregate they number perhaps three
hundred to four hundred volumes.   Unique among them is
the "American Journal of Science," started in 1818 under
Prof. Silliman, who did so much for science in the first half
of the present century.   It embraces the circle of the "physical sciences, and their application to every useful purpose."
Its one hundred and thirty-three volumes form a work of
permanent value as exhibiting the progress of American
science in the century.   The "Journal of the Philadelphia
Academy of Science," which is one year older, admitting to
its pages "only that which is new, or is thought to be
so," in natural history, has for sixty years had a wide
circulation both in Europe and America, and has been
pronounced "absolutely indispensable to every American
naturalist."

The published documents of the Massachusetts Historical
Society number forty-four volumes, include the Winthrop
and Sewall and Belknap papers, and are of more than local
importance.   Together with like collections by other colonies, they have been the (original) sources of most of the
early historical literature of this country.   The "Plymouth
Colony Records" comprise ten volumes, and those of Massachusetts and Rhode Island, the "New Hampshire Provincial
Papers," and the records of the town of Boston, aggregate
fifty more.   Broadhead's "Documents of the Colonial History of New York," a similar set of papers in New Jersey,
the publications of the New York Historical Society (com-
piled by Mr. George Bancroft), including the noted "Lee
Papers," and the archives of Maryland, have all been the
work of either historical societies or of Legislatures and individuals, at the suggestion of such bodies.   Their labors are
invaluable, not for the number of volumes they represent,
but for the indispensable fund of historical information,
town and church histories, political papers and correspondence, biographies, records and diaries, glimpses of the past,
data for the comparative study of institutions and custom
and progress.

2. Libraries.

When one considers that, exclusive of parish and Sunday-school libraries, all private collections, and public and school libraries of less than three hundred volumes each, there are in the United States twenty million volumes, the magnitude of the library interest is apparent. And yet these millions of books, in more than five thousand libraries, have been gathered in a century and a half.

A. COLONIAL BEGINNINGS.

Though rich in the sources of suggestion and example, the colonial history is both short and of meager details.

The earliest community-libraries were, doubtless, suggested by the occasional choice private libraries of public-spirited citizens. Of historic note among these were: 1. The Sharp Library of New York, which was presented to the town in 1700, and fifty years later became the nucleus of the New York Society Library. 2. The Logan Library of Philadelphia; a valuable collection of classical works, owned by a learned Quaker, who conveyed three thousand volumes to the village in 1745, with an endowment. 3. The Prince Library, the property of a pastor of the Old South Church, Boston. This was rich in the annals of New England; and, after being held by the church a hundred years, was finally deposited with the Boston Public Library.

It is not likely these were all. Among the colonists were scholarly men. But, at any time before the Revolution, libraries must have been small, for their collection was both difficult and expensive. In 1723 there was but one printer in New York, and two only in Philadelphia. Practically all books were brought from England. It is not strange, then, that in the first one hundred and fifty years from the founding of Jamestown, the country had barely six libraries, besides what might be found in the colleges. It is estimated that there were in the colonies, all told, in 1775, about forty-three thousand volumes, forty-five per cent of which were in the colleges.

The most fruitful collections of this period were the social or subscription libraries. The oldest of these was that in Philadelphia, which Franklin said was the "mother of all North American subscription libraries." It had its suggestion in the "Junto," * a reading and debating club of Franklin and his companions, and was started in 1732. The selection was chiefly of reference-books, though they circulated among "subscribing members." † Of theological works and controversial, it is said the library had none ; something of polite literature, and much of science, travels, the mechanic arts, and philosophy. The same general character is still preserved, while it has been much enriched by certain rare collections, newspaper files (one set continuous from 1791), pamphlets of the Revolution, etc. The society has now one thousand members and one hundred and fifty thousand volumes.

Next to this, both in time and influence, is the Redwood Library, of Newport, Rhode Island (1747). It had large donations before the middle of the century, and was the recipient of substantial favors from the English bishop. George Berkeley. This gentleman was both philosopher and theologian. Coming to America (1729), his scholarly tastes ‡ early made him the center of the culture and learning of Rhode Island and Connecticut—colonies noted for their learning and refinement. A society for literary and philosophical intercourse was founded the next year. Aspiring to the possession of a library, its members contributed a

---

* The basis of the American Philosophical Society, perhaps, started ten years later.

† Mr. James Parton's "Triumphs of Enterprise" contains (p. 177) a very readable and trustworthy chapter on the "Rise of Circulating Libraries."

‡ "So much understanding, so much knowledge, so much innocence, and such humility, I did not think had been the fashion of any but angels till I saw this gentleman."—ATTERBURY.

few books, and in 1747, through the generosity of Abraham
Redwood, the library was established, said to have been one
of the choicest collections on theology, history, and the arts
and sciences of its day.   Scholars came to it "from the
Carolinas and the West Indies, from New York, and even
from Boston,"* to replenish their stores of knowledge.   It
is still flourishing, with nearly thirty thousand volumes in
the library, extensive galleries of painting and sculpture,
and a liberal yearly income.

About the same time, and probably inspired by the Newport and Philadelphia ventures, a number of young men in
South Carolina associated themselves for mutual improvement; a library was formed, which, though destroyed during the Revolution, became, in organization, the nucleus of
the present Public Library of Charleston.

The present New York Society Library was incorporated
(1754) as the "City Library," and was chartered under its
present name just before the Revolution.   In half a century from 1800 it had increased from six thousand to forty
thousand volumes, has now more than twice as many, and
ranks as one of the earliest and most successful loan-libraries
in the country.   It contains rare editions, valuable newspaper files, and is withal the "library of the old Knicker-
bocker families of New York city."

One other library deserves mention in this connection, as
indicating the intelligence and general refinement which
might then be found in not a few New England communities.   The "Social Library" of Salem, Massachusetts, was a
club organization (1760), limited in its membership, and philosophical.   Its books were few, but well chosen, numbering,
fifty years afterward, but eight hundred volumes; though
including the memoirs of the French Academy, the Royal
Society transactions from the beginning, and the memoirs
of the Berlin Academy, besides philosophical works of indi-

---

* Stockwell's "History of Public Education in Rhode Island,"
p. 269.

viduals and the publications of contemporary literary institutions.

B. RECENT LIBRARIES.

Between the Revolution and the second war with England, little more was done in improving libraries than other
educational agencies. But the period since has shown interesting developments. New agencies for increasing knowledge were devised; new means of spreading it. School and
church, government and trade, social interests and established forms were put to the test—out of the ordeal emerged,
if not new institutions, vastly modified and improved old
ones.

Within this period, besides those named, have started
the Mercantile, Mechanics', and Apprentices' Libraries; endowed and public libraries; school and free town libraries;
most of those in colleges and professional institutions; State
and national libraries. The aggregate is enormous, and
constitutes one of the most available of educational agencies.

(1.) Mercantile Libraries.

The first of these, as the principal libraries of the colonial
period, are supported by subscription, but differ from those
already noted in belonging generally to or taking their members from a guild or class. Three such were established in
the year 1820—the Boston and the New York Mercantile, and
the New York Apprentices' Library. The Philadelphia Mercantile was founded a year later. After the example of the
English society, mechanics' institutes were formed in this
country, which frequently took advantage of the library interest to hold their members together; but no large collections resulted.

The two oldest of these mercantile library institutions
are also representative of two distinct types of control.
Most of them are principally for merchants' clerks or mechanics, and, as in Boston, are managed by them. In New
York, on the contrary, the Clinton Hall Association of the

City of New York is an organization of prominent merchants, who own the building and "hold in trust and manage all property, real and personal, for the benefit of the library." The officers of the library control their own affairs, financial and administrative, as a distinct organization, having free rent, and holding the books equally open to members of both associations. The institution has two hundred and twenty-five thousand volumes, nine thousand members, its own bindery, property to the value of half a milion, and ranks fifth in size in the United States. Of the same class is the St. Louis Mercantile Library (seventy-five thousand volumes). The Brooklyn organization is pecular in that, while a' class institution in name and control, it is free to all on equal terms. It has ninety thousand volumes ; San Francisco sixty thousand, and Philadelphia as many as both. This last is famous for the large bibliographical department numbering five thousand volumes. There are thirty-five libraries belonging to this class, and as many more that, while social in their organization, are somewhat more literary, and go by the name of young men's associations, athenæums, etc. Of the former is the Young Men's Association Library at Albany, New York, founded in 1833. The Boston Athenæum is a unique institution. Primarily devoted to its reading-room, it has a library of one hundred and fifty thousand volumes. It is proprietary, owning real estate, library, and fine-art collections, and invested funds to the amount of a quarter of a million of dollars.

(2.) Public Libraries.

The Public Library in Boston "sprang," says Mr. Henry Barnard, "from a feeling on the part of its most thoughtful and judicious citizens that the system of public education, so liberally provided for the young, might be and should be extended to those of more mature age." The sentiment took form in 1847, when Mayor Quincy offered to give to the city $5,000 in order to initiate a library, provided $10,000 should be otherwise raised for the same purpose. The gift was accepted, and a legislative act secured authorizing its establishment. In fifteen years it numbered nearly one hundred thousand volumes. Besides cash donations from Mr. Joshua Bates ($100,000) and others, it has received some valuable gifts of books. The famous mathematical collection of Prof. Bowditch was presented by his sons. Theodore Parker bequeathed to it his own scholarly library of over eleven thousand volumes. Mr. George Ticknor donated seven thousand volumes of ancient classics, Spanish and Portuguese. It received, also, the Prince Library from the Old South Church, and the Boston Shakespeare Collection. It comprises four hundred and fifty thousand volumes, and is, next to the Library of Congress, the largest in the United States. The Cincinnati Public Library, of one hundred and fifty thousand volumes, and the Public Library of Chicago, nearly as large, are both public (free) and tax-supported.

(3.) Endowed Libraries.

The endowed libraries of the United States—either founded or maintained, or both, by private benefaction—form a large class. Among the oldest and most widely known of these are the Astor and Lenox Libraries of New York, the Case Library of Cleveland, Ohio, the Peabody Libraries in Baltimore, Maryland, and Danvers and Peabody, Massachusetts, and the Sutro Library, San Francisco, California.

John Jacob Astor, of New York, died March 29, 1848. One codicil to his will said: "Desiring to render a public benefit to the city of New York and to contribute to the advancement of useful knowledge and the general good of society, I do, by this codicil, appoint $400,000 out of my residuary estate to the establishment of a public library in the city of New York." Eleven trustees were appointed, whose first president was Washington Irving. The institution was opened (1854) with eighty thousand volumes, selected wholly for reference, a character which the library still retains. It has since received from the Astor family (three generations) two large and well-equipped buildings and $300,000 in cash donations and bequests. The library is a general, not special one, but with history constituting about one fourth of the whole (two hundred and twenty-five thousand volumes). It has a permanent invested fund of $775,-000.

Of the same general character, both as to organization and books, is the Peabody Library, Baltimore, established in 1857. It has approximately one hundred thousand volumes, free to any one within the building. The proposed Newberry Library, Chicago, comes of the half part of an estate left to the city, in a residuary bequest, by Walter L. Newberry in 1868. The trustees have just come into possession of $2,149,200, out of which are to be furnished buildings and a reference library similar to the last.

(4.) School District Libraries.

It has been generally said that libraries supported by public funds began in England (1850). But the State of New York, fifteen years before, had a working law for providing and supporting free-school libraries throughout the State. Three years afterward, $55,000 a year was ordered turned from the general school fund for their maintenance, on condition that the districts raise an equal sum. Within fifteen years they numbered a million and a half of volumes. These were to do for the rural districts of the Empire State what Boston meant to do for the city—contribute to out-of-school improvement. The limit of their efficiency was soon reached. In 1860 only seven hundred thousand volumes were reported, notwithstanding more than a million dollars had been expended in their support.

Following New York, Michigan (1837) authorized the establishment of township libraries, and Massachusetts immediately after. Connecticut passed a similar law in 1839, Rhode Island in 1840, and Iowa the same year, while yet a Territory. Indiana's first law was enacted in 1841, but supplemented eleven years after, by ordering a tax of one fourth of a mill on each dollar, and twenty-five cents on each poll, to be levied for two years, and the proceeds applied to the purchase of books for the school districts. Within three years half a million volumes had been distributed. Ohio made substantially the same provisions in 1848, and Wisconsin also, whose legislation Mr. Barnard pronounced " altogether in advance, in its practical bearings and completeness, of anything then attempted." Of twenty States which, prior to 1875, had made some attempt to provide books for the school districts, eleven had sent out more than three million volumes. In a general way it may be said that, while they fell short of the expectations of their friends, these libraries yet served to prepare the way for the more recent town libraries that promise to be a needed and wholesome supplement to the common schools.

(5.) Free Town Libraries.

New Hampshire initiated the plan of town libraries maintained by public tax, or municipal appropriation (1849), the amount of the grant in any case being left to the town. This was a year before the so-called Public Libraries Act of England. Previous to this, single communities in New Hampshire * had assumed the responsibility, and by public vote had established and by annual appropriation supported exactly similar libraries. Castine, Maine, had one in 1827, and the Bingham Library, at Salisbury, Connecticut, in 1803, antedated the State law by sixty-six years. Such instances were not unknown even in the West, though they came later, and were generally given private aid.

The State Library law of Massachusetts (1851) grew out of an attempt to establish a library at Wayland, in that State, a few years before. New Bedford first organized under this law a library that has now fifty thousand volumes. Maine, Vermont, Ohio, Wisconsin, Connecticut, Indiana, and Iowa had all made similar enactments before 1870 ; perhaps a dozen others have done so since.

---

* Peterborough had then had a free public library for fourteen years.

(6.) Professional Libraries.

Another class, far less numerous, and more special, are those belonging to the professions—law, medicine, and theology.

Of the last, there is but one not connected with seminaries or theological departments. This is the General Theological Library of Boston, founded in 1860 by members of different denominations, "looking toward Christian union by first promoting a better understanding among the sects." Altogether the United States has seventy-six theological libraries, including both independent seminary and department libraries, with an aggregate of eight hundred thousand volumes.

Of the function of medical libraries, it has been asserted : * "Few persons have any adequate idea of the amount of medical literature in existence, or its proper and true value. The result is that the same ground is traversed over and over again ; cases are reported as unique and inexplicable which, when compared with accounts of others buried in obscure periodicals, or collections of observations, fall into their proper places, and both receive and give explanation."

The medical library is indispensable to the practitioner or student who would know his profession ; and yet, for the most part, the collections are very insignificant. Of the two hundred and fifty or three hundred thousand volumes in the United States, the three cities—Washington, New York, and Philadelphia—contain four fifths ; one third of the one hundred and twenty-six schools reporting none. The collection in the last city is regarded as valuable, though that in the Surgeon-General's office, at Washington, is incomparably superior, not only to all others in that city, but, in numbers and character, outranking any other in this country. It contains eighty thousand volumes.

To the bar, the need of well-stocked libraries of the profession becomes daily more urgent. The rapid multiplica-

---

* Dr. Billings, "Public Libraries of the United States," p. 171.
20

tion of reports complicates incalculably the practice of the profession. It is estimated that, including the judicial reports of the English, Irish, Scotch, and American courts, standard treatises and digests and the statute laws of these countries, "a fairly complete library would embrace, approximately, seventy-five hundred volumes, and cost not less than fifty thousand dollars. The principal center for this class of literature is New York, with its eighty-two thousand volumes. Boston has fifty thousand, and San Francisco forty thousand. The Bar Association Library of Washington—the only one in the city—catalogues but five thousand volumes ; though it is supplemented by a vast collection of books more or less closely bearing upon the profession, and a large number, the most valuable of all, in the Government departments, estimated at two hundred thousand volumes. Of the forty-five law schools, fourteen report no libraries. Harvard (1817) has twenty-two thousand volumes, particularly full in Roman jurisprudence and the commercial law of Continental Europe. That of Yale, formed later, is much smaller (nine thousand volumes), but fairly complete in English and American reports and international law. The earliest collection seems to have been that of the Philadelphia Law Association (1802), though the Social Law Library of Boston is nearly as old. Besides these, two Courts of Appeals in New York, Middlesex County, Massachusetts, and Harvard, possessed the only ones prior to 1825.

(7.) State Libraries.

Supplementary to collections of law books proper are several State libraries, which because of their character very naturally follow them. There are forty-seven of these in the several States and Territories, having nearly a million volumes. They include public documents of every kind— local and national, legislative, judicial, and administrative. Some of them were formed very early, though perhaps none before the Revolution. There was one in Philadelphia in 1777, others in New Jersey and New Hampshire twenty

years later, and similar ones in Pennsylvania, Ohio, New
York, Illinois, Kentucky, Virginia, and Indiana, all before
1825.

(8.) Government Libraries.

Government Libraries are of two kinds: 1. The Congressional Library; 2. The department libraries.

While the seat of the national Government was at Philadelphia, officials used the local City Library. Immediately
upon the removal to Washington (1800), Congress appropriated five thousand dollars to be expended in the purchase
of books " for the use of the two Houses of Congress and the
members thereof." Two years later an annual appropriation
was ordered and permanent regulations adopted. It was
provided that the library should be open freely to the President, heads of departments, judges and *attachés* of the courts,
members and officers of the two Houses, the diplomatic
corps, and, later, to the Secretary and Regents of the Smithsonian Institution.

The library grew slowly, having twelve years after (1814)
but three thousand books, which in the one day's occupation
of the city by the British were entirely destroyed by fire.
The year following, Jefferson's private library was pur-
chased. A generation later (1851) a second fire destroyed two
thirds of the collection, including works on English and
European history, the arts, sciences, literature, and voyages,
leaving but twenty thousand volumes. *Then* was erected
an iron finished building. In eight years the library had
added fifty thousand volumes, and was receiving an annual
appropriation of ten thousand dollars. In 1866 it was given
the Smithsonian deposit, and the next year the Peter Force
Library of " Colonization and History of the United States,"
numbering sixty thousand volumes. The enactment of the
copyright law (1870), requiring the deposit of two copies of
each published work, makes about twelve thousand entries
annually. The books now number nearly six hundred thousand, besides two hundred thousand pamphlets, and are open
in the room to all who choose to use them.

Besides the Congressional Library, most of the departments have special collections, some of which are very complete and valuable. In addition to those indicated in the table there are libraries at each military post and garrison, at army headquarters, at the National Soldiers' Homes, and on naval and merchant vessels, aggregating two hundred thousand volumes.

Government Department Libraries.

DEPARTMENTS.	Volumes.	Character.
1. State......................	23,000	Diplomatic history, economics, voyages ; 1,000 volumes English newspapers.
2. Treasury..................	15,000	
3. Senate....................	20,000	A complete set of state papers.
4. House	100,000	Legislative and executive.
5. Executive Mansion	2,000	
6. Coast Survey..............	5,000	Scientific works and journals.
7. War......................	15,000	
8. Military Academy	30,000	
9. Naval Observatory	10,000	
10. Naval Academy	10,000	
11. Bureau of Education........	25,000	Large pedagogical collection.
12. Patent-Office..............	30,000	Best technological library in the United States.
13. Judiciary	15,000	
14. Agriculture	20,000	Very complete in agricultural science and reports of agricultural and scientific societies in Europe and America.

(9.) College Libraries.

Among the most important of all the classes named is the college library. It was also one of the earliest. John Harvard's private collection started the first one simultaneously with the first college. Among the first donations to Virginia education were books and maps for the "college." Yale had a like beginning ; and yet in a different sense the modern college library is important. It is both less and more valued; less a general possession, more as a special instrument. It is not now always the first step in the founding of colleges. Forty existing institutions report none.

The total catalogue of three hundred and six libraries is something over three million volumes. Twenty-four institutions, only, report more than twenty-five thousand volumes each; nine have sixty thousand or more.

A good college library is a thing of growth. But four of these twenty-four larger ones were started since 1860: Lehigh (1866), Cornell (1868), University of California (1869), and Johns Hopkins (1876).

This is one of the characteristics of the contemporary library: it is coming to be adapted in kind and conditions to the use to be made of it. It is made a laboratory, a workshop. To the student it becomes the starting-point for research, the source of adjustments and verifications of knowledge. It is indispensable in the study of history and language, but scarcely less to the student of science who would avoid the needless repetition of observations and established conclusions. Much use of books by associated departments tends to set off the mass of books into special libraries, each with a particular character. So a university will have its general library, society libraries, and professional libraries. It may have, further, its mathematical references or biological or psycho-physical; its historical and philosophical; appliances made constantly available for special studies; not so many catalogued volumes, but trusted authorities. This is true of all the eight or ten largest collections. Not that they are kept in separate buildings or under independent management; indeed, they are not generally so controlled. But, with the greater independence of departments and the larger option among courses and the narrowing of specialties, comes the need for a more systematic use of technical authorities and references and an adapted literature. With such interpretation the library is no longer a place in which to lounge, but an instrument to be used; and so around well-managed libraries have grown up seminaries for special inquiry, and societies, and a contributing literature, and subject alcoves, of great variety and of yet greater service.

Another device for making the library more generally available and useful is the classified subject index. Not a few small libraries of well-chosen books are made doubly serviceable through the use of catalogues so arranged as to place within easy reach their material. ' Next in importance to the free use of books is the very extensive utilization of magazine, newspaper, and other current literature as sources of information bearing upon studies. Judiciously selected pamphlet collections are of incalculable value. The geographical and educational and economic bureaus of the Johns Hopkins University illustrate this function. Most colleges sustain reading-rooms of substantial literature, also brought by index into the regular current of the library service. Columbia has ten thousand pamphlets, Cornell fifteen thousand, Michigan as many, Yale forty thousand, and Harvard two hundred and seventy thousand.

So important are the management and use of these collections considered in the best colleges, that in more than one institution they have come to be subjects of study. The Columbia College " School of Library Economy " (1883) is a well-organized enterprise that in a more or less complete way is being tried at Johns Hopkins University, Cornell, Harvard, Michigan, and elsewhere, both East and West. Rochester University, New York, has given annual lectures on the founding, control, and development of libraries since 1880. At Columbia the faculty of the School of Library Economy consists of nine instructors, including the director and twenty to thirty special non-resident lecturers annually.

The course includes lectures and observations on:

1. Library economy.
2. The scope and usefulness of libraries.
3. The founding and extension of libraries.
4. Buildings.
5. Government and service.
6. Regulations for readers.
7. Administration, catalogue, references, loan, etc.

8. Libraries on special subjects.
9. General libraries.
10. Libraries of special countries or sections.
11. Reading and aids.
12. Literary methods.
13. Bibliography.
14. Catalogues of general collections.

Bibliography.

" The Literary Influence of Academies," by M. Arnold ; " Learned Societies," by J. Farrar, " North American Review," vol. viii, p. 157 ; Warren and Clark, " Public Libraries in the United States," 1876 ; " College Libraries as Aids to Instruction," published by the Bureau of Education ; " Free Public Libraries," T. Greenwood, 1886 ; " Libraries and Schools," by S. S. Green, 1883 ; " Libraries and Readers," by W. E. Foster, 1883 ; " District School Libraries," Horace Mann, Lecture VI ; also " Relation of Libraries to General Education," Horace Mann, " Third Report," 1839. Of incalculable value is the " Library Journal," edited by M. Dewey, New York.

CHAPTER XVII.

THE GENERAL GOVERNMENT AND EDUCATION.

THE modern representative Government, like the contemporary Church, is an organized protest against the dominance of unreasoning authority, from whatever source. Nevertheless, the national Government in this country has had a large share in the control and direction of educational thought and institutions.

It has created and repeatedly enlarged school funds, first and directly, by appropriations of land, to the common schools, academies, and universities; and indirectly, through the surplus revenue deposit, and the three per cent of public land sales. It is officially charged with the education of the Indians and Alaskans; provides generously for military and naval education, both in the two national institutions and in established colleges and universities in the States; furnishes homes and instruction to many hundred soldiers' orphans, and has with rare wisdom contributed millions to the schooling of the impoverished South. The true spirit of republicanism has never opposed any centralization that looked to the greater general good. And to the service of the Government in the particulars named, must be added another chapter treating of the National Bureau of Education, the Smithsonian Institution, and the general scientific work carried on through its departments.

1. The Bureau of Education.

Pinckney, of South Carolina, Madison, of Virginia, Morris, of New York, the wise Jefferson, and a half-dozen other contemporary statesmen, advocated the establishment of a national university, "for the advancement of useful knowledge, and the promotion of agriculture, commerce, trades, and manufactures." The idea, in some form, has since come up in almost every administration.

In his message to the two Houses of Congress in 1790, Washington's often-quoted words were full of wisdom and rare foresight. "Knowledge," he says, "is in every country the surest basis of public happiness. In one in which the measures of government receive their impressions so immediately as in ours, from the sense of the community, it is proportionally essential. . . . Whether this will be best promoted," he continued, "by affording aid to seminaries of learning already established, by the institution of a national university, or by any other expedients, will be well worthy a place in the deliberations of the Legislature." Six years later he urged immediate attention to the improvement of agriculture as a fundamental concern in this country, and recommended "the creation of a national central agency, charged with collecting and diffusing information, and enabled by premiums and small pecuniary aids to encourage and assist a spirit of discovery and improvement." Twenty years after the address just quoted, M. Julian, a Frenchman, urged upon his Government the comprehensive and comparative study of educational questions through a national establishment, whose duty it should be "to collect the material for a general report on the scholastic institutions and on methods of instruction in the different European states."

The need for such an agency in this country early attracted the attention of educators. The teachers of Essex County, Massachusetts, in association 1849, voted to petition Congress to established a "bureau in the home department for promoting public education." Fifteen years later, at the sixth meeting of the National Educational Association, a paper was read and discussed on the subject of a "National Bureau of Education," for the establishment of which the intelligence and interest of the country were pledged. The year following, Bishop Fraser, after emphasizing the importance of a more general supervision, commended the growing sentiment in the States in favor of a central agency. In 1866 the attention of the National Educational Association was turned toward the subject in a practical way. At the first meeting of the Section of School Superintendents, held in Washington that year, a committee, of which State School Commissioner E. E. White, of Ohio, was chairman, was appointed to memorialize Congress on the establishment of such a bureau. This memorial was presented in the House of Representatives, in June of the same year, by Hon. James A. Garfield, in a speech which is rich in the history of the educational sentiment of this country. After some unimportant modifications the bill passed both Houses, and on the 16th of March, 1867, Hon. Henry Barnard was appointed first "United States Commissioner of Education."

Originally created a Department, it was two years later made a Bureau of the Interior, as it remains. Mr. Barnard held the office but three years, and was succeeded by Hon. John Eaton, who resigned in 1886. The present commissioner is Hon. N. H. R. Dawson. The function of the bureau is: 1. To collect such statistics and facts as shall show the condition and progress of education in the several States and territories ; and, 2. To diffuse such information respecting the organization and management of schools and school sys-tems, and methods of teaching, as shall aid the people of the United States in the establishment and maintenance of effi-cient school systems, and otherwise promote the cause of education throughout the country.

A. BUREAU PUBLICATIONS.

The office issues an annual report, and publishes occa-sional circulars of information, besides carrying on an ex-tensive correspondence in both hemispheres. Its nineteen reports make a valuable statement of a most interesting period of our educational history. They completely cover the quarter of a century since the war, and shed a flood of light upon the saving influences of a right training of youth. Among the sixty or seventy circulars are included discus-sions of American and foreign systems; elementary, sec-ondary, and collegiate instruction, and various phases of them ; industrial, physical, and art training ; Kindergar-ten and normal schools; school architecture, expositions, and legislation ; besides methods in particular branches of the curriculum. Its special reports on " Medical Education," " Public Libraries," " Education and Labor," and " Education and Crime," the " Theory of American Education," and " City School Systems of the United States," would be of incalculable service if studied by every teacher.

B. PEDAGOGICAL LIBRARY.

In the prosecution of its official duties there has been collected an educational library, in size and richness unsur-passed in this country. It contains eighteen thousand vol-umes and about fifty thousand pamphlets. It is full in more or less disconnected and diffuse but original material for the history of American education. This includes State and city reports, American and foreign educational journals, catalogues and special publications of colleges and other educational bodies, scientific periodicals and papers, besides a large collection of American text-books and foreign school documents.

C. PEDAGOGICAL MUSEUM.

In addition to the library and supplementing it, the bureau has the beginnings of an admirable educational museum. It consists of clay and other models of primitive and civilized industry; art-work from city schools; globes, maps, charts, herbaria, school cabinets, portraits and busts of educators ; Kindergarten and industrial exhibits, besides specimens of apparatus and furniture.

2. The Smithsonian Institution.

About this institution cluster some of the most grateful recollections and the most cherished hopes of science. Its history is a record of enviable service.

In the year 1829 there died in Genoa an Englishman, James Smithson. He had spent his life in travel and study. Devoted to science, and a man of leisure, he became an investigator and author. In an authorized biography of him is given a list of twenty papers published by him, monographs chiefly, on scientific subjects, showing not only a comprehensive interest and knowledge, but a familiarity with the latest achievements of science. He was educated at Oxford, and was a member of the Royal Society. He remained unmarried, never visited the United States, and, so far as known, in political sympathies was undemocratic. He belonged to the English aristocracy, and to the house of Percy made famous by Scott and Shakespeare.*

A. THE SMITHSON BEQUEST.

Notwithstanding his English citizenship and his undemocratic instincts, upon his death the United States Government was made by provisional bequest the trustee of his large es-

---

* "Smithsonian Miscellaneous Collections," vol. xvii, pp. 151, 152.

tate. The property was to go to his nephew; but, if he should die without heirs, should be committed to the United States (save a small annuity) " to found at Washington, under the name of the Smithsonian Institution, an establishment for the increase and diffusion of knowledge among men." Upon the death of this relative, Henry James Hungerford (1835), the United States Government was informed from London of the conditions of the bequest, and the Hon. Richard Rush dispatched to receive it. The net amount was five hundred and eight thousand three hundred and eighteen dollars, to which were afterward added some small sums, making in the aggregate about five hundred and fifty thousand dollars.

B. PLANS PROPOSED.

Much doubt existed as to the original design of the testator and yet more as to the means to be employed. It took Congress nine years to decide upon its disposition. The one condition, to provide " for the increase and diffusion of knowledge among men," is very general.

The impression almost uniformly present at first was that Mr. Smithson meant to bestow his fortune upon the cause of education, and that a school or college or university was the only mode of meeting the condition. So it was argued that this should be one of a number of colleges toward the creation of a national university, the possession of which had been the hope of statesmen and scholars from the times of Washington and Jefferson. Others would have the annual income used to maintain a cabinet of natural history, a museum, or a general accumulating library. Indeed, this last had the strongest minority support from Rufus Choate and others. It was suggested that the money be made a primary school fund for the city of Washington or for infant and Sunday school encouragement throughout the United States, or that it be applied to geographical or other explorations. One party (to the credit of our representatives a small one) proposed to refund the money to James Smithson's brother, his proper heir, on the ground that the United States could not legally become a trustee for individual benefactors. It is needless to say the better judgments prevailed. The trust had been accepted, and its right use was a sacred obligation.

It was early agreed by the committee to whom the whole question was referred, and of which John Quincy Adams was chairman, that "no part of the fund should be applied to the education of children or youth nor to the establishment or support of any school, college, or university, institute of education, nor ecclesiastical establishment." It was then proposed that there should be founded an institution for physical research, contributing to agriculture, war, engineering, architecture, mining, commerce, and manufactures. John Quincy Adams pleaded for a great astronomical observatory rivaling those of Greenwich and Paris; Mr. Tappan for an institution after the plan of the Jardin des Plantes in Paris. The best educated sentiment was converging upon an agency of physical or general research; that a part or all of the proceeds of the fund should be appropriated "to a system of annual awards" for original contributions to science and the useful arts, scientific collections, the publication of scientific communications, and provisions for lectures. The very approach to the final organization in its deliberation, and the all-sided regard for ultimate efficiency, are prophetic of the conservative and comprehensive service of the subsequent management.

C. THE ORGANIZATION.

The formal act establishing the institution passed in 1847, the corporation being made to consist of the President, Vice-President, members of the Cabinet, the Chief-Justice of the Supreme Court, the Commissioner of Patents, the Mayor of Washington, and such other persons as these may elect to honorary membership. The immediate supervision rests with a Board of Regents composed of the Vice-President and Chief-Justice, the Mayor of Washington, three senators, three representatives, and six other persons, two of whom shall be residents of Washington, D. C., and four from the

States, no two from any one. From the Board of Regents one is chosen to be Chancellor, and by them a local executive officer called "secretary."

The plan of internal organization as submitted by Prof. Joseph Henry, first secretary, and as finally adopted, included the following provisions: Toward the *increase* of knowledge—1. Such systematic encouragement should be given as would stimulate to original research by rewards for scientific memoirs; 2. An annual appropriation of money should be made sufficient to generously compensate physical research. Further, looking to the *diffusion* of knowledge, there should be published: 1. Regular reports on the progress of different branches of knowledge; 2. Occasionally, as may be advisable, separate and less formal treatises on subjects of general interest. More specifically the organization was made to include: 1. A museum; 2. A chemical laboratory; 3. A library; 4. A gallery of art; 5. Lecture-rooms.

The botanical collection was, after some years, transferred to the Agricultural Department, and to the Army Medical Museum certain articles of professional interest. The library early acquired a valuable and, for this country, a rare collection of books, including philosophical and scientific transactions of learned societies throughout the world. These were finally turned over to the Congressional Library (1866), where are annually deposited copies of its exchanges, and publications of whatever kind. Carrying out the spirit of the original design—to co-operate with existing societies and institutions as far as possible—the accumulations of the Art Gallery were deposited with the Corcoran Art Exhibit, in Washington; and, upon rebuilding in 1865, after the fire, by which both buildings and records were destroyed, it was decided to discontinue the regular lectures. There remains, then, the simple and single function of carrying forward, on a liberal scale, systematic physical research, and the publication to the world of its verified conclusions. It has been from the founding, and remains, the policy of the regents and the secretary to do no work of investigation or collection or diffusion of knowledge, that is being done, or can be as well undertaken, by existing agencies.

Extensive researches have been made in the broad field of ethnology, in the much-worked but promising one of astronomy, besides the more common fields of science and meteorology ; most of the last, however, being recently transferred to the Signal-Service Bureau.

D. PUBLICATIONS.

The publications of the institution are of three kinds: 1. Contributions to knowledge. 2. Miscellaneous collections. 3. Annual reports. Of the first there have been about one hundred and fifty volumes, in which appear only memoirs, records of extensive original investigation and researches resulting in what are believed to be new truths, and to constitute positive additions to the sum of human knowledge. The miscellaneous collections comprise a series begun in 1862, to present reports on the current state of our knowledge on particular branches of science; instructions for collecting and digesting facts; lists and synopses of species in the organic and inorganic worlds; museum catalogues; reports of explorations; aids to bibliographical investigations, etc. Of these there are something more than a hundred volumes; and of the annual reports thirty-eight. Besides these there are the occasional bulletins of the National Museum, and reports of special bureaus; the latter including ethnological studies of great value.

E. THE NATIONAL MUSEUM.

Not the least important part of the Smithsonian organization is the "National Museum." In the original act of establishment (1846) it was provided that "all objects of art, and of foreign and curious research, and all objects of natural history, plants, and geological and mineralogical specimens, belonging or hereafter to belong to the United States, which may be in Washington, and such like collections made by the Coast and Interior Surveys, or by any other parties for the Government of the United States, shall be deposited in the rooms provided by the Smithsonian Institution." This large accumulation of materials, besides being a record of past investigations, and affording a stimulus to and opportunity for research, is an educational agency of the most comprehensive reach. The materials are arranged in five divisions:

I. Anthropology, with three departments.
II. Zoölogy, with ten departments.
III. Botany, in two departments.
IV. Geology, in three departments.
V. Exploration and Experiment, in four departments.

Every precaution is taken to make its resources serviceable to their intelligent use. Persons not officers of the institution may obtain access to the collection, for purposes of study, by filing an application, which must be indorsed by the director. It has been described as "the best record of original research and investigation ever made in this country."

Altogether, it may be said, no institution in this country has more perfectly accomplished its object, and none contributed more generously to either the increase or the diffusion of knowledge, than the Smithsonian Institution. Its studies of the antiquities of America, and the encouragement given to such studies by others, have more than justified its establishment and recognition by Government.

3. Special Scientific Work.

A. THE COAST SURVEY.

Among the earliest departments, and, at that time, in an undeveloped country, the most important, as it is to-day perhaps the best matured of any in the comprehensive system of scientific work by the General Government, is that of the

United States Coast Survey. Its inauguration marks an epoch in the growth of a national spirit. It dignified national interests and influence.

The enterprise was established under President Jefferson (1807), and was designed primarily to furnish accurate maps of the coast ; to determine positions for, and establish nautical and other signals ; to determine and mark the course and conditions of shore-currents, tides, and prevailing winds, and whatever should contribute to the safety and efficiency of domestic and foreign commerce in our ports. The survey was put in charge of the Secretary of the Treasury, and work ordered after plans submitted by Prof. Hassler, a Swiss resident in this country, and who was made superintendent. Operations were begun on the New Jersey coast in 1816. The commission being transferred almost immediately, however, to the army and navy, the work was checked. It was revived in 1832, and Mr. Hassler reappointed superintendent. At his death (1844) he was succeeded by Prof. A. D. Bache, with whom the present system may be said to have commenced. For twenty years he was center and compass of the greatest single educational and scientific enterprise the Government has ever undertaken. Under his direction both Pacific and Atlantic coast lines were cut into sections, each with its own base-line ; and the survey set about making a systematic exploration and map of the entire shore. Triangulation frequently reached far inland, and through subsequent years has covered adjacent States in a way to form the basis of their topographical surveys—thus rendering a double service. About the year 1870 the province of the survey was enlarged by Congress, and the triangulation carried farther inland, with a view of covering the intervening section, " so as to form a geodetic connection " between the eastern and western coasts, determining points in each State of the Union for needed local, geological, and topographical surveys.

In addition to the immediate service it was meant to render—the location of the coast-line, the mapping of harbors

21

and other inlets, and the location of danger-signals—it has
made numerous valuable hydrographic and magnetic observations ; carried on deep-sea soundings and dredgings ;
studied minutely, and for years, the tides from nine hundred
stations ; mapped the Gulf Stream; perfected determinations
of latitude and longitude ; contributed data for calculating
the measurements and curvature of the earth, and corrected
variations of the magnetic needle. How much has been accomplished in all these respects, or in each, and how eminently serviceable have been the conclusions both to economics and to abstract science, can not easily be overstated;
its contributions to the "general welfare" give it a prominent place in the functions of the national Government. It
has been pronounced by Mr. J. D. Whitney "the only great
scientific work in this country, which has been uninterrupt-
edly carried on for any considerable time ; and one of the
few things done under the authority of the General Government in which every American citizen can take pride."

B. GEOGRAPHICAL SURVEYS.

The Department of the Interior early made surveys and
explorations in the unoccupied territory of the Great West.
At the opening of the present century much of the territory
lying between the Mississippi and the Pacific was a wild
region.   Till the second quarter of the century the Utah
Basin was unknown, and far into the third quarter much
of Nevada and adjoining parts.   To map its domain was
one of the first needs of the Government toward its settlement.

Very early, therefore, geographical exploring parties had
been sent into the more accessible of the little known parts.
Lewis and Clark made their memorable expedition along
the upper Missouri and the Columbia in the three years
from 1804 to 1806. Major Pike, a year later, explored the
source of the Rio Grande. Major Long mapped the Platte
River in 1820, and Lieutenant Allen the head-waters of the
Mississippi twelve years later. About the same time Captain

Bonneville, on leave of absence from the army, at his own cost, and for love of science, went into the Great Basin region, and, though he has rarely been noticed in its history, discovered and described Salt Lake. Nicollet, under Government, again, explored and surveyed Minnesota; and Fremont, in that fruitful transcontinental tour to the Pacific, gave his country (1842–1847), besides new views of the Platte and the Utah Basin, the now magnificent California. Then came the gold discovery of 1849, and the Pacific Railroad survey of 1852–'57 ; the fixing of the Northwestern boundary line, and resurveys and mapping of the larger Western rivers ; and the only really great geographical survey of the century in the United States—that of the fortieth parallel—begun in the year 1867, by Clarence King, under the direction of the War Department.

This survey covered a belt one hundred miles wide from north to south, and along the line of the Central Pacific Railway, from the western boundary of Nevada to the eastern base of the Rocky Mountains. Its work covered seven years, and furnished material for the most accurate information then had, not only of the topography, but of the geological and biological conditions as well, of the entire section. The published report comprises six large volumes, with numerous elaborate illustrations. These volumes are :

    I. Systematic Geology.
   II. Descriptive Geology.
  III. The Mining Industry.
  IV. Paleontology and Ornithology.
   V. Botany.
  VI. Microscopic Petrography.

C. GEOLOGICAL SURVEYS.

Many years before any such interest was shown by Government, more or less systematic attempts were made by States or individuals to effect local geological surveys. About the time of the organization of the Coast Survey, Mr. William

McClure made a painstaking examination of the Appalachian chain and the Piedmont region, together with the adjacent States and Territories. He continued his observations for several years, and into the West, visited the mining centers of Europe and America, and gave withal a permanent direction to geological study in the United States. Amos Eaton, also, under the generous patronage of Stephen Van Rensselaer, surveyed the regions about Albány, New York, and the route of the Erie Canal. Resulting, no doubt, from these exhibitions of local interest, and suggested by the geographical explorations then making, fifteen years later (1834) a national survey was undertaken, in the appointment of G. W. Featherstonhaugh, an Englishman, to examine geologically the Arkansas Territory; he became, therefore, the first "United States Geologist." David Dale Owen was employed to explore and survey public mineral lands in the upper Mississippi Valley, an expedition which revealed a rich lead supply, as a few years later from two other surveys were made known the resources of copper.

The systematic study of the Rocky Mountains began, under Dr. F. V. Hayden, in the year 1853, along with the paleontological investigations of Mr. F. B. Meek. Fifteen years later Dr. Hayden was appointed United States geologist, and given charge of a scientific corps for the survey of the Territories. In the mean time, however, the researches begun by him were the commencement of the real geological investigation of the Great West. Besides his geographical and geological researches, he made large contributions also to the ethnography and philology of the numerous Indian tribes which he met along the Yellowstone and in neighboring regions. In 1879 this and the previous commission were combined into the "United States Geological and Geographical Survey," in which the two forces co-operate under one management.

The work of Mr. J. W. Powell, present director of the survey, began twenty years ago in an exploration of the Colorado River, which was repeated the next year. In 1869

he was employed by the department to make an extended
tour and study of that region, which he did in its geology,
botany, zoölogy, and ethnology, publishing the results in
1878 in five large and valuable volumes. The survey is organized under eleven departments, comprising general gla-
cial and volcanic geology, archæan geology of the Appalachian and Lake Superior regions, structural and historical
geology of the Appalachian region, topographical * and
geological survey of Yellowstone Park, paleontology in five
sections, chemical and physical laboratories, microscopical
lithography, and economic geology.

D. THE SIGNAL SERVICE.

Since the survey of the fortieth parallel the most important service of the Bureau of Engineers has been in the
establishment and maintenance of the "Signal Service."
This term originally meant—still means in militant governments and in the United States in war-times—an organized
system of transmitting reports and messages between officers
and the army or between posts of an army. It has come to
signify, in this period of our national peace, a system of
communicating intelligence of storms or other approaching
weather changes by flags or other device. The bureau has
five hundred stations within the territory of the United
States, twenty-five in Canada, three hundred and thirty-three
foreign stations, and five hundred and sixty-three naval and
merchant marine vessels, with all of which it co-operates in
collecting simultaneous meteorological observations and
publishing information.

In addition to the familiar but little understood weather
predictions, which, contrary to popular belief, constitute but
a part of its service, the bureau's studies include the nature

---

* For an interesting presentation of the changed meaning of "topography" see "Science," September 23, 1887. The issue of the same journal
also, for July 29, 1887, has an elaborate statement of the work of the party
in perfecting a new map of the United States from these surveys.

and conditions of earthquakes, tornadoes, floods, etc. ; it con-
structs charts, sailing directions, and light lists for uses in
navigation, and is coming to be recognized as one of the
serviceable scientific bureaus of Government. From the
central office tri-daily reports are made of weather, wind-
direction, and temperature to the New York Associated Press,
to the United States Associated Press, to two telegraph com-
panies, to nine individual papers, and to the Secretary of
War.

E. NAVAL EXPEDITIONS.

In the effort to add to scientific knowledge the United
States navy has been an active agent. Its expeditions have
been numerous and fruitful. Under its authority the Ant-
arctic was explored by Wilkes in 1835–'42, and the Arctic
by Kane and Hall in the years 1854 and 1872 respectively.
Rodgers visited the Pacific in 1852, and Captain Lynch,
Africa and the Dead Sea four years earlier. The Amazon
was explored about the same period, and shortly afterward
Mordecai went to the Crimea. In 1854 was made Captain
Perry's historic voyage to Japan, which did so much toward
opening up that country to Western influence. The Howgate
Expedition to the North in 1877–'78, and the recent Greely
cruise of three years in the same region, are well known.

F. THE NATIONAL OBSERVATORY.

A service more in the line of pure science, if not of
greater immediate economic utility, has been rendered in
the establishment and continued generous use of the National Observatory at Washington.

Its organization was authorized (1842) as a "depot of
charts and instruments for the navy." * It is located at
Washington, with a branch observatory on Mare Island for
the Pacific coast. Among its instruments are mural and

---

* It is said that the repugnance of the dominant political party to satisfying the long-cherished desire of John Quincy Adams, prevented its
being called at once the National Observatory.

transit circles ; meridian transit, and prime verticals ; and two (a nine-inch and a twenty-six-inch) equatorial telescopes. Its prime object was and remains the improvement of navi gation. For fixing boundaries, and determining the latitude and longitude of cities it co-operates with the Coast Survey; and for the position of points abroad, with the navy. From its chronometers, time-balls are dropped at noon in Phila delphia, Baltimore, New York, New Orleans, Washington, Hampton Roads, Savannah, and Newport, Rhode Island. It has a very complete library of twelve thousand volumes. Connected with the observatory is the Nautical Almanac Division, which publishes the "American Ephemeris," the "American Nautical Almanac," the "Atlantic Coasters' Nautical Almanac," and the "Pacific Coasters' Nautical Almanac."

G. THE BUREAU OF AGRICULTURE.

Skill in farming and related industries, and familiarity with the principles which underlie them, are obviously fundamental in the United States. Washington has already been quoted as urging Government attention and encouragement to these interests.

Recognition has been given in the establishment of a Bureau of Agriculture in the Department of the Interior (1862), and though its services have been both numerous and widespread, and at times exceedingly fruitful, it is perhaps of all departments of the Government least understood and most depreciated. The act creating it declares its functions to be, "to acquire and diffuse among the people of the United States useful information on subjects connected with agriculture, in the most general and comprehensive sense of that word, and to procure, propagate, and distribute among the people new and valuable seeds." It has twelve specialized departments, besides an extensive museum and library. The former are : 1. Pomological Section. 2. Contagious Diseases of Animals. 3. Fertilization. 4. Entomology. 5. Seeds. 6. Forestry. 7. Chemistry. 8. Ornithology. 9. Plant Diseases. 10. Satistics. 11. Microscopy. 12. Animal Industry.

Besides a botanic or propagating garden at Washington, its organization includes two experiment farms, one maintained in the South, and the other in the West.

4. Special Publications.

Besides these organized services contributed by the national Government to the enlargement of the sphere of natural science, and the general diffusion of its beneficent uses, there are certain incidental and secondary ones, though not the less positive in their educational bearings.

This larger service is shown first in the abundant literature of the departments, the annual and special reports, and the particular and general histories of their respective duties. The decisions of the Supreme Court, for example, number one hundred and twenty volumes and form the standards of law and equity for the bars of the entire country; and the special reports of the Interior Department on the Indians, railroads, public lands, and labor, constitute a fund of valuable information. When Audubon's "Birds of America" was ready to publish, the magnitude of the undertaking, both in expense and execution, must have exceeded the possibilities of ordinary means; but the generosity of Astor, and the aid of the Department of State, gave the public one of the rarest works, and immortalized American science. Serviceable in a different way have been the publications by this department of reports on the three great expositions—Paris in 1867 and 1878, and Vienna in 1873. In the publication of Wheaton's "International Law," also, the office rendered timely aid. The decennial census has been shown by Dr. Harris to be full of the most significant educational information to every locality. Three years before the first census, a volume was published containing information on foreign countries ; in 1820 another on "Home Industries." The treasury reports on commerce and navigation were made the same year. The first inquiries on education were made in the sixth census (1840), whose answers contributed to the general educational awakening of the period.

The anthropological studies also made by Surgeon Baxter, among civil-war recruits, deserve mention as among the most careful and comprehensive of the kind made in this or any other country. The " Medical and Surgical History of the War of the Rebellion," in six volumes, and the general " Official History of the Civil War," in one hundred volumes, will furnish an authoritative statement of the occurrences of an eventful period. It is safe to say that the Government itself, from the administrative side alone, is one of the greatest educational forces of the country.

Bibliography.

" The United States Bureau of Education—Answers to Inquiries about its Work and History," 1883 ; "Origin and History of the Smithsonian Institution," W. J. Rhees ; concerning the Smithsonian bequest and the final organization of the institution, much valuable material is contained in the memoirs of John Quincy Adams, edited by C. F. Adams. " Organization of the Scientific Work of Government," by J. W. Powell, 1885 ; "Government Geological Surveys," " Nature," vol. xii, p. 265 ; also " North American Review," vol. cxxi, p. 270 ; the " United States Coast Survey," "American Journal of Science," vols. xlix, lv, lix, lxii, and lxxv ; "What has the Coast Survey done for Science ? " " Science," December, 1885, p. 558 ; "Catalogue of Government Publications," by Ben. Perley Poore ; and "What has been done for Education by the Government of the United States," John Eaton, "Education," vol. iv, p. 276.

PART FOUR.

CURRENT EDUCATIONAL INTERESTS.

CHAPTER XVIII.

COMPULSORY SCHOOL ATTENDANCE.

On the plane of the State, enforced attendance is an attempt to make good citizenship certain, by making education universal. It is not a modern device, though it has its recent applications and new conditions. In its most unyielding and narrow sense, it was authorized and enforced among the Hebrews by Joshua. Under Solon, the Athenians were enjoined to reach every child; and, "with the Spartans," says Mitford, "attendance upon the schools was made every man's concern." *

Among more recent nations, German states had made experiment of compulsory legislation as early as 1732; Bavaria in 1802. The cantons of Switzerland, always forward in promoting the general welfare, have had like provisions for more than half a century, and Denmark since 1814.†
The German system was introduced into Greece twenty years after, and into Sweden in 1842. Norway, since 1869, has required even that pupils from private schools attend the public examinations; and, if found deficient, enter the public schools. England authorizes local boards to require the

---

* "History of Greece," vol. i, p. 286.
† Attempted as early as 1793, but ineffectually.

attendance of children between six and thirteen years of age. Following the example of England, Scotland almost immediately revised the "Parochial and Burgh School Act" of 1869, and, while still retaining school fees, inserted a compulsory clause, providing that no child under thirteen may be employed in any labor, except it be shown that he has attended school at least three years, from five to thirteen, and is able to read and write. In more recent years the same principle has been tried with greater or less success in Italy, Japan, France, and other European and Oriental countries.

So much has been given of foreign educational legislation to afford a kind of setting for the numerous recent attempts in the United States to make really general participation in the benefits of a free education. It will be seen that the problem is an old one; most of the applications are both recent and Western; the whole exceedingly complicated by the diffusion of authority, which characterizes our republican institutions. Yet how much simpler is the question in a new community, among a homogeneous people, without fixed institutions and with a high notion of learning and the regenerations of culture, may be seen in the prevalent sentiments of New England under the first administrations.

The Massachusetts law of 1647, and the Connecticut code of 1650, were, both theoretically and practically, coercive, and efficiently administered. They early recognized and formulated the now common sentiment that the permanence of a representative government also demands an education coextensive with its sovereignty; that universal suffrage is meaningless if not wedded to universal education. That the public school is the only agency for securing such citizenship has been sometimes questioned; that it is the most available means is generally accepted. The steps toward compulsory education have been taken, more or fewer of them, in most States.

In the older sections the legalizing of free schools by authorizing localities to tax themselves for the common school-

ing was thought to be and was a great advance on the casual
instruction which had prevailed. It was an admission of
the supremacy of the common need. Still, the law was only
permissive. Schools might be established and they might
not. Such a statute was on the books in Rhode Island for
twenty years, leaving no trace of its existence other than
the system in Providence. It was simply inoperative. The
history of Pennsylvania is similar, and that of most States
South prior to 1870. The more recent provisions of State
Constitutions (since 1820), especially those in the Northwest,
are mandatory upon school officials, formulating the system,
appointing the administration, fixing a minimum time, and
regulating the tax, but not at the same time always equally
constraining upon children and parents.

Massachusetts requires that in every town there must be
kept at the public expense a sufficient number of schools,
and for a minimum time, for the instruction of all the children who may legally attend. Michigan, Minnesota, Oregon, and other States have somewhat similar provisions.
Nineteen States name a minimum school term, in some uniform throughout the State, elsewhere varying with the den-
sity of the population. The average required term in these
States is nearly four months and a half. Nine of them *
withdraw from delinquent communities any sharing in the
State school fund. Four States have enacted truant laws,
upon the principle that, by establishing separate schools for
the offending or truant or disturbing class and enforcing
their attendance, that of the majority would be satisfactory.
The like general results also have been sought in the
effort to accommodate the public, to make attendance easy.
Schools and school surroundings have been made both more
attractive and more safe. They have been multiplied and
so brought to each man's home. Tasks have been modified

---

* Colorado, Kentucky, Mississippi, New York, Oregon, Rhode Island,
Wisconsin, and Arizona. In Michigan the offending party is prosecuted as
for any other violation of law.

and courses revised to fit the general want.   Industrial practice and the principles underlying it have been introduced into the better secondary schools, and an immediate value thus set upon their training.

The ultimate object of all these is the same as that of, and justifies, compulsory attendance laws. Though considered only as devices, these indirect efforts have accomplished something. Attendance grows more regular. Terms have been lengthened (something more than a month since 1880). Teachers have improved. Nevertheless, thousands remain away from, while within easy reach of, the best schools.

In populous districts, and especially manufacturing centers where it has been found profitable, child labor has robbed the school to replenish the family purse. To meet this injustice, factory laws and the like restrictive enactments have been passed, most of which have an educational aspect. New Hampshire and Rhode Island make it unlawful for any child under ten years of age to be employed in any manufacturing industry. In Pennsylvania children under thirteen are excluded from silk, cotton, paper, and other specified factories and from the mines. Eight States * prohibit the employment of children under a designated age in *any* industry except upon evidence of recent prescribed schooling, the Pennsylvania law (a typical one) providing that no child from thirteen to sixteen may be employed more than nine calendar months in a year, nor except after twelve weeks of schooling. This, again, is only a negative compulsion, and, as a means of securing a more general use of the schools, ranks with their multiplication and bettering, the improvement of teachers, and the revision and rationalizing of the school course. By one class of men it is urged that such indirect control is the only legitimate republican management. To others, positive enactments, the fixing of

* Connecticut, Michigan, New Hampshire, New Jersey, New York, Ohio, Pennsylvania, and Rhode Island.

a minimum attendance, as well as a minimum term, presents itself as a possible means.

With a conservatism born of the masses, the States have been slow to enact, and the administration slower to enforce, the more coercive laws. A large and not unwholesome *laissez-faire* is implicit in our State and local life. But, when it shall be found that conditions of danger no longer right themselves, or involve more dangerous delay, it is safe to confide in the certainty that an organized public will take them vigorously in hand. Upon the part of no small number of thinking tradesmen and educators, legislators and patrons, the time seems impending when the State, as a means to universal education, and so a means to public safety, should make the acceptance of that education obligatory.

Seventeen States have such statutory provisions. Massachusetts, in the act of 1852, required that every child between the ages of eight and fourteen years should attend school for twelve weeks each year, six of which must be consecutive. A penalty was imposed for violation, and twenty years later the term lengthened. South Carolina passed a similar law in 1868, and Connecticut and New Hampshire immediately after; New York in 1874, and California, Kansas, New Jersey, Rhode Island, and Vermont, the same year; Maine and Wisconsin (1875), Michigan and Nevada (1879), Ohio (1880), Dakota (1882), Montana and Washington Territories (1883), and Illinois (1885).

Justice compels the admission that, as it stands on most statute-books, the law is at best inefficient, if not unmeaning. Its execution is irregular, half-hearted, or ignored; the duty of its enforcement is often indefinitely placed, while the law not unfrequently carries no penalty for its infraction, either by officers or patrons.

Bibliography.

On compulsory education and allied topics consult "Social Science," G. L. Harrison, 1877; "Dynamic Sociology," L. F. Ward, 1883; "Social

Statics," Herbert Spencer, 1865; "Higher Ground," Augustus Jacobson, 1888; "Relation of Education to Crime in New England," Rev. A. S. Fiske; "Compulsory Education in Relation to Crime and Social Morals," Dr. W. T. Harris; "Compulsory Education," C. E. Norton, "Nation," vol. v, p. 191.

CHAPTER XIX.

THE GRADATION OF SCHOOLS.

VIEWED from the side of organization, the acme of wise supervision is the working adjustment of each part of the system to its antecedent and subsequent stages—a process termed grading. Given the various attainments of pupils on the one side, and the logical or economic sequence of subjects on the other, gradation results in the co-ordination of the two into classes with their appropriate work. The classification may be more or less conventional, and the nomenclature wholly so—though, historically, the terms in use have a fairly definite content. The names "high-school," "grammar-school," "elementary," "primary," "intermediate," and "secondary," at first descriptive only, have been more or less specialized into terms of individual significance.

From the standpoint of the college, "elementary" and "secondary" name two successive stages in the educational preparation for college studies; the "high-school" is one of the secondary agencies. As part of a city system, on the contrary, assuming the primary and higher grades, the high-school is the culmination only.

1. Primary Schools.

Prior to about 1818, speaking generally, the only public schools were the so-called "grammar-schools." They were in reality schools of mixed grades, with a comprehensive course of elementary and secondary instruction, often fitting for college, but to which children were not admitted except they had "learned in some other school, or in some other way to read the English language by spelling the same." The "other way" was the private or dame school, or home —the only means of primary instruction for many years.

The first low-grade school in New York city was opened in 1828, by the "Infant School Society." Four years later it was assisted by public tax, and ultimately became a part of the common system. In most other communities its adoption came later. In the West, of course, it came in with the organization of States, and the original enactments of school laws. That it was not at first regarded as an essential part of the public-school system appears in that, both in and out of New England, for many years, it was—as is the modern Kindergarten—managed independently of other schools : in Boston, until 1854.* Moreover, it appears that among the earliest infant-schools were the Sunday classes among poor children, who were brought together for instruction. These were only semi-religious at most, and on the instructional side, in some towns, grew into the public primary school. Notwithstanding its occasional exotic origin, it is now a part of every public-school system, whether rural or urban. In cities it includes about one half of all the pupils doing elementary work, commands the best preparation and experience of teachers, and most patient temper ; and is, withal, peculiarly characteristic of the contemporary common school.

2. The Kindergarten.

As another phase of child education belonging to the recent period is the Kindergarten. It is a recognition of the importance of a rational nurture of the young. The system originated with Friedrich Froebel. He was the embodiment of its idea. With all its changes, it remains essentially his discovery. The first Kindergarten was that opened by Froebel

---

* "Annals of the Primary Schools in Boston," by J. Wightman, is a representative sketch, and very suggestive of improvements in primary instruction, covering a period of nearly forty years.

himself at Blankenburg, in Thuringia, barely half a century ago. After ten years, by invitation of royal patronage, he removed into Liebenthal, where, connected with his school, he began the training of young women as Kindergarten teachers. Froebel dying in 1852, the cause of infant education was enthusiastically espoused and generously promoted by the Baroness Marenholtz-Bülow. Her zeal and intelligence interested all Europe. She became the Kindergarten apostle of the Continent. France, Italy, and England adopted it.

It was introduced into this country by pupils of Froebel himself, and his immediate European successors. Mr. Carl Schurz came to the United States in 1852. Three years afterward he settled in Watertown, Wisconsin, where his wife— "herself an adept in the theory, and expert in practice, by attending *con amore* Froebel's own lectures and Kindergarten in Hamburg " *—founded among the Germans a Kindergarten. Through Mrs. Schurz, Miss Peabody became acquainted (1859) with the Kindergarten idea, studied it from every available source, and the year following, "without a knowledge of the details of Froebel's system," opened a school in Boston, which, with about fifty children, was maintained for many years. During this period Miss Peabody published the "Kindergarten Guide," through which her school became known far and wide.

Becoming convinced, in 1867, that she had not the full Froebel idea, she went to Europe to study the system for herself. "An hour," she says, "in the Hamburg Kindergarten, opened her eyes." Upon her return to Boston she began anew her advocacy of the system. What Baroness Marenholtz-Bülow did for Europe, Miss Peabody has done for America. She was the earliest, as she has been one of the most persistent, advocates of its merits. Hers was the first literature on the subject—hers a pioneer labor.

---

* For this item, as for others here and there in this paragraph, the author gratefully acknowledges indebtedness to Miss Elizabeth Peabody.

In the mean time some attempts had been made by German-speaking communities in Hoboken (1861) and New York (1864) to introduce the Kindergarten ; but it met with little success for a time, although the two schools named are yet in existence. About 1870 Mrs. Kriege and her daughter—the latter a graduate of the training-school of Baroness Marenholtz - Bülow—opened in Boston the first true Kindergarten. The school still continues. A year later a Kindergarten was attached to a private school in New York city, and Miss Boelte (now Mrs. Kraus-Boelte) made director. Miss Boelte was a graduate of the Froebel Training School, maintained by the widow of the founder. In this New York school Miss Susan E. Blow, of St. Louis, was a pupil. Upon her graduation, she returned home to introduce the system into the public schools of St. Louis.* Dr. W. T. Harris, Superintendent of the St. Louis Schools, had urged it for three years ; and in 1873 Miss Blow offered "to undertake gratuitously the instruction of one teacher appointed by the board, and to supervise and manage a Kindergarten, provided the board would furnish the rooms and a salaried teacher." The offer was accepted, and the first school opened ; the year following, three others. During the centennial year, thirty such classes were reported, and in the school year 1879-'80 the entire number enrolled in the St. Louis free public Kindergartens was 7,828.

Such were the beginnings in Boston, New York, and St. Louis—initiative centers. Outside these cities into others, large and small, the interest was communicated, and schools established. A half - dozen enthusiastic, sensible teachers

---

* Miss Blow was already well trained in the theory of the Kindergarten, and more or less familiar with the practical details of its management. She had made, the year before the arrival of Miss Boelte, the offer to supervise a Kindergarten and instruct one teacher gratuitously, provided that the board would furnish rooms and pay the salary of the pupil-teacher, but postponed beginning her work for a year, in order to avail herself of the advantage of another year's study of the system in the excellent Kindergarten of Miss Boelte.—EDITOR.

had found place in American education for a new influence ; had erected a new institution—the public, free infant-school ; had introduced it into fifteen cities, in one hundred and thirty classes, and over four thousand pupils.

In the five years, from 1874 to 1878, ninety-three new Kindergartens were established. Since the centennial year, the number of schools has more than doubled, with five times as many pupils.

The first Kindergartens in the United States were private, and patronized chiefly by the well-to-do families able to pay a tuition. Soon were undertaken schools for the poor and the uncared-for—charity Kindergartens, that have done so much to put best influences and refined standards within the reach of the waif and the neglected. Later came public Kindergartens.

Of the first class are the Model Kindergarten, of San Francisco ; the Garfield Kindergarten, at Washington ; the La Porte Kindergarten, at La Porte, Indiana ; and the Kraus Model Kindergarten, New York city. Among the largest of charity Kindergarten enterprises are, or have been, those of San Francisco, Chicago, Philadelphia, and the Quincy Shaw Free Kindergartens of Boston and Cambridge. Besides, St. Louis, San Francisco, Washington (D. C.), Des Moines (Iowa), Portland (Maine), Boston, Worcester, Ionia (Michigan), New York city and Oswego (N. Y.), Columbus and Dayton (Ohio), Lancaster (Pennsylvania), Austin (Texas), and Janesville and Milwaukee (Wisconsin), support one or more public Kindergartens. Boston has recently adopted the Quincy Shaw Kindergartens, which will hereafter be supported as part of the common-school system. In Philadelphia,* of the forty schools, nine are private, four are charity, and eight public ; of the other nineteen, there are combined private and charity classes, and sixteen under the management of the Sub-Primary-School Society, partly sustained by public funds.

---

* They have just been made public in their adoption by the Public School Board.

Altogether, of the four hundred and seventeen schools, forty per cent are public, thirty per cent private, and the others charity or mixed classes. These public Kindergartens represent sixteen States and twenty-five cities. Besides these, seven other cities contribute more or less of public money to Kindergarten instruction, and so are pledged to the idea. These, in the aggregate, represent a city population of four million, and a wide reach of country from Massachusetts to California. After the individuals named, much credit for its introduction is due to the voluntary societies that, in most cities, have espoused the cause of free Kindergartens. The Sub-Primary-School Society in Philadelphia, the Free Kindergarten Association of Chicago, and the half-dozen similar organizations in San Francisco, are examples of this co-operative spirit. Prof. Felix Adler and the Society of Ethical Culture in New York have made the Twenty-second Street Free Kindergarten a historic confirmation of the regenerative power of cleanliness and innocent play, and directed interests, and refined example, even among the lowest.

The work of Mrs. Quincy A. Shaw (daughter of Prof. L. Agassiz), in Boston, was a remarkable charity. In 1877 she started four schools among the poor at her own expense. The year following she opened fourteen more. All were among the laboring and poorer classes, all free, and all an individual charity. The work extended to Cambridge, and included about thirty schools, at an annual expense of from thirty thousand to fifty thousand dollars. Their adoption by the city * seems to be a forward movement.

In addition to the four hundred and seventeen Kindergartens there are several reliable training-schools for teachers. The first of these was that of the Krieges, in Boston, already noted. In 1876 there were five; there are now forty-one, with four hundred and fifty-two pupil-teachers. Nine State normals have Kindergartens attached.

---

* May, 1888.

Table of Kindergartens* in the United States.

STATES.	Schools.	Teachers.	Pupils.	Supported by public funds.	Kindergarten training-schools.	Pupil-teachers.
Alabama	1	3	35	....	1	2
California	56	121	2,815	1	2	33
Colorado	1	3	105	1	....	....
Connecticut	13	30	519	3	1	10
Dakota	1	2	28	....	....	....
Delaware	1	2	21	....	....	....
Georgia	2	3	31	....	....	....
Illinois	48	157	2,684	1	4	101
Indiana	12	31	446	....	2	32
Iowa	8	22	368	4	1	5
Kansas	2	3	51	....	....	....
Kentucky	1	1	27	1	....	....
Louisiana	3	11	192	....	1	4
Maine	3	5	69	1	....	....
Maryland	10	19	286	....	1	13
Massachusetts	46	86	1,446	1	5	34
Michigan	16	31	725	11	1	4
Minnesota	10	19	336	1	3	9
Missouri	71	244	6,081	68	1	25
Nebraska	1	4	50	1	....	....
Nevada	1	1	30	....	....	....
New Jersey	15	28	680	2	....	....
New York	60	124	2,813	10	11	72
North Carolina	1	1	30	....	....	....
Ohio	34	74	850	5	2	29
Oregon	6	13	192	....	1	8
Pennsylvania	63	108	1,899	26	5	83
Rhode Island	5	15	186	2	1	12
Tennessee	2	2	32	....	1	4
Texas	4	6	116	1	....	....
Vermont	1	2	17	....	1	13
Washington	1	1	10	....	....	....
Wyoming	1	1	10	....	....	....
Wisconsin	31	58	2,491	17	....	....
District of Columbia	11	22	195	1	3	11
Indian Territory	1	1	26	....	....	....
New Mexico	1	1	10	....	....	....
Utah	1	1	50	....	1	30
Total	544	1,256	25,952	158	49	524

* Inasmuch as the Kindergarten is in a state of transition, the table represents rather the distribution by States than the actual number of institutions, or the number made public, though as far as possible the materials have been corrected for the present condition.

3. The High-School.

The oldest of the existing high-schools is the Boston Latin School, which admirably represents the classical side of this secondary training. To Boston, also, must be credited the first typical high-school—an institution of the nineteenth century cast, representing the best English education. The English High-School, Boston, was founded in 1821. Among all secondary schools it marks almost the first reaction against the mediæval classicism of the previous two centuries. It is the American "real-school," founded with the design of "furnishing young men of Boston, who are not intended for a collegiate course of study, and who have enjoyed the usual advantages of the other public schools, with the means of completing a good English education." Its three years' course was made to include, besides English, the French and Spanish languages; physics; mathematics, pure and applied; mental and moral science, rhetoric, and general history. It is emphatically a people's college, the thoroughness of whose instruction led Tillinghast to say that "West Point was the best place in this country to get an education, and that the English High-School in Boston was the next." For almost twenty years, among all the cities, Boston stood alone in this public secondary education. New York, early in the century, incorporated certain of her academies, and so postponed the adoption of the high-school; though the organization of the Rochester and Buffalo Seminaries (1827) was under this name. As far as known, the next city to follow was Philadelphia (1837). Both in its inception and management the Central High-School was particularly fortunate. Its course of study and constitution were largely the work of Prof. Bache, then of Girard College. Prof. J. S. Hart was the first principal. In this school Philadelphia, and Pennsylvania indeed, first broke away from the damaging charge of "pauper schools," by declaring that "the benefits of the school were not to be confined to the poor." Two years later Baltimore City College (the Boys' High-School) was founded, and in 1849 the New York Free Academy, now the City College. The high-schools of the four cities named were for boys exclusively, and maintain their original rank as the best of their kind.

An attempt was made by Boston, in 1826, to establish a high-school for girls. It failed, however, in a year, and the enterprise was abandoned because of its great success—to give such an education to both sexes involved too great expense. Providence opened its high-school for boys and girls in 1843. It was many years before another community took up the interest.* Philadelphia, three years after the opening of the Central High-School (for boys), established a similar one for girls (1840). It was organized, it seems, chiefly as a training-school for teachers, but with an extended academic course. It is known as the Girls' High and Normal School, whose graduates receive principal's and assistant's certificates. With the election of a city superintendent (1852) and the readjustment of her school system, Boston re-established the Girls' High-School, but gave it, like that of Philadelphia, a professional bias. Twenty years after, the school was set off into two schools, one for academic instruction, the other as a training-school proper. Boston has now ten high-schools—six open to both sexes, and one classical and one non-classical school for each sex. Cincinnati has two, dating from 1847, and St. Louis (1853), Chicago (1856), and Detroit (1858), one each, besides branch high-schools. By 1860, all of New England, and most States West, had accepted the principle.†

The "St. Louis School Report" for 1878 publishes a list of one hundred and forty-one cities, each with a population of seventy-five hundred or more, which then had public high-

---

* The Lowell High-School (1831) was opened to both sexes, but seems to have been rather a mixed academy than a specialized secondary school.

† Mr. J. F. Babcock, Secretary of the New Haven (Connecticut) School Committee, having made a careful and extended inquiry into the subject, said he was not aware of any city of the size of New Haven that had even a tolerable system of schools that had not then (1856) its high-school also.

schools; adding that in smaller cities, and other large ones
not reporting, there were more than twice as many. The
latest educational reports from cities of five thousand inhabitants and upward, show three hundred and forty-two cities
having high-schools, with more than seventy thousand
pupils.

A. THE LEGAL ASPECT OF THE HIGH-SCHOOL.

By public schools in the United States are meant those
maintained at public cost, or under public control—usually
both. School management everywhere has led uniformly
to some sort of gradation. The several grades are so adjusted as to form together a system which, under the control
of the State, is known as the common-school system. That
the high-school, in some form, is as legitimate a part of this
system as is the primary school, has frequent historical confirmation. It is recognized not only in the published sentiments of educators and statesmen, in school and college
texts, courses of study, and systems of promotion, but in State
Constitutions, and national and State appropriations of land
and money. Of the thirty-eight State Constitutions, twenty-
two specify high-schools as an object of legislative and general interest ; three others direct a "general, suitable, and
efficient system," which shall be gratuitously open to all
children between six and twenty-one years of age; and one,
"such grades of schools as are for the public good."

Nevertheless, there have not been wanting those who
deny the right of the State—certainly its duty—to provide
free secondary education. To understand the history and
general conditions of the legal phase of this question it is
necessary to summarize briefly the objections which have
been made to the school.

The first one seems to have been founded upon the assumption that public schools are essentially charitable institutions, and that their patrons have no right to demand or
expect more than elementary instruction. Others, with a
tinge of like assurance, have insisted that such considerable
learning has the effect to educate children out of their des-

tined sphere in life, and for the industrial good of society should be withheld. One class objects that, as the high-school formed no part of the system of free schools as originally established, it has now no constitutional right to exist; and that tuition should be charged for all instruction beyond the rudiments. It has been claimed, further, that but few children are found in these schools, and it is manifestly unjust to tax the general public for their maintenance. In this same spirit also it has been argued that, as the few who do attend come from families of affluence, it is unfair to tax the poor for their support.*

All these questions, in some or other of their phases, have come up for settlement before the law. Without commenting upon any of them, the following reports of cases are cited as showing the attitude of the courts, historically, upon the subject:

COMMONWEALTH OF MASSACHUSETTS *vs.* THE TOWN OF DEDHAM, 1817.

Indictment was found in the lower court against the town, in its corporate capacity, for failure to maintain at public expense a "grammar-schoolmaster, of good morals and well instructed in the Latin, Greek, and English languages, to instruct children and youth in such languages." The finding was sustained by the Supreme Court, and the principle held that "every inhabitant had the right to participate in both descriptions of schools" † (lower and higher).

CUSHING *vs.* NEWBURYPORT, 18—.

In a suit brought to restrain the collection of a tax for the support of a high-school, it was held that the "schools established by the town of Newburyport, Massachusetts,

---

* In 1848, in Norwich, Connecticut, it was said, when steps were taken to establish a high-school, "It's a shame to tax the poor to pay a man eighteen hundred dollars a year for teaching children to make *x*'s and pothooks and gabble *parley-vous*."

† Tyng's "Reports," Massachusetts, vol. xvi, p. 141.

though extending instruction to branches of knowledge beyond those required by the statutes, were yet town (public)
schools, within the proper meaning of that term, provided
for the benefit of all the inhabitants, and that the taxes levied
for the support of them were not illegal." *

STUART *et al. vs.* SCHOOL DISTRICT No. 1, Kalamazoo,
   Michigan, 1874.

This was a case similar to the last, brought to restrain
the collection of such portion of the school-taxes assessed
against complainants for the year 1872 as was voted for the
support of the high-school in that village, and for the payment of the salary of the superintendent.

"While nominally this is the end sought," said Judge
Cooley, in his decision, "the real purpose is wider and vastly
more comprehensive, . . . inasmuch as it seeks a judicial
determination of the right of the school authorities, in what
are called 'union school districts' of the State, to levy taxes
upon the general public for the support of what, in this
State, are known as 'high-schools,' and to make free, by such
taxation, instruction in other languages than the English."

It was held, in confirming the decision of the lower court,
that "neither in our State policy, in our Constitution, nor in
our laws do we find the primary school districts restricted in
the branches of knowledge which the officers may cause to
be taught, or the grade of instruction that may be given, if
the voters consent, in regular form, to bear the expense and
raise taxes for the purpose." †

RICHARDS *vs.* RAYMOND, La Salle County, Illinois, 1878.

This was a bill in equity to test the constitutionality of
section 35 of the school law of Illinois, providing for the es-

---

* Metcalf's " Reports," Massachusetts, vol. x, p. 508.

† A full report of this interesting case may be found in the " Michigan
School Report" for the year 1874, p. 409. It was also held in this case that
"the power to appoint a superintendent was incident to the full control
which, by law, the board has over the schools of a district."

tablishment of high-schools to be operated under special charters. It was held that "the law was constitutional, and the levy and collection of a tax to maintain the school was proper, although the course of study prescribed was different from that contemplated by the law." *

POWELL *et al. vs.* THE BOARD OF EDUCATION OF SCHOOL DISTRICT No. 4, St. Clair County, Illinois, 1880.

This case rested upon the right to require the study of German in the public schools, and was brought by a number of tax-payers against the village Board of Education to enjoin what they alleged was a misappropriation of the school-funds. The Supreme Court affirmed the judgments of the lower court, holding that there was nothing "to show that the school was not an English school, in which the common medium of instruction is the English language"; and, further, that "the mere fact that the German language is one of the branches of study prescribed does not change its character as an English school." †

B. THE FUNCTION OF THE HIGH-SCHOOL.

Among secondary schools the American high-school is unique. It shares with academies and normal schools and college preparatory departments the privilege of fitting for university studies, but has also an independent function. The two services are not always distinct, though usually so. The institution is now emphatically an industrial agency, fitting for business or trades; and, again, a school of English culture, but excluding what is not narrowly American. Here it is classical and complete, looking to the college or the profession; there, honored as the apex of the common-school system—the goal of school life. Usually its course is overcrowded, often with a bias that obstructs general de-

---

* "Ninety-second Illinois," p. 612.

† For a full presentation of this case and the text of Judge Scott's decision, see "Illinois School Report," 1881–'82, p. 107.

velopment; but, variously modified by material considerations or culture environments, by wealth and ancestry, it
has yet certain well-marked functions, and falls into classes
fairly discriminated.

Its origin, its aims, its methods, all mark its kinship with
institutions below rather than above it. It appears as the
completion of the one system rather than an introduction to
the other. Viewed from the side of its organization it pre-
pares for life, not for learning; it fits for industry, not
study. And yet it seldom loses sight altogether of the end
of culture. If the two ends are one, or if the means to those
ends coincide, then will the function be single. With a
somewhat homogeneous organization, however, it frequently
exercises very diverse functions.

That, in the one view, the demand for industrial training,
for business courses, studies in government, economics, etc.,
has not always been an intelligent one, goes without saying;
but whether a rational or instinctive insight, the intimate
organic relation of the high-school with the grades below,
has emphasized with many the impression that the system is
all one; that, for the people, by a large majority, the high-
school is a finishing school, and, as such, should be adapted
to the immediate and pressing and understood wants of the
people.

On the contrary, there is discernible a marked educational tendency toward centralization. No part of our educational policy is better defined than the constant, generous
governmental support and encouragement accorded to institutions of learning. The conviction grows, in a most wholesome way, that every child of every Commonwealth should
have access gratuitously, and without needless restriction, to
every grade of education, from the most elementary to the
most comprehensive, which public wealth can buy; that no
step shall be wanting; that no part shall be left wholly to
chance or to private enterprise. Each stage of the system
should fit itself to its neighbor. The elementary must not
attempt the work of the high-school, nor this of the college;

no more must gaps be left between. This is the State's ideal.
As a matter of fact, circumstances determine more or less of
modification.   In sections where other secondary agencies
fail, and the college spirit prevails, the high-school becomes
the legitimate fitting school.

The attempt to give permanence and system to this relation of the high-school and the university has worked out
in what is called the diploma system in Michigan, the High-
School Board in Minnesota, and commissioned high-schools
in half a dozen States.

(1.) Michigan High-Schools.

Dating from 1837, the University of Michigan was authorized to establish, in the State, branch schools, to be under
its direction, with uniform courses of study and tributary to
it. In three years seven such branches had been established.
The reason assigned twelve years after for their decline was
that "they were not able at the same time to perform the
functions of a common school and those of a branch of the
university." *

Nevertheless, as the years went on, the Superintendents
Mayhew and Gregory and Shearman, and President Tappan,
favored a closer union of the academies and public schools
on the one hand, and the university on the other. In 1870
it was recommended by the faculty of the university that a
"commission of examiners" be appointed who should visit
annually such schools as desired it, giving certificates to
those pupils who were successful in examination, which
should admit directly to the university. The year following
a plan very similar was adopted. Pupils have since been
received upon the diplomas of accredited schools. In 1876
there were eight such high-schools; four years later there
were sixteen. Since 1884 the same conditions have been
extended to, and accepted by, certain schools in New York,
Illinois, Minnesota, and California. The experiment in

---

* " Report of Regents of the University," 1852.

Michigan is wholly voluntary, having its origin and its development in the readiness of both lower and higher schools to co-operate for their mutual advantage.

(2.) Minnesota High-Schools.

Seven years ago (1881) the State of Minnesota attempted to effect a similar union by legislation. A "High-School Board" was constituted for the encouragement of liberal education in the State. Through this board the law provides for the rendering of pecuniary aid to such schools as shall have "regular and orderly courses of study, embracing all the branches prescribed as requisite for admission to the collegiate department of the university." The New York plan is similar to this, the distribution of funds being made and certificates given by the "Board of Regents of the University of the State of New York."*

(3.) Commissioned High-Schools.

Following the experiment in these States, and especially in Michigan, as the first attempt, the idea has been adopted in Indiana, Nebraska, Iowa, Kansas, and perhaps other States — not always, unfortunately, with careful guards thrown about its application, like those in Michigan and Minnesota.

Since 1881 graduates of approved high-schools in California have been admitted to the State University; and since 1878 graduates of the Hopkins Grammar-School, New Haven, to Yale. Dartmouth has for ten years had a like arrangement with local schools, and recently Rutgers.

Bibliography.

"Annals of the Boston Primary School Committee," by J. Wightman, 1860 (comprises the history of primary education for a large part of New

---

* For a general discussion of this subject, see " Relations of High-Schools and Colleges," in " Proceedings of National Educational Association," Chicago, 1887, p. 282.

England, and is of general interest); "Courses and Methods for Primary, Grammar, and Ungraded Schools," J. T. Prince, 1886; "District Schools," J. O. Taylor, 1834; "Graduating System for Country Schools," A. L. Wade, 1881; "The Kindergarten in America," Steiger, 1872; "The Kindergarten in the United States," by Kate B. Ford, "Michigan School Report," 1877, p. 287; "Lectures in the Training-School for Kindergartners," Miss E. P. Peabody, 1886; "Reports of the St. Louis City Schools for 1875-'76, 1876-'77, and 1878-'79," by Dr. W. T. Harris, on the "Philosophy of the Kindergarten" and the "History of the System in St. Louis"; "The High-School and the College," C. W. Tufts, "New England Journal of Education," February 12, 1885; "Relation of Secondary Education to the American University Problem," A. F. West, "Proceedings of the National Educational Association," 1885; "The Function of the High-School as a Factor in Public Education," H. H. Morgan, "New England Journal of Education," vol. xii, No. 24; "Report on Preparation for College," "Proceedings of the National Council of Education," 1884, p. 36; "City School Systems in the United States," by J. D. Philbrick, 1885.

CHAPTER XX.

EDUCATION IN THE SOUTH.

THERE are three well-defined periods in the educational history of the South: 1. The colonial period; 2. The ante-war period; 3. The period of reorganization.

During the first of these, if the systems of Massachusetts and Connecticut be excepted, parts of the South were even better supplied with the means of education than most colonies North. This means only that throughout this period and for almost the entire country the only established agencies were private and parochial schools, and these, in the early days of Georgia, South Carolina, and Virginia, were superior. The reorganization came a quarter of a century later in most of these States than in the North and West.

1. The Ante-war Period.

In the second period began the educational divergence between the two sections. The South perfected existing institutions, adapting them to the peculiar social and governmental conditions. The North founded new ones—the public free schools. The colleges and academies and denominational seminaries met the common want of the financially independent planter, and, for anything more, sons were sent to the North or abroad. It was estimated in 1855, by eminent authority,* that for many years before the war the South paid annually to the North for books and education not less than five million dollars. And yet in most States something had been done looking toward common schools; but it was done half-heartedly, as will appear, and in the midst of the most unfavorable conditions. To those familiar with these conditions and the prevalent social and ethical standards, the common sentiment concerning public schools can not seem strange.

Georgia as early as 1792 had taken steps for a high-grade school in each county, and in 1821 appropriated two hundred and fifty thousand dollars to their maintenance. Two years later a like fund was set apart for the use of the elementary or " poor schools." Beginnings were made in Virginia for a literary fund in 1810, and a decade later in Kentucky. Louisiana, Mississippi, and Tennessee made appropriations of land. Seven of the States—Alabama, Delaware, Georgia, Kentucky, Missouri, North Carolina, and South Carolina—applied their shares of the surplus revenue in whole or in part to education. This alone aggregated three and a half millions, and under favorable conditions would have been a powerful factor in their school administration. Maryland as early as 1825 had a State School Superintendent and others later. Georgia, North Carolina, Louisiana, Mississippi, Tennessee, Alabama, and Kentucky each spent annu-

---

* J. B. De Bow, " Review," vol. xviii, p. 664.

ally on common schools for many years from one fourth to
three fourths of a million dollars. The result of the effort
was the establishment of systems in Baltimore, St. Louis, and
Louisville, with beginnings in New Orleans and Charleston.

Speaking broadly, all attempts at public education, as is
seen now, were stamped with failure from the beginning—
with failure, if by success is meant making the schools free
and equally open to all without class implications.* First,
the general better class sentiment of these States was, if not
antagonistic, at least indifferent to a free education. In
1859 it was asserted that the New England system was not
adapted to Louisiana and the South. A Southern review
said: "After ten years' trial it has been proved that the laws
can not be carried out, that more than half the families in
Louisiana will not accept of the mental food the State offers
to her children. Some parishes will not receive any of it."†
It was said of Texas about the same time that, while taxed
sixteen thousand dollars for public schools, there was not
one in the State. Yet nearly every planter had a school in
his own house. That the feeling sometimes appeared in
stronger antagonism is shown by another extract from the
same authority (1858). After quoting those who, while admitting that the system had failed in rural districts, yet
asserted its success in New Orleans, the writer said, "If the
tree be judged by its fruits, it is poisonous instead of salutary
to republican institions in our great cities."

Further, under the most favorable circumstances, the
laws that were enacted were, almost without exception, permissive only. In a report made to the Delaware Convention
in 1843 was a section on education showing how fundamentally the citizenship of that State rested upon optional taxation. It said:

"The report of the Massachusetts Board of Education declares that the cardinal principle which lies at the founda-

---

* Of course, no consideration is had of the negro in this period.
† "De Bow's Review," vol. xvii, p. 278.

23

tion of their educational system is that all the children of the State shall be educated by the State. Let it be distinctly remarked that this is not the principle of our school system, but that our system is founded upon the position that the people must educate their own children; and that all the State should do or can do for any useful effect is to organize them into communities, so as they may act together for that purpose and help and encourage them to act efficiently. The school of every district is thus in the power of its voters. They can have as good schools as they wish, or an inferior school, or no school." *

Most States, however, provided some means of schooling the children of those who were unable to educate their own. In South Carolina the schools were for all, preference being given to the poor. In Virginia these were paid for by the State at the rate of four to eight cents per day. In general this was the " pauper system " that had worked such disaster in one or two Northern States, and those who could do otherwise would have nothing of it. The tendency to large plantations also and small towns negatived the free-school impulse, while "the existence of slavery," says Ramáge, " prevented the growth of a large middle class, out of whose ranks the patrons of the common school are so strongly recruited."

2. The Period of Reorganization.

With the close of the war came new conditions, new institutions, and new standards of public policy and administration. Taxable property had depreciated sixty per cent at a stroke, and four million illiterates were added to the school population. The educational problem set for solution, it has been said, was how to educate three times the number of children with one third the money. School funds had been wasted in the conflict to the amount of millions. Banks were gone, investments of every sort swept away, and per-

---

* Delaware has no State School Superintendent, and but little system in State schools.

sonal security was valueless. There was no currency, no independent industry. Labor was disorganized. There was no skill in the use of tools, no co-operation. Private schools, once the pride of the South, were closed for want of patron-age. There were no public schools, but in their stead an overmastering ignorance of their beneficent influences; ignorance of their management and their accompanying institutions; and, next to the want of efficient teachers and funds and the prevailing indisposition to taxation, the absence of an established authority that could be used to gather data for an intelligent organization and oversight of educational forces was the most serious obstacle. For ten years in educational affairs the executive energy and control were from without. That it has not remained so is an index of the marvelous elasticity of the Southern mind.

A. THE FREEDMEN'S AID SOCIETY.

In the year 1861 was opened a school at Fortress Monroe for colored youth—fugitive slaves—by the American Missionary Association. Immediately almost was formed the Freedmen's Aid Society, which, all through the war, and afterward until 1869, established schools and furnished houses and teachers, and may be said, along with the Missionary Association, to have initiated the work of negro education in the South. At the close of the war the society had six hundred teachers and many thousand pupils.

In the eight years of its existence it expended $1,350,000 on its work, which at its dissolution passed into the hands of denominational agencies, by whom, during the war even, schools and churches had been planted in half a dozen States.

B. GOVERNMENT AGENCY.

The Freedmen's Bureau was a Government institution, created by act of Congress, March 3, 1865, as a "Bureau of Refugees, Freedmen, and Abandoned Lands." It soon took the shorter name, and, while having other functions, also, was predominantly serviceable as an educational agency.

It took hold of schools already established, co-operated with the churches and other corporations, built houses and hired teachers. During the first year (1865-'66) the Bureau schools—those under Government supervision, and partially or wholly supported by it—had nine hundred and seventy-five teachers and ninety-seven thousand five hundred pupils. In four years it had developed into a great system, with twenty-five hundred teachers and two hundred and fifty thousand pupils. At first its work was elementary only. Both day and evening schools were established, and industrial schools; and later, even Sunday-schools—whatever was demanded, or could be used to dispel the appalling ignorance of the freed blacks. Still later, by acting with the religious denominations, it assisted in the founding of institutions for superior instruction also. It contributed in this way to Howard University and Wayland Seminary, at Washington; Claflin University, South Carolina; Fisk University and the State Central College, in Tennessee; Straight University, Louisiana; and Hampton Normal and Agricultural Institute, Virginia.

The great service rendered by the Bureau was not in hiring teachers, or meeting any current expenses, but in erecting buildings. In respect to this first need, the Government was a strong arm and a ready purse in an emergency. It did easily and at once for the South what it must have taken them years to accomplish unaided or through private beneficence alone. The general functions of the office ceased in 1869, its educational support continuing in certain States a year longer. It had done a great work, one of the pronounced benefactions of the General Government. In the five years of its existence it had contributed to the schools $5,250,000.

C. DENOMINATIONAL AGENCIES.

Increasingly, the oversight, much of the support, and the enlargement of the established institutions passed into the hands of the missionary organizations, chiefly of the churches, though not a few of the foundations were unsectarian; and ultimately drifted into or were absorbed by the public systems. Prominently active among these agencies were:

1. The American Missionary Association.

2. The Freedmen's Aid Society of the Methodist Episcopal Church.

3. The Presbyterian Board of Missions for Freedmen.

4. The American Baptist Home Mission Society.

5. The work of Congregationalists, Friends, Unitarians, etc.

The first of these, the American Missionary Association, was organized in 1866 for Southern work, and, next to the national Government, has been the largest contributor to education in that section. In twenty years it has spent $6,000,000, and has now under its control nine institutions for superior and professional instruction, more than a dozen normal schools, and fifty elementary and academic schools, with an aggregate of nearly three hundred teachers and twenty thousand pupils.

The Freedmen's Aid Society of the Methodist Episcopal Church was organized in 1866 also, with a fourfold purpose (among negroes primarily, though their recent interest has extended to whites also): 1. The preparation of ministers. 2. The preparation of teachers. 3. The education of physicians. 4. The elevation of colored women of the South. The society has charge of seven chartered university organizations in as many States—the Central Tennessee College, Clark University, Georgia, Claflin University, South Carolina, New Orleans University, the Philander Smith College, Arkansas, Rust University, Mississippi, and Wiley University, Texas. In addition to these, it supports three theological schools, one medical college, two normal schools, and eleven seminaries and academies. It has more than half a million dollars invested in permanent school property, and has collected and disbursed in twenty years $2,000,000.

The Presbyterian Board expends annually in this section

from $30,000 to $50,000, and the Baptist Society about as much, the latter having institutions at Washington, Richmond, Baltimore, Raleigh, Columbia, Augusta, Nashville, and New Orleans.

D. THE PEABODY FUND.

Few men have given more to benevolent purposes, none more wisely, than George Peabody. Besides two and a half millions to organized charity in London, $10,000 to the Kane Arctic Expedition, and $15,000 to the London Exposition of 1851, he distributed in life and at his death nearly $6,000,000 for education in the United States. A table of these benefactions is presented, setting forth his numerous large gifts, and the magnitude of his service to the South:

Benefactions of George Peabody.

INSTITUTION.	Amount.
1. Library at Thetford, Vt	$5,500
2. Library at Newburyport, Mass.	15,000
3. Library at Georgetown, D. C.	15,000
4. Library at Peabody, Mass.	125,000
5. Library at Danvers, Mass	125,000
6. Museum at Harvard, Mass.	150,000
7. Museum at Yale, Conn.	150,000
8. Kenyon College, Ohio	25,000
9. Washington and Lee University, Virginia.	145,000
10. Phillips Academy, Andover, Mass.	25,000
11. Peabody Academy, Salem, Mass.	140,000
12. Peabody Institute, Baltimore, Md.	1,400,000
13. Massachusetts Historical Society	20,000
14. Maryland Historical Society	20,000
15. Peabody Fund for the South	3,100,000
16. London Charity	2,500,000
17. Memorial Church, Georgetown, Mass	100,000
18. Kane Arctic Expedition	10,000
19. London Exposition, 1851	15,000
20. United States Sanitary Commission	10,000
21. Commission to Maryland	60,000
22. To uphold the credit of the South	40,000
Total	$8,195,500

Impressed with the need of the more favored and wealthy portions of our nation to assist the less fortunate, Mr. Peabody gave (February, 1867) to R. C. Winthrop and fourteen others—trustees—one million dollars to be held in trust, and "the income thereof applied and used for the promotion of intellectual, moral, and industrial education among the more destitute portions of the Southern and Southwestern States of our Union." His purpose was as generous as his purse; and, with the bias of a philanthropist only, he charged that the benefit should be "distributed among the entire population, without other distinction than their needs and the opportunities of usefulness to them." The same year was added to this amount another $1,100,000 in Mississippi State bonds, and two years afterward, upon his death, a bequest of $1,000,000 in railroad, State, city, and bank bonds of various descriptions, and completing the total of $3,100,000.

Dr. Barnas Sears, then President of Brown University, was immediately made general agent of the board, and began one of the grandest educational experiments and the most successful labors of the century. At the same time, donations of school text-books were tendered by prominent publishing houses to the amount of nearly one hundred and fifty thousand volumes.

It was early agreed by the board that only those should receive aid who had first contributed to the support of their own schools, and that the amount raised by the district must be twice that received from the fund. Further, schools aided must have at least a hundred pupils, with a teacher for every fifty; they must be graded, and must continue through the school year with an average attendance of not less than eighty-five per cent. With these careful guards against waste, the Peabody beneficence "gave the earliest impulse to the cause of common-school education, which was vital to the regeneration of the States impoverished and devastated by war." By requiring the best, and insisting upon local effort, it set standards and initiated habits of fundamental importance. By 1872 the cities of Savannah and Columbus,

Georgia, Natchez and Vicksburg, Mississippi, and a few others, had already become self-supporting.

It was early felt that, with public schools begun and laws formulated, the furnishing of capable teachers, and some skill in industry, were of importance. So that, in addition to appropriation to common schools, aid was applied (1875) to institutions having in view these special trainings. In the twenty years aid has been given to twelve States, as shown in the table:

Distribution of the Peabody Fund.

STATES.	Amounts.	STATES.	Amounts.
1. Alabama	$95,200	8. South Carolina	$77,950
2. Arkansas	103,475	9. Tennessee	306,975
3. Florida	72,075	10. Texas	122,350
4. Georgia	123,127	11. Virginia	267,599
5. Louisiana	96,870	12. West Virginia	137,010
6. Mississippi	88,383		
7. North Carolina	138,315		$1,629,249

E. THE SLATER FUND.

In the year 1882, fifteen years after the Peabody donation, Mr. John F. Slater, of Norwich, Connecticut, conveyed to trustees $1,000,000 cash to be invested for the education of the freedmen of the South. Rev. Atticus G. Haygood has been agent of the trust from the first. Its appropriations have been principally devoted to the industrial elevation of the colored youth, and to their medical education. These have averaged $30,000 a year, and extended to eleven States, omitting Florida and West Virginia in the Peabody list, and including Kentucky and the District of Columbia. Its aid has been given to about forty institutions annually (all for colored students), among which are State universities and normal schools, the Meharry Medical College, industrial schools, and female seminaries—the best in the South. By its assistance have been introduced into Central Tennessee College carpentry and printing; shoemaking, smithing, and a workshop into Claflin University; carriage and harness making and painting into Clark University, and into most of them sewing and general housework for the girls. Two such benefactions, of so wide-spread influence and so economically disposed as the Peabody and Slater funds, has the world scarcely seen elsewhere.

F. PUBLIC-SCHOOL SYSTEMS.

In the mean time much had been accomplished by the people for themselves. Even before the centennial, and but ten years after the war, there were creditable beginnings of, both State and city systems of graded schools; there were superintendents of State, city, and county; established systems of taxation, courses of study, institutes, associations, etc. To this end were and have been all the services of the North to the South, to make them independent, to establish self-supporting institutions. Fundamental ideas in regard to education had to be given in regard to schools, and teachers, and taxation, and State co-operation. Legislation must be directed, and legislators themselves brought to right views. These, combined with wholesome industrial and social interests and more liberal governmental administration, have done much to help on the new South.

Before 1870 every Southern State except Delaware had made constitutional and somewhat of legislative provision for free schools and a general system. Twelve States had some form of State control; eight had county supervision. Normal schools had been started in six States, and some progress made in grading schools in the larger cities. Of the last, the best specimens here, as elsewhere, were in cities. The sixteen States show systems in cities whose combined school census aggregates nearly seven hundred thousand, and having a school enrollment of about three hundred thousand. These same cities report forty-five high-schools, with a membership of over eight thousand. Of these, Louisville, New Orleans, Baltimore, St. Louis, and Richmond have nearly one half.

Table showing Growth in Public School Patronage, 1872–1885, in Sixteen Southern States.

STATES.	Consti-tution.	School cen-sus, 1872.	Enroll-ment, 1872.	School cen-sus, 1885.	Enroll-ment, 1885.
Alabama.............	1868	340,000	150,000	450,000	253,000
Arkansas	1868	180,000	62,000	358,000	176,000
Delaware	......	40,000	19,000	46,000	31,000
Florida	1865	62,000	14,000	124,000	61,000
Georgia..............	1868	260,000	77,000	509,000	319,000
Kentucky............	1873	340,000	181,000	581,000	283,000
Louisiana............	1868	182,000	50,000	311,000	103,000
Maryland............	1864	276,000	80,000	341,000	175,000
Missouri.............	1865	634,000	330,000	813,000	569,000
North Carolina.......	1868	268,000	51,000	535,000	306,000
South Carolina.......	1868	197,000	76,000	275,000	184,000
Tennessee............	1867	350,000	121,000	623,000	383,000
Texas................	1869	230,000	64,000	350,000	261,000
Virginia	1867	350,000	167,000	610,000	308,000
Mississippi...........	1868	246,000	120,000	450,000	304,000
West Virginia........	1863	125,000	77,000	243,000	172,000
Total	......	4,080,000	1,639,000	6,619,000	3,888,000

G. NORMAL SCHOOLS.

Thirteen of these States maintain thirty-six public and eighteen private normal schools, enrolling in the aggregate ten thousand to twelve thousand students. West Virginia and Alabama have each six, and North Carolina and Missouri five. Kentucky, Georgia, and Delaware report none, either public or private.

Some of these schools have acquired a national reputation for the preparation they give and for the wide-spread influence of their graduates. The State Normal College of Tennessee was founded in 1875, and has sent out one thousand teachers. The Tuskegee Normal and Industrial School (Alabama) is for colored students, of whom it has three hundred to four hundred, with a faculty of twenty, all colored. The Baltimore Normal School for Colored Teachers was established in 1864—two years before the State Normal School for White Teachers in the same city. Of the five State schools for teachers in North Carolina, four are for the negroes.

H. COLLEGES.

This section has one third of the colleges and universities of the country, and nearly one third the instructors and students. Prominent among the institutions are Tulane University, New Orleans, to which Mr. Paul Tulane generously gave a million and a half of dollars for the education of the white youth of Louisiana; the Vanderbilt University, the recipient from the Vanderbilts of one million dollars; the University of the South, at Sewanee, Tennessee; the University of Mississippi, the University of Virginia, and Johns Hopkins. In addition to the usual collegiate work, nineteen institutions in this group of States have three hundred graduate students doing special work.

I. PROFESSIONAL SCHOOLS.

Besides the institutions for general culture, the section has its full quota of professional schools. Of these, forty-eight are medical colleges, or departments, Delaware, Mississippi, South Carolina, Texas, and West Virginia, reporting none, and Maryland, Missouri, and the District of Columbia, thirty of them.

Twenty-five are law-schools, representing every Southern State except Delaware and Florida. The theological schools number forty-two.

Altogether, the professional schools report nearly eight thousand students, more than half of whom are in the medical colleges.

3. General Condition.

Without doubt a great work has been going on in the South these years. No form of education is without its representative. There are thirty-six business schools, sixteen for deaf-mutes, twelve for the blind, one, in Kentucky, for the feeble-minded, and five reformatories, two thirds of all of which have been founded and three fourths of them developed in the last score of years. The section has been profitably active in educational publications, and issues one third the educational journals of the United States. Its five hundred libraries have an aggregate of three million volumes. Its university properties are valued at eleven million dollars, and their productive endowments at twelve million dollars; or, with one third the superior institutions (128 out of 361), it has one fourth the endowments.

The relatively generous provision for the colored race, also, where the great ignorance centers, emphasizes the magnitude of the work going on. Their schools are, for the most part, separate, though coeducation of the races is not unknown. Besides thirty-three normal schools, forty-four secondary schools, and eighteen colleges, they have twenty-three theological seminaries, four schools in law, and six in medicine. Of the twenty-eight institutions for the deaf-mute and blind, nine are for the negroes. These, with the public elementary schools open to them, represent a school attendance of more than a million of the colored race.

School Expenditures.

STATES.	1878.	1883.	1886.	Property valuation.
Alabama............	$358,697	$522,727	$741,244	$167,124,594
Arkansas...........	148,393	561,745	866,892	126,826,394
Delaware...........	216,540	215,161	215,161	....
Florida............	134,880	172,178	385,800	76,611,409
Georgia	411,453	613,647	711,990	329,489,505
Kentucky	1,130,000	1,248,524	700,790	....
Louisiana	558,231	466,930	450,030	....
Maryland	1,593,260	1,686,640	1,832,383	469,593,225
Mississippi..........	592,805	803,876	840,776	140,000,000
Missouri	2,406,133	4,288,135	4,328,596	725,775,259
North Carolina	324,287	535,200	671,116	202,752,622
South Carolina	319,030	423,273	425,903	149,973,365
Tennessee..........	794,232	955,470	1,047,223	226,844,184
Texas..............	747,534	1,661,476	2,166,633	....
Virginia...........	963,865	1,321,537	1,453,103	341,735,707
West Virginia	687,275	997,431	1,036,874	159,514,752
Total...........	$11,386,645	$16,472,050	$17,875,514	$3,116,241,016
New York...........	$10,755,905	....	$13,284,886	$3,224,682,343
Ohio...............	7,995,125	....	9,327,549	1,688,676,168
Michigan...........	3,116,519	....	4,332,968	945,450,000

Another interesting and suggestive phase of Southern education appears in a comparative study of the expenditures for schools in the various States. In the decade just closed the actual outlay in the sixteen States has increased from $11,400,000 in 1878 to about $20,000,000 in 1888, or seventy-five per cent. Again, the assessed valuation of taxable property in twelve Southern States from which returns are available aggregates a little less than that of the State of New York; the former nevertheless spent on the public schools, for the year 1885–'86, $1,058,000 more than the latter. Mississippi, Missouri, and West Virginia each spend more mills to the dollar than does New York, and the last of them three times as much as does Michigan.

The South is rapidly settling for itself the vexed problem of education.

Bibliography.

"Schools and Universities North and South," "De Bow's Review," 1855, p. 545; "Opposition to the Free-School System in the South," "American Social Science Journal," vol. ix, p. 92; "Sketch of Education in South Carolina," R. Means Davis, 1882; also, in "Creoles of Louisiana," by G. W. Cable, see "The Schoolmaster," chap. xxxiii, p. 256, for a picture of education before the war.

Upon the later period consult "The Freedmen during the War," General O. O. Howard, "Princeton Review," May and September, 1886; "Our Southern Colleges and Schools," C. F. Smith, "Atlantic Monthly," October, 1884, p. 542; "Proceedings of the National Educational Association," 1884 (fifty pages by Robert Bingham, Rev. A. D. Mayo, B. T. Washington, Miss Clara Conway, and others, in a very valuable discussion); "Twenty Years of Negro Education," J. M. Keating, "Popular Science Monthly," November, 1885; "The Case of the Negro," Rev. Atticus G. Haygood; "The South, the North, and the Nation keeping School," Rev. A. D. Mayo; "The Negro Question," by G. W. Cable, "New York Tribune," March 4, 1888; "Education in South Carolina," by Mayor Courtney. On the question of "Federal Aid to Education," see discussion by J. L. M. Curry, "Circular of Information, No. 3," 1884; H. R. Waite, "Princeton Review," May, 1884, p. 215; and D. H. Chamberlain, "Princeton Review," March, 1887. Consult also the "Annual Reports of the Peabody and Slater Funds," and of the "Freedmen's Aid Society of the Methodist Episcopal Church."

CHAPTER XXI.

THE HIGHER EDUCATION OF WOMEN.

THE caption is here used in its most general significance, to include the educational recognition accorded to girls and women in the United States. The popular sentiment touching the question has been an index to the attitude of the public upon many others. Woman's right to the highest culture has shared the national creed—the privilege of every individual to make the most of himself. A century of her education admirably illustrates the evolution of an idea among a people already committed to the doctrine of personal sovereignty, predisposed to a wholesome recognition of individual rights. It is in keeping with the character of a free people that no class, and no one of any class, shall be hindered in a rational participation in all manner of good and enjoyment. In the degree that the people have become less selfish and more rational, less individual and more personal, the privileges of superior training have become less exclusive.

In the last century the United States stood beside other nations touching the education of girls. No European government made anything like the same provision for the two sexes. The educational institutions of Prussia were first co-ordinated into a state system in the common law of 1794. There had been schools of a kind for girls for a hundred years, but " far less efficient than for boys." And it is said that not till 1804 had any one in Prussia courage to start a seminary for female teachers. The English schools came even later, Girton College being opened eight years after Vassar. It can not seem strange, then, that American schools have been only recently opened to girls.*

---

* Mayor Quincy, in closing the Girls' High School, Boston (1822), after a year's trial, said : " It is just as impracticable to give a classical education

The steps in the development of this best sentiment, from indifference to interest, while not always distinctly apparent, are distinguishable. There came first the girls' academies, many of which remain. Within the same generation, this secondary training had the effect to greatly increase the demand for the advanced. Refused admission to the established colleges, women sought to found others for themselves. With so much granted, access to institutions for young men was not long delayed—not to all, but to the younger colleges, and, generally, those most in sympathy with the spirit of the time. It was to be expected that the older and more conservative institutions, the product of a long past, and with established functions and courses, should more slowly accept the change. Even these, however, form an interesting class, making concessions recently, and giving assurances of their good intentions. Further, to concede the general education of women is, among a busy, practical, here-and-now people, to concede the *use* of that education, looking toward the general welfare. The professional training of women easily follows their admitted general culture.

The subject is resolved, then, under the several heads enumerated, viz. :

1. Girls' seminaries and academies.
2. Colleges for women only.
3. Colleges admitting women.
4. College "annexes," and examinations.
5. Women in the professions.

1. Girls' Seminaries.

The story of the rise of girls' schools in the United States is almost biographical, so interwoven is it with the lives of four women in the first half of the century, whose names and services have become historical. Mrs. Emma Willard,

---

to all the girls of a city whose parents would wish them to be thus educated at the expense of the city, as to give such a one to all the boys at the city's expense ; no funds of any city could endure the expense of it."

in Vermont and New York; Miss Catherine E. Beecher, in Connecticut and Ohio; Mary Lyon, in Massachusetts; and Miss Grant, in New Hampshire, did for girlhood and woman what Horace Mann did for school systems—brought them to consciousness; what Mary Carpenter and Mary Somerville did in England.

After a short service in Bradford Academy (1804), Mrs. Willard (then Miss Emma Hart) opened a school for young ladies at Middlebury, Vermont (1808). Six years later it was made a boarding-school, and the curriculum extended. In 1819 she removed, by invitation, to Waterford, New York, and two years later founded the celebrated Troy Female Seminary,* to which, for seventeen years, says a recent Regents' Report, "she brought unparalleled success." While here she prepared and published, in an address, a "Plan for improving Female Education," which, being submitted to the New York Legislature, secured to Waterford Academy, and a few other proposed girls' schools, a share, for the first time, in the Literature Fund, or State appropriation for academies. The "Plan" was a sensible and comprehensive discussion of the " education of girls."

Her published address and the fame of her teaching reached other States, and similar institutions were founded in Georgia, Kentucky, Illinois, Michigan, etc., besides one at Bogotá, in South America, and another at Athens, Greece, as a school for the preparation of native teachers. She visited Europe twice, first in 1830, and again twenty-three years later, to attend the World's Educational Conference at London—both times inspecting schools, conferring with the most eminent foreign educators, and studying systems; received in France as the friend of Lafayette, and everywhere welcomed, both for her womanhood and her profession.†

---

* For a very interesting sketch of Mrs. Willard's school and her educational doctrine, see Barnard's "American Journal of Education," vol. vi, pp. 125–168.

† Mrs. Willard was a successful author, also, of two histories of the

Miss Beecher, born in 1800, and educated in Connecticut, opened, when twenty-two years of age, at Hartford, in that State, an academy for young ladies, which is said to have been for ten years so successful as to have attracted students from every State in the Union. She was assisted by her sister Harriet, the pupils frequently numbering more than one hundred and fifty. In 1832, settling in Cincinnati, she again opened a seminary, which failing health, after two years, compelled her to abandon. She immediately gave her influence to the forming of public sentiment on the subject of female education, and, through a National Board and Society, to the enlargement of its facilities. For forty years she was a controlling spirit in the organization, which sent hundreds of teachers to Western schools, to the Territories, and to the South.*

Since the active period of these two women, young ladies' seminaries have become both fashionable and numerous. There are reported two hundred and seven institutions now of about the same grade as the Troy Seminary, most of which have been founded within a generation. Of these, Kentucky, Virginia, Georgia, Tennessee, and Missouri have each more than a dozen ; Ohio has eleven, and North Carolina, New York, and Alabama, ten each, these nine States having more than half the whole number. In seven Southern States are forty-seven per cent of them. About two thirds of them are authorized to confer degrees, though the course is various as to scope and fullness.

2. Colleges for Women.

One of the oldest of the higher grade schools was the somewhat famous Wesleyan Seminary and Female College

---

United States, a universal history. a number of historical charts, and works on physiology, astronomy, and morals.

* Miss Beecher was the author of text-books on arithmetic, mental and moral science, a " Course of Calisthenics " for young ladies, and one or two books on female education.

at Kent's Hill, Maine, founded in 1821. In the West was one at Granville, Ohio (1834); but as all earlier and contemporary services were eclipsed by the beneficent earnestness of Emma Willard, so the later founding of colleges was insignificant beside Mary Lyon and Mount Holyoke.

Three years the senior of Miss Beecher, Mary Lyon began teaching while yet a girl, and from 1821 for thirteen years was continuously in the school-room, ten years of the time with Miss Grant at Londonderry and Ipswich, New Hampshire, teaching and studying. During these years originated the idea of a seminary "which should be to young women what the college is to young men." After many delays and much opposition, funds amounting to eight thousand dollars had been collected; South Hadley, Massachusetts, was fixed upon for the location, and Mount Holyoke Female Seminary was incorporated February 10, 1836. It was opened the following year, all students being required to live within the institution and to assist in domestic duties.

The course occupied three years, and received graduates from other seminaries and academies of New England. For many years it was mainly devoted to preparing teachers for public and private schools, furnishing in the first twenty years (1837–'57) seven hundred and twenty-four teachers out of ten hundred and sixty pupils leaving the institution. Beyond this, however, the school was designed to give and did afford a solid, extensive, and well-balanced English and classical education to its pupils. It provided three years of Latin, two of mathematics, three each of general history and literature, three of physical science and mental and moral science. The instruction was meant for culture, not mere accomplishments. The whole work and management of the institution were adapted not to girls, but to women of mature character and considerable attainments.

The seminary has recently been incorporated as a college and authorized to confer degrees.

Elmira Female College, founded in 1855, claims to have been "the first in this country, and, so far as known, the first in the world that offered to women the same advantages and adopted the same standard for graduation as colleges and universities for the other sex."* The course was a small advance over that of Mount Holyoke.† It required more Latin, added Greek and the modern languages, and gave more mathematics, all included in a four years' course, and leading to degrees.

There was noticeable a growing spirit of approbation in the public. Interest was here and there manifested by the investment of capital, by Legislatures and churches, in the "new experiment." The sentiment was spreading beyond the centers where it originated, and schools were multiplying, perhaps too rapidly. Of the two hundred institutions of this class now in existence, more than half had their origin prior to Vassar College, which dates from this period (1861). The preceding decade had witnessed a great wave of interest on this subject.

As the earlier standards were set by Troy, Hartford, and Mount Holyoke, so the more recent date from Vassar, Smith, Wellesley, and Bryn Mawr.

Of these, Vassar came first by almost ten years, the act of incorporation dating January, 1861. The war coming on, the work was hindered, though never entirely stopped, the institution opening in 1866 with three hundred students. The founder, Matthew Vassar, looking to the "necessity of providing such an education for the women of this country as would be adequate to give them a position of intellectual equality with men in domestic and social life," purposed, he says, to devote a liberal portion of his estate "to promoting their education in literature, science, and art," endowing an institution so liberally as "to secure to it the elevated character, the stability, and the permanency of our best col-

---

* "New York Historical and Statistical Record" (1885), p. 269.

† Mount Holyoke has recently taken steps to expand the course and confer degrees. For a fresh and reliable sketch of this school see "Education," April, 1888, p. 477.

leges." * The buildings are located on a farm of two hundred acres, beautifully situated, near Poughkeepsie on the Hudson, the whole valued at seven hundred and fifty thousand dollars. It is supplied with an observatory, over which from the first Prof. Maria Mitchell has presided, a museum, a library of fifteen thousand volumes, a large and well-endowed art-gallery, music-rooms, and gymnasium.

The collegiate course covers four years, and has nine departments, besides music, drawing, and painting. Its faculty numbers twenty-two professors, among whom have been from the foundation some whose names are familiarly known to the educated public, and give guarantee of the excellence of the Vassar work : Prof. Sanborn Tenney, the naturalist ; Prof. T. J. Backus, now President of Packer Collegiate Institute, Brooklyn; Prof. Cooley, the physicist; and Dr. Maria Mitchell,† the well-known astronomer and mathematician.

Wellesley College, a few miles out of Boston, is the gift, so far as grounds and buildings are concerned, of Mr. Henry F. Durant. The farm consists of four hundred acres, with groves and lakes and lawns, and, with improvements, is estimated to be worth two million dollars. The first and largest structure was intended to accommodate three hundred students. For some years the average attendance has been twice that. To provide for this increase, cottages have been built in the place of large structures, and a system of home-life management introduced, not the least attractive of the Wellesley administration.

The institution is well supplied with apparatus, laboratories—physical and chemical—a hall with a capacity of seven hundred, and a library of thirty thousand volumes, admirably catalogued after the Dewey system. The college was opened to students in 1875 with a faculty of thirty, and an extended course of study. The first experience of Well-

---

* " Official History of Vassar College " (1876), p. 6.
† Resigned, 1888.

esley coincided with that of Vassar—young ladies were poorly fitted to do the work offered. Of the three hundred and fifty who entered Vassar ten years before, less than a third were well prepared. Fitting-classes were a necessity. That in Wellesley, however, was dropped in 1881, and the present faculty of seventy-five is engaged in collegiate instruction only.

The course is very complete—covers five years, including, besides four modern languages, Greek and Latin (with postgraduate courses), science and history, embracing an extended course in political and social science and constitutional history. The work in botany requires three years, and is enforced and supplemented by a morphological laboratory and a working library of more than one thousand volumes. The physical laboratory, with its special library, is quite as complete. Of mathematics, the president, in her report for 1883, said: "I know of no American college where more intelligent or more advanced undergraduate work has been attempted than that accomplished by those seniors who have been reading Doster's 'Determinants,' Howison's 'Analytics of Three Dimensions,' Watson's 'Theoretical Astronomy,' and calculating the orbit of the new comet from data obtained at Harvard."*

Smith College was established about the same time as Wellesley, through the beneficence of Sophia Smith. It has an endowment of $400,000, an art-gallery costing $30,000, and a full collegiate course of instruction. The professorships are equally divided between the sexes. Wells College, of like grade, was founded two years earlier.

Bryn-Mawr, the most recent institution of this class, was opened in 1885. It is located near Philadelphia, and was founded by the late Joseph W. Taylor, M. D. It has a limited number of students, a productive endowment of nearly a million dollars, and opens with great promise. No prepara-

---

* See article "Wellesley College" in "Education," January, 1887, p. 313.

tory class is sustained. For undergraduates, the "group system"* of studies is employed. Graduate study is provided for and encouraged, the institution conferring no honorary degrees, but offering annual fellowships in history, biology, Greek, and mathematics. The gymnasium is pronounced by Dr. Sargent the largest and most complete for women in the United States.

3. Coeducation of the Sexes in College.

Whatever later means may accomplish for woman's education, the first schools and seminaries, with all their frequent show and little careful study, with much of accomplishment and little of discipline, fitted the general mind and the feminine mind for something better.

The something better came, not all at once, nor without opposition, nor equally throughout the land, but occasionally, with varying success, at Middlebury and Hartford; in Maine, Ohio, and Michigan; in Vassar and Wellesley; an occasional success compelling confidence; sometimes failing; always working with limited means, but with every favorable experiment answering questions of health, capacity, and demand. With these settled or settling, the next question was that of coeducation. Is its intellectual competition safe for the girl? Morally, is it wise? Physically, is it prudent?

From Oberlin came an early answer. The institution was opened as the Collegiate Institute (1833). Both sexes have been admitted from the first. After seventeen years the school was incorporated as Oberlin College, under the presidency of Rev. Charles G. Finney. From the start it has been an ultra-radical—since 1835 no distinction being made either as to sex or race. In addition to the preparatory department, which has always been large, are theological, classical, philosophical, and literary departments, and a "ladies' course."

---

* The name originated with Miss Thomas, the dean of the institution, though now in common use.

This last differs from others in that it omits all the Greek, most of the Latin, and, in mathematics the calculus, adding French and drawing. It leads to no degree, but is followed by a certified diploma. Since 1837 women, upon application, have been admitted to the regular academic courses as candidates for a degree. The present attendance is from twelve hundred to fourteen hundred, fifty-five per cent of whom are women.

The table, indicating the selection of work by the two sexes, is taken from the official report of the institution for 1886–'87 :

COURSES.	Men.	Women.
1. Classical	160	50
2. Philosophical	2	22
3. Literary		157
4. Music	85	389
5. Art	3	68

Next to Oberlin as a pioneer in coeducation, though two decades later, was Antioch, at Yellow Springs, Ohio. The institution was opened (1853) under Horace Mann, one of whose aims was to make its advantages, whatever they were, equally open to both sexes. About one third of the attendance since its establishment has been of young women, usually mature and efficient. It is not too much to say that no one has seriously questioned coeducation at Yellow Springs. The conditions may have been different, the circumstances more favorable than those found elsewhere, but it appears that Antioch, whether from the point of view of intellectual capacity, or physical endurance, or moral purity, affirms the wisdom of the experiment in coeducation. So entirely satisfactory and without criticism have been the moral influences, that a prominent literary man* was led to say, some years since, that " young men were first called gentle-

---

* Moncure D. Conway.

men at Antioch." The present faculty consists of sixteen, five of whom are women.

In 1846 Earlham College, Indiana, a Friends' school, admitted both sexes, and the Indiana State University in 1867. The next year women were admitted to Boston University, and two years later to Swarthmore College and the University of Missouri. They were formally admitted to Michigan University in 1870, and to Cornell in 1874. In the last quarter of a century, even, it has been the rule rather than the exception to grant them full privileges in the newly established institutions. Most State endowments are coeducational. Of three hundred and forty-five colleges and universities reporting to the National Bureau of Education, and exclusive of those for women alone, two hundred and four are coeducational. Thirty-eight of the forty-eight schools of science endowed with the national land grant are coeducational, as are eleven of the independent schools of the same class.

4. *Examinations and Annexes.*

Contemporary with the founding of Smith and Wellesley, an organization was formed in Boston (1872) whose aim was to aid in the more liberal and thorough education of woman in the higher branches. Arrangements were made with the Harvard authorities to hold examinations for women similar to those, and under the same conditions, accorded them by the Edinburgh, Oxford, and Cambridge Universities. These were first held (1874) in Cambridge, Massachusetts, though similar ones are now offered annually at New York, Philadelphia, and Cincinnati, also by the Harvard authorities, in all respects equivalent to and on the same conditions as the regular examination of men for admission to university classes.

After five years' experience it was proposed to provide for instruction as well as examination, the new organization being incorporated as the "Society for the Collegiate Instruction of Women by Professors and other Instructors of Harvard College." The former has recently dissolved, the functions being assumed and the duties performed by the later organization. A dozen Harvard professors are members of the corporation, of which Mrs. Elizabeth Agassiz is president. The "Annex" bears no official relation to Harvard; the names of its graduates do not appear in the college catalogue. Instruction is given by Harvard professors who have taken a personal interest in the matter, and are under contract with the "Society." Fifty members of the university faculty are on the "Annex" staff, and offer eighty-one courses, as follows: Hebrew (two), Sanskrit (two), Italian (two), astronomy (two), philosophy, political economy, music, physics, and chemistry (three each), fine arts (four), German (five), Greek, French, mathematics, and natural history (six each), Latin (seven), English (eight), and history (ten).

The first year twenty-seven women were admitted, and twenty-four courses taken; most of the students were mature; many have been teachers. The second year the courses were doubled, and the attendance increased, there being one hundred students now; the average for nine years has been above fifty. In 1883–'84 the students were drawn from twelve States, seven outside of New England. The Harvard Annex has been called the "American Girton," and is said by Prof. Goodwin to offer "better advantages to women than any institution [in this country] offered young men in 1865." Tuition is two hundred dollars a year. The society owns its building, and has one hundred thousand dollars' endowment.

Next to the Harvard examination for women, both in time and in the dignity of the undertaking, is that of Columbia College. After an entrance examination, a course of study (without instruction) is offered, embracing the following nine groups:

1. The English language and literature.
2. Modern languages and foreign literature.
3. The Latin language and literature.

4. The Greek language and literature.
5. History and political science.
6. Moral and intellectual philosophy.
7. Mathematics.
8. Physics, chemistry, and hygiene.
9. Natural history, geology, paleontology, botany, and zoölogy.

The course covers four years, and is prescribed for the first two; in the Harvard Annex the instruction offered is altogether elective. Arrangements have been recently shaping in Columbia to offer instruction also, as in Harvard.

5. Association of Collegiate Alumnœ.

Seven years ago (1882) there was formed in Boston an "Association of Collegiate Alumnæ," representing Vassar, Wellesley, Smith, Oberlin, Wisconsin, and Boston Universities. Within one year it enrolled two hundred and sixty-four members, admitting graduates, also, from Cornell, Michigan, Massachusetts Institute of Technology, Wesleyan University, Syracuse, Kansas, and Northwestern. The object is said to be "to unite alumnæ of different institutions for practical educational work." It offers advantages for home and advanced study, and covers a wide range of investigation. The present membership is about five hundred, representing fifteen institutions in nearly as many States. Branch organizations have been formed in Washington, Chicago, New York, San Francisco, Philadelphia, Poughkeepsie, and Cleveland, and perhaps one or two other places. Members have been doing more or less special and graduate work in political and sanitary science, in a study of the "Occupations of Women," "Health Statistics," and "Local Histories." There has been recently organized, also, by the society a "Bureau of Collegiate Information," whose object is "to collect trustworthy facts and statistics concerning the history of the movement for the collegiate education of women."

6. The Professional Education of Women.

A. THEOLOGICAL.

Of the departments for special training of women, that of medicine is best established, and of the ministry least. Yet among Friends, for more than two centuries, women have performed ministerial functions, as among Moravians also, there being one instance at least of a woman holding regularly and discharging the duties of a bishopric. The like may be said in general of women among Universalists and Unitarians, who have ordained them preachers and pastors, as have the Protestant Methodist and Baptist Churches. Mrs. Antoinette Brown Blackwell, a graduate of Oberlin in 1847, finished the theological course also in the same institution three years afterward. At first refused a license to preach, she was subsequently ordained pastor of a church in New York. Rev. Olympia Brown, Rev. Phebe Hanaford, and others followed both in the seminary and in the pulpit. In 1880 there were in the United States one hundred and sixty-five pulpits regularly occupied by women, most of whom had taken more or less of theological training in the schools of their respective churches.

Boston University, Northwestern University, Chicago, and St. Lawrence University, New York, have been especially forward in extending the privileges of their divinity courses to women.

B. MEDICAL.

To the Drs. Blackwell, Elizabeth and Emily, sisters, is due more than to any other single agency the early though slow recognition accorded to women by the medical institutions of the country. In the year 1847, the former and elder of the two, having read in Charleston and Philadelphia, applied for admission to the medical schools of the latter and afterward of New York and Boston, being uniformly refused. She was finally admitted to the Medical

School of Geneva, New York, by vote of the students. She graduated in 1849, and, upon going abroad, studied in Paris and London, practiced successfully in foreign hospitals, and returned in 1854 to the United States. In New York she was instrumental in establishing the "Infirmary for Women and Children," to which was attached thirteen years afterward a medical college.

During the studies of Miss Blackwell in Geneva College, there had been organized in Boston a "Female Medical Education Association," which led (1848) to the establishment of the New England Female Medical College. In 1874 it was merged in the Boston University. The Woman's Medical College of Pennsylvania, founded in 1850 and graduating its first class the next year, has now a faculty consisting of both men and women of high social and professional standing and scientific attainments, buildings and apparatus, lecture-rooms, and laboratories of modern completeness and design. The University of Michigan organized a medical department about 1850, and twenty years later admitted women to it, as to all other departments, on equal terms with men. In the same year also was opened the "Woman's Hospital Medical College," Chicago. In twenty years from Miss Blackwell's graduation at Geneva, half a dozen institutions received women regularly, and more than five hundred graduates were practicing their profession. There are now about one thousand in practice, and of one hundred and twenty-six medical schools, exclusive of dental, pharmaceutical, and veterinary courses, thirty-six admit both sexes on equal terms. These schools represent eighteen States and the District of Columbia, and such large cities, with all their hospital and clinical advantages, as New York, Philadelphia, Boston, Chicago, St. Louis, Baltimore, Louisville, Cincinnati, and Washington. Besides these coeducation schools there are six independent institutions, as shown in the table, for women only:

Medical Colleges admitting Women.

Allopathic.

University of Southern California, Los Angeles.

Cooper Medical College, San Francisco, Cal.

University of California, San Francisco.

University of Colorado, Boulder.

Howard University, Washington, D. C.

National Medical College, Washington, D. C.

Quincy College of Medicine, Quincy, Ill.

Iowa College of Physicians and Surgeons, Des Moines, Ia.

College of Physicians and Surgeons, Keokuk, Ia.

College of Physicians and Surgeons, Boston, Mass.

University of Michigan, Ann Arbor, Mich.

Minnesota Hospital College, Minneapolis, Minn.

University of Nebraska, Lincoln, Neb.

Omaha Medical College, Omaha, Neb.

Leonard Medical School, Raleigh, N. C.

University of Wooster, Cleveland, O.

Columbus Medical College, Columbus, O.

Toledo Medical College, Toledo, O.

Willamette University, Portland, Oreg.

Eclectic.

California Medical College, Oakland, Cal.

Georgia College of Eclectic Medicine and Surgery, Atlanta, Ga.

Bennett College of Eclectic Medicine and Surgery, Chicago, Ill.

Indiana Eclectic Medical College, Indianapolis, Ind.

Iowa Medical College, Des Moines, Ia.

American Medical College, St. Louis, Mo.

American Eclectic Medical College, Cincinnati, O.

Eclectic Medical Institute, Cincinnati, O.

Homœopathic.

Hahnemann Medical College and Hospital, Chicago, Ill.

Boston University, Boston, Mass.

University of Michigan, Ann Arbor, Mich.

Medical College of Missouri, St. Louis, Mo.

University of Nebraska, Lincoln, Neb.

Pulte Medical College, New York, N. Y.

Homœopathic Hospital College, Cleveland, O.

Physio-Medical.

Physio-Medical Institute, Chicago, Ill.

Physio-Medical College, Indianapolis, Ind.

Independent Schools for Women.

Woman's Medical College, Chicago, Ill.

Woman's Medical College, Baltimore, Md.

Woman's Medical College of New York Infirmary, N. Y.

Woman's Medical College of Pennsylvania, Philadelphia, Pa.

New York Medical College and Hospital, N. Y.

School of Pharmacy for Women, Louisville, Ky.

C. LEGAL EDUCATION.

The history of the legal education of woman is brief.*
About twenty years after Dr. Blackwell left Geneva College, Washington University, St. Louis, admitted a young
lady to the department of law. The next year one was
admitted to the Iowa bar, and three others enrolled as students of the Law School of Chicago University. The same
year from the same institution Mrs. Ada H. Kepley was
given the degree of Bachelor of Laws, though she was refused for two years permission to practice.

Women were first admitted to the Iowa University Law
School in 1872. Seven years later Miss Clara Foltz received
judgment to compel the directors of Hastings College of Law,
in the University of California, to admit her as a student.

Now, after twenty years, though comparatively few use
the privilege, women are admitted to most law schools, and
are practicing at the bar in Maine, Massachusetts, Connecticut, Ohio, Illinois, Indiana, Iowa, Minnesota, California,
Oregon, Michigan, Missouri, Wisconsin, Texas, District of
Columbia, and the Territories of Wyoming, Washington,
and Utah. A woman is Professor of Commercial Law in
Rockford, Illinois, and the principal legal *newspaper* of
Chicago and the West is edited by a woman. The Equity
Club of Michigan and the Woman's International Bar Association are organizations of women lawyers, both with a
considerable membership.

D. WOMEN AS TEACHERS.

One accompaniment and consequence of the long neglect
of female education was the great preponderance of male
teachers in the schools, both public and private. The eighteenth century had its dame-schools both in England and
her colonies. Bright girls occasionally taught in a quiet

---

* It is a fact of history that one Margaret Brent, attorney to Lord Baltimore, was admitted to the Maryland bar in 1648.

way, and the mothers themselves, learning of pastor or
father, sometimes instructed their own children.   From the
later schools of Mrs. Willard, and especially from Mount
Holyoke, young ladies went out to teach more than sixty
years ago.   The teachers sent West by Miss Beecher were
principally well - educated young women.   Nevertheless,
they were not only few, as compared with the great body
of teachers, but they were indifferently regarded among
patrons and school officers and even among teachers themselves.   Women were not allowed to take part in the teachers' gatherings, though toward the middle of the century it
was granted that they might submit communications to be
read by their gentlemen friends.

As late as 1845 Mr. Barnard asserts that in the entire
State of Rhode Island, except Providence and the primary
departments of a few large central districts, there were probably not more than a dozen female teachers employed.   A
like state of affairs existed throughout the newer West and
the South.

Yet there were forces at work in most sections to change
this arrangement.   When the first State Normal School was
opened at Lexington, Massachusetts, it was, as it has remained, for women only.   Of twenty-nine students who entered at Albany a few years afterward, sixteen were women.
A like proportion obtained at New Britain, Connecticut, in
1850.   Before the middle of the century the New York
academies also began sending out young women from their
teachers' classes; and after twenty years' experience in Massachusetts with four normal schools, eighty-seven per cent
of the students were found to be women.   So rapidly had
the proportion of men decreased that it attracted the attention of the Swedish visitor, Siljeström, in 1854, who com-
mented upon it favorably; of Bishop Fraser, ten years
later; and of Francis Adams, who criticised it in his recent
visit to this country in 1875.   The impulse was a part of
the general movement which established normal schools,
State systems, supervision, etc., in the first half of the cent-

ury. Below is presented a tabulated statement of the change noted in thirteen typical States:

Table showing Per Cent of Female Teachers in Thirteen States.—
Growth in Thirty Years.

No.	STATES.	1855.	1875.	1880.	1886.	Increase.
1	Vermont....................	21	85	83	88	67
2	Pennsylvania	33	50	52	83	50
3	New Jersey	39	71	76	79	40
4	Iowa......................	44	63	67	76	32
5	Indiana...................	21	42	48	49	28
6	Illinois..................	39	57	61	67	28
7	Rhode Island..............	60	80	78	87	27
8	Missouri..................	21	39	43	40	19
9	Connecticut...............	64	76	76	82	18
10	Massachusetts.............	74	88	87	89	15
11	New Hampshire.............	74	86	83	88	14
12	Ohio......................	46	46	52	56	10
13	Maine	61	69	67	65	4

In noting the increasing proportion of women teachers between 1855 and 1875, it should be remembered that it includes the war period, when there was a large withdrawal of male teachers:

Table showing Per Cent of Women Teachers in each State, 1885–'86.

No.	STATE.	Per ct.	No.	STATE.	Per ct.
1	Alabama................	36	20	Mississippi............	45
2	Arkansas...............	23	21	Missouri...............	40
3	California.............	76	22	Nebraska...............	75
4	Colorado...............	73	23	Nevada.................	77
5	Connecticut............	82	24	New Hampshire..........	88
6	Delaware...............	57	25	New Jersey.	79
7	Florida................	45	26	New York.............	81
8	Georgia................	33	27	North Carolina.........	40
9	Illinois...............	67	28	Ohio	56
10	Indiana................	49	29	Oregon.................	83
11	Iowa	76	30	Pennsylvania..........	62
12	Kansas	58	31	Rhode Island	87
13	Kentucky...............	47	32	South Carolina.	46
14	Louisiana.....	54	33	Tennessee.............	32
15	Maine	65	34	Texas	31
16	Maryland...............	67	35	Vermont................	88
17	Massachusetts..........	89	36	Virginia...............	50
18	Michigan...............	75	37	West Virginia..........	34
19	Minnesota	89	38	Wisconsin	79

In thirteen States, it will be seen, male teachers yet pre-
dominate; these are all Southern States except Indiana.
Yet even here the gain in the proportion of women teachers
is scarcely less than for the thirteen States shown in the
preceding table. Georgia, Massachusetts, New Hampshire,
and Vermont made no gain, and Arkansas and Maine present the anomaly of employing constantly fewer women
teachers for the last twelve years.

In cities, especially the larger ones, the preponderance of
female teachers is most noticeable. In sixty-nine cities of
the United States, employing more than one hundred teachers each, more than ninety-one per cent are women. In but
twelve of them does the proportion fall below ninety per
cent, while in seventeen of them it is ninety-five per cent or
over. A few cities are typical of the most radical policy of
employing women. Twelve cities in seven States reporting
an aggregate of three hundred and nine teachers, and representing a school population of thirty-three thousand five
hundred, employ women teachers only.

7. *School Suffrage of Women.*

As showing a different relation of women to education,
but promising, in its consequences, their school suffrage and
service on educational boards of control, are deserving of
attention.

Fifteen States — California, Colorado, Illinois, Iowa,
Louisiana, Michigan, Minnesota, Nebraska, New Hamp-
shire, New York, Oregon, Pennsylvania, Rhode Island,
Vermont, and Wisconsin, and the Territories of Idaho,
Montana, and Washington — admit them to both these
privileges.

In Iowa the State Board of Examiners, created to encourage training in the science and art of teaching, is composed of four *ex-officio* members and two others, one of
whom must be a woman. In Oregon the privilege among
women of voting upon school questions is confined to
widows. Twelve States extend their educational service to

25

county superintendency, and six make women eligible to
any educational office in the State.

Bibliography.

"Intellectual Education for Women," by E. Shireff, 1862; "The College, the Market, and the Court," by Caroline H. Dall, 1867; "The Liberal Education of Women," by J. Orton, 1873; "Schools for Girls and
Colleges for Women" (English), by C. E. Pascoe, 1879; "Smith College," Caroline E. Hilliard, "Education," September, 1887; "Wellesley
College," Jean Kincaid, "Education," January, 1887; "Bryn-Mawr College," "Education," September, 1886; "Women in Colleges," "Proceedings of the New York University Convocation," 1883, p. 417; "Women
in English Universities," "Yale Review," July, 1886; "The American
Girl Graduate," T. W. Higginson, "Critic," December 4, 1886; "Women
of the Twentieth Century," F. K. Carey, "Princeton Review," September
and November, 1884; "Progress of Coeducation," "The Forum," August, 1887, p. 631; "The Harvard Annex," G. C. Eggleston, "The Century Magazine," September, 1884; also "Education," vol. vi, p. 568;
"Michigan School Report," 1879, p. 142, and "Education," May, 1886;
"Women as Professional Teachers," May Mackintosh, "Education,"
April 4, 1887. Consult, also, "Heredity," by W. K. Brooks, chap. x,
on "Intellectual Differences between Men and Women"; "Female Education from a Medical Point of View," T. S. Clouston, "Popular Science
Monthly," December, 1883, and January, 1884; "Higher Education of
Women" (adverse), by Mrs. E. Lynn Lynton, "Popular Science Month-
ly," December, 1886; and "Advanced Education for Women," by Kate
Stevens, "Forum," March, 1889.

CONCLUSION.

WHATEVER confidence one may feel in the general soundness of the idea of education here sought to be sketched, or
however well satisfied one may be with the work of existing
schools, from this brief study of them no conclusion could
be less warranted than that this New World idea of education is altogether the best, or that our school systems have

reached a final form. With three teachers in four having
no special fitness for the work; schools but six months in
twelve; the average school period less than five years; but
sixty-one per cent of minors over six years of age in school;
and two million (sixteen per cent) illiterate voters in the
country, there is abundant room for criticism—not, indeed,
upon the schools as such, but upon the general public sentiment which makes these things possible, and even common.
The schools come in for their share of this responsibility.

Along with this deficiency, and perhaps the occasion of
it, are certain unsettled social and educational questions that
are of peculiar interest, and may well claim the most serious
attention of every one : ·

1. It betrays neither lack of confidence, nor want of appreciation of what has been done, to say that no sufficient
means has yet been found to provide a supply of qualified
teachers.

2. How best to honor the complex nature of the child,
and, while shaping the understanding mind, to bring up
youth with sound bodies and a love for truth, is still in the
stage of personal opinion.

3. There is no general agreement among legislators or
educators as to the relation which the public schools should
sustain to industrial training, either manual or technical.

4. The supreme importance of infant and primary education is only beginning to be appreciated by the community, and this only in cities.

5. Free public higher, and professional education, has
still numerous opponents; as does anything like coercive
legislation in the interests of school attendance.

6. Closely related to this is the question of extra-school
training, which is daily assuming graver proportions. How
may the hundreds of thousands be reached who, too old for
school, or prevented by industry and poverty—the day-labor-
er, the recent immigrant, the street Arab, the orphan, the
young offender—are practically illiterate ? How accommodate the intelligent and willing, but half-educated workman,

who seeks higher skill in his trade ? The uses to which public libraries, and lectures, and evening schools, and university faculties, may be put for this extra-school education, have been but recently tried outside the few centers of cities where first introduced.

7. Finally, what constitutes a citizenship education—how to compass an education with special civic and administrative aptitudes—is only beginning to claim general and systematic attention, and chiefly of the colleges. That the common elementary schools have a definite citizen-making function is by no means generally accepted.

Notwithstanding all this indecision, and sometimes disagreement, and perhaps because of the fact, there is a widespread public interest in education in all its phases, such as has not been before for half a century. The public education societies in large cities are only conspicuous examples of an impulse that is stirring rural as well as urban communities alike. It means faith in the common school as a civilizing and purifying agency ; it means a patriotic interest in home industry ; an unselfish concern for the next generations.

Much of this general activity may be ascribed to a common familiarity with the systems of other states and nations. Acquaintance with one's neighbor's success is a great quickener to home enterprise. A generation since, European schools were chiefly known to Americans through a half-dozen volumes. How great a service these few did ! But now, what with the easier intercourse, the frequent intermigration, the translation of foreign literature, the prominence given to modern-language study, and the interchange of views in international expositions and conferences, the school systems of Europe are, in a general way, more familiar to many an American teacher than are those of his own country.

This comparative study of educational institutions, very elementary and very superficial it may be, gives a kind of perspective to the nearer views of one's own schools—a chance

to look at them in their universal relations. This concern,
it has already been suggested, is not monopolized by the
profession; but instances of it may be seen in every State,
and in all sections, among business men, and lawyers, and
the clergy, physicians, and laborers. Common-school questions are being studied by college presidents and professors,
as related to their own labors; by economists and historians; and the outlook is hopeful.

Only this comprehensive study of education in all its
relations can save our people from a national tendency to
run to extremes and ride hobbies. These problems and
others, with which the public is still experimenting, and in
whose presence wise men stand confounded, confronted
the early settlers also, with every subsequent generation.
Some of them have been settled before, but "are constantly recurring," it has been said, " because of our ignorance of
that fact."

SYLLABUS OF BOONE'S
EDUCATION IN THE UNITED STATES.

From the International Reading Circle Course of
Professional Study.

Pages 1 to 43.

1. What conditions made the New World more favorable than the Old for the advancement of popular education?
2. What conditions rendered the seventeenth century an especially favorable time?
3. To what extent may our American public-school system be said to be of Holland origin?
4. Where and under what circumstances was the first free public school in the United States established?
5. What steps were taken toward founding schools in the early Virginia colonies?
6. What were the earliest provisions for schools in New England?
7. What were the circumstances of the founding of Harvard College?
8. How was the establishment of William and Mary College secured?
9. What names prominent in American political history are associated with the early history of William and Mary College?
10. What aids and what difficulties attended the founding of Yale College?

Pages 43 to 78.

11. What provisions for an educational system were made by the Massachusetts laws of 1642 and 1647?

12. What were the characteristic features of the Connecticut law of 1650 ?

13 What were the earliest recorded movements toward establishing schools in New York ?

14. From what origin in each case have Columbia College in New York and Princeton College in New Jersey sprung ?

15. What was the attitude of the Southern colonies toward the establishment of free public schools ?

16. What class distinctions interfered with the progress of the early public schools ?

17. What were some of the earliest notable text-books ?

Pages 79 to 116.

18. What principle most influenced educational thought in the period of transition from colonial to national existence ?

19. How did the provision of school funds in the early years of the century differ generally from the present provisions ?

20. What were some of the earliest provisions for permanent school funds ?

21. What declaration has been adopted into most State Constitutions from the ordinance for the government of the Northwest Territory?

22. What definite contributions has Congress made to the funds of the several States for educational purposes ?

23. In what proportion are the schools now supported from these general funds as compared with local taxation ?

24. What is the basis of argument for legal supervision of schools ?

25. What chief influence has supervision by appointed authority had upon the methods and results of school work ?

26. What especial advantages and what disadvantages are possessed by the " District System " of supervision ?

27. What seems to be the greatest need in the line of perfecting State supervision ?

28. What do you deem the strongest argument in favor of strictly professional superintendence of city and country school systems ?

Pages 117 to 157.

29. What chief benefits have resulted from educational associations ?

30. What valuable work was done by the early societies for the promotion of schools ?

31. Why were the members of these societies usually business and professional men, not teachers ?

32. What work was accomplished by the earlier associations of teachers ?

33. What is your estimate of the value and your view of the right work of the teachers' institute ?

34. What was the origin of the normal schools ?

35. What were the first steps in this country toward the establishment of normal schools ?

36. To what extent are the normal schools of to-day fulfilling the purpose for which they are established and supported ?

37. To what extent should the curriculum of the normal school include academic work ?

38. What provision have colleges been led to make for the professional instruction of teachers ?

39. What is the most valuable form of educational literature?

40. In what respect do educational reports constitute a valuable class of professional text-books?

Pages 158 to 209.

41. Upon what chief lines has the college curriculum been extended during the present century?

42. What was the extent of science teaching at the beginning of the century?

43. Where were the earliest advances made in the instruction in physics?

44. Under what circumstances was chemistry made a separate branch of college instruction?

45. What have been the notable steps in the advance of geology, astronomy, and biology instruction?

46. How has the recognition of the utility and the disciplinary value of modern language study led to advances upon this line of college work?

47. What teachers and what schools have been most prominently instrumental in advancing the study of history and of economics?

48. What conditions made necessary the provision for elective college courses and studies?

49. How have the "group systems" and the graduate courses grown out of the system of elective studies?

50. In what relations do the principles of self-interest and of philanthropy severally underlie the foundation of state established and privately endowed institutions of learning?

Pages 209 to 243.

51. What guiding relation have the professional schools borne to the general teaching of the universities?

52. Why is this guidance less marked at the present day than formerly?

53. In what special lines has the current of modern thought influenced theological education?

54. What notable interest has the general public in the extent and thoroughness of legal education?

55. What line of progress is at present most noticeable in regard to preparation for the profession of law?

56. In what respect has the medical profession allowed itself to take the lowest rank educationally?

57. How does technological education differ from and in what particulars does it resemble professional edution?

58. What was the distinctive nature of the earliest industrial schools organized in this country?

59. What has been the greatest advance made within the last quarter of a century in the nature of this class of schools?

60. What are the two opposing views as to the proper purpose of manual training schools?

61. What relation should the public schools bear to the several classes of professional and technological schools?

Pages 243 to 272.

62. In what manner is education preventive of crime?

63. Aside from the charitable view, what is the economic argument for the care and education of the mentally unfortunate classes?

64. Through whose efforts and from what beginning was the first institution in America for the instruction of deaf-mutes founded?

65. What are the two characteristic methods of deaf-mute instruction in speaking and reading?

66. By whom was the instruction of the blind introduced into the United States?

67. What do you know of Dr. Howe's efforts and success in the case of Laura Bridgman?

68. How much is being done in this country for the instruction of feeble-minded children?

69. What three distinct lines of training are essential in the reformatory schools?

70. What have been the chief steps of progress in providing for education among the Indians?

71. What classes of private schools seem necessary in relation with the public schools?

72. What marked difference between the Catholic Church and the other denominations in the matter of denominational schools?

73. What is the argument for evening schools, and what classes of evening schools should be maintained?

Pages 272 to 307.

74. What chief causes have led to the establishment in recent years of museums of art and science?

75. What educational ends do such museums serve in their relation to the general public?

76. To what extent or in what manner may the "museum idea" be wisely cultivated in the public school?

77. In what does the educational value of organized clubs or societies lie?

78. When and whence came the idea in this country of the organized reading circle?

79. What was the immediate purpose of the first reading circle organized in this country?

80. What are the characteristics of the Chautauqua organization?

81. How have the professional needs of teachers in these respects been provided for ?
82. What service have the various learned societies rendered in the advance of general education ?
83. How may the work of our schools be adjusted to the opportunities for later study supplied by the public libraries ?

Pages 307 to 325.

84. Upon what principle would you base an argument for national aid to the State public-school systems ?
85. What special educational demands has the General Government been called to meet ?
86. What names have been most prominently associated with the successive steps in the establishment of the National Bureau of Education ?
87. What are the two chief functions of the Bureau of Education ?
88. Would you deem it desirable that any supervisory authority over the State systems should be possessed by the National Bureau ?
89. What remarkable fact is connected with the fund for establishing the Smithsonian Institution ?
90. What were the plans most prominently urged for using the Smithson bequest ?
91. What is the present chief function of the Smithsonian Institution ?
92. How has the United States Coast Survey work been productive of general scientific progress ?
93. Under what Government organizations have the advances in our geographical and geological knowledge been chiefly made ?
94. For what chief purpose was the bureau, now the Department of Agriculture, organized ?

95. Besides those of the National Bureau of Education, what publications of the national Government are of highest general educational value?

Pages 326 to 385.

96. By what right may the State justly require the attendance upon schools of those who are of school age?

97. What have been the chief obstacles to the due enforcement of compulsory attendance laws?

98. What has been the general order of development of the system of gradation in public schools?

99. To what extent should the kindergarten be adopted as a part of the public-school system?

100. Upon what grounds is the public high school justly supported by general taxation?

101. Should the course of study of the public high school be organized essentially as completing a public-school course, or as preparatory to the higher course of college education?

102. How does the public provision for education in the Southern States now compare with that of two decades ago?

103. What has been the specific work accomplished by each of the four women whose names are most prominently identified with the early provisions for the higher education of women in the United States?

104. How does women's work in the colleges now compare with that of men?

105. From your study of this work upon the history of education in the United States, what do you consider the line of our greatest progress?

INDEX.

Abbott, Benjamin, 72.
Abderrahman I, 4.
Academe, the, 278.
Academia Virginiensis et Oxoniensis, 32.
Academic studies in normal schools, 136.
Academies, endowment of, 72; in England, 71; in New England, 72; in New York, 132, 364; of science, 285; of the Revolutionary period, 70.
Academy of Arts and Sciences, 286.
Academy of Natural Science, 286.
Academy, the scientific, 286.
Acrelius, Israel, 55.
Adams, C. K., in Michigan University, 177; "Washington and Higher Education," 149.
Adams, Francis, 62, 64, 123.
Adams, H. B., 6, 36, 43, 177, 183.
Adler, Prof. Felix, Twenty-second Street (N. Y.) Kindergarten, 336.
Agassiz Association, 284.
Agassiz, Mrs. Elizabeth, President of the Society for the Collegiate Instruction of Women, 373.
Agassiz, Prof. Louis, 274.
Agricultural colleges, 233; curriculum, 234; education, 227, 232; land grant, 233; museum, 273; schools, 234.
Alaska, education in, 262.
Albany (N. Y.) Normal School, 132.
Alcott, A. Bronson, 151, 278.
Alcott, William A., 151.
Alfred the Great, 4.
American Association for the Advancement of Science, 286; Asylum for Deaf-Mutes, 245; Entomological Society, 289; Ethnological Society, 256; Geographical Society, 286; Historical Association, 291; idea of free schools, 1, 8; Institute of Instruction, 122; Journal of Education, 6, 51, 60, 150, 152; Journal of Psychology, 153; Journal of Science, 292; Missionary Association, 353; Museum of Natural History, 274; Philosophical Society, 286, 294.
American history, instruction in, 178.
American Preceptor, the, 167.
Andover Normal School, 129.
Annex, Harvard, 373.
Ante-war period in the South, 348.
Antioch College, 371.
Apprenticeship schools, 231.
Architecture, education in, 227.
Arithmetic texts, 67.
Army Medical Museum, 273.
Art and design, schools of, 229.
Articulation in deaf-mute instruction, 245.
Artillery school at Fortress Monroe, 239.
Art, museums of, 272; normal schools, 229.
Associates of Cooper Union, 290.
Associations, classification of, 118; educational, 117; State, 121.
Astor Library, 298.
Astronomy, 158, 164.
Athenian education, 7, 326.
Atterbury quoted, 294.
Authority, withdrawal of, 186.
Awakening, educational, 182.

Bache, Prof. A. D., Superintendent of Coast Survey, 317; visit to Europe, 129, 149.

Baker, Miss Alice, 279.

Bancroft, George, 7; editor of New York colonial MSS., 11, 241, 292; History of the United States, 177, 198.

Baptist Western Educational Association, 119.

Barbarism, New England idea of, 17.

Bar, fitting for the, 213.

Barnard, Henry, 6; in Connecticut, 104; in Rhode Island, 106; Principal of Connecticut Normal School, 132; American Journal of Education, viii, 150, 152; Commissioner of Education, 309.

Barre (Mass.) Normal School, 131.

Bartram, John, 167.

Bates, Joshua, gift to Boston Library, 298.

Battle Creek School, Md., 59.

Beecher, Miss C. E., 365.

Beers, Samuel, 106.

Bell, Andrew, 127.

Benefactions, educational, 206; of George Peabody, 354; to Harvard, 29; to William and Mary, 35; to Yale, 41; to the South, 353.

Berkeley, Bishop, 14, 41; donation to Newport Library, 279; founds the New Haven Club, 286.

Berkeley, Governor of Virginia, 59.

Bermuda Islands, school on, 14.

Bible study in elementary schools, 66; in Harvard, 25.

Bibliography of early colonial schools, 19; colonial colleges, 42; colonial school systems, 60; college curricula, 184; compulsory education, 330; education for women, 382; education in the South, 361; education of dependent classes, 263; elective courses, 208; elementary and secondary instruction, 346; learned societies and libraries, 307; national education, 325; normal schools and institutes, 141; professional education, 221; Revolutionary period, 78; school funds, 93; school supervision, 116; supplementary agencies, 284; technological training, 242; university pedagogy and educational literature, 157.

Bickmore, Dr., 274.

Bicknell, T. W., 94.

Billings, Dr., 301.

Bingham, Caleb, The American Preceptor, 67; The Columbian Orator, 67; girls' school, Boston, 69; Young Ladies Accidence, 68.

Biological studies, 166.

Bishop, Nathan, superintendent of Boston schools, 110; superintendent of Providence schools, 110.

Blackboard used by Christopher Dock, 56.

Blair, Rev. James, 33.

Blackstone on deaf-mutes and blind 244; sale of "Commentaries" in America, 214.

Blackwell, Dr. Elizabeth, 375.

Blanqui, J. A., quoted, 275.

Blind, education of the, 246; industrial training of the, 247; methods of instruction, 248; occupations of the, 248; work at the New Orleans Exposition, 247.

Blow, Susan E., 334.

Blue Laws of Connecticut, 49.

"Boarding 'round," 64.

Board of Education, Connecticut, 105; functions of, 108; Massachusetts, 104.

Boelte, Miss (Kraus); 334.

Bopp's Indo-Germanic studies, 173.

Boston Academy of Science, 288.

Boston evening schools, 270; Latin School, 9, 14, 338; lectures in pedagogy, 146; primary schools, origin of, 332; Public Library, 297; school superintendent, 110; training-school, 140.

Botanical science, 167; in Harvard, 25, 167.

Botany, museum of, 273.

Boucher, characterization of early Maryland teachers, 64.

Bowdoin teachers' class, 130.

Bowen, Francis, 179.

Boyle fund for educating Indians, 254.

Bridgewater (Mass.) Normal School, 131.

Bridgman, Laura, 249.

Broadhead's Documentary History of New York, 5, 292.

Brooklyn school-tax, 10.

Brooks, Rev. Charles, 129.

Brooks, Rev. Phillips, 9.

Brothers of the Christian Schools, 268.

Brown, Goold, 122.

Browning clubs in the United States, 278.
Browning, Oscar, 150.
Brown University, 94.
Bryant and Stratton Business Colleges, 266.
Bryn Mawr College, 369; group system of, 200, 370.
Buffalo, school supervision, 109.
Bureau, Indian schools, 258; of Agriculture, 323; of Education, 308; museum, 311; library, 310; of collegiate information, 374; publications, 310.
Burlington (N. J.) school-funds, 56.
Business schools, 265.

Cabell and Jefferson, 190.
Cadets in the United States Military Academy, 237.
California, exploration of, 319; history of education in, 150; Lick Observatory, 166; naval training-ship, 242.
Calvin, John, 6, 7.
Calvinism in New England, 28.
Cambridge, England, 8.
Cambridge (Mass.) early school, 16.
Carlisle Indian School, 261.
Carolus, Alexander, 11.
Carter, Rev. James G., 130.
Catalogue, of students, alphabetic, 76; of Philadelphia Pedagogical Library, 151.
Catalogues, library, 306.
Catechism, Mather's, 52.
Catholic, estimate of public schools, 98; Indian missions, 253; parish schools, 267; university, 268.
Census, school, 154.
Centralization in education, 44.
Centralizing tendencies, 79, 83.
Chaldee in Harvard, 28.
Chandler Scientific School, 226.
Charity schools in Pennsylvania, 55-63; in England, 62.
Charlemagne, 3, 4.
Charles X, 4.
Charter, Harvard, 27; Penn Colony, 54; William and Mary, 34; Yale, 39.
Chase, Dr. P. E., 188.
Chauncy, President of Harvard, 26.
Chautauqua, 281; Teachers' Reading Union, 284; University, 281.
Chauvenet, Prof., 241.
26

Cheever, Ezekiel, 18, 51, 68.
Chemistry, in college, 158, 162; a branch of medicine, 162.
Chicago High-School, 339; Kindergarten, 335, 336; library, 298; school reports, 155; supervision, 111, 112.
Child labor, legislation on, 329.
Children's reading circles, 284.
Chipman's "American Moralist," 67.
Christian Brothers, 126, 268.
Church, lotteries, 88; schools, 266.
Cincinnati school reports, 155.
Circulating libraries, 294.
Citizenship education, 384.
City, reports, 155; school histories, 150; supervision, 119-123; teachers' institutes, 140; training-schools, 140.
Civilization fund, Indian, 255.
Civil Liberty and Self-Government, 175.
Clark Institution for the Education of Deaf-Mutes, 246.
Clark University, Worcester, 206.
Class distinctions at Harvard, 195.
Cleveland, Ohio, supervision in, 110.
Clubs and circles, 275.
Coast Survey, 316.
Coeducation of races, 262, 360, 370; of sexes, 69, 131, 339, 370.
Cokesbury College, 267.
Colburn, Warren, 122.
Collections, art, 272; scientific, 274, 431; of Massachusetts Historical Society, 291.
College-bred colonists, 20.
College Corner Club, 278.
College, curricula, 158; histories, 150; journals, 153; libraries, 304; of professional teachers, 121; organization, 202; reports, 157; training in pedagogy, 144.
Collegiate Alumnæ, Society of, 374.
Colleges, colonial, 20; for women, 365; of Revolutionary period, 73; table of, 77; recent, 158; Southern, 359; Western, 195.
College Society of Yale, 119.
Colonial school systems, 43; libraries, 293; period, 9.
Colonists, early English, 7.
Colorado Agricultural College, 235.
Colored schools in the South, 356-360.

Columbia College, 53, 73; electives, 197; examinations for women, 373; French in, 171; graduate courses, 201; history in, 175; legal studies in, 215, 216; Lieber in, 176; School of Library Economy, 306; School of Political Science, 180.

Columbian Orator, the, 67.

Common-school controversy, 154.

Common - school system, principles of, 43.

Commissioner of Education, United States, vii, 309.

Comparative Zoölogy, Museum of, 274.

Compulsory education, 7, 326.

Concord School of Philosophy, 278.

Concord Teachers' School, Hall, 128.

Congregationalism, 28; in South Carolina, 59; schools of, 267.

Congress, land grants of, 88; Library of, 304; Morrill Act of 1862, 233; act of 1841, 90.

Connecticut Asylum for Deaf-Mutes, 245; Code of 1650, 47, 327; fee bills, 64; first schools, 18; normal school, 132; school-fund, 85; supervision in, 104; union of colonies of, 48.

Contract Indian schools, 261.

Controversial spirit of New England, 29, 30.

Cooper, Peter, 271.

Cooper Union, 271, 290.

Copeland, Rev. Patrick, 13, 31.

Corcoran Art Gallery, 273.

Corlett and Cheever, 51.

Cornell University, elective courses in, 196; graduate courses, 196, 202; organization of, 196; School of Political Science, 181; science and art of teaching in, 146.

Correspondence University, 281.

Council of education, 123.

County superintendent, election of, 115; duties of, 116.

County supervision, 113-115.

Courses of study, in colonial schools, 52; early colleges, 24, 35, 41; high-school, 343; law-school, 216; medical school, 220; normal school, 136; pedagogy, 147; recent colleges, 158; technological schools, 227; theological schools, 211.

Current educational interests, 326.

Curriculum of agricultural schools, 234; Columbia College, 74; Cooper Union, 272; Harvard Annex, 373; Naval Academy, 241; night-schools, 270; reform schools, 252; schools of science, 228; United States Military Academy, 238; University of Virginia, 189.

Cutler, Dr. Manasseh, 203.

Cutler, Timothy, rector of Yale, 42.

Cuttings Museum, 273.

Cyclopædia of Education, 150.

Daboll's Arithmetic, 67.

Dana, James D., 163.

Dana, James F., 161, 163.

Darlington, William, estimate of early teachers, 64.

Dartmouth College case, 75.

Dartmouth College, origin of, 75, 254; physics in, 160.

Davenport, John, 8, 37, 40.

Davenport (Iowa) Training-School, 141.

Dawson, N. H. R., United States Commissioner of Education, 309.

Deaf-Mute College, 246.

Deaf-mute education, 244; schools, 245.

Deaf-mutes at New Orleans Exposition, 246; legal status of, 244; public education, 245.

De Bow, J. B., 60, 348, 349.

Decentralization, 98.

Dedham High-School case, 341.

Degrees, collegiate, 25, 199, 367.

Delaware, convention of 1843, 349; State control of, 107; prior to the Revolution, 57, 58; school-fund, 86.

Democratic tendencies of Revolutionary period, 76.

Denman, J. F., 124.

Denominational agencies in education, 266, 352.

Department Libraries of Government, 304.

Departments, collegiate, in Harvard, 29; of National Educational Association, 123.

De Pauw University Normal School, 144.

Dependents, education of, 243.

Depot of charts for the navy, 322.

Design, schools of, 272, 361, 363.

Dewey, Chester, 163, 167.

Dexter, F. B., 177.
Dickinson College, physics in, 160.
Didactics in college courses, 143, 145; in Iowa University, 145.
Dillaway, C. K., history of Roxbury free school, 16.
Dillworth, Schoolmaster's Assistant, 67; Speller, 66.
Dissenters, influence on colonial education, 54.
District libraries, 299.
District system, 84, 96, 99, 115.
Dix, John A., 101.
Dock, Christopher, 56, 149.
Doddridge, Master, 65.
Domestic economy, 230.
Dorchester, early schools of, 15.
Dorchester (S. C.) Seminary, 59.
Dordrecht Latin School, 5.
Dorr, Thomas W., 110.
Dort, Synod of, 5.
Double-headed school system, 70.
Drawing, industrial, 229.
Drew Theological Seminary, 267.
Dudley, Joseph, 28.
Dummer School, 71.
Dunshee, H. W., 11.
Dunster, Henry, 23–26.
Durant, Henry F., 368.
Dutch, the, in New York, 58; West India Company, 9.
Dwight, Edmund, 131.
Dwight, Nathaniel, geography, 68.
Dwight, Timothy, 21, 65.

Earlham College, 372.
Early colleges, table of, 77.
Eaton, Amos, 163; Survey of New York, 320.
Eaton, John, United States Commissioner of Education, 309.
Eaton, John, 8.
Eaton, Nathaniel, 23.
Ecclesiastical history in early colleges, 175; societies, 97.
Economic associations, 291; studies, 179.
Edinburgh High-School, 71.
Educational associations, 117; histories, 150; journalism in New England, 151; literature, 148; periods, 347; reports, 154; revival, 149.
Education and sovereignty, 3; and the General Government, 307; in the South, 347; of defective classes,

243; of girls, 68; of women, 362; universal, 4.
Edwards, Jonathan, 30, 42.
Elective courses, 186, 198.
Elementary instruction a private interest, 59.
Elementary schools of Europe, Stowe, 130.
Eliot, John, the Indian teacher, 254.
Elizabeth Aull Seminary, 231.
Elmira Female College, 366.
Emerson, G. B., 18.
Endowed libraries, 298.
Endowment of colleges, 35, 76, 204, 207, 208.
Engineering, instruction in, 227.
English academies, 71, 72; elementary schools, 62; local government, 3; occupation of New York, 53; origin of American schools, 1; schools for women, 362; technical training, 223; youth in Harvard, 26.
English High School, Boston, 338.
English Reader, the, 67.
English, the study of, in colleges, 173.
Episcopacy in New York, 54, 73; in Virginia, 13.
Erasmus Hall, 72.
Erie Canal, geology of, 164.
Essays on popular education, 130.
Essential studies, 194.
Essex County Teachers' Association, 121.
European schools (Bache), 129.
European university pedagogy, 144.
Evening schools, 269, 271.
Everett, Edward, oration on John Harvard, 22.
Examinations, Harvard, for women, 372
Expenditures for education in the United States, 92.
Expositions, industrial, 123, 274; and education, 274.

Factory legislation, 329.
Featherstonhaugh's survey of Arkansas, 320.
Feeble-minded, education of the, 249.
Fees, school, 63.
Fellows, Dr. S. N., 145.
Felt, J. B., 46.

Female academies, Boston, 339, 362; Hartford, 364; Ipswich, 366; Mount Holyoke, 366; Philadelphia, 69; Waterford, 364.
Female teachers in the United States, table of, 380.
Field, D. D., 212.
Fiftieth Report of Massachusetts Board of Education, 155.
Finance and Economy, Wharton School of, 180.
Fine-art schools, 229.
Finney, Rev. Charles G., 370.
"First Fruits of New England," 25.
Fisk, John, 22.
Fitting for the bar, 213.
Fitting-schools, 344.
Five Nations, schools of the, 261.
Flatbush Academy, 71.
Fleming's Spelling-Book, 66.
Fortieth parallel, survey of, 319.
Framingham Normal School, 131.
Francke, Hermann August, 126.
Frankfort, University of, 5.
Franklin, Benjamin, 55, 277, 294.
Fraser, Rev. James, 62, 94, 204.
Free, early academies not, 73.
Freedmen's Aid Society, 351; of the Methodist Episcopal Church, 353.
Freedmen's Bureau, 351.
Freeman, Edward A., 181.
Free schools, 46.
"Free schools of the United States," 62.
Free School Society of New York, 119.
Free school system in the South, 58.
Fremont, explorations of, 319.
French language, instruction in, 171.
Friends' school in Philadelphia, 55.
Froebel, 2, 332.
Froebel Kindergarten, 333.
Frothingham, 3.
Froude, J. A., 181.

Gallaudet, Rev. T. H., 128, 244.
Garfield, J. A., 266.
Geneva, education in, 7.
Geographical surveys, 318.
Geographies, 68.
Geological surveys, 319.
Geology, 158, 163.
German immigration, 171.
German influence in Pennsylvania, 55.

German local self-government, 3.
Germantown Academy, 56, 72.
Germany, parochial schools of, 6.
Gilman, D. C., 1, 106, 285; classification of universities, 202.
Girls, education of, 4, 68; High-School of Boston, 339, 362; in Boston schools, 108; in Pennsylvania Charter School, 69.
Goldsmith, Roman history, 67.
Goths, the, 3.
Government, the, and education, 307; Indian schools of, 255; libraries of, 303; publications, 324.
Grading schools, 331; colonial schools, 52.
Graduate courses, 200.
Graduates of Harvard, 26; of William and Mary, 36.
Grammar in Boston schools, 68.
Grammar-schools, 18, 46, 52, 72, 331.
Gray, Asa, 167.
"Great schools" of Holland, 5.
Greek Societies, origin of, in United States, 76.
Greeley Arctic Expedition, 322.
Green, Prof. S. S., in Brown University, 145.
Gregory, J. M., lectures on pedagogy, 145.
Grimke's arraignment of the classics, 121.
Grimm brothers, 171.
Group system of studies, 199.
Gustavus Adolphus, 4.
Guyot, Arnold, lectures on geography, 201.

Hall, James, 164.
Hall, expedition to the Arctic, 322.
Hall, G. S., 249; bibliography of education, 150; Boston lectures on pedagogy, 146; resignation of, 147; university lectures at Johns Hopkins, 146.
Hall, S. R., 128; the American Hecker, 129.
Hamilton College, origin of, 254.
Hammond, Charles, 72.
Hammond, Governor of South Carolina, 62.
Hampden, 8.
Harris, W. T., exposition of the Kindergarten, 156; lectures on pedagogy, 146; school reports of, 156; Summer School of Philoso-

phy, 278; Superintendent of St. Louis Schools, 111.

Hartford, first schools in, 18; Teachers' Institute, 124.

Harvard College, 20; and William and Mary, 35; charter, 28; curriculum, 24, 25, 28, 194; elective courses, 191; graduate courses, 200, 201; hastens the Revolution, 30; instruction in economics, 183; instruction in history, 174; lectures in pedagogy, 146; lotteries of, 88; museum of, 274; opposes the founding of Williams College, 75; physics in, 160.

Harvard, John, 21-23.

Hassler, Prof., Superintendent of Coast Survey, 317.

Hawley, Gideon, 101.

Haworth, J. M., superintendent of Indian schools, 257.

Hayden, F. V., survey of Rocky Mountains, 320; United States geologist, 320.

Haygood, Rev. A. G., 356.

Hecker, J. J., 126.

Henrico College, Virginia, 15, 31.

Henry, Prof. Joseph, at Princeton, 161; Secretary of the Smithsonian Institution, 314.

Herriot, Thomas, 167.

Heterogeneous population of Pennsylvania, 56.

Hunt, Helen, work among Indians, 253.

High-School, Edinburgh, 71.

High-schools, evening, 270; list of, noticed, 339; commissioned, 346; of Michigan, 345; of Minnesota, 346.

High-School, the, for girls, 339; function of, 343; legal aspect of, 340; objections to, 340; of Michigan, 345; of Minnesota, 346.

Hill, Thomas, 193.

Historical libraries and seminaries, 183.

Historical societies, 291.

Historical transactions, Webster, 67.

Histories of education, State, 150.

History, a branch of philosophy or language, 175; in American colleges, 175; in Harvard (early), 174; of education in the United States, 176, 178, 184.

Hobart College, physics in, 160.

Hodder's Arithmetic, 67.

Holland, idea of free schools, 1, 6; and Dutch West India Company, 10.

Hollis, Thomas, benefactions to Harvard, 29; professorship of Natural Philosophy, 160.

Holmes's American Annals, 81.

Homes, children's, 251.

Horn-book, the, 52.

Houses of refuge, 250.

Howe, Dr. S. G., 247, 249.

Howgate Arctic Expedition, 322.

Howland, John, 49, 62.

Hubbard's "History of New England," 23.

Illinois College, 119.

Illinois Industrial Convention, 232; University, 145; high-school decisions, 342; petition to Congress, 232; reading circle, 283; school reports, 155.

Improvement of colleges, 149; of schools, 118; of teachers, 120.

Indiana lotteries, 87; normal school, 138; School Journal, 152; Teachers' reading circle, 283; Teachers' Seminary, 130; University, 200.

Indiana University, 371; chair of Pedagogy, 145; co-education in, 371; group system of studies, 200.

Indian agency, 256; bureau, 255, 260; education in Virginia, 14; land in severalty bill, 256; massacre in Virginia, 13, 31; missions, 253; school of William and Mary, 35; schools, 258, 260.

Indians, education of, 15, 253, 259; Government control of, 255; industrial education of, 260; normal training - school, 259; table of schools, 260; theological education, 211.

Indian Territory, schools of, 261.

Industrial education, nomenclature of, 222; of Indians, 260; beginnings of, 223; for teachers, 141; of deaf-mutes, 246.

Industrial expositions, 274.

Infantry and Cavalry School, 239.

Infant School Society, New York, 332.

Information bureaus, 184.

Institutes, at Hartford, 124; compulsory attendance at, 125; in New

York, 124; mechanics, 282; of civics, 291; of technology, 290.
Institutional history, 174.
Instruction of the blind, 247.
Iowa University, didactics in, 145.
Ipswich, early schools of, 15.

Jackson, Mrs. H. H., 253.
Jackson, "Stonewall," 239.
James I, letter to English bishops, 30.
Jamestown (New York) schools, 228.
Jefferson, Thomas, 36, 59, 81; and the University of Virginia, 190; essay on instruction in Anglo-Saxon, 174; interest in science, 287.
Jersey City, supervision, 111.
John C. Greene School of Science, 227.
John of Nassau, 4.
Johns Hopkins University, history in, 183; pedagogy in, 146; the group system of, 199.
Johnson, Samuel, 54.
Johnson, W. R., 128.
Jones, Miss M. E. M., 137.
Jones, Prof. Hugh, 65.
Jones, Dr. Hiram K., 279.
Jordan, Dr. D. S., 149, 187.
Journalism, educational, 151.
Journal of Biology, 153; of Chemistry, 153; of Economics, 153; of Mathematics, 153; of Philadelphia Academy of Science, 292; of Philology, 153; of Psychology, 153; of Speculative Philosophy, 278.
Journals, school, 150, 152.
Julian, M., idea of central bureau, 309.
"Junto," The, 277, 294.

Kalamazoo College, 145; high-school case, 342.
Kane Arctic Expedition, 322.
Kansas Normal School, 137; University, 198.
Keller, Helen, 249.
Kent, Chancellor, 81, 82, 215; lectures in Columbia College, 214; Commentaries, 215.
Kentucky school-lands, 87.
Kindergarten, The, 2, 332; training-schools, 141, 336; associations, 336; table of, 337.
King, Clarence, survey of fortieth parallel, 319.

King's College, 53, 73.
Kitchen Garden in New York, 231.
Knox, John, 7.
Krieges, the, Kindergarten of, 334.
Krüsi, Hermann, 122.

Laboratory practice, 160-162, 166.
Laboulaye, 176.
Ladies excluded from early teachers' associations, 121; seminaries, 363.
Lafayette College, language studies in, 172.
Laissez faire in education, 330.
Lancaster, Joseph, 127, 132.
Lancasterianism, 127.
Land grants for education, 88, 90, 233, 240, 245.
Land in Severalty Bill for Indians, 256.
Lane Theological Seminary, 120, 267.
Langley, J. P., 161.
La Salle, Abbé J. B. de, 126.
La Salle Seminary, 231.
Latin accidence, Bingham, 68; Cheever, 51, 68.
Latin in early Harvard, 25.
Latin schools, 5, 11, 18, 51.
Laurie, S. S., 150.
Law a learned profession, 209, 216; libraries, 301.
Law of 1642 in Massachusetts, 16; of 1647, 44; of 1650, in Connecticut, 47.
Lawrence, Eugene, 2.
Lawrence Scientific School, 226.
Law schools, early, 214.
"Laws" of Plato, 7.
Lawyers in Revolutionary period, 214.
Learned societies, 285; publications of, 291.
Learned professions, 209, 221.
Lectures on School-Keeping, 129.
Legal aspect of high-schools, 340.
Legal education, 212; of women, 378.
Leibnitz, 173.
Lending Library, The, 280.
Leverett, President of Harvard, 28.
Lewis and Clark Expedition, 318.
Lewis, Samuel, 121.
Leyden, University of, 5.
Liberal education, 159, 188.
Libraries, 293; and learned societies, 285; colonial, 293; college,

304; congressional, 304; circulating, 294; departmental, 304; Economy, School of, 306; endowed, 298; governmental, 303; historical, 184; mercantile, 296; of Bureau of Education, 310; professional, 301; public, 297; recent, 296; school district, 299; State, 302; town, 300.

Lick Observatory, 166.

Lieber, Francis, 1, 175, 179.

Lincoln, President, 233.

Lindsley, Philip, 128.

Lip-reading by deaf-mutes, 245.

Literary Club, Cincinnati, 277.

Literary Fund of Virginia, 62, 86.

Literature funds, 85, 86.

Literature of education, 148.

Local taxes, 92.

Locke, John, 8.

Lodge, H. Cabot, 178.

Logan, James, 167; library, 293.

"Log College," New Jersey, 58, 73.

Longfellow at Bowdoin, 172; at Harvard, 189.

Long, Major, explorations, 318.

Lotteries, 87.

Louisiana school lands, 87; State University, 204.

Lowell Institute Lectures, 18.

Luther, Letter to Magistrates, 6, 7.

Lynch Expedition to Africa, 322.

Lyon, Mary, 366.

MacAlister, James, Superintendent of Schools, Philadelphia, 111; Pedagogical Catalogue, 151.

Maclean, John, 162.

McClure, William, Geological Survey, 320.

McCormick Observatory, 165.

McMaster's "History of the People of the United States," 65, 178.

Maine, school system, 50; school-funds, 86.

Mann, Horace, 2, 18, 43; and the Massachusetts system, 96, 103, 122; controversy with the thirty-one Boston schoolmasters, 154; reports, 104, 154.

Manual-labor schools, 223, 224.

Manual-training schools, 228, 230.

Marenholtz-Bülow, Baroness, 333.

Marietta College, 120.

Marine zoölogy 168.

Marsh, George P., 201.

Maryland, Act of 1726, 62; teachers of Revolutionary period, 64.

Massachusetts Agricultural School, 235; Board of Education, Fiftieth Report of, 103; supervision, city, 111; supervision, State, 103; colony, 8; Historical Society, 291; law of 1642, 16; law of 1647, 44, 327; nautical schools, 242; normal schools, 125, 130, 133; school-fund, history of, 85; school system, 4; Teachers' Institute, 123; Teacher, the, 152.

Mather, Cotton, 51.

Mather, Increase, 28.

Maude, Danyell, 15, 265.

Mechanics, education in, 227.

Medical Colleges admitting women, 377.

Medical education, 217; of women, 375.

Medical instruction in Columbia, 219; in Michigan, 220.

Medical libraries, 301.

Medical Museum, Army, 273.

Medical schools, curriculum of, 220; distribution of, 219, 377; early, 218.

Mennonites in Pennsylvania, 56.

Mercantile libraries, 296.

Metallurgy, instruction in, 227.

Methodists, schools of, 267.

Michigan, high-school system, 345; history of education in, 150; lotteries in, 87; normal schools, 133, 137; school reports, 155.

Michigan University, co-education in, 372; electives, 195; graduate courses, 201; history in, 176; law lectures in, 215; School of Political Science, 181; science and art of teaching in, 146; seminaries, 183; special courses, 196.

Middlesex County Teachers' Association, 121.

Military academies, 237, 239; education, 237; Institute of Virginia, 289; post schools, 240; tactics in schools, 233, 240.

Millersville (Pa.) Normal School, 136.

Milton, John, 71.

Minimum school term, 328.

Minnesota high-school system, 346.

Missouri, coeducation in, 372; University Normal School, 144; visitors to schools, 114.

Mitchell, Miss Maria, 165.
Mitford, 326.
Model schools of S. R. Hall, 129, 138; recent, 138.
Modern language studies, 169, 170.
Modern normal schools, 138.
Moravian schools for girls, 69; theological education, 210.
Morse, S. F. B., 161.
Morse, Jedediah, Geography, 68.
Motley, 4, 5.
Mount Holyoke Seminary, 366.
Murray, English Grammar, 68; English Reader, 67.
Museum, National, 274, 315; New York, 431; of Comparative Zoölogy, 274; of Science and Art, 272; Pedagogical, 274.
Music-Teachers' Institute, Boston, 124.

National Educational Association, 122: recommends a Bureau of Education, 309.
National land grant, 88, 232; Museum, 274, 315; Observatory, 322; University proposed, 308.
Natural history, 160, 176, 194.
Naval Academy, 241; architecture in University of Michigan, 242; education, 240; expenditures in the United States, 322; observatory, 322; war college, 242.
Nautical training, 240.
Navy, department of the, 241.
Nebraska school lands, 91.
Neef, Joseph, "Plan of Education," 149.
Negative compulsory legislation, 328–330.
Neill, E. D., 13, 19, 31, 32.
Neshaminy, Log College, 58.
Netherlands, idea of free school, 6.
New Amsterdam, 10.
Newberry Library, 299.
New Britain Normal School, 106, 132.
Newburyport high-school case, 341.
New Connecticut, 89.
New England Primer, 52, 66.
New England Psalm-Book, 66.
New England, early schools in, 14.
New Hampshire, early schools in, 50; school-fund, 85.
New Harmony (Indiana) Community School, 149.

New Haven colony, 18, 51; Training School, 221.
New Jersey, College of, 73; fee bills, 64; Newark, early schools, 57; pauper-tax, 62; prior to the Revolution, 57; reading circle, 283; school-fund, 86.
New Mexico, State school officer, 107.
New Orleans, supervision in, 110.
New World, the, 2.
New York, colonial, 53; city supervision, 109; county supervision, 114; fee bills, 64; high-school system, 338; history of education in, 9, 150; Industrial Training-School, 141; lotteries, 87; school-funds, 85: school lands, 85; school reports, 155; Society Library, 295; State system, 101; vs. New England, 59.
Night-schools, 269.
Nomenclature of industrial education, 222.
Non-sectarianism in colleges, 77, 203, 206; in schools, 104.
Normal schools, 125; art, 141; Connecticut, 132; curriculum of, 136; early promoters of, 128; idea in the United States, 127; in the South, 358; in New York, 132; in the university, 143; modern, 133; objected to, in Boston, 132; of the University of North Carolina, 145; origin of, 126; private, 134; public, 133; State, 130; table of, 135.
North American Review, 80.
Northend, Charles, 122.
Northwestern Educational Association, 122.
Norwood, teacher on Somers Island, 14.
Nott, Dr. E., 188.
Nurses' schools, 231.

Oberlin College, 370.
Objections to free schools, 58; to high-schools, 340; to the Normal School in Boston, 131.
Observatories, 164, 322.
"Odious Rate Bill," 63.
O'Fallon Polytechnic Institute, 225.
Officers, civil, as school officers, 102.
Ohio, charity education clause, 63; school agent, 121; School Journal, 152; school system, origin of, 102;

teachers' institutes, 124; teachers' reading circle, 282; university, 203.

"Old South" movement, 279.

Olmsted, Denison, 81, 122, 164; graduating thesis, 128.

Open system, the, 188.

Ordinance of 1785, 88, 89; of 1787, 89.

Organization of Smithsonian Institution, 313; of universities, 202.

Origin of normal schools, 126.

Oswego Training-School, 137, 141.

Ottawa University, Kansas, pedagogics in, 145.

Owen, D. D., survey of mineral lands, 320.

Page, David P., 132.

Palmer, Edward, island school of, 32.

Palmer, Prof. G. H., concerning electives, 198.

Pamphlet literature in college libraries, 306.

Parallel courses in college, 189, 199.

Pardee School of Science, 227.

Parishes in Connecticut, 97, 98.

Parish schools in the United States, 268; of Germany, 6.

Parton, James, 294.

Pauper schools, 62.

Patroons, Dutch, in New York, 10.

Payne, Joseph, 150.

Payne, W. H., 124.

Peabody fund, 354; distribution of, 356.

Peabody, George, benefactions of, 354.

Peabody Library, Baltimore, vii, 298.

Peabody, Miss E., and the Kindergarten, 333.

"Peace policy" with the Indians, 255.

Pedagogical library, 310; museum, 274; literature, 148.

Pedagogy, college training in, 144; in European universities, 145; in University of City of New York, 147; in Johns Hopkins, 146; in Michigan, 146.

Peers, B. O., 121.

Penalty under Massachusetts law of 1647, 46; in New Hampshire, 1693, 50.

Penn Charter School, 55, 63, 69.

Pennsylvania, county supervision, 115; history of education in, 54, 150; Historical Society, 287; pauper schools, 62, 63; prior to the Revolution, 54; school-funds, 86; School Journal, 152; school-tax, 92; university of, 74.

Periodicals, educational, 151; in colleges, 153.

Perkins's Institution for the Blind, 249.

Permanent funds and local taxes, 92.

Permissive school legislation, 328.

Perry, Captain, expedition to Japan, 322.

Phi Beta Kappa Fraternity, 76.

Philadelphia, academy founded, 74; Academy of Natural Sciences, 286, 292; city school system, 111; normal school, 132; pauper schools, 63; public library, 294.

Philbrick, J. D., 112, 117, 155.

Phillips Academies, 71.

Philological studies, 173.

Philosophical clubs, 277; societies, 287.

Philosophy, as related to education, 148; in American colleges, 169.

Physical sciences, 159.

Physics, 160; in early Harvard, 24, 29.

Physics and Chemistry in the Schools of the United States, 159.

Pickering, Prof., laboratory of, 161.

Pickett, Albert, 121.

Pierce, spelling-book, 66.

Pierce, J. D., Superintendent of Michigan, 104.

Pierson, Rev. A., Rector of Yale, 39.

Pike, Major, expedition of, 318.

Pike's Arithmetic, 67.

"Plan of Education" (Neef), 149.

Plato, 3, 7.

Plymouth Colony schools, 15.

Plymouth masters, 50.

Political education, 179.

"Political Ethics" (Lieber), 175.

Political Science, Columbia School of, 180; Johns Hopkins School of, 183; Michigan School of, 181; Quarterly Journal, 153; White school of, 181.

Politics in early Harvard, 30.

Polytechnic schools, 228.

Population, growth of, 79.
Porter, Noah, 169.
Powell, Major J. W., Director of Geological Survey, 320.
Practice schools for teachers, 139.
Pratt, Captain R. H., 260.
Praying towns, 254.
Preparation of teachers, 117, 142.
Preparatory schools, 70, 338, 369.
Presbyterian Board for Freedmen, 353.
Presbyterian schools, 267.
Prescribed course, the, 199 ; of Harvard, 194.
Primary schools, 331 ; of Boston, 82, 132, 332.
Prince, J. T., "Courses and Methods," 113.
Prince Library; the, 293.
Princeton College, 73, 227 ; first chair in chemistry, 162 ; graduate courses, 202.
Principles of the common-school system, 43.
Printing press, the, at Harvard, 27.
Privately endowed universities, 202, 204, 208.
Private schools, 264 ; normal schools, 134.
Professional libraries, 301 ; education of women, 375 ; schools in the South, 359 ; studies, 136.
Professions, the, 209 ; liberal, 221 ; women in, 375.
Pofessorships of pedagogy in colleges, 144.
Protestantism and free schools, 2.
Protestant Reformed Dutch Church, school of, 10.
Providence, R. I., school report of, 155 ; supervision in, 110.
Provinces, Catholic, 268.
Prussian school system, 129.
Psalm-Book, the New England, 66.
Psychology in normal schools, 139, 148 ; Journal of, 153 ; pedagogical, 140 ; school of, in the University of the Pacific, 144.
Publications of Bureau of Education, 310 ; of Smithsonian Institution, 315.
Public Education Society of Philadelphia, 111.
Public (free) Kindergarten, 335.

Public, libraries 297 ; normal schools, 133 ; schools in the South, 357 ; libraries in the South, 360.
Public School Society of New York, 82, 127.
Puritans, 2.
Purmont, Philemon, 14, 16, 265.

Quakers, the, in Pennsylvania, 55.
Qualifications of teachers, 50, 64, 117, 120, 136, 147.
Quarterly Journal of Economics, 184.
Queen's College founded, 75.
Quick, R. H., 144, 150.
Quincy, Josiah, 21, 51.

Rafinesque, 149.
Raleigh, Sir W., 8.
Rate bills, 15, 19, 45, 55, 63.
Reading books, 67.
Reading circles, 279, 284.
Reading schools, Boston, 70.
Recent colleges, 158, 186.
Redwood Library, 294.
Reformation, the, and free schools, 2.
Reformatories, 250 ; industrial training in, 252.
Reformed Dutch Church, 10.
Reform schools, 251 ; curriculum of, 252.
Regents of the University of the State of New York, 202.
Regulations in early Harvard, 25 ; in William and Mary College, 36.
Religious tests in Yale, 42.
Renaissance, the American, 82.
Rensselaer School, the, 224.
Reorganization, period of, 79 ; in the South, 347.
Reports, of educational institutions, 154 ; of city systems, 155 ; of colleges, 157 ; of Horace Mann, 154 ; of St. Louis, 155.
Representative town government in New England, 14, 16.
"Republic," the, of Plato, 7.
Reservation Indians, 256.
Review courses in college, 143.
Revolutionary period, 61.
Rheims, normal school at, 126.
Rhode Island, first schools in, 19, 49 ; history of education in, 150, 295 ; lotteries in, 88 ; early idea of education, 62 ; School Commissioner, 106 ; school fees, 64 ; school-funds, 86 ; school reports, 155 ;

school system, 49, 58; teachers' institutes, 124; reading circle, 283.
Richards, Zalmon, 122.
Rickoff, A. J., and the Ohio schools, 112.
Riley, J. B., 258.
Riparian lands, New Jersey, 91.
Rittenhouse, David, 287.
Ritter, 158.
Roebling, W. A., 224.
Robinson, John, 8.
Roelandsen, A., 10, 12.
Roman history, Goldsmith, 67.
Round Table, the, of the West, 279.
Roxbury School, the, 16; early teachers of, 50.
Royal Society of London, 28, 40; origin of, 286.
Rumford chair of Science, 225.
Russell, J. Scott, 223, 234.
Russell, William, 128, 158.
Rutgers College, 75.

St. Louis philosophical club, 277; school reports, 155, 156; training-school, 140.
St. Mary's Nautical School, 241.
Salaries of early college presidents, 29; of teachers, 12, 15, 52.
Salem, early schools of, 15; library, 295.
Saline lands, 91.
Sandys, Sir Edwin, 12, 31.
San Francisco Training-School, 141.
Saracens, the, 2, 4.
Saybrook school, 39.
Scharf, Thomas, 64.
Schmidt's "History of Education," 5.
School-books, 66.
School district libraries, 299.
School fees, 13.
School-funds, 83; Burlington, New Jersey, 57; commissioner of, in South Carolina, 86.
School journals, 151.
School lands unsold, 91.
Schoolmasters' Club, the, 279.
School of Design, the, for Women, 225.
School of library economy, 306.
School of Mines Quarterly, 153.
School of psychology, 144.
School societies, 96, 98, 100.
School suffrage for women, 381.

School system, American, 1; State, 101.
School-tax, 10, 92.
School term, 19, 49, 329.
"Schul-ordnung," 56, 149.
Schurz, Mrs. Carl, 333.
Science and the arts, 225; in early Yale, 41; in the college course, 168; museums of, 272; teachers' class in, 274.
Scientific academies, 285; departments in colleges, 225; journals, 153; work of government, 316.
Scotland, education in, 7.
Sears, Barnas, agent of Peabody fund, 355.
Secondary schools, 338; of the Revolutionary period, 70.
Sections of National Educational Association, 123.
Seeley, Prof., 170.
Seminaries, ladies', 363; in the university, 183.
Seventeenth century, 2.
Sewing, instruction in, 230.
Seymour, Attorney-General, 34.
Sharp Library of New York, 293.
Shaw, John A., Superintendent of New Orleans Schools, 110.
Shaw, Mrs. Q. A., Kindergartens supported by, 336.
Sheffield Scientific School, 197, 226.
Shepard, Thomas, 20.
Sherman, General W. T., 239, 256.
Sibley Scientific School, 227.
Signal Service, 321.
Sign-method in deaf-mute instruction, 245.
Sigourney, Mrs. L. H., 121.
Silliman, Benjamin, 65, 162; Journal, 292.
Slater fund, 356.
"Small schools" of Holland, 5.
Smart, J. H., 124.
Smith College, 369.
Smith, Goldwin, 181.
Smith, Prof. Walter, 229.
Smithson bequest, the, 311.
Smithson, James, 311.
Smithsonian, the, 285, 311, 312; museum, 274, 315; Prof. Henry in, 314; the publications of, 315.
Societies for the promotion of schools, 118; general, 285; scientific, 286; teachers', 120.

Society for the Propagation of the Gospel, 53, 74.
Society for the Collegiate Instruction of Women, 372.
Society of Arts in Massachusetts Institute of Technology, 290.
Society to encourage Studies at Home, 280; for home culture, 280.
Soldiers' orphans' homes, 252.
Somers Island, school on, 14.
South Carolina, College of, 163, 171, 176, 179, 202, 204; colonial education, 58, 59; colonization of, 58; modern languages in, 171; normal schools in, 135; public schools in, 358; recent education in, 360; school-funds of, 86.
South, J., introduction to English, 68.
South, the colonial, 58; ante-war period, 348; education in, 347; general condition of, 359; period of reorganization, 350; public-school system of, 357.
Spanish, instruction in, at Columbia, 172.
Sparks, Jared, 175.
Special Indian schools, 260.
Specializing in normal training, 140.
Spelling-books, 66.
Springfield, supervision of, 111.
Spring Garden Institute, 225.
Squadrons in Rhode Island, 96.
Stages in the development of school systems, 94.
Stanford, "The Art of Reading," 67.
State Control, Boards of, 107; general view of, 107.
State Libraries, 302.
State Normal Schools, 130.
States of Northwest Territory, 89.
State Universities, 203, 207, 208.
Statistics, school, 154.
Stiles, Ezra, 65.
Story, Joseph, 122, 175, 188.
Stoughton, 20.
Stowe, Prof. C. E., 121, 130.
Studies in history and political science, 179, 184.
Stuyvesant, 11.
Subscription schools, 265.
Sully, J., 150.
Sumner, W. G., 257.
Superintendent of Schools, 103; Boston, 110; Indian, 257; mode of choosing, 115.

Supervision of schools, 94, 101, 109, 113; city, 109; county, 113; early, 102, 113; forms of, 96; in New York, 101, 114; State, 101, 107, 109.
Supervisory university, 202.
Surplus revenue, 91, 348.
Survey, Coast, 316; geographical, 318; geological, 319.
Swamp-land grant, 90.
Swarthmore College, co-education in, 372.
Sweden, education in, 4.
Swedes in Pennsylvania, 55.
Swiss Cross, the, 284.
Switzerland, early schools of, 6.
Symmes, Benjamin, 14.
Syriac, instruction in, at Harvard, 25.
Systems, colonial school, 43.

Table of State Universities, 204.
Tappan, David, 72.
Tappan, Henry T., President of Michigan University, 195, 201.
Taxes, local school, 92.
Teachers, colonial, 50; female, 380; efficient, 127; Institute of, in Ohio, 124; of the Revolutionary period, 64; preparation of, 117, 120, 136, 142; proportion of the sexes, 380; reading circles, 282; respect for, 50; services and pay, 12.
Technological education, 221; societies, 289.
Tennent, Rev. William, 57, 73.
Tennessee land grants for colleges, 86; University of, 204.
Terms, school, 19, 49, 52, 329.
Territorial claims of the colonies, 88.
Territory, growth of, in the United States, 79.
Texas school lands, 91.
Text-books, elementary, 52, 66.
Theological curriculum, 211; education, 210; libraries, 301; training for women, 375; Chautauqua School of, 281.
Theology as a learned profession, 209, 211; in early colleges, 29, 35. 39, 41, 76.
Theory of education, Plato, 6.
Thirty-one Boston schoolmasters, 154.
Three-per-cent fund, 91.
Ticknor, Elisha, 127.

Ticknor, Miss A. E., 280.
Ticknor, George, 188, 189.
Tillinghast, 338.
Tompkins County (N. Y.) Institute, 124.
Topography, changed meaning of, 321.
Towne Scientific School, 227.
Town meeting, the, 16.
Township system, the, 99, 115.
Town, the, in New England, 97; libraries, 300.
Town, Salem, 124.
Tractate, Milton, 71.
Trade, growth of, in the United States, 80.
Trade-schools, 231.
Transition, period of, 79.
Translation of pedagogical works, 150.
Treaties with Indians, 256.
Trinity School, New York, 53, 74.
Troy Female Seminary, 364.
Truant laws, 328.
Tulane University, 200.
Types of university, 202.

Unfortunate classes, education of, 243.
Union of Connecticut colonies, 48.
Union of Utrecht, 5.
Union College, engineering in, 226; French in, 171; physics in, 160.
University Convocation, 121.
University, Chautauqua, 281; normal schools in, 143; of North Carolina, 145, 160; of Pennsylvania, 77, 178, 180; of the city of New York, 145, 189; of the Pacific, 144; of the State of New York, 74, 202; of Virginia, 189; organization, 24, 202; privately endowed, 204, 208; the function of, 77.
Unsettled educational questions, 383.
Unsold school lands, 91.
Utica Convention, 121.
Utility of modern languages, 170.
Utrecht, Union of, 5.

Vassar College, 367.
Vermont, colonial system, 50; fee bills, 50; local supervision, 114; University of, 204.
Veterinary schools, 220, 234, 236.
Virginia, colonial university, 13, 30; early schools, 12, 14; land cession, 89; literature fund, 86; University of, 189, 208, 215.
Virginia Company, 12, 32.

Wabash College, 120.
Wade, L. S., 113.
Wagner Free Institute, 225.
Wait, Green & Co., Journal of, 151.
Wallace, S. T., 222.
Warner Observatory, 166.
War of 1812, 79.
Washington Academy, 72.
Washington, George, 308; Chancellor of William and Mary College, 34, 77; on higher education, 149, 308.
Watts, Isaac, 65.
Wayland, Francis, 149, 151.
Weather predictions, 321.
Webster, Daniel, 44.
Webster, Noah, 127; text-books of, 66.
Wellesley College, 368.
Western Academic Institute, 121.
Western Baptist Educational Association, 119.
Western colleges, 195.
Western College Society, 119.
Western Literary Institute, 121.
Western Reserve, 85, 89; College of, 120.
Westfield Normal School, 131.
West Point Military Academy, 237.
Wharton School of Finance and Economy, 180.
Wheaton, "International Law," 324.
Wheedon, Professor. 176.
Wheelock, Eleazar, 75, 254.
White, Andrew D., 176, 181, 184.
White, E. E., 3, 8.
Whitefield, 30, 42.
White School of History and Political Science, 181.
Wigglesworth, 30.
Wightman, Joseph, 232.
Wilkes (Captain) Expedition, 322.
Willard, Mrs. Emma, 121, 264.
Willard, President of Harvard, 29.
William of Holland, 5.
William and Mary of England, 33.
William and Mary College, 30; Chancellor of, 34; curriculum of, 35, 160; French in, 171; marriage of professors, 37; physics in, 160; vs. Harvard, 35.

Williams College founded, 75 ; exploring parties, 164 ; history in, 175 ; language chairs, 171 ; physics in, 160.
Wilson, John, 20.
Windsor, Justin, Narrative and Critical History of America, 178.
Winterbotham, 72.
Winthrop, John, 8, 20.
Wisconsin University, training in pedagogy, 145.
Woodbridge, W. C., 151.
Woolman's "First Book," 66.
Woolsey, T. D., 197.
Women, colleges for, 365 ; excluded from early teachers' associations, 121 ; higher education of, 362 ; theological education of, 375 ; medical education of, 375 ; in normal schools, 379 ; in European schools, 362 ; as teachers, 51, 378 ; legal

education of, 378 ; school suffrage for, 381.
Wouter Van Twiller, 10.
Writing-schools, Boston, 69.

Yale College, founding of, 37 ; aided by the State, 77 ; chemistry in, 162 ; courses in economics, 183 ; early embarrassments of, 39 ; elections in, 197 ; graduate instruction, 201 ; history in, 175 ; modern languages in, 172 ; physics in, 160, 161 ; theological instruction in, 163.
Yale College Society, 119.
Yale, Elihu, 40.

Zealand school law, 3.
Zimmermann, Comparative Grammar, 173.
Zoölogy instruction, 166 ; Museum of, 274.

THE END.